No. 2776
$18.95

1001 THINGS TO DO WITH YOUR ATARI® ST™

MARK SAWUSCH AND LINDA SCHREIBER

TAB BOOKS Inc.
Blue Ridge Summit, PA 17214

FIRST EDITION
FIRST PRINTING

Library of Congress Cataloging in Publication Data

Sawusch, Mark.
1001 things to do with your ATARI ST.

Bibliography: p.
Includes index.
1. Atari ST (Computer) I. Schreiber, Linda M.
II. Title. III. Title: One thousand one things to do
with your ATARI ST. IV. Title: One thousand and one
things to do with your ATARI ST.
QA76.8.A824S29 1986 004.165 86-23002
ISBN 0-8306-0476-6
ISBN 0-8306-2776-6 (pbk.)

Contents

Preface

Every good book begins with a bit of historical perspective, as does this one, although it does not necessarily follow that this is a good book. However, the phenomenal success of *1001 Things To Do With Your Personal Computer,* with over 100,000 copies in print, indicates a need for the information it has provided. Since the time of publication of the first book, nothing short of a revolution has taken place. Personal computers have joined the American love affair with the television and automobile and now occupy a coveted spot in more than five million homes. Many of the applications in the first book are now commercially available programs; the home computer software market now includes some 50,000 entries, a bewildering assortment of programs for those from every walk of life.

The continued unawareness of the large number of applications a personal computer can be used for has prompted me to prepare this expanded book, which is fully updated and includes the many new BASIC programs and ideas incorporated in the ATARI ST.

Acknowledgments

The authors would like to thank the following people for suggesting ideas and improvements or providing material: Steve Witham, Larry Hughes, Jack Atwater, George Gross, Dr. E.P. Miles and his associates, Janis Qualls, Dr. and Mrs. Robert Sawusch, Bob Johnson, Dwight Sawusch, Ed Manning, and Louis Brasovan. Thanks also are in order for the many readers who kindly sent letters suggesting improvements. We have incorporated these changes whenever possible. And special thanks go to Alan B. Clements, Peter T. Mueller, and Stephen H. Schreiber.

The following firms also provided illustrative material for the book: AMI Corp., Bally Manufacturing, Colorado Video, Inc., Compucolor Corp., Computer Portraits, Inc., Video Brain Corp., ECD Corp., Interstate Electronics Corp., RCA, Magnavox, and Apple Computer Corp.

Introduction

"What can it do for me?" is probably one of the most common yet subtly annoying questions asked by the would-be customer of the personal computer salesman, sometimes leaving him speechless. It is a difficult question, to be sure. It's certainly much easier and lucrative to expound on the advantages of this computer versus that one "because it has 512K." Enter this book—a unique, comprehensive guide to the marvelous (yet scarcely explored elsewhere) home computer applications that in the words of the media, "will greatly change the way you live and work." It's not just a "how-to-do-it" book, but a "what to do" book; over 1000 different imaginative ideas are presented and explained herein on the premise that one idea spawns another.

Not only the salesman, but the personal computer manufacturers themselves are often insecure about just *what* can be done with their product. The standard, meager manual on BASIC and perhaps a few sample programs come with their computer, but little of reassurance about applications is included, leaving the buyer in a quandary. Something is missing from the whole brave new world he had breathlessly imagined. No, the video display, keyboard, cables, papers, and other paraphernalia is probably all there and functional. It's the *applications* that are missing. You didn't buy a computer as a conversation piece, to keep up with the Joneses, or because it had 64K; you bought it as a gadget of the future, an appliance of the mind, the ultimate game machine, an adult pacifier, or a business partner; you got it to save the world from another computer illiterate, or you wanted it to save something—be it time, effort, headaches, or money.

There is good news. Among the seemingly endless numbers of personal computing books available today, this book remains a unique browser's catalog of potential applications for your computer. Allow it to spawn, identify, and tailor new uses for your system and to serve as an operator's manual for *the* appliance that is your mind. It provides the background you need to become more adept, more versatile, and more creative in using your computer's problem-solving capabilities. As an *idea* book, it will stimulate your own creativity, helping you stretch your own limits and those of your system; the usefulness of your computer will be limited only by your ingenuity. I venture to say that virtually all the uses to which personal computers are being put today are discussed briefly or illustrated within this cookbook, save the *pate de foie de volaille*, that is, the more restricted, specialized uses (although there are many of those inside, too).

Lest I be accused of exaggeration, I'll amend the above claim to "virtually *almost* all of the applications . . ." and invite readers to send in their latest mousetrap, regardless of whether or not the world is beating a path to their door.

This book should appeal to anyone interested in or owning a microcomputer—on three levels. The *skeptical buyer* may use it in deciding whether the possible applications will justify the cost of a computer or he may use it to decide between various brands of computers on the basis of the software available for a listed application. The *person interested in using computers* but not in programming can use this book as a source of applications that may warrant further investigation, or he can type in the many BASIC programs for his computer included within. The *advanced personal computer user* has the opportunity to sharpen his programming skills using the many useful, interesting, and often challenging program suggestions found throughout the book or to develop commercial software for the burgeoning microcomputer market.

Your computer is an extension of your mind, a mind appliance. Use it to do complex calculations you would not have previously done manually (for example, the amateur or professional photographer may calculate more precise values for camera settings to achieve a certain effect). Examples of simple formulas are presented herein and are intended to be part of larger, more complex programs to be written for your own personal application. In some cases, due to space regulations, the advanced reader is left to find the information necessary to write a program based on an idea given; all information should be readily available at a local library. In other cases, the program itself or the formulas and methods necessary to write the program are provided to illustrate an idea and set you on the right track. Analyze and adapt the program within; learn to write an applied program.

Some of the program ideas are intended not only for microcomputers, but for programmable calculators as well. Although anyone who has programmed a calculator will realize the tremendous advantages of a microcomputer system, the programmable calculator does have its place. For those applications where portability is important (for example, marine navigation), the calculator comes in handy.

Promises, promises—that's all you can hear from the alluring ads and articles generating countless wonders from a personal computer at the tap of a key. Everything from tending your garden to filling out form 1040 has been claimed as a time- or cost-justifying excuse to buy a computer. Yet these applications are often genuinely easier, faster, or cheaper to do by hand. This has led to the claim by newspaper and magazine critics that computers are not the common man's electronic panacea and are, at best, toys for the man who has everything, the computer hacker, the math wiz, or the gadget freak.

There is a bit of truth to this assertion. It's certainly possible that you don't need a personal computer at all (skip ahead if you've already taken the plunge). The time-honored means of managing a household—typewriter, file folders, index cards, address book, check-book, bulletin board—can often perform just as well as or better than their computerized equivalents. It's senseless to patiently spend 15 minutes loading and reloading programs, referencing commands, and remembering keywords, only to eventually call up your spouse's birthday. Likewise, it wouldn't be practical to use a $2000 computer for the purpose of computing your automotive miles per gallon or to store a couple dozen recipes; miles per gallon can easily be computed in your head; index cards are much better for storing a typical small collection of recipes and can be thumbed with wet or sticky hands. A checkbook can be carried along and filled out on the spot—not an easy match for a home computer.

"But," you say, "I see some of those applications listed in this book," and you may have the urge to fold, spindle, or mutilate this page. The answer to this seeming contradiction is that these applications are practical uses of a computer for *some* people. For instance, if you ran a delivery service, a miles per gallon calculating program that included statistical analysis for each truck and driver could be useful in improving efficiency. If you happen to be a professional chef or gourmet cook, you might need a computer program that could automatically organize hundreds of recipes and even calculate the amount of each ingredient necessary for a given number of people. Using a computer to balance a checkbook would be a case of electronic overkill. However, a program fed with your financial data on a regular basis could serve as your personal accountant, giving you a rundown on clothing costs for each individual family member, a comparison of monthly utility bills, and a complete year-end list of tax-deductible expenditures—and yes, your bank balance.

Impractical programs thus become practical in specialized applications, as interesting, educational examples of programming, and as idea stimulators for better applications. Therefore they are included in this book, but with a warning that they can often be considerably more time and effort consuming than the old-fashioned way.

It is when the size of your project or hobby becomes large enough that computing can offer solutions. The typewriter is a simple, easy tool for creating short memos; the word processor becomes useful in preparing 100-page theses. When your application demands many mathematical calculations, it's important to consider computing power. However, to many hobbyists, the writing of a program, whether or not it has any real value, is an end in itself. To them, the computer is the most enticing combination crossword puzzle, chess game, Rubik's cube, and balsa-wood airplane kit yet devised.

Within the pages of *1001 Things to Do with Your ATARI ST*, you can discover and exploit the virtually boundless potential inherent in your personal computer. Move *ahead* of the times, extend your reach, open up new avenues of personal growth, enjoy! This book is here to help you expand your horizons and to answer the paramount question, "What can it do for me?"

THE PROGRAMS

All the programs in this book are written in ST-BASIC and require you to be in medium- or high-resolution mode for them to work properly. You can set the resolution from the GEM™ Desktop. Move the mouse cursor to the OPTIONS menu and click Set Preferences. When the menu is displayed, set your option and go to BASIC to begin typing these programs.

If your computer has a RAM version of TOS, you will have a disk titled TOS™ System Disk. In this case, you must go to the BASIC Run menu and click the Buf graphics option. Failure to do so will cause an out-of-memory error message to be displayed.

You may want to stop the program while it's running. You will find that, unlike most computers, Control-C or Control-Break will not stop program execution. Simply move the mouse cursor to the Run menu and click the Break option. To continue, you can either type "cont" in the command window or go back to the Run menu and click the Continue option.

Good luck and happy programming!

Chapter 1

Applications for Everyone

In this increasingly complex world, a personal computer is most useful in organizing and simplifying the minutia of everyday life. In this chapter you will find an eclectic collection of applications for everyone, each designed to streamline daily life.

PERSONAL REFERENCE SOURCE

Reference information that is often referred to but too complex to memorize could be stored for instant retrieval. Possibilities are endless, but examples of charts, tables, and lists that have been stored in personal computers include:

1. Caloric and nutritional content of selected foods.
2. Appointment itinerary.
3. Important articles and books (stored by author, title, topic, and date).
4. Sports statistics, amateur or professional.
5. Product sources, specifications, and prices from various suppliers, for comparison.
6. Names, addresses, and phone numbers.
7. Stock market data including name, symbol, shares, price, and historical data.
8. Recipes and shopping lists.
9. Postal and shipping rates, requirements, and regulations for the businessman.
10. Metric conversions and information.
11. Time differences and phone rates between cities.
12. Words commonly misspelled or misused (as a quick reference writer).
13. Ham radio log of contacts, locations, and times.
14. Collection inventory, including name of item, age, values, and identifying information.
15. Private pilot flight planning data.
16. Household inventory for insurance and financial purposes.
17. Astronomical and astrological data.
18. Things to be done, ordered, or checked, with times available and deadlines.
19. Fishing log.
20. Quotations by topic and source.
21. References from literature, the Bible, and so on.

22. Dates of birthdays, anniversaries, and other special occasions.
23. Automotive service information, especially for business car fleets.
24. Patient laboratory data over time, differential diagnoses, or drug data for physicians.
25. Credit cards, with numbers to call in the event of theft.
26. Safety deposit box contents.
27. Physical contents, chemical data, formulae.
28. Emergency phone numbers.
29. Poison antidotes.
30. Computer software/hardware comparisons.
31. Cumulative weather data.
32. Abbreviations.
33. Wine information for the connoisseur.
34. Horse racing statistics.
35. Anecdotal material for those obliged to make speeches.
36. Insurance policy inventory including coverage, cost, account numbers, and deductibles for house, car, health, and other kinds of insurance.

This list isn't exhaustive, and only a few of these applications may be of use to you, but it serves to illustrate the multiple possibilities primarily involving the storage of information. How would you store this information? Use the *Electronic Memorandum* program Listing 1-1, or the *Data Base Demonstration* program, Listing 1-14, for your own tailor-made application.

Listing 1-1. The Electronic Memorandum Program.

```
10      REM LISTING 1-1: The Electronic Memorandum Program
50      REM E$=FLAG TO INDICATE WHETHER DATA ID HAS BEEN USED
60      REM Z=ID NUMBER FOR ENTRY
70      REM M AND M$ USED TO COUNT ITEMS PRINTED TO SCREEN
90      FULLW 2:CLEARW 2:GOTOXY 1,1
95      PRINT,"       Electronic Memorandum":PRINT:PRINT
100     PRINT,"          SELECT AN OPTION:"
105     PRINT
110     PRINT,"COMMAND","FUNCTION"
115     PRINT
120     PRINT ,"INPUT","INPUT A NEW ITEM"
130     PRINT ,"CAT","GENERATE A CATALOG OF COMMON ENTRIES"
140     PRINT ,"FIND","FIND A PREVIOUSLY STORED ITEM"
150     PRINT ,"REDO","EDIT A PREVIOUSLY STORED ITEM"
160     PRINT ,"DEL","DELETE A PREVIOUSLY STORED ITEM"
170     PRINT ,"END","END THE PROGRAM"
180     PRINT ," ";:  INPUT A$
190     IF A$="INPUT" THEN 270
200     IF A$="CAT" THEN 660
210     IF A$="FIND" THEN 960
220     IF A$="REDO" THEN 460
230     IF A$="DEL" THEN 1140
240     IF A$="END" THEN END:REM CLOSE THE FILE
250     PRINT"ILLEGAL COMMAND--PLEASE ENTER"
255     PRINT"     ONE OF THE FOLLOWING:"
260     GOTO 110
265     REM Routine to input data
270     CLEARW 2:GOTOXY 1,1
275     INPUT "Enter a keyword (may be up to 20 letters long) ";B$
280     IF LEN(B$)>20 THEN 270
285     REM lines 290-310 are for verification of catalog when inputtin
        g-you may wish to delete these lines to save time
```

```
290     INPUT"Is this correct (1=YES , 2=NO):";D
310     IF D<>1 THEN 270
320     PRINT "Enter the data for this record (may be up to 105 letters
        long)"
325     INPUT C$
330     IF LEN(C$)>105 THEN 320
340     D$=LEFT$(B$,1)
360     OPEN "R",1,D$
370     Z=LOF(1)+1
380     FIELD #1,3 AS E$,20 AS F$,105 AS G$
400     LSET F$=B$
410     LSET G$=C$
420     LSET E$="999":REM this marks the record
430     PUT #1,Z:REM store the entry
440     CLOSE #1
450     GOTO 90
455     REM routine to edit data
460     CLEARW 2:GOTOXY 1,1
465     INPUT "ENTER THE KEYWORD FOR THE DATA TO BE EDITTED ";B$
470     D$=LEFT$(B$,1)
480     Z=1
490     OPEN "R",1,D$:IF LOF(1)=0 THEN PRINT "FILE END":CLOSE #1:GOTO 1
        00
500     FIELD #1,3 AS E$,20 AS F$,105 AS G$
510     IF Z>LOF(1)          THEN PRINT "FILE END":CLOSE #1:GOTO 100
520     GET #1,Z
530     IF E$<>"999" THEN Z=Z+1:GOTO 500:REM if no entry go on
540     IF LEFT$(F$,LEN(B$))<>B$ THEN Z=Z+1:GOTO 500:REM if no match go
        on
550     CLEARW 2
560     PRINT,"MEMORANDUM:"
570     PRINT G$:PRINT
580     INPUT "Do you wish to edit this item (1=YES, 2=NO)";Y
590     IF Y<>1 THEN Z=Z+1:GOTO 500
600     INPUT "Re-enter all data: ";C$
610     IF LEN(C$)>105 THEN PRINT "DATA TOO LONG -- MUST BE LESS THAN 1
        05 LETTERS"
620     LSET G$=C$:LSET F$=B$:LSET E$="999"
630     PUT #1,Z
640     INPUT "Edit another item with this keyword (1=YES, 2=NO) ";Y
650     Z=Z+1:IF Y<>1 THEN CLOSE #1:GOTO 100 ELSE 500
655     REM Routine to list catalog of entries
660     CLEARW 2:GOTOXY 1,1
665     PRINT "SELECT: 1)LIST A CATALOG OF ALL ITEMS ON FILE"
670     INPUT "          2)LIST ALL ITEMS WITH A SPECIFIC KEYWORD ";Y
680     ON Y GOTO 810,690
685     GOTO 660
690     INPUT "enter the keyword ";H$
700     D$=LEFT$(H$,1)
710     Z=1:M=1:?:?"ITEM #","ITEM"
720     OPEN "R",1,D$:IF LOF(1)=0 THEN ?"FILE END":CLOSE:GOTO 100
730     FIELD #1,3 AS E$,20 AS F$,105 AS G$
740     IF Z>LOF(1) THEN PRINT"--------------":PRINT:CLOSE:GOTO 100
750     GET #1,Z
760     IF E$<>"999" THEN Z=Z+1:GOTO 730
770     PRINT Z,F$:M=M+1
780     IF INT(M/17)=M/17 THEN INPUT "MORE TO COME; PRESS ENTER WHEN RE
        ADY:";M$
```

```
790   Z=Z+1
800   GOTO 730
810   CLEARW 2:GOTOXY 1,1
820   PRINT "RECORD #","KEYWORD"
830   X=65
840   J$=CHR$(X)
850   D$=J$
860   Z=1
870   CLOSE #1
880   OPEN "R",1,D$:IF LOF(1)=0 THEN X=X+1:IF X<=90 THEN GOTO 840 ELS
      E CLOSE #1:GOTO 100
890   FIELD #1,3 AS E$,20 AS F$,105 AS G$
900   IF Z>LOF(1) THEN X=X+1:IF X<=90 THEN 840 ELSE CLOSE:GOTO 100
910   GET #1,Z
920   IF E$<>"999" THEN Z=Z+1:GOTO 890
930   PRINT Z,F$
940   Z=Z+1
950   GOTO 890
960   CLEARW 2:GOTOXY 1,1
970   INPUT "Enter keyword ";B$
980   D$=LEFT$(B$,1)
990   Z=1
1000  OPEN "R",1,D$:IF LOF(1)=0 THEN ?"FILE END":CLOSE #1:GOTO 100
1010  IF Z>LOF(1) THEN PRINT"FILE END":INPUT"Press RETURN to continue
      ";M$:CLOSE:GOTO 90
1020  FIELD #1,3 AS E$,20 AS F$,105 AS G$
1030  GET #1,Z
1040  IF LEFT$(F$,LEN(B$))=B$ THEN 1080
1050  IF E$<>"999" THEN Z=Z+1:GOTO 1010
1060  Z=Z+1
1070  GOTO 1010
1080  PRINT "KEYWORD: ";F$,"ITEM #: ";Z
1090  PRINT G$
1100  PRINT
1110  Z=Z+1:M=M+1
1120  IF INT(M/5)=M/5 THEN INPUT "more to come; press RETURN when
      ready ";M$
1130  GOTO 1010
1140  CLEARW 2:GOTOXY 1,1
1150  INPUT"Enter keyword, record number: ";B$,Z
1160  D$=LEFT$(B$,1)
1180  OPEN "R",#1,D$
1190  FIELD #1,3 AS E$,20 AS F$,105 AS G$
1200  GET #1,Z
1210  IF LEFT$(F$,LEN(B$))<>B$ THEN ?"Keyword and item number don’t
      match":CLOSE #1:GOTO 100
1220  CLEARW 2
1230  PRINT "Keyword ";F$
1240  PRINT G$
1250  PRINT
1260  INPUT "If you want to delete this record type ’1’";Y
1270  IF Y<>1 THEN CLOSE #1:GOTO 100
1280  FIELD #1,3 AS E$,20 AS F$,105 AS G$
1290  LSET E$="":REM erasing
1300  LSET G$="":REM information
1310  LSET F$="":REM from this record
1320  PUT #1,Z
1330  CLOSE #1
1340  GOTO 100
```

THE ELECTRONIC MEMORANDUM PROGRAM

In Listing 1-1 you will find a program that should be useful to everyone; think of it as a memory extension. The program allows you to store any type of information (household, business, financial) under a "keyword" for instant retrieval at a later date. For instance, if you had an appointment on a certain date, the pertinent information could be stored under the keyword "9/11/85;" on that date you would simply type "9/11/85" to receive a printout of all appointments or reminders stored under that keyword. Likewise, a remainder for an annual occasion could be entered under a keyword specifying only the month and day. Keywords may be dates or words such as "MARKS BIRTHDAY." Telephone numbers, business contacts, important dates, and many other bulletin-board type scraps of information could be stored so that they could not be forgotten or misplaced. This information could include the number and expiration date of your driver's license, the serial numbers of credit cards (and whom to notify if they are lost), expense account information, information about insurance policies, warranty information on all appliances, names and addresses of dealers, magazine subscription dates, handy home repair tips (for example, the size of the air conditioner filter), lock combinations, special codes, the method of resetting a digital watch, Christmas gifts and to whom they were given, eyeglass prescription, and so on, *ad infinitum*. Additionally, information may be stored under more than one keyword to ensure the ability to retrieve it.

AN INDEX TO YOUR LIBRARY

How often do you remember reading an important article or chapter, yet you can't remember the name or date of the magazine or book? A personal computer can easily organize and cross-reference your books and articles for instant retrieval using only the name, subject, author, or other parameter to retrieve the entries you are interested in. With the wealth of personal computer magazines available, an index to pertinent articles will ease the difficulty of finding that special patch or program.

A program to accomplish indexing could store information regarding items as a continuous string of data, each string being composed of several "fields," and each field separated by a comma. An example of a string with fields describing a magazine article could be as follows:

The Stock Market,	name of article/book
Business Today,	name of magazine/book
5,	volume no.
6/84,	date
I,	category #1
S,	category #2
1,	storage location
Smith	author

If data is formatted on disk in a manner similar to this example, *random access* disk commands will allow the computer to search through a selected field to find all entries with a given field. For example, the user could specify a search for all entries having an author named "Smith." The computer would then search through the entire disk file examining all the fields containing author's names (the last field in the above example) and printing all those with "Smith" as the author. The disk commands used for random access for the above format are shown in Listing 1-2.

Likewise, the computer could examine more than one field to limit the search to more specific entries. As an example, you could request a list of all articles published after 1980 concerning the stock market. The computer would search both the category and date fields for data meeting these requirements. A listing of all the information concerning each item would be output at the conclusion of the search. Diskettes or high-speed fixed disks are best-suited for this application.

WORD PROCESSING

Pencil and paper have never been the ideal servants of the mind. Paper refuses to accept instant

Listing 1-2. The Random Access Sample Routine.

```
10      REM Listing 1.02 The Random Access Sample Routine
15      FULLW 2:CLEARW 2:GOTOXY 1,1
20      OPEN "R",1,"FILE":REM open a file for random access ("R") using
        buffer #1 named "FILE"
30      REM format buffer #1 as 30 letters for the name of the article/
        book, 30 letters for the name of the magazine
40      REM two letters for volume no., 5 letters for date, 1 for categ
        ory#1, 1 for category #2, 1 for storage location
50      REM and 10 for author name
60      FIELD #1,30 AS NME$,30 AS MAG$,2 AS VOLUME$,5 AS DTE$,1 AS C1$,
        1 AS C2$,1 AS WHERE$,10 AS AUTH$
65      REM set file counter to 1 to begin at beginning of file
67      X=1:GOTO 120
70      REM if reach end of file, then end search
80      IF EOF(1) THEN GOTO 500
110     REM read the next entry into buffer #1
120     GET 1,X
130     REM is the author "SMITH"? if so, print out that entry
140     IF AUTH$="SMITH" THEN PRINT NME$;MAG$;VOLUME$;DTE$;C1$;C2$;
        WHERE$;AUTH$
150     REM increment counter
160     X=X+1:GOTO 80
500     CLOSE:REM continue program from here
```

changes at the whim of the writer. Instead, the writer must resort to erasing, inserting, cutting, and pasting.

But no longer are we restricted to pencil and paper. Word processing programs can allow rearrangement of words at the touch of a finger; erasures are a thing of the past. Correction fluid has likewise been replaced by the DELETE key. Word processors give you the ability to write spontaneously. Whereas most people try to edit their words before committing them to paper, the advent of word processors allows you to type as you think, and later rearrange words, sentences, and paragraphs in a painless fashion. Thus, the writer can make ideas concrete by displaying them on the video screen and later attend to the grammatical aspects, before printing out a manuscript. Many writers feel that this enhances creativity and makes writing easier and more enjoyable.

After your manuscript, letters, or documents are corrected on the video screen, you may assign various codes determining page widths, page lengths, page numbering, margins, and so on; the printer will reproduce the document perfectly, as you have specified. You can then edit the document and print it out again, without having to devote time and effort to retyping it. Additionally, this information can be stored on a floppy disk for later review and retrieval.

Anyone who writes professionally, or composes a letter each day, should investigate the use of a word processor. Most are very easy to use and can be tremendous time, labor, and money savers. Many experts consider this application one of the most useful for personal computer owners.

With most word processors you can:

- **Block Move.** This feature lets you move pieces of your text—from a word to several paragraphs—around like blocks. You can also delete a block at whatever point you designate, and the rest of the text will fill in the "hole." Conversely, you can add new blocks at any point. Think of a word processor as a processor writing, capable of slicing, chopping, and dicing for the language with ease.

- **Word Wrap.** As you type on a word processor you can forget hitting the carriage return key at the end of each line, as the computer automatically puts as many words as possible on one line and then starts a new one. This, in computerese, is called *word wrap.*
- **Search and Replace.** You can instruct the word-processor program to search the entire text or a portion of it for the occurrence of a particular word or phrase. Suppose you would like to correct a misspelled name throughout a six-page letter: just type in the name as you misspelled it and again as spelled correctly; the program will automatically correct this error throughout the text. The search command may also be used to rapidly locate a section in a large manuscript.
- **Typeover.** When you want to substitute one word or phrase for another, you can type your change right over the existing text, and the unwanted letters will vanish as the new ones appear to fill their places.
- **Justify.** Some programs will automatically adjust the spacing between words or letters so that each line can be printed out at the same length. This process is called *right justification.* Left justification simply means that the lines are aligned at the left margin as usual, although some programs can create special effects by aligning text only at the right margin or by centering all text.

These are the most basic features found on word processing programs. Many other special features come with certain word processing packages. For example, a *mouse* can be used to position the cursor at any point on the screen to facilitate editing. An automatic dictionary program can check the spelling of each word you write against its vocabulary and make corrections. An automatic thesaurus program can, at your command, display five to ten synonyms for thousands of common English words. Other programs are designed to correct faulty grammar—for those who don't mind having a computerized English teacher—or allow you to design type fonts and integrate graphs and pictures with your text. Several typesetting firms will also accept word processor output directly via modem or floppy disk for instant, money-saving typesetting jobs.

LETTER WRITING

A specialized text editor, designed to edit and format your letters, could expedite the process considerably. For example, if you are writing a business letter, the address of the recipient could be stored when it is typed at the beginning of the letter and later recalled to print the envelope. If you are writing the same letter to several people, the body could be stored in the computer. You need type only the addresses and other personalized information, and this information would be integrated with the text to form a complete letter. Additionally, the editing features of a word processor facilitate the correction of mistakes while you are entering the body of the letter or the personalized information. A mailing list program can be integrated with such a program to automatically produce personalized letters.

CATEGORIZING INFORMATION

The purpose of the *subroutine* in Listing 1-3 is to categorize information stored in random access format on a floppy disk. Data is stored on disk with, for instance, a 10-character keyword preceding 240 characters of descriptive information (many random access disk systems have a string length limit of 255 total characters). The subroutine searches through the disk files to find and print all entries having a given keyword. This subroutine operates on the same principle as the *Electronic Memorandum* presented earlier in this chapter, but it is simplified for this application. Listing 1-4 is a simple categorizing program.

Why is a categorizer program useful? Businessmen, writers, and other professionals who need to categorize information for presentations, reports, outlines, or organizational purposes may find that a program incorporating this subroutine is helpful. A similar program was used in the preparation of

Listing 1-3. Categorizer Subroutine.

```
10      REM LISTING 1.03 Categorizer Subroutine
15      REM uses disk commands
20      REM incorporate with a data base which stored information
30      REM in the format of (E.G.) 10 characters for keywords
40      REM and (E.G.) 240 characters for descriptive information
900     REM select keyword/category to search for
950     FULLW 2:CLEARW 2:GOTOXY 1,1
960     INPUT "ENTER KEYWORD/CATEGORY:",A$
1000    REM open a file for random access ("R") using buffer #1 and
        file named "DATA"
1010    OPEN "R",1,"DATA",110:X=1:REM set file counter to 1 to begin at
        beginning of file
1020    REM format buffer #1 as 10 characters for the category name
1030    REM and 100 characters for descriptive information
1040    FIELD #1,10 AS CAT$,100 AS INFO$
1070    REM if reach end of file the end search
1080    IF EOF(1) THEN 2000
1110    REM read the next entry into buffer #1
1120    GET 1,X
1125    REM if this item is the desired category then print out
1130    IF CAT$=A$ THEN PRINT INFO$
1140    REM INCREMENT COUNTER
1150    X=X+1:GOTO 1080
2000    CLOSE:REM continue program here...
```

Listing 1-4. Categorizer Program.

```
10      REM LISTING1.04 Categorizer program
15      REM uses disk commands
20      FULLW 2:CLEARW 2:GOTOXY 1,1
30      DIM A$(1000)
40      PRINT "SELECT: 1)ENTER STRINGS"
41      PRINT "         2)CATEGORIZE"
42      INPUT "         3)END           ",A:X=1
50      ON A GOTO 60,200,400
55      GOTO 40
60      OPEN "O",1,"CATEGORY.DAT":REM open sequential file -no append
        function
70      PRINT "Enter up to three lines of text with keyword at the
        beginning"
75      A$=" ":PRINT #1,A$
80      LINE INPUT A$
90      IF A$="END" THEN 120
100     PRINT #1,A$:REM writes strings with embedded commas to file
110     GOTO 80
120     CLOSE:GOTO 40
200     INPUT "ENTER KEYWORD ",B$
205     ON ERROR GOTO 260
210     OPEN "I",1,"CATEGORY.DAT":REM open sequential file for input
220     WHILE NOT EOF(1):REM checking for end of file
```

```
230   LINE INPUT #1,A$
240   IF B$=LEFT$(A$,LEN(B$)) THEN A$(X)=A$:X=X+1
250   WEND
260   CLOSE #1
270   INPUT "OUTPUT TO 1) PRINTER OR 2) DISPLAY ";A
280   ON A GOTO 290,340
285   GOTO 270
290   INPUT"READY PRINTER; PRESS RETURN TO CONTINUE ",C$
300   FOR K=1 TO X-1
310   LPRINT A$(K)
320   NEXT K
330   GOTO 40
340   CLEARW 2:GOTOXY 1,1
345   FOR K=1 TO X-1
350   PRINT A$(K)
360   IF INT(K/17)=K/17 THEN INPUT "MORE TO COME; PRESS RETURN TO
      CONTINUE",C$:CLEARW 2
370   NEXT K
380   GOTO 40
400   END
```

this book. Many other applications, including categorizing income tax deductions, are possible.

A RECIPE INDEX AND CALCULATOR

A collection of your favorite recipes can be stored on your computer for rapid and selective retrieval. A list of the characteristics of each recipe could be included (for example, time required for preparation, hot or cold, number served, meal (dinner, lunch, or breakfast), expense, and calories). Using these characteristics, the computer could index recipes and print lists of recipes with a selected characteristic for a special occasion.

A recipe calculator could change the amounts of each ingredient so that the proper amount of the recipe will be made for a given number of people. A simple recipe calculator subroutine is presented in Listing 1-5. It can be used alone or can be incorporated in a recipe database program.

If the costs for various ingredients were stored in your computer, the cost of a given recipe could be instantaneously computed; allowance would also be made for the number of persons to be served. This type of program could be especially useful to those with a sideline or full-time bakery or catering service, as the costs for any recipe for any number of people can be quickly estimated.

A sample information record for one recipe might look like Fig. 1-1. Note how commas are used to separate fields and, in the ingredients field, how asterisks separate the sub-fields.

MEATLOAF,	6,	1.5 lb.gr.beef*1 cup milk*.5 cup onion*egg,
name of item	no. servings.	abbreviated ingredients
350	1.5 hr.,	Bill's favorite
oven temp.	bake time	comments

A program to store information used in selecting and mixing *drinks* for instant retrieval could be created. Such a program could even store pictures of the size and shape glasses to use with each drink. The computer could also suggest an appropriate cheese to accompany a selected wine.

ITINERARY ASSISTANT

A list of appointments, deadlines, and various tasks could be stored in a computer and displayed in a specified format to assist you with your itinerary. The electronic memorandum program may be used for this task. Another format could be that of a calendar; each day-block would be filled with things to do. Is there something you must do peri-

Listing 1-5. Recipe Calculator Program.

```
10    REM LISTING1.05 Recipe Calculator
20    REM could be improved to convert units of measurment (E.G. pints to quarts)
25    DIM A$(30),B(30),C$(30)
30    INPUT "How many servings is the original recipe intended for ";S1
40    INPUT "How many servings are to be prepared ";S2
50    R=S2/S1
60    N=1
70    PRINT
80    PRINT
90    PRINT "Enter the name of each ingredient, the amount, the measure, (E.G. MILK,1,PINT).":PRINT
100   INPUT A$(N),B(N),C$(N)
110   IF A$(N)="END" OR A$(N)="end" THEN 130
120   N=N+1:GOTO 100
130   FOR X=1 TO N
140   PRINT A$(X),R*B(X),C$(X)
150   NEXT X
160   PRINT
170   END
```

odically, but often forget? Program the computer to automatically remind you each time.

A program could also printout a *daily* appointment calendar of your custom design. It could include beginning and ending times, time intervals, and provisions for recording expenses, and comments. Incorporate the day-of-the-week program found in this chapter.

The professional may use a more sophisticated program for the purposes of billing clients for time. The computer can also be used as a medication reminder, signaling with an audible alarm, for those on complex therapeutic regimens.

PHONE TIMER

When you are making long-distance phone calls, keeping track of the elapsed time can save you a considerable amount of money. Usually the first one or three minutes is charged at a flat rate, but for the remainder of the call the charges are

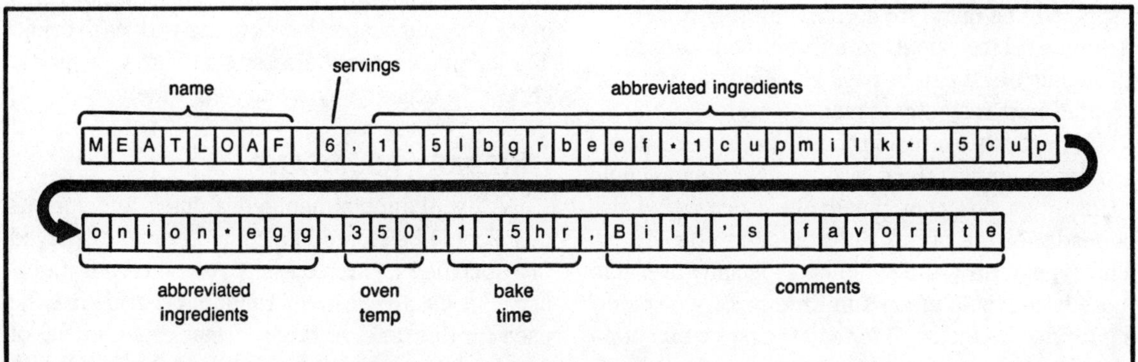

Fig. 1-1. An information record in a recipe file might look something like this.

updated by the minute. A countdown timer that makes use of a *timing loop*, such as FOR X = 1 to 500: NEXT X (which requires approximately 1 second), can display the amount of time remaining until the next charge. Also, a record could be kept of the number called and the cost for the call, for use with income tax deductions or for comparison with the telephone bill. The program in Listing 1-6 will time your calls and keep track of the charges.

TELEPHONE FILE, DIALER, AND ANSWERING MACHINE

Listings of emergency and frequently used telephone numbers could be stored if the list is sufficiently long to warrant computer search capabilities.

The data strings used to store this information could be formatted as shown in Fig. 1-2.

For those with a hardware bent, the addition

Listing 1-6. Long Distance Telephone Call Tally.

```
10     REM LISTING1.06 Long Distance Telephone Call Tally
15     DEFSNG B
20     FULLW 2:CLEARW 2:GOTOXY 1,1
25     INPUT "Need telephone tips (Y/N) ";A$
30     IF A$="Y" THEN 300
35     IF A$<>"N" THEN 25
40     PRINT:PRINT,"TELEPHONE COST TALLY"
50     INPUT "IS THIS AN OPERATOR ASSISTED CALL (Y/N) ";A$
60     IF A$="Y" THEN O=1 ELSE O=0
70     INPUT "ENTER INITIAL FLAT RATE ";B
80     INPUT "ENTER CHARGE PER ADDITIONAL MINUTE ";C
90     INPUT "ENTER DISCOUNT AS PERCENTAGE#",D:D=100-D
100    D=D*.01
110    PRINT "TO BEGIN TIMING PRESS 'RETURN'"
120    PRINT "TO END TIMING MOVE MOUSE TO RUN WINDOW"
130    INPUT A$
135    CLEARW 2
140    GOTOXY 1,4:PRINT "ELAPSED MIN","CURRECT COST","SECONDS TO ADD
       CHARGE"
150    S=60:B1=B*D
160    GOTOXY 1,6:PRINT T,B1,S
165    REM LINE 170 ACTS AS A TIMING LOOP; ADJUST TO YOUR BASIC
170    FOR X=1 TO 1250:NEXT X
180    S=S-1
185    IF S<>0 THEN 160
190    T=T+1:S=60
200    IF (O=1) AND (T<3) THEN B1=B1+B*D:GOTO 160
210    B1=B1+C*D
240    GOTO 180
300    CLEARW 2:GOTOXY 1,1
305    PRINT "The flat rate for operator assisted calls is for the
       first"
310    PRINT "3 min and for the first min on direct-dial calls"
315    PRINT "discount times for calling are:"
320    PRINT "60%--8AM-5PM SUNDAY / 8AM-11PM SATUDAY / 11PM-8AM DAILY"

340    PRINT "35%--8AM-11PM ON HOLIDAYS / 5PM-11PM SUNDAY-FRIDAY"
345    REM check with your long distance provider for correct figures
350    PRINT:GOTO 40
```

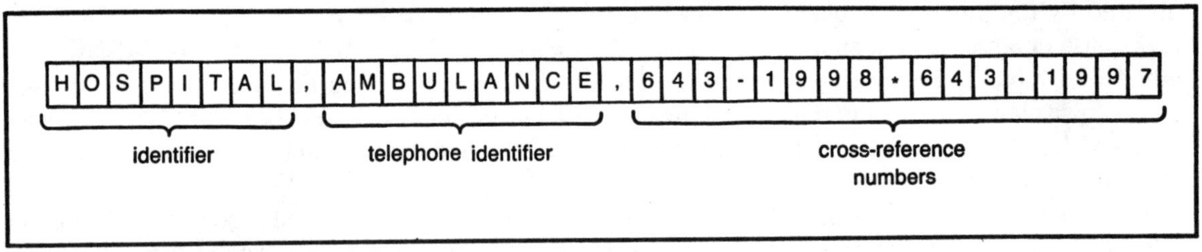

Fig. 1-2. Possible record format for a telephone number utility program.

of a pulse or tone dialing circuit for a modem with automatic dialing capability could allow a computer to search and then automatically dial a desired number. In connection with a burglar/security alarm system, the computer could be instructed to dial the police or fire departments and deliver a tape-recorded message. You could also construct a computer-controlled, programmable telephone answering machine with capabilities far exceeding those on the market.

GREETING CARD/INVITATION LIST

A mailing list program could be used to address your Christmas greeting cards. If your list is large enough, the computer could sort zip codes, allowing you to send your cards under the bulk mail rate. (This would probably only be practical for businesses with large customer files.) Additionally, the computer could print a short "hello" note on the back of each card. The same idea could be applied to producing an invitation list for a party or meeting.

Similarly, a list of dates of birthdays and anniversaries could be stored and each month could remind you of the important dates for the upcoming month.

PERSONAL TIME MANAGEMENT SYSTEM

A personal time management system would assist you in planning the most effective schedule for completing a list of tasks. Input could include the description of each goal, the priority of that goal (using A, B, or C to represent categories of importance) and the deadline date. The program could use *PERT* (Program Evaluation and Review Technique) or *critical path analysis* to plan and output a schedule most evenly distributing the work load. PERT is described in numerous computer programming texts; PERT programs are available for many personal computers. Many people have found that they can accomplish much more if they make schedules and deadlines for themselves; PERT analysis will make all of that much simpler.

DECISION MAKER

Complex decision making may be facilitated through the use of the computer. In the program in Listing 1-7, the computer first requests you to enter a list of the factors involved in making a decision. Next, you are asked to rate the relative importance of each of these factors on a scale of ten. Finally, for each possible outcome to the decision, you are asked top rate the favorability of each factor on a scale of ten. This data is then analyzed, and the outcome with the highest "favorability" score for the most important factors is the one chosen as the final decision.

The most favorable decision will have the highest score, computed by summing the "rate of favorability" multiplied by the relative importance for each factor.

For example, if you had several locations in mind for building a home and could not come to a decision, you could form the following chart of factors for making the decision; these factors would be the input to the decision-making program.

Shopping: Are there adequate facilities nearby?
Churches: Are they available and convenient?
Neighbors: Are they likely to be compatible with your lifestyle?
Police and fire protection: Are they adequate for the area?

Listing 1-7. The Universal Decision-Making Program.

```
10      REM Listing1.07 - The Universal Decision Making Program
20      DIM A$(100),B(100),C(100),D$(100)
30      INPUT "Enter the number of factors used in making the decision
        ";NUM
40      PRINT "Enter factors and relative importance on scale of ten:"
50      FOR X=1 TO NUM
60      PRINT "#";X;" ";:INPUT A$(X),B(X)
70      NEXT X
80      INPUT "Enter number of possible outcomes ",X
90      PRINT "Enter name of each outcome:"
100     FOR I=1 TO X
110     PRINT "#";I;" ";:INPUT D$(I)
120     NEXT I
130     PRINT "Now, let's rank each factor for each possible outcome:"
140     FOR I=1 TO X
150     PRINT "for outcome #";I;" ";D$(I);","
160     PRINT "rank these factors on a scale of ten:"
170     FOR J=1 TO NUM
180     PRINT A$(J);:INPUT R
185     C(I)=C(I)+B(J)*R
190     NEXT J
200     PRINT
210     NEXT I
220     PRINT
230     PRINT "rankings of outcomes are (highest ranking=best decision)
        :"
240     FOR I=1 TO X
250     PRINT D$(I),C(I)
260     NEXT I
270     PRINT:PRINT"TO BREAK POINT MOUSE TO RUN WINDOW"
275     REM ENDLESS LOOP KEEPS OUTPUT ON SCREEN
280     GOTO 280
```

Schools: Are the schools your children will attend nearby?

Hospital: Is there a medical center nearby?

Hazards: Are there hazards such as oil tanks or streams that might overflow?

Recreation: Are there suitable facilities within walking distance?

Traffic: Are the streets quiet and safe?

Transportation: Is public transportation available?

Lay of land and landscaping: Is the land well-drained and not subject to erosion?

Water: Is there an adequate pressure and is it drinkable?

Nuisances: Are there nearby sources of excessive noise, smoke, soot, dust, or odors that will degrade your environment?

If this process is still too complex, try this program:

```
.
.
 5  PRINT "THE DECISION IS:"
10  X = RND (0): IF X < .5 PRINT "NEGATIVE"
    ELSE
    PRINT "AFFIRMATIVE"
.
.
```

If you need help in making a decision that many people have to make, at least once in a lifetime, you may want to use the program in Listing 1-8, which

Listing 1-8. The Gas Guzzler Program.

```
10      REM LISTING1.08 - The Gas Guzzler Program
20      REM determines the economic incentive in trading off a
30      REM gas guzzler for a more economical car
35      FULLW 2:CLEARW 2:GOTOXY 1,1
40      INPUT "Enter the new car's m.p.g, current car's m.p.g. ";R,M
50      INPUT "Enter the cost of the new car in dollars ";C
60      INPUT "Enter the average number of miles you drive per year ";D
70      INPUT "Enter the current price par gallon of gasoline ";P
80      R=R/(R-M):Y=(C*R*M)/(D*P)
90      PRINT:PRINT "If ";Y;" years is greater than the number of years
        you"
100     PRINT "were planning on keeping your car, you should stick with
        "
110     PRINT "your gas guzzler for the time you normally would have"
120     PRINT "kept it.  Otherwise, you should trade it in now."
```

determines the economic incentive for trading off a gas-guzzling car for a new, more economical car sooner than you would if gas prices were not a factor.

HEALTH

Your personal computer can even help you maintain your health. A listing of the caloric or nutrient content of various foods could be stored and subsequently referenced for determining the nutritive value of the food you eat. Additionally, data on the sugar or salt content of foods could be stored for the diabetic or person on a salt-free diet. Of course, such a program lends itself well to diet planning.

"Nutritive Value of Foods," Home and Garden Bulletin No. 72, Agricultural Research Service, is an excellent source of nutritive values for all foods and is available from the Superintendent of Documents, U.S. Govt. Printing Office, Washington, D.C., Stock #001-000-03667-0. It lists the water, calorie, protein, fat, carbohydrate, mineral, and vitamin composition of all foods.

A low-calorie diet planning program could compute the number of calories you use per day (on the basis of weight, sex, height, and activities). Of course, if you eat more calories than you use up in energy, you build up reserves in the form of fat. Thus, weight control is primarily based on calorie balance. The amount of weight you could lose by either reducing intake or increasing activities would be mathematically calculated. The following data should be helpful in writing a program to help you lose weight or maintain health through exercise.

A complete nutritional analysis program would allow you to input the types and amounts of foods you have eaten during the day, would compute the total intake of proteins, carbohydrate, fats, fiber, vitamins, and minerals, and would determine your average daily intake of each per day. Similarly, it would compute your average energy expenditure (see Table 1-1) and then subtract this from your average daily nutrient intake to determine your calorie balance and to compare your intake with the recommended daily allowances for your age, sex, and weight (see Table 1-2). Thus, areas for improvement could be easily identified. A diet plan could then be determined to achieve these improvements.

One hobbyist uses a computer to determine his pulse rate and lead him through an exercise session, acting as the coach and timer. Along similar lines, another hobbyist computes the aerobic points he earns in bicycling.

A general-purpose data plotting subroutine could graph morning resting pulse on the X axis

Table 1-1. Energy Consumption Table.

Intensity Exercise	Heart (Beats Minute)	Respiration (Breaths/Minute)	Energy Consumption (Calories/Hour)
maximum	200	50	1440
very	150	30	1008
heavy	140	25	864
fairly heavy	130	20	720
moderate	120	18	576
light	110	16	432
very light	100	14	288
resting	70	10	100

versus minutes run previous day on the y axis, miles run versus subjective feeling at end of day, or many other inputs to allow you to see where you've been and where you are going!

Listing 1-9 is a simple program that will help you calculate your pulse rate.

The beginning runner is often unsure how fast he should run. Pulse taking can be helpful to assure beginners that they're doing the right amount of work—not too much or too little. First, determine your *base training pulse* using this formula

$$[220 - (\text{your age})] \times .65$$

Table 1-2. Recommended Caloric Intake Table.

Mean heights and weights and recommended energy intake

Category	Age (years)	Weight (kg)	(lb)	Height (cm)	(in)	Energy needs (with range) (kcall)	(MJ)
Infants	0.0-0.5	6	13	60	24	kg × 115 (95-145)	kg × .48
	0.5-1.0	9	20	71	28	kg × 105 (80-135)	kg × .44
Children	1-3	13	29	90	35	1300 (900-1800)	5.5
	4-6	20	44	112	44	1700 (1300-2300)	7.1
	7-10	28	62	132	52	2400 (1650-3300)	10.1
Males	11-14	45	99	157	62	2700 (2000-3700)	11.3
	15-18	66	145	176	69	2800 (2100-3900)	11.8
	19-22	70	154	177	70	2900 (2500-3300)	12.2
	23-50	70	154	178	70	2700 (2300-3100)	11.3
	51-75	70	70	178	154	2400 (2000-2800)	10.1
	76+	70	154	178	70	2050 (1650-2450)	8.6
Females	11-14	46	101	157	62	2200 (1500-3000)	9.2
	15-18	55	120	163	64	2100 (1200-3000)	8.8
	19-22	55	120	163	64	2100 (1700-2500)	8.8
	23-50	55	120	163	64	2000 (1600-2400)	8.4
	51-75	55	120	163	64	1800 (1400-2200)	7.6
	76+	55	120	163	64	1600 (1200-2000)	6.7
Pregnancy						+ 300	
Lactation						+ 500	

One gram of Carbohydrate = 4 calories
One gram of Fat = 9 calories
One gram of Protein = 4 calories

Listing 1-9. The Pulse Rate Program.

```
10    REM LISTING1.09 - The Pulse Rate Program
20    FULLW 2:CLEARW 2:GOTOXY 1,1
30    INPUT "Enter your age ",AGE
40    INPUT "Enter the number of beats per minute ";N
50    PRINT "Training pulse=";INT((.6)*(220-AGE))
```

Anyone who makes sure that his or her pulse does not rise above this value is in the safety zone where the heart is being strengthened rather than overtaxed.

SHORTHAND TRANSLATOR

You could develop a shorthand system that your computer could be programmed to understand and translate. The system could be similar to that used by court reporters, in which a single key represents a word or part of a word. In this manner, you could quickly commit your thoughts to paper, and the computer could quickly analyze the shorthand and print the English equivalent.

The basic stenographer's character and word assignment is given in Table 1-3.

In a like manner, a machine language program could translate a single keystroke into a full command. For instance, such a program could translate a Control-P or shifted P to the word PRINT, thereby facilitating the input of a program.

KITCHEN INVENTORY

A file of all food items on hand (pantry inventory) could be useful in determining whether or not a given recipe can be prepared. As each item is added or subtracted, the transaction would be entered into the computer. If a desired level of inventory

Table 1-3. Basic Steno Character Assignment Chart.

Character	Word	Suffix	Character	Word	Suffix
A	and	able	V	very	ver
B	been	bility	W	with	ward
C	can	cial	X	experience	
D	down	day	Y	you	
E	even	ent	Z	the	zation
F	from	ful	0	zero	
G	good	ght	1	one	
H	have	hood	2	two	
I	into	ing	3	three	
J	just		4	four	
K	know		5	five	
L	like	less	6	six	
M	more	ment	7	seven	
N	not	ness	8	eight	
O	other	ous	9	nine	
P	people		!	hundred	
Q	quite		@	thousand	
R	right	rent	#	million	
S	said	self	$	dollar	
T	that	tion	%	percent	
U	united	ugh	¢	cent	

is specified, the computer could automatically print out a shopping list of items that are below desired quantity levels. An inventory program of this type would be best suited for the gourmet cook who must have a wide variety of seasonings and other ingredients on hand. The inventory of a wine collection or food in the deep freezer may also be maintained.

RATING CALCULATIONS

An equation to determine a rating for a particular stock, car, horse, home, or any item of value could be computerized if it is referred to often or is complex. For example, the horse racing fan could use the following empirically derived equation to determine an objective rating for a particular horse:

$$\text{Rating} = (W + P/3 + S/6) \times 100/R + E/850$$

where W = the number of wins
P = the number of places
S = the number of shows
R = the number of races
E = the amount of earnings in dollars

Rating equations are empirically derived or are determined by finding the statistical correlation between a set of factors and the outcomes that the factors influence.

INVENTORY OF POSSESSIONS

A file of your personal property could be stored in computer format for insurance purposes or for determining your net worth. A database program could record the date of purchase, the place of purchase, the length of the warranty, description of item, price, serial number, and model number. For instance, you could set up a simple database for tracking possessions by using these four fields: date, store, item, and price. This information could be entered from sales receipts or from your checkbook. At the end of the year, the database could be printed and a backup disk or cassette put in safe keeping. This could save you $10,000 or more in the event of a major disaster, because you will have excellent documentation of what you've owned.

The computer may also be useful in comparing various insurance policies to determine which plan offers what you need at the lowest cost. Professionally prepared insurance-planning programs are available for a variety of personal computers.

The advantage to using a personal computer is that items may be easily added, deleted, or categorized, and a cassette or floppy disk copy of the inventory may be stored in a safe-deposit box. If you own a business, use this type of program to inventory your business equipment.

INDEX TO IMPORTANT LITERATURE

Your favorite lines of literature, passages from the Bible, quotations, scientific and business journal references, anecdotes, and other literary miscellany could be collected, categorized, cross-referenced, and indexed for rapid retrieval. A specialized database program could be used for this purpose; see the database demonstration program at the end of this chapter. Sophisticated database programs are commercially available for searching the King James Bible for selected passages and references.

DAY OF THE WEEK CALCULATION

Calculation of the day of the week corresponding to a given date is useful to the businessman, vacation planners, historians, and others. For the sake of curiosity, some have found amazing correlations between the days on which U.S. Presidents were born and other significant events in history.

To calculate the day of the week for a specific date in the twentieth century, either use the program in Listing 1-10 or use the following formula:

$$N = D + M + Y[(0.8(2M + 1)] + [Y/4]$$

where D = day of the month
M = Month, where March is considered the first month, April the second, and February the twelfth
Y = Last two digits of the year
[ ] = The integer part of the result

Next, divide the sum N by 7. The remainder from

Listing 1-10. The Day of the Week Program.

```
10     REM LISTING1.10 - The Day of the Week Program
20     REM applicable to any date in the 20th century
25     FULLW 2:CLEARW 2:GOTOXY 1,1
30     INPUT "Enter the month, day, year, (MM,DD,YY) ",M,D,Y
40     IF M>2 THEN M=M-2 ELSE M=M+10:Y=Y-1
50     N=D+M+Y+INT(.8*(2*(M+1))+INT(Y/4))
60     A=(N/7-INT(N/7))*7.1
70     FOR X=0 TO 6
80     READ A$(X)
90     NEXT X
100    PRINT "The day is ";A$(A)
110    INPUT S$
120    DATA SATURDAY,SUNDAY,MONDAY,TUESDAY,WEDNESDAY,THURSDAY,FRIDAY
```

the division gives the day of the week. Count 0 as Sunday, 1 as Monday, and so on.

Programs to calculate the date of Easter for forthcoming years have been written, and this remains an interesting programming challenge; hint—incorporate the above formula.

A simpler program could calculate the day of the year for a given date; the businessman may find such calculations useful.

FOOD STORE SHOPPING AID

Your programmable calculator can sum and categorize prices and types of items as they are removed from the shelf at the supermarket. Provision could be made for categorizing items into meat, groceries, produce, and taxable subdivisions. Additionally, there may be provisions for multiple entries, unit price calculations and comparisons, error correction, and a warning if a preset cash limit has been exceeded. Outputs could include total cost, tax, item count, and subtotals in each category.

COUPON FILE

For those who have the money-saving habit of collecting food coupons, a computerized list of your coupons could be helpful. Enter each coupon by its amount, brand name, product name, and location in your coupon folders or envelopes. Next, enter your shopping list. A computer search between your list and the available coupon list should yield a roster of coupons that may be used and where each one is.

Alternatively, the computer could store coupons by type of product, using categories such as these: restaurants, pasta products, drinks, cereals, snacks, meat, poultry, vegetables, fish, condiments, dairy products, baking items, pet food, cosmetics, paper goods, cleaning products, medicine, and miscellaneous. The shopper may call up the list of coupons within a category to select the coupons he is interested in and find out which brand name each one is filed under.

HOME PLANNING

An interesting program could be written to help a family design a house to fit their needs; the expense of a house certainly justifies an in-depth analysis of the design before construction is started. You could use video graphics to draw and transform basic house plans (preferably with a light pen).

Square footage could be calculated with the following guidelines in mind: the minimum square footage should equal the number of family members times 200; the desirable square footage should equal the number of family members times 300. An activity list such as the one below could be included to ensure that the family's activities will not conflict and that there will be provisions for all activities. The program could request the user to enter the activities that are to be done in each room and the times involved; conflicts could thus be analyzed, and the plans could be altered accordingly. The following activities could be included in the program:

Group Activities

1. Lounging—indoors and outdoors
2. Television watching
3. Listening to stereo, tapes, or radio
4. Playing a musical instrument
5. Meals
6. Children's play areas

Social Activities

1. Holding a meeting in the home
2. Children's/adult's games
3. Viewing movies/slides
4. Visiting with guests

Work Activities

1. Meal preparation and clean-up
2. Household business
3. Food preparation
4. Laundry
5. Ironing, sewing, or drying clothes
6. Workshop area

Private Areas

1. Study of reading areas
2. Grooming or dressing facilities

Traffic patterns and storage requirements could also be analyzed.

Storage Requirements:

Bedrooms—minimum of 4′ × 6′ × 24″ closet space/person

Utility areas—about 36″ wide and 16″ deep

Kitchen—approximately 10 linear feet of base and wall cabinets

PRIVATE INFORMATION STOREHOUSE

Almost everyone has some private—financial information, diaries, or important numbers—that they would like to keep more securely than in a filing cabinet. A program could be written to store this information in coded form so that it could only be retrieved by someone with the proper password. Copies of such data could be stored in a safe-deposit box.

GENERAL-PURPOSE CLOCK OR TIMER

If your computer is equipped with a real time clock, it could be used as an electronic timer or time controller for scientific research, sporting events, or other applications requiring a stopwatch. The capabilities that computers have but stopwatches don't include the automatic storage and printout of selected times and the automatic control of instruments or other devices that must be turned on or off at given times.

Even without a real time clock, your computer can still keep track of elapsed time for long distance telephone calls or act as a simple timer for applications in which accuracy is not a major factor. When they are not using their computers for more practical tasks, some hobbyists have transformed them into very expensive clocks, with graphic displays of hour and minute hands, digital displays, simulated sundials, or even sand timers. Digital watch circuits may be interfaced with computers to facilitate time keeping.

BLOOD ALCOHOL CONTENT

It would be a good idea to calculate your blood alcohol content after a few drinks, before attempting to drive. The formula used to calculate the percentage alcohol content in the blood is:

$$C = \frac{OZ \cdot p \cdot 0.037}{W}$$

where C = blood alcohol content in % wt./vol.
OZ = ounces of drink consumed
p = proof
W = body weight (lbs.)

The program in Listing 1-11 will automatically calculate your blood alcohol content.

Listing 1-11. Blood Alcohol Content Calculator.

```
10      REM LISTING1.11 - Blood Alcohol Content Calculator
15      FULLW 2:CLEARW 2:GOTOXY 1,1
20      INPUT "Enter the number of oz. consumed, the proof of the drink
        ",OZ,P
30      INPUT "Enter your weight in pounds ",W
40      C=(OZ*P*.037)/W
50      PRINT "Your estimated blood alcohol content=";c
60      PRINT:PRINT
70      IF C<=.05 THEN PRINT "A level below .05 is not considered as in
        toxication."
80      IF C>.05 AND C<.1 THEN PRINT "A level between .05 and .1 is con
        sidered borderline intoxication.
90      IF C>=.1 THEN PRINT "A level greater than .1 is conclusive into
        xication."
95      INPUT "PRESS RETURN TO END",A$
```

CARPENTERS' AND MECHANICS' HELPER

Your computer can expedite the numerous calculations required by carpenters and mechanics when they perform tasks such as changing the dimensions of a set of plans, converting anglo to metric measures or vice versa, and estimating the amount of in many other situations building materials needed.

Some useful formulae include

English/metric conversions

1 meter = 39.37 inches
= 3.281 feet
= 1.0936 yards
1 inch = 2.54 cm
1 foot = 30.48 cm
= .3048
1 yard = .9144 m
1 mile = 1609 m
= 1.609 km

Wall paper estimator

$$N = \frac{8640}{W \cdot (H + R)} \qquad P = \frac{S}{W \cdot N}$$

where N = the number of strips in one roll
W = the width of the paper
H = the height of the wall
R = the repeat length of the pattern
P = the number of double rolls needed
S = the width of the wall to be covered

Concrete block estimator

$$N = \frac{H \cdot L \cdot 1.25}{125}$$

where N = the number of blocks
H = the height of the wall
L = the length of the wall

Concrete yardage estimator

$$Y = \frac{L \cdot W \cdot W \cdot T}{324}$$

where Y = the volume of concrete in cubic yards
L = the length (ft.)
W = the width (ft.)
T = the thickness (in.)

CAR MAINTENANCE CALCULATIONS AND RECORD KEEPING

In addition to calculating and recording your car's miles per gallon, the computer could keep track of mileage statistics and signal you when a periodic check-up, overhaul, or oil change is necessary. For people having the privilege of deducting automotive expenses, the computer could keep tabs on amounts spent.

RAFFLE TICKET PRODUCER AND DRAWER

If your organization is sponsoring a raffle drawing, your computer could print out serialized raffle tickets and then draw the winning ticket based on a random number generator.

LIFE EXPECTANCY CALCULATOR

Listing 1-12 presents another program of interest to guests. Your life expectancy in years is

Listing 1-12. Life Expectancy Calculator Program.

```
10    REM LISTING 1.12 - The Life Expectancy Calculation Program
20    REM estimates how long you will live
30    REM program is based on scientific data
35    FULLW 2:CLEARW 2:GOTOXY 1,1
40    PRINT "LIFE EXPECTANCY CALCULATION FOR ADULTS 20-65 YEARS OF AG
      E"
50    PRINT "PRESS 1 for YES, 2 for NO to answer questions."
60    A=72
70    INPUT "Are you male";B
80    IF B=1 THEN A=A-3 ELSE A=A+4
90    PRINT "Do you live in an urban area with a population more"
95    INPUT "than two million";B
100   IF B=1 THEN A=A-2 ELSE INPUT "Do you live in a town with a popu
      lation less than 10,000";B
105   IF B=1 THEN A=A+2
110   PRINT "If you work behind a desk type 1"
120   INPUT "if your job requires regular, heavy physical labor type
      2";B
130   IF B=1 THEN A=A-3 ELSE IF B=2 THEN A=A+3
140   PRINT "If you exercise strenuously more than 5 half hour sessio
      ns per week.,"
150   INPUT "type 1.  If you exercise 2-3 times per week type 2; othe
      rwise type 3";B
160   IF B=1 THEN A=A+4 ELSE IF B=2 THEN A=A+2
170   INPUT "Do you live with a spouse or friend";B
180   IF B=1 THEN A=A+5 ELSE INPUT "How many decades have you lived w
      ithout others since 25 years old";B
185   A=A-B
190   INPUT "Do you sleep more than 10 hours per night";B
200   IF B=1 THEN A=A-4
210   PRINT "If you are intense, aggressive, easily angered, type 1"
220   INPUT "If you are easy-going, relaxed, follower, type 2";B
230   IF B=1 THEN A=A-3 ELSE IF B=2 THEN A=A+3
240   INPUT "Have you had a speeding ticket within the last year";B
270   IF B=1 THEN A=A-1
280   INPUT "Do you earn more than $50,000/year";B
290   IF B=1 THEN A=A-2
```

```
300    INPUT "If you've finished college type 1; grad school type 2";B
310    IF B=1 THEN A=A+1 ELSE IF B=2 THEN A=A+2
320    INPUT "If you're 65 or over and still working type 1";B
330    IF B=1 THEN A=A+3
340    INPUT "If any of your grandparent have lived to 85 type 1";B
350    IF B=1 THEN A=A+2:INPUT "Did all four live to be 80";B:IF B=1 T
       HEN A=A+6
360    INPUT "Did either of your parents die of stroke/heat attack bef
       ore 50";B
370    IF B=1 THEN A=A-4
380    PRINT "Have any of your parents or siblings under 50 have a"
390    INPUT "heart condition, cancer, or childhood diabetes";B
400    IF B=1 THEN A=A-3
410    PRINT "If you smoke more than 2 packs/day type 1, 1-2 packs typ
       e 2"
420    INPUT "1/2 - 1 pack/day type 3.  If none, type 4";B
430    IF B=1 THEN A=A-8 ELSE IF B=2 THEN A=A-6 ELSE IF B=3 THEN A=A-3
440    INPUT "Do you drink the equivalent of 1/4 bottle of liquor/day"
       ;B
450    IF B=1 THEN A=A-1
460    PRINT "If you are overweight by more than 50 lbs, type 1, 30-50
       lbs, type 2"
470    INPUT "10-30 lbs, type 3.  Otherwise type 4";B
480    IF B=1 THEN A=A-8 ELSE IF B=2 THEN A=A-4 ELSE IF B=3 THEN A=A-2
490    PRINT "If you're male and have an annual check-up type 1, and i
       f"
500    INPUT "female, type 1 if you see a gynecologist annually";B
510    IF B=1 THEN A=A+2
520    PRINT "If you're between 30-40 type 1, 40-50 type 2, 50-60 type
       "
530    INPUT "3, more than 70 type 4";B
540    IF B=1 THEN A=A+2 ELSE IF B=2 THEN A=A+3 ELSE IF B=3 THEN A=A+4
       ELSE IF A=4 THEN A=A+5
550    PRINT
560    PRINT "Your life expectancy if ";A;" years."
570    PRINT:PRINT:PRINT:INPUT Q$
```

calculated on the basis of life insurance studies. This program is interesting to run with data supplied for your present condition, and then run with data about yourself assuming you had kept your New Year's resolutions (stop smoking, lose weight, and so on). The difference in years is often surprising.

DATABASE DEMONSTRATION

Many of the program ideas described in this chapter can be implemented with a general purpose *database* computer program. This type of program should be able to store information pertaining to many items on a tape or disk and retrieve selected information.

The usual method of storing data on a cassette or disk involves the use of one string of information containing several *fields* of separate data. A field is an item of data. For example, a string containing five fields might look like this:

Boolean Algebra*Byte Magazine*25*Schwartz*Feb 1978

The first field signifies the title of the item (in this case a magazine article); all of the strings to be stored would be formatted in the same way, with the title of the item in the first field. Also, a limit is usually set on the length of any field (so that the data will fit neatly on a cassette or disk). If the information in one field does not contain enough characters to fill the allocated space, extra spaces are added. The longer the fields, the fewer records the disk or cassette can hold. You'll learn to make fields as short as possible when you are dealing with a large database.

The second field in the example above contains the name of the source of the item. The third, fourth, and fifth fields contain the page number, author, and issue date, respectively. An adequate database program should be able to search through many such strings and output those that contain items you want. For example, you can store an index to your library on a database system and subsequently obtain a listing of all the references pertaining to the stock market and written after a specific date. You would simply instruct the computer to search for all items that contain *stock market* in a certain field and a date later than the date specified in another field. Because the position of each field in all strings is fixed, the computer can search through a string (using the MID$ command, for example) to the beginning of the proper field: specific information can easily be accessed in this manner.

Lines 1790-1850 in Listing 1-13 summarize the variety of commands available in this chapter's database management program; these may be summoned to the screen by typing HELP in response to COMMAND?

Listing 1-13. The Database Program.

```
10      REM LISTING1.13 - The Database Program
20      REM may be used to maintain mailing lists, collections
30      REM inventory, etc.
40      REM the command HELP provides instructions
50      FULLW 2:CLEARW 2:GOTOXY 1,1
60      REM initialize for up to 200 records with 30 fields each
90      REM alter these dim statements to allow for more records
100     DIM M$(100),D$(200)
110     DIM P$(30),C$(31),F(31)
120     FULLW 2:CLEARW 2:GOTOXY 1,1
140     INPUT "SELECT:  1) BEGIN ANEW,  2) LOAD OLD DATA FILE";V
150     IF V=2 THEN 1890
160     IF V<>1 THEN 120
170     F1$="      ":C$="":P$(0)="BUFFER EMPTY":N=0
190     PRINT:PRINT
200     PRINT "Input field name, field type (A=Alpha, N=Numeric)"
210     REM
220     FOR I=1 TO 30
230     PRINT I;")    ";
270     E$="":INPUT E$,RS$
280     IF E$="" THEN 420
290     IF RS$<>"A" AND RS$<>"N" THEN 330 ELSE 340
330     PRINT "INCORRECT SYNTAX, PLEASE RE-ENTER":GOTO 270
340     E$=LEFT$(E$+F1$,4)+" "+RS$
350     GOSUB 2470 :REM routine to throw out extraneous spaces
390     P$(1)=E$
400     NEXT I
410     GOTO 430
420     P$(I)="END"
430     PRINT:PRINT "THE RECORDS AND FIELDS ENTERED WERE:"
460     FOR I=1 TO 10
470     IF LEFT$(P$(I),3)="END" THEN 500
480     PRINT I;":";P$(I)
490     NEXT I
500     PRINT:GOTO 540
```

```
530   PRINT "INCORRECT SYNTAX, PLEASE RE-ENTER YOUR COMMAND"
540   INPUT "COMMAND";E$
550   N1=0:PRINT
560   RESTORE
580   READ Z$,T
590   IF Z$="##" THEN 530
600   IF LEFT$(Z$,3)<>LEFT$(E$,3) THEN 580
610   ON T GOSUB 750,1120,1120,1120,2090,3340,1310,1220,3180,1120,2620
620   GOTO 540
630   DATA ADD,1,LIST,2,CHANGE,3,LABELS,4,HELP,5,END,6,SEARCH,7
640   DATA SUM,8,SAVE,9,RUBOUT,10,SORT,11,##,-1
750   REM ADD RECORD ROUTINE
755   PRINT "BEGIN ADDING RECORDS.  TYPE 'END' WHEN FINISHED."
760   N=N+1:N1=N1+1:E$=""
790   PRINT N;")    ";
810   FOR I=1 TO 30
820   IF LEFT$(P$(I),3)="END" THEN 980
830   PRINT TAB(7)P$(I);": ";
840   RS$="":INPUT RS$
850   REM
860   IF RS$="" THEN RS$=" ":REM ADD A SPACE
870   IF RS$="END" THEN 1060
880   IF MID$(P$(I),6,1)<>"N" THEN 920
890   IF ASC(RS$)>43 AND ASC(RS$)<58 THEN 920
900   PRINT "THIS IS A NUMERIC FIELD--ENTER NUMBERS ONLY":GOTO 830
920   REM
950   IF LEN(E$)+LEN(RS$)>245 THEN 1010 ELSE E$=E$+CHR$(126)+RS$
970   NEXT I
980   P$=STR$(N)
990   E$=P$+E$+CHR$(126)
1000  GOTO 1030
1010  PRINT "YOU HAVE EXCEEDED THE ALLOWED RECORD LENGTH, PLEASE RE-ENTE
      R":GOTO 790
1030  M$(N)=E$
1040  PRINT
1050  GOTO 760
1060  REM END OF ADDITION TO RECORDS
1070  N=N-1:N1=N1-1
1090  PRINT "YOU ADDED ";N1;" RECORDS"
1100  RETURN
1110  REM ROUTINE TO LIST RECORDS
1120  GOSUB 2170:REM DETERMINE RECORD RANGE TO LIST
1125  IF T=10 THEN 2081
1130  IF T<>4 THEN 1360
1135  INPUT "WOULD YOU LIKE TO TEST LABEL ALIGNMENT ";Z$
1137  IF Z$="NO" THEN 1360
1140  FOR I=1 TO 2
1150  INPUT "ALIGN PRINTOUT AND PRESS 'RETURN' WHEN READY";W$
1160  FOR J=1 TO 5
1170  LPRINT "XXXXXXXXXXXXXXXXXXXXXXXXXX"
1180  NEXT J
1190  LPRINT:NEXT I
1210  GOTO 1360
1220  REM ROUTINE TO SEARCH RECORDS AND PERFORM SUMMATIONS
1230  INPUT "ENTER THE NUMBER OF THE FIELD TO BE SUMMED ";SM
1240  IF MID$(P$(SM),6,1)="N" THEN 1270
1250  PRINT "INCORRECT TYPE OF FIELD, PLEASE RE-ENTER"
1260  GOTO 1230
1270  INPUT "DO YOU WANT TO SUM OVER ALL RECORDS? (Y/N)";S1$
```

```
1280  IF S1$="N" THEN 1310
1290  IF S1$="Y" THEN SO=0:GOTO 1330
1300  GOTO 1270
1310  INPUT "ENTER THE FIELD NUMBER AND EXPRESSION TO BE COMPARED ";SO,EX$
1320  INPUT "ENTER THE EXPRESSION TO BE COMPARED ";EX$
1330  T1=1:SM=0:T2=N
1360  FOR I=T1 TO T2
1370  RS$=M$(1)
1410  E$=LEFT$(RS$,5)
1420  T3=VAL(E$)
1430  E$=RS$
1440  RS$=CHR$(126)
1450  GOSUB 3050 :REM ROUTINE TO PARSE STRING
1460  GOTO 1490
1463  REM RUBOUT COMMAND ROUTINE
1465  GOSUB 2081
1488  RETURN
1490  IF T<=4 THEN 1570
1500  IF SO=0 THEN 1520 :REM SUM THE RECORDS
1510  IF C$(SO)<>EX$ THEN 1850 :REM GO TO SEARCH ROUTINE
1520  IF T=7 THEN 1650
1530  PRINT "(";I;")";
1540  T3=VAL(C$(SM))
1550  SM=SM+T3
1560  GOTO 1850
1570  ON T-1 GOTO 1650,1650,1580
1580  REM ROUTINE TO PRINT LABELS
1590  FOR J=1 TO 5
1595  IF C$(J)="END" THEN 1620
1600  LPRINT C$(J)
1610  NEXT J
1620  LPRINT
1630  GOTO 1850
1640  REM
1645  PRINT "YOU HAVE EXCEEDED THE ALLOWED RECORD LENGTH, PLEASE RE-ENTER"
1650  PRINT I;") "
1670  FOR J=1 TO 10
1680  IF LEFT$(P$(J),3)="END" THEN 1760
1690  PRINT P$(J);": ";C$(J)
1700  IF T<>3 THEN 1740
1710  INPUT RS$
1720  IF RS$="-" THEN 1740
1730  C$(J)=RS$
1740  NEXT J
1750  REM
1760  IF T<>3 THEN 1850
1770  P$=C$(0):REM ROUTINE TO ADD A CHANGED RECORD
1780  PRINT P$
1790  E$=P$+CHR$(126)
1800  FOR J=1 TO 10
1805  IF LEN(E$)+LEN(C$(J))>245 THEN 1645
1810  E$=E$+C$(J)+CHR$(126)
1820  IF P$(J)="END" THEN 1840
1830  NEXT J
1840  M$(I)=E$
1850  NEXT I
1860  IF T<>8 THEN 1880
```

```
1870  PRINT "THE SUM OF RECORD ";P$(SM);"=";SM
1880  RETURN
1890  REM LOAD DATA FROM DISK
1900  CLOSE:J=-1
1910  INPUT "ENTER FILE NAME ";F$
1920  OPEN "I",1,F$
1930  INPUT #1,E$
1940  J=J+1
1950  INPUT #1,E$
1960  IF E$="EOF" THEN 1990
1970  M$(J)=E$
1980  GOTO 1940
1990  E$=M$(0)
2000  RS$=CHR$(126)
2010  GOSUB 3040
2020  FOR I=1 TO 30
2030  P$(I)=C$(I)
2040  IF LEFT$(P$(I),3)="END" THEN 2060
2050  NEXT I
2055  I=I-1
2060  N=VAL(C$(I+1))
2070  CLOSE:GOTO 540
2081  FD=T2-T1+1
2082  FOR I=T2+1 TO N+1
2083  M$(I-FD)=M$(I)
2084  NEXT I
2085  N=N-FD
2086  RETURN
2090  REM HELP SEQUENCE
2100  PRINT "COMMANDS AVAILABLE:"
2150  PRINT "ADD:ADDS RECORDS TO THE FILE":PRINT "CHANGE:CHANGES RECORDS
      IN FILE"
2155  PRINT "RUBOUT:DELETES RECORDS FROM THE FILE":PRINT "SAVE:SAVES DAT
      A ON DISK"
2157  PRINT "SORT:SORTS RECORDS INTO ALPHANUMERIC ORDER BY SPECIFIED FIE
      LD":PRINT "SUM:SUMS A SPECIFIED FIELD OVER A GROUP OF RECORDS"
2159  PRINT "HELP:BRINGS YOU HERE":PRINT "END:ENDS THE PROGRAM"
2160  RETURN
2170  REM DETERMINE THE RANGE
2180  IF N=0 THEN PRINT "EMPTY FILE"
2190  IF N=0 THEN 540
2200  PRINT "ENTER MODE: A(ALL), O(ONE), R(RANGE)"
2210  INPUT E$
2220  IF E$<>"A" THEN 2260
2230  T2=N:T1=1
2250  GOTO 2430
2260  IF E$="O" THEN 2310
2270  INPUT "ENTER NUMBER OF RECORD";T1
2280  IF T1>N THEN 2440
2290  T2=T1
2300  GOTO 2430
2310  IF E$="R" THEN 2340
2320  PRINT "IMPROPER SYNTAX, PLEASE RE-ENTER
2330  GOTO 2200
2340  PRINT "INPUT THE LOWER BOUND"
2350  INPUT T1
2360  IF T1<1 THEN T1=1
2370  IF T1>N THEN GOSUB 2440
2380  INPUT "INPUT THE UPPER BOUND ";T2
```

```
2390  IF T2>N THEN 2440
2430  RETURN
2440  PRINT "THERE ARE ONLY ";N;" RECORDS IN THIS FILE"
2450  GOTO 2200
2460  REM
2470  REM ELIMINATE EXTRANEOUS SPACES FROM STRINGS
2480  T1=LEN(E$):C$=" ":IF T1=0 THEN 2600
2510  FOR T2=2 TO TI
2520  IF MID$(E$,T2-1,1)<>C$ THEN 2550
2530  E$=MID$(E$,2,T1-1)
2540  NEXT T2
2550  TI=LEN(E$)
2560  IF T1=0 THEN 2600
2570  IF RIGHT$(E$,1)<>C$ THEN 2600
2580  E$=LEFT$(E$,T1-1)
2600  RETURN
2610  PRINT "PLEASE RE-ENTER DATA"
2620  INPUT "INPUT THE FIELD NUMBER TO BE SORTED ";SO
2630  PRINT "THE FIELD NAME IS: ";P$(SO)
2660  T2=N:T1=1
2670  T2=N
2690  FOR I=T1 TO T2
2700  E$=M$(I)
2710  RS$=CHR$(126)
2720  GOSUB 3040
2730  D$(I)=C$(SO)
2740  NEXT I
2750  IF MID$(P$(SO),6,1)<>"A" THEN 2780
2760  SR=1
2770  GOTO 2820
2780  IF MID$(P$(SO),6,1)="N" THEN 2810
2790  PRINT "ERROR: THE WRONG FIELD TYPE WAS ENTERED"
2800  GOTO 540
2810  SR=2
2820  REM SORT ROUTINE
2830  M=N
2840  M=INT(M/2)
2850  IF M=0 THEN 3020
2860  J=1
2870  K=N-M
2880  I=J
2890  L=I+M
2900  IF SR=2 THEN 2930
2920  GOTO 2940
2930  IF VAL(D$(I))<VAL(D$(L)) THEN 2990
2940  E$=D$(I)
2942  D$(I)=D$(L)
2944  D$(L)=E$
2950  E$=M$(I)
2952  M$(I)=M$(L)
2954  M$(L)=E$
2960  I=I-M
2970  IF I<1 THEN 2990
2980  GOTO 2890
2990  J=J+1
3000  IF J>K THEN 2840
3010  GOTO 2880
3020  GOTO 540
3040  REM
3050  REM STRING PARSING ROUTINE
```

```
3060  K=-1
3070  FOR J2=1 TO LEN(E$)
3080  IF RS$=MID$(E$,J2,1) THEN 3110
3090  NEXT J2
3100  RETURN
3110  M=J2-1
3120  K=K+1
3140  C$(K)=MID$(E$,1,M)
3150  E$=MID$(E$,J2+1)
3160  J2=0
3170  GOTO 3070
3180  REM ROUTINE TO SAVE DATA
3190  INPUT "INPUT A NAME FOR FILE BEING SAVED ";F$
3200  OPEN "O",1,F$
3215  E$="00000"
3220  FOR I=1 TO 10
3230  E$=E$+CHR$(126)+P$(I)
3235  RS$=LEFT$(P$(I),3)
3240  IF RS$="END" THEN 3255
3250  NEXT I
3255  E$=E$+CHR$(126)+STR$(N)+CHR$(126)
3256  PRINT #1,CHR$(34)+E$+CHR$(34)
3260  FOR J=1 TO N
3270  PRINT #1,CHR$(34)+M$(J)+CHR$(34)
3280  NEXT J
3285  PRINT #1,"EOF"
3290  CLOSE:RETURN
3340  END
```

Table 1-4. Uses for Database Management Systems.

BUSINESS USES	EDUCATIONAL USES	HOME & HOBBY USES
Customer filing	Student records	Personal records
Prospect lists	Grade records	Check lists
Master files for . . .	Teacher lists	Club rosters
General Ledger	School lists	Telephone directories
Accounts Receivable	Program design	Recipes files
Accounts Payable	Tuition data	Medical information
Payroll Records	Enrollment data	Property records
Personal data	Property/equipment	Appliance warranties
Telephone logs	Athletic schedules	Insurance records
Telephone lists	Player assignment	Christmas lists/gifts
Hotel/travel data	Games schedules	Appointments
Reservations	Player statistics	Articles indexes
Property control	Mailing lists	Tax records/data
Library catalogues	Test scores	Expenses
Inventory	Menus	Book ownership
Key Employee data	Diet selections	Utility records
Advertising data	Inventory	Deposit files
Source files	Seating charts	Due dates
Sales leads	Cataloguing	Travel records
Mail lists	Laboratory data	Meal planning
Private records	Inspection data	Mortgage data
Corp. records	Experimental data	Auto records
Directories	Attendance data	Crop yields

BUSINESS USES	EDUCATIONAL USES	HOME & HOBBY USES
Billing information	Course description	Source files
Delivery schedules	Purchase orders	Magazine Article index
Routes	Requisitions	Estimate files
Territories	Vacation records	Investments
Quotations	Budgets	
Applintments	Maintenance data	
Conventions	Locker assignment	
Workshop data	Field trips	*. . . Plus all the Business and Educational Uses overlaps*
Assets lists	Vehicle records	
Marketing data	Tenure records	
Insurance data	Parking assignment	
Pricing schedules	Violation records	
Formulas	Meeting schedules	
Production data	Facility schedules	
Processes		
Cross referencing		
Commission records		
General filing		

Database programs are perhaps the most useful personal computer programs because of their wide application. In what applications could you use a database? The list in Table 1-4 names a number of the thousands of types of information that may be stored, indexed, organized, or cross-referenced by a database program. Many of these applications are discussed in more detail throughout the book.

Sophisticated database programs are commercially available, but the following database demonstration program should be adequate for most home uses. Unlike most commercial programs, which rely upon machine language commands for added speed, this program is written in BASIC for easy modification. It is designed for use with floppy disks.

Chapter 2

Business and Financial Applications

Personal computers have greatly altered the business world by permitting rapid calculation of numerous "What if?" questions involving financial formulas, in addition to providing accounting functions. Likewise, the homeowner will find the personal computer useful in analyzing loans, budgets, and investments. Calculations that were previously time-consuming and open to error can now be accomplished with ease and permit better decision making.

FINANCES AND INVESTMENTS

A growing number of investors are using their personal computers to help them manage their stock and bond portfolios, analyze trends in the financial markets, and investigate individual stocks and decide when to buy or sell. A personal computer connected to a database can sort out enormous quantities of market and company statistics for an investor; within seconds, the results may be projected on the screen as charts, tables, or graphs, enabling an investor to evaluate a buying opportunity—or a must-sell situation—quickly and probably more accurately than if the calculations were done by hand. The personal computer can sometimes make your life as an investor more rewarding, and often much easier. Additionally, the cost of investment programs may be counted as a business expense for tax purposes, as can part or all of the cost of your computer.

Stocks, Bonds, and Securities

The personal computer has come to the aid of the individual investor in three areas: portfolio management, technical and fundamental analysis, and database access. Making investment decisions or recommendations requires accurate technical analysis of large amounts of data on a timely basis. Compiling information in standard formats concerning stock performance or company finances, doing statistical computations to update individual stock files, tracking moving averages, and maintaining complete records of one or a number of portfolios are all tasks ideally suited to the personal computer. Professional brokers as well as individuals have witnessed the significant impact that the personal computer can have on the analytical functions on which they base their recommendations. With the advent of the bull market of the early 1980s and the rise of the discount broker, professional software packages have become available to help investors at home make the investment decisions that used to be made by their full-service brokerages.

Portfolio Management

Portfolio management programs are really just electronic notebooks. They keep a complete record of the stocks you own and show how well you're doing at the game. They are especially useful at tax time; their compilations of your losses, gains, dividends, brokerage commissions, etc., make it easy to account to Uncle Sam for your Wall Street activity.

The limitations on most packages involve the number of stock characteristics maintained or computed for each stock. Most packages will allow for a virtually unlimited number of stock records (letting you track your own portfolio as well as that of several financial advisors), as long as you are willing to maintain them on a number of disks.

The simplest individual portfolio management programs provide a means of recording the basic information on stocks in your own portfolio or on any other stocks you wish to track for comparison. When you choose to update—on a daily, weekly, or other periodic basis—the program will automatically perform certain calculations, such as present value of the issues, or long- and short-term gains and losses (as if you sold the stock on that date). It can automatically remind you of a stock that will go long-term within 30 days, or maintain other information such as dates and number of shares purchased, total number of shares owned, dividends, growth rate, and percentage appreciation or depreciation. The following analysis factors may be computed for the entire portfolio: sum of cost prices, sum of current value, sum and percentage difference between cost and current price, percentage return on a cost basis, and percentage return on the current value. A report may be automatically prepared for attachment to IRS forms, and the portfolio information may be printed in a variety of formats for ready reference.

More advanced portfolio management packages allow hundreds of open tax lots in a system that matches your transactions against open positions to let you make investment decisions that minimize your tax liability. You can track stocks, options, bonds, treasuries, and mutual funds; the system can accommodate buy, sell, short sell, and buy-to-cover transactions. Return on investment for each stock and the entire portfolio may be computed as well as the total net earnings. Sophisticated programmers could make use of Sharpe's method (or another method) in determining the proportion of funds that should be allocated to each security in a portfolio to maximize returns.

Technical and Fundamental Analysis

Fundamental analysis assumes that the price fluctuations of stocks are based on the basic financial health of the economy and the performance of the individual company. Thus, fundamental analysts look at such factors as earnings, sales, assets, and liabilities and use these to predict future price movements.

Technical analysts argue that these factors affect stock prices only over the long run. Short-term fluctuations, they maintain, are governed by psychological conditions in the market itself, not external factors. Therefore, they believe the study of the past market behavior can determine the way to profits in the future. There are many different theories that promote various indicators as the key to future price movement. Some of the major indicators are the relationship between price and volume, market averages, and new highs versus lows.

Both fundamental and technical analysis call for extensive number crunching and are well suited for being handled by computers, although fundamental analysis exceeds the capacity of most personal computers. In fact, almost all of the analysis programs available on the personal computer market do technical analysis. In technical analysis, computers can be especially useful in charting various relationships between individual stock prices and trading volumes. A personal computer can turn a pile of statistics that might take several hours to plot by hand into a chart within seconds. In this chapter I will discuss some popular means of technical and fundamental analysis. Interested readers are referred to popular manuals on investment analysis, statistics, and these publications on computer-assisted stock analysis for further information:

*L.R. Schmeltz, *Playing the Stock and Bond Markets With Your Personal Computer,* TAB BOOKS Inc., Blue Ridge Summit, PA 17214.

*Leslie E. Sparks, *Investment Analysis With Your Microcomputer,* TAB BOOKS Inc., Blue Ridge Summit, PA 17214.

**The Microcomputer Investor,* The MicroComputer Investors Association, 902 Anderson Dr., Fredericksburg, VA 22401.

**Computerized Investing on the Stock Market* from Investment Software Concepts, P.O. Box 27, Bronxville, NY 10708.

*Woodwell, Donald, *Automating Your Financial Portfolio: An Investor's Guide to Personal Computers,* Dow-Jones-Irwin, 1818 Ridge Rd., Homewood, IL 60430.

With a microcomputer at your disposal, you can now develop and test a market theory without countless, error-prone manual calculations! A "paper portfolio," or collection of stocks to track that are not actually owned, was once too time- and effort-consuming for the individual investor to experiment with. When you experiment, each "buy and sell" decision can be based on actual market performance and serve as a "lesson learned" in developing your own trading strategies.

Moving Averages

Moving averages provide a measure of the movement of a stock relative to itself (in price, dividend, or volume), a composite summary of a key factor (for example, the average price of a stock group), and a ratio of two or more key factors (for example, P/E ratios). The moving average is often most useful in predicting the buy versus sell position of a stock in regard to its past trend. If the current stock price drops below the moving average, a sell position would be taken and vice versa for a buy position. The program in Listing 2-1 computes the moving average for a stock or other security given a set of successive daily prices and the

Listing 2-1. Moving Average Calculator Program.

```
10     REM LISTING2.01 - The Moving Average Calculator Program
15     FULLW 2:CLEARW 2:GOTOXY 1,1
20     PRINT "Enter price values successively, 9999 to end."
30     DIM A(200),B(200):X=0
40     X=X+1:PRINT "#";X;:INPUT A(X)
50     IF A(X)<>9999 THEN 40
60     X=X-1:INPUT "Enter span length";C
70     E=(1+C)/2:D=1:G=C
80     F=0:FOR I=D TO G
90     F=A(I)+F:NEXT I
100    G=G+1:B(E)=INT(.5+F/C):E=E+1:D=D+1
110    IF G<1+X THEN 80
140    PRINT "  WEEK #     WEEKLY  PRICE AVE.     MOVING AVE"
150    A$="  ####          ####                  ####"
160    FOR I=1 TO X:PRINT USING A$;I,A(I),B(I)
170    NEXT I
180    INPUT "Type 1 to choose new span";ZZ
190    IF ZZ<>1 THEN END
200    FOR I=1 TO X:B(I)=0:NEXT I
210    GOTO 60
```

length of the span over which the average is to be computed.

Price/Volume Trace

In this analysis technique, the daily stock price and volume data are considered as (x, y) data points. Probability rules may be developed as clues to the immediate future performance of the stock price as it relates to volume.

Rate of Change

The rate of change is a measure that involves price fluctuations of a stock to itself and may be used to compare stocks in terms of price, sales, or earnings. On this basis you can find the stock with the best potential to increase in price in the immediate future, barring any information or indication that the current stock trend will change or reverse. It is computed as follows:

$$\%\ \text{Rate of Change} = \frac{\dfrac{\text{Ending} - \text{Starting Price}}{\text{Starting Price}}}{\text{No. of trading days}} * 100$$

This value may be determined for daily, weekly, monthly, yearly, or other periods by alternating the denominator.

Change Distribution

This analysis technique compares the distributional change of individual stocks within a group to the average change of the group for a given time period. This provides a probabilistic measure of the rate of change in either relative or absolute terms.

The stock distribution, like a normal distribution, is described by the factors of price average and standard deviation; the standard deviation usually increases as the length of time considered increases and as the market rate of change increases. By knowing the typical stock price distributions for different market index rates of change, the probability of success in short-term trading is increased; the investor is equipped with the probability distribution of the price change.

Price Indexes

Price indexes are indicators of the central drift of a set of stocks or the market as a whole. These include the Dow Jones, New York Stock Exchange, American Stock Exchange, Standard & Poor index, and other indexes. They can be best applied to determine a consensus of individual stock trends within a given stock category. An indicator that is well suited for computation on your personal computer would use the formula

$$\text{INDEX} = \sum^{\text{all stocks}} \frac{x_n\, y_n}{y}$$

where x_n = stock price
y_n = number of shares traded at x_n
y = total shares traded

The moving average and indexing concepts may be used as powerful decision-making tools in determining whether the investor should be anticipating a trading decision, trading, or investigating other investments.

Ratio Relationships

The use of ratios is popular in business and finance because they afford a means of comparison of two or more factors that influence investment decisions. A well-known example is the price/earnings (P/E) ratio used in measuring the potential of a stock. Others include the ratio of sales growth, the ratio of consecutive period earnings, the yearly high stock price versus the low price, and the relative strength of a stock versus the market index. The personal computer may be used in automatically calculating many of the popular ratios and in forecasting changes of ratios through the use of statistical regression. For instance, the future price of a stock may be computed given current value per share, projected earnings, and projected percent change in the P/E ratio using this simple formula:

$$V_p = \frac{V_c E_p^2}{E_c^2}$$

where V_c = current value per share
E_p = projected earnings
C = projected percent change of P/E ratio
E_c = current earnings
V_p = projected value per share

Note that all projected values must be for the same length of time.

Trend Line Analysis

Trend-line analysis is a major statistical computation in financial analysis and is accomplished by using the method of *linear least squares* fitting of data. Suppose you obtained a set of data listing the value of one stock over a period of time. If these values were plotted versus the Dow Jones Index the result could appear as shown in Fig. 2-1.

A trend line analysis would determine the equation of the line that best fits or describes the data, telling you how one variable is related to another. This equation, in the form of $y = a + bx$, provides a means to estimate the value of a variable (y) given the value of the other variable (x). The values of a and b are determined using these regression equations:

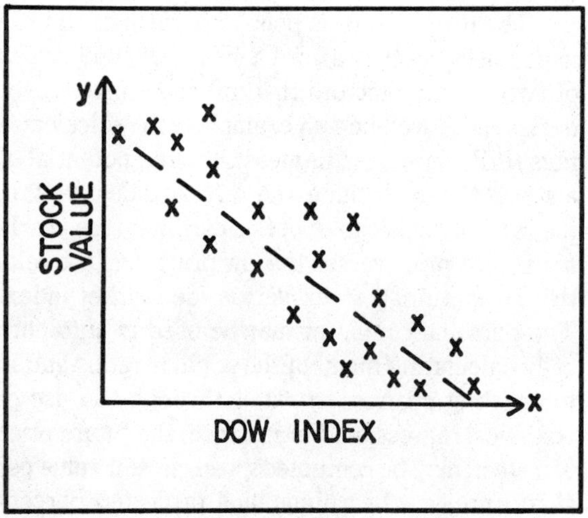

Fig. 2-1. A trend line graph.

$$b = \frac{n\Sigma XY - \Sigma X \Sigma Y}{n\Sigma X^2 - (\Sigma X)^2}$$

$$a = \frac{1}{n} (\Sigma Y - b\Sigma X)$$

where n = no. of (x,y) pairs
X = individual x values
Y = individual y values
b = slope of line
a = y axis intercept

As described in the chapter concerning mathematical and statistical applications, the standard error may be calculated for a regression line to determine how well it describes the data.

The technique of multiple linear regression is used by investors in determining the influence of more than one variable ($x_1 - x_n$) on another variable (y). The total variation in y may often be better explained through the use of multiple x variables ($y = a + b_1x_1 + b_2x_2 + \ldots b_nx_n$), allowing more precise prediction than is possible through the simple linear regression discussed above. For instance, one investor using microcomputer techniques has developed a four-variable regression equation describing the stock market average:

$$\log V = a + b\log E + c\log G - d\log R$$

where V = Value of the average
E = Earnings of the average
G = Growth rate of the average's earning
R = Yield of quality long-term bonds

In this example, the variables (E, G, R) are regressed on V. The constants a, b, c, d are determined and used in predicting future values of V based on past relationships to E, G, and R. Multiple linear regression is also computed using the least squares method. For more information on the least squares method, refer to a textbook of statistics.

Investors using multiple linear regression techniques have developed modeling equations that reflect the influence of a wide variety of factors, with high correlations, on stock and security prices, earnings, and P/E ratios. These include

- The current month's interest yield of the Moody's AAA Bond Index.
- The ratio of pretax corporate profits for the preceding twelve months to pretax corporate profits adjusted for inventory profits for the same period.
- The ratio of current dollar gross national product for the preceding twelve months to current dollar gross national product for twelve months ending one quarter into the future.
- The average yield on taxable U.S. Government 3-5 year issues for the preceding six months.
- The average year-to-year percentage gain of the Consumer Price Index.
- The equity of the S&P 400 one-year previous divided by the earnings of the S&P 400 for the latest twelve months.
- The relative consistency of divided growth for 10 years, in terms of the ratio of the correlation of the stock's dividend growth with time to that of the S&P Industrial Stock Average's dividend growth.
- The relative consistency of earnings growth for 10 years, computed as above.
- The relative profit margin for the latest report 12 months.
- The relative rate of earnings growth for the previous 10 years on a per-share basis.
- The relative size measured by net income for the latest 12 months.
- The relative return on equity, as earnings less dividends divided by equity at the beginning of the 12-month period.
- The relative 5-year earnings-per-share least-squares growth rate.
- The relative prospective return on equity in the year for which earnings are being estimated.
- The relative prospective earnings growth for the next quarter.
- The relative investment rate in the latest year.
- The relative prospective earnings growth for the next 2 quarters.
- The relative dividend payout ratio for the latest 12 months.
- The relative earnings growth for the latest 12 months.

Of course, many other variables could be used at the investors discretion, including DJIA, specific industrial indicators, GNP, employment statistics, disposable personal income statistics, indexes of industrial production, bank deposits, money supply, interest rates, inventory levels, accounts receivable/payable, and railroad freight usage. With a large selection of apparently useful variables to employ, you can now build a multiple regression equation on your personal computer, seeking both the highest possible correlation and confidence level and the least interaction among variables chosen. The variables may be regressed against individual stock performance, group stock performance, and market indices or other securities. Those variables that are generally most useful include measures of preceding and following interest rates, inflation, economic activity (such as GNP), industry health, and rates of change.

Database Searching

With the advent of databases available to the individual investor at low rates, a personal computer can be instructed to search for stocks fulfilling any combination of investment criteria. If, for example, you are a conservative investor, you could have a program hunt for companies whose shares have a P/E ratio of 5 or less and annual yields of 10 percent or more—both of which can signify undervalued companies.

Financial Ratio Analysis

Financial ratio analysis is an ideal, simple method of determining how well a particular company has performed in relation to other companies in its industry or in relation to its own past performance and of predicting future performance. Described below are several popular financial ratios that can be determined using figures from corporate annual reports and a simple BASIC program that does the necessary divisions and tabulations or comparisons with figures concerning other corporations. Over the years, security analysts, brokers, and investors have found that financial statements become more meaningful when ratios between various values on the income and balance sheets are computed. These ratios may be divided into four categories, as shown below:

Liquidity Ratios

Current ratio
Quick ratio
Inventory to working capital

Leverage Ratios

Debt to total assets
Times interest earned
Current liabilities to net worth
Fixed assets to net worth
Debt to equity

Activity Ratios

Cash velocity
Inventory turnover
Fixed assets turnover
Average collection period
Total assets turnover

Profitability Ratios

Net operating margin
Net income margin
Return on assets
Return on net worth

Liquidity ratios are designed to measure a firm's ability to meet its obligations as they mature and relate to the amount of cash and assets convertible into cash in the near future.

Leverage ratios measures the financing provided by owners as compared with the financing provided by the firm's creditors. Creditors look at the owner-supplied funds to provide them with a margin of safety, but by raising funds through debt, the owners are able to maintain control of the firm with a small investment. The return of the owners is magnified when the firm earns more on the borrowed funds than it pays in interest.

Activity ratios determine how effectively the firm utilizes the resources available.

Profitability ratios demonstrate the result of the policies and decisions of the firm's management. Both operating margins and new profits are calculated to distinguish between the results of operating policies and the results of financial policies.

The input data needed for computation of these ratios is usually found in the financial statements of a company and includes:

Cash: all cash on hand plus cash in the company's bank accounts. Any cash in certificates of deposit or other short-term deposits should be included.

Marketable securities: investments in obligations that are readily marketable and can be converted into cash on short notice.

Receivables (beginning): receivables should be net of any reserve for doubtful accounts and be fully collectible within one year. Beginning receivables are those that were due to the company at the beginning of the operating year.

Receivables (ending): those receivables due to the company at the end of the operating year.

Inventory (beginning): inventory that is on hand at the beginning of the operating year.

Inventory (ending): inventory that is on hand at the end of the operating year.

Current assets: the total of cash, marketable securities, receivables, inventories, and other assets of the company that are expected to be converted into cash in the normal course of business within the current operating year.

Fixed assets: assets such as land, buildings, leasehold improvements, equipment, fixtures, furnishings, vehicles and other assets with lives longer than one year that are used in the operations of the company.

Total assets: the total of all assets of the company, including current assets, fixed assets, and other assets.

Current liabilities: debts of the company that

must be paid within one year, usually consisting of trade accounts payable, payroll taxes withheld, accrued expenses, and that portion of long-term debt coming due within one year.

Total liabilities: the total of all the debt of the company, including current as well as noncurrent liabilities.

Net worth: (also called owner's equity or stockholders' equity) the difference between total assets and total liabilities.

Sales: the total revenues earned by the company during the year, net of all sales discounts and returns.

Gross operating profit: found by subtracting cost of sales from sales. It represents the difference between the sales price of all items sold and the cost of the items sold.

Interest charges: the total amount of interest that has been paid by the company on its indebtedness.

Profit before income taxes: the net income of the company for the year after all expenses have been considered. It is commonly referred to as the "bottom line."

Current Ratio. This ratio is computed by dividing current liabilities into current assets. This ratio is the generally accepted measure of the ability to satisfy short-term obligations and indicates the extent to which the claims of short-term creditors can be covered by assets that can be expected to be converted to cash in a period corresponding to the time obligations become due.

Quick Ratio. This ratio is computed by deducting inventories from current assets and dividing the remainder by current liabilities. This is a measure of the ability to pay short-term obligations without relying on the sale of inventories and is a better guide to short-term liquidity than the current ratio.

Inventory to Working Capital. This ratio demonstrates the proportion of working capital tied up in inventory and is used to find the possible loss to the company resulting from a decline in inventory values; a low ratio is desirable.

Debt to Total Assets. This ratio measures the company's obligations to creditors in relation to all the funds provided to the company; the lower the ratio, the greater the protection from losses being incurred by creditors in the event of liquidation. Generally, the maximum debt ratio should be 50%.

Times Interest Earned. This ratio is determined by dividing earnings before interest and taxes by interest expense. This measures the extent to which earnings could fall before the company is unable to pay annual interest costs; the lower the ratio, the more difficulty the company will have in raising additional funds. A manufacturing company should cover interest more than four times and public utilities should cover interest about three times.

Current Liabilities to Net Worth. This ratio determines the amount of funds supplied by owners compared to funds provided by current debt; if the owners have not put enough funds into the company, long-term creditors will be less willing to provide funds, and the company will have to utilize short-term financing to a great extent, resulting in greater time before current bills are paid. Lower ratios are favorable.

Fixed Assets to Net Worth. This ratio indicates the extent to which owner's funds are invested in assets with little turnover. Higher ratios will result for industries that are capital intensive versus companies that are labor-intensive.

Debt to Equity. This ratio demonstrates the relation between total debt of the firm and funds provided by the owners; the lower the ratio, the greater the protection against creditor's losses in the event of liquidation. Owners may desire a high ratio because this will magnify earnings and prevent possible dilution of control of the company if additional equity must be raised.

Cash Velocity Ratio. This ratio is computed by dividing cash and cash equivalents into sales. This ratio indicates the number of times cash has turned over within the year; a high cash velocity indicates cash is being used effectively.

Inventory Turnover. This ratio is computed by dividing the cost of sales by inventory. This ratio indicates the liquidity of inventory; a high inventory turnover shows that inventories are being held to a minimum, and a low ratio may indicate obsolete or slow-moving stock.

Fixed Assets Turnover. This ratio is computed by dividing sales by fixed assets. This measures the utilization of fixed assets; a low ratio may indicate the plant isn't being utilized as effectively as possible, unless the company is labor-intensive.

Average Collection Period. This ratio is computed by dividing accounts receivable by average daily sales. This represents the average time period after making a sale before cash is received, indicating the effectiveness of credit and collection policies; these may need to be strengthened if this ratio is on the increase.

Total Assets Turnover. This ratio is computed by dividing sales by total assets. This shows the effectiveness of the firm in utilizing resources to generate sales; a high ratio may indicate overutilization of assets, and a low ratio may indicate an excessive investment or idle assets.

Gross Operating Margins. This ratio is computed by dividing gross operating profit by sales. This ratio determines how far unit selling prices may decline without resulting in a loss from the sale of units and how products are priced in relation to their cost.

Net Operating Margin. This ratio is computed by dividing profit before taxes by sales. This shows the amount each sales dollar provides to the continuing operation of the firm before consideration of income taxes.

Net Income Margins. This ratio is determined by dividing net profits after taxes by sales. A lower ratio indicates selling prices are relatively low and total costs are relatively high; thus, a small percentage drop in sales may result in losses. This ratio indicates the profitability after taking into account all income taxes and expenses and measures the return on all sales.

Return on Assets Ratio. This ratio is computed by dividing net profits after taxes by total assets. This measures rate of return on total resources.

Return on Net Worth Ratio. This ratio is computed by dividing net profit after taxes by net worth. This ratio is indicative of the company's earning on the investment of shareholders. A high or increasing value is favorable, although a very high value may indicate intense competition. Additionally, temporary inventory profits may be the result of increasing commodity prices. A high value could also be caused by general prosperity or a declining position.

Combined Coverage. Combined coverage is computed by dividing annual interest and debt costs plus preferred dividends into the adjusted operating profit after taxes and before interest. A combined coverage of four is considered acceptable for an industrial company; a coverage of three times the combined requirements would make a utility stock high-grade.

Dividend Payout. The dividend payout is the percentage of earnings on common stock that are paid out as dividends. Industrial companies average about 55 percent, utilities 70 percent, and growth companies less than 55 percent.

Book Value Per Share. The book value per share is determined by adding the stated or par value of the common stock to the additional paid-in capital and retained earnings accounts and dividing by the number of common shares. The book value would be lower for companies in which preferred stock is entitled to share in additional paid-in capital. The book value is not as important an indicator as earnings and prospects for industrial companies. However, the book value of stock for financial institutions and utilities is important in analysis.

Additional Investment Applications

On the following pages you will find ten more ways in which you can use your microcomputer as a tool for making profitable financial decisions.

Company Growth Rates. The program in Listing 2-2 may be used to calculate company growth rates using historical financial data:

The Intrinsic Value of a Stock. This value is calculated with this formula:

$$I = \frac{TC \cdot AMT}{CS}$$

Where I = intrinsic value
TC = total corporation capital

Listing 2-2. Growth Rate Calculator Program.

```
10    REM LISTING2.02 - The Growth Rate Calculator Program
90    FULLW 2:CLEARW 2:GOTOXY 1,1
100   REM CALCULATION OF THE GROWTH RATE
110   A=0
120   INPUT "Enter the number of data points ";z(0)
130   PRINT "Enter data points successively"
140   FOR B=1 TO Z(0)
150   INPUT Z(B)
155   IF Z(B)<=0 THEN PRINT "DATA LESS THAN ZERO NOT ALLOWED":GOTO
      150
160   NEXT B
170   FOR B=1 TO Z(0)
190   A=A+LOG(Z(B))
200   NEXT B
210   A=(1/Z(0))*A
220   Z6=0:Z7=0
230   FOR B=1 TO Z(0)
240   Z6=Z6+(LOG(Z(B))-A)*(B-(Z(0)/2))
250   Z7=Z7+((B-(Z(0)/2))^2)
260   NEXT B
270   V=Z6/Z7
280   PRINT "The growth rate is ";INT((100*V)+.5);"%"
290   PRINT:INPUT A$
300   END
```

AMT = price per share
CS = amount in dollars of capital stock

A Stock Valuation Program. A program of this type could find current and future values of a stock and the rate of return before and after taxes. Commissions would be considered in all calculations.

Brokerage Commissions. Commissions could be calculated on standard and odd lots, as well as for stocks selling below one dollar per share.

Earnings Per Share Estimation. A historical balance sheet and income data could be used to estimate future earnings for a given stock; future estimations may be made with trend-line analysis.

An Options Valuation Program. Using the Black-Scholes or another economic model, an options valuation program could determine the optimum hedge ratio and spread of any options. When selling partially covered calls or when selling puts and shortening stock, an options writing program could be used to find the maximum profit and upper and lower break-even points.

A program of this type is presented in Listing 2-3. The purpose of this program is to assist the investor in planning the most profitable stock option buy and sell strategy. The strategy used by the program involves the selling of options against stock bought; this is usually considered the least risky strategy and it is often the most profitable one. For example, you could buy 100 shares of stock to use as collateral for each call option sold. A *call option*, which is sold at a premium, allows the purchaser the right to buy the stock at a certain price (called the *strike point*), no matter what the true stock price becomes. However, the option is valid only for a certain length of time, known as the life of the option. This computer program will request information pertaining to the stock and will calculate the value of the stock and return on investment (ROI) over a range of 40 percent to 160 percent of the current value. Using this data, the investor should be able to decide the probability

Listing 2-3. Stock Option Analysis Program.

```
10    REM LISTING2.03 - Stock Option Analysis Program
20    FULLW 2:CLEARW 2:GOTOXY 1,1
30    DIM D(12),A$(20),B(10),F(12),K$(12)
40    FOR D4=1 TO 12
50    READ D(D4):F(D4)=D4:READ K$(D4)
60    NEXT D4
70    INPUT "Enter the numerical month, day, year ",M1,D9,Y1
80    INPUT "Is the stock to be bought on margin (1=YES, 2=NO)";M
90    INPUT "Enter the % margin rate ",M2
100   IF M=1 THEN D5=.5 ELSE D5=1
110   PRINT "Enter the name of the stock or ID, the dividend in $'s
      per share"
115   INPUT " per quarter ",D6$,D7
120   PRINT "Enter the number of shares to be purchased (multiple
      of "
125   INPUT "100 shares) ",D8
130   INPUT "Enter the price per share ";P9
140   INPUT "Select market 1) NYSE, 2) OTC ) ",E
150   INPUT "Select the expiration month (E.G. 1=January, 2=February
      ...) ",E2
160   INPUT "Enter the strike price ",E3
170   INPUT "Enter the cost per option (multiply price by 100) ",E4
180   E5=D8/100
190   INPUT "Enter the January, April, July, October, Premiums ",
      B(1),B(4),B(7),B(10)
195   C4=100:C3=100
200   FOR C8=1 TO 10 STEP 3
210   IF B(C8)=0 THEN 590
220   C9=B(C8)
230   A4=C8*30.4225
240   A8=A4+A7-((M1-1)*30.4225)-D9
250   C=P9*C3
260   FOR A9=1 TO 2
270   C4=A9*C4
280   D=C4*C9
290   B4=D*.034+.017*C
300   B5=B4+C-D
310   B6=B5*.085*A8/365
320   D1=B6+B5
325   INPUT "More--press RETURN ",A$:CLEARW 2:GOTOXY 1,1
330   PRINT "Month of call";C8
340   PRINT "Initial investment ";B5
350   PRINT "Total investment ";D1
360   PRINT "Effective writing ratio ";A9
370   PRINT
380   PRINT"Stock Price    Return            ROI                    ROI/YR"
390   FOR D2=-4 TO 6
400   A1=(1-(.1*D2))*C
410   IF A1/C3>(.25+E3) THEN 460
420   B9=0
430   B7=A1-D1
440   GOTO 480
450   D1=(1-A9)*A1+D1
460   B7=C3*E3-D1-100*(A9-1)*E3
470   B9=(((A1/C3+1)-(1.068*C9))*100)/(1.068*C9)
```

```
480   B8=B7/D1*100
490   C2=A1/C3
500   D3=B8/(A8/365)
510   PRINT USING"#####.##          #####          #######               ###
      ####";C2,B7,B8,D3
520   NEXT D2
530   NEXT A9
590   NEXT C8
600   IF A8>180 THEN PRINT "Long term"
610   PRINT
620   E6=INT(E5*E3*100)
630   E7=INT(E4*E5)
640   E8=Y1*365
650   E9=D9+D(M1)+E8
660   F=E8+20+D(E2)
670   F1=F-E9:IF F1<0 THEN F1=F1+365
680   F2=INT((F1/90)+.5)
690   F3=INT(F2*D7*D8)
700   F5=INT(P9*D8)
710   F6=INT(D5*F5)
770   GOSUB 1150
780   G1=G2:F9=E6:G=D8/100:GOSUB 1150
820   G3=G2:F9=E7:G=E5:F8=3
830   GOSUB 1150
860   GOSUB 1150
870   G4=G2
880   G5=F7-E7-F3+G3+G4+G1
900   IF D5=1 THEN G6=0 ELSE G6=INT(((M2/100)*G5)*F1/365)
910   G7=G6+G3+F7+G4+G1+F6
920   G8=F4-G7
930   G9=F6-F3-E7+G6+G3+G1+G4
940   H=INT((G8*1000)/G9)/10
950   H2=INT(((G7-F3-E7)*100)/D8)/100
960   H1=INT(3650*H/F1)/10
970   INPUT "Press RETURN to continue ",A$:PRINT
980   PRINT "Covered write:";D6$;" DATE (MMDDYY):";M1;D9;Y1
990   PRINT "Hedge strategy:"
1000  PRINT "Buy ";D8;" shares. (price=$";P9;")"
1010  PRINT "Sell ";E5;" ";K$(E2);E3;" 's ($";E4;" apiece)"
1020  INPUT "Press RETURN to continue ",A$
1030  CLEARW 2:GOTOXY 1,1:PRINT "EXPENSES:"
1040  PRINT "  IMMEDIATE      $";F6
1045  PRINT "  LOAN (50%)     $";F7
1050  PRINT "  BROKER'S FEES  $"
1055  PRINT "     OPTION      $";G4
1060  PRINT "     IN          $";G1
1065  PRINT "     OUT         $";G3
1070  PRINT "  MARGIN COST    $";G6
1080  PRINT "TOTAL            $";G7
1100  PRINT "INCOME:":PRINT " STOCK $";E6
1105  PRINT "  OPTION     $";E7
1110  PRINT "  DIVIDENDS  $";F3
1115  PRINT "TOTAL        $";F4
1125  PRINT:PRINT "The return on your money is ";H;"% ($";G8;" on $";
      INT(G9);")"
1130  PRINT "for ";F1;" days, ";H1;"% annually."
1140  PRINT "The break-even point is a price of $";(INT(H2*10))/10:
      GOTO 1310
1150  G2=((.009000001#*F9)+22)+(6*G)
```

```
1160  ON F8 GOTO 1180,1190,1200
1170  IF G2<25 THEN G2=25
1175  RETURN
1180  G2=INT(.7*G2):RETURN
1190  G2=21*G:RETURN
1200  G2=INT(.82*G2):RETURN
1300  DATA 0,JANUARY,31,FEBRUARY,59,MARCH,90,APRIL,120,MAY,151,JUNE,1
      82,JULY,212,AUGUST,243,SEPTEMBER,272,OCTOBER,304,NOVEMBER,334,
      DECEMBER
1310  PRINT:PRINT:INPUT A$
```

that a certain buy and sell strategy will be profitable. In the final analysis, the program uses a set of financial formulas to recommend a specific buy-sell strategy and then prints an itemized listing of all costs, brokerage fees, proceeds, and returns. To make the best use of this program, it is suggested that you study references concerning stock-option strategies.

Computation of Short-Term Insolvency. In this "Z-Score" computation based on an American Institute of Certified Public Accountants timesharing program, the short-term liquidity trend score indicates whether a company is likely to face financial difficulties in the near future.

$$Z = .012*((G-L)/I) + .014*(W/I) + .033*((P+E)/I) + .006*(W/M) + .999*(S/I)$$

where G = current
L = current liabilities
I = total assets
W = net worth
P = profit before income taxes
E = interest changes
M = total liabilities
S = sales
Z = "Z score"

Stock Alpha and Beta. In this approach to analysis, the investor compares movement of a stock over a period of time with movement of a market average. This can be best measured by comparing the percent change in a given stock's price with the percent change in the market as a whole over several large recent market fluctuations and deriving a result in the form $y = a + bx$ where y = percent change in a stock's price given x as the percent change in the market level.

The constant a is called *alpha* and is a measure of the stock's absolute continuing movement; high positive alphas are always attractive in stocks. The coefficient b is called the stock's *beta* and is a measure of the riskiness of a given stock. High betas should produce good relative performance in a bull market, but relatively poor performance in a declining market.

Betas may be calculated separately as a function of such factors as size of the company involved, its capital structure (for example, its debt/equity ratio), return on equity, earnings consistency, and so forth. You may experiment with multiple linear regression in determining the relationship between beta's and these or other variables. In general, the greater the beta, the cheaper the stock should seem to be and the greater the appreciation potential. A risk versus benefit analysis may be conducted, with, for example, betas charted versus potential appreciation based on present discounted value of the price of the stock.

Equations used to independently determine stock betas are as follows and are well-suited for incorporation into a portfolio analysis program:

Stock Beta

$$\text{Beta} = \frac{\text{Covariance of market and stock risk premiums}}{\text{Variance of market risk premium}}$$

$$\text{Variance} = \sum_{\text{time}} (\text{market risk premium-ave. market risk premium})^2$$

$$\text{Convariance} = \sum_{\text{time}} (\text{SRP-ave. SPR}) * (\text{MRP-ave. MRP})$$

$$\text{SRP} = \text{stock risk premium}$$

$$\text{MRP} = \text{market risk premium}$$

$$\text{risk premium} = (\text{rate of return}) - (\text{risk free rate of return})$$

$$\text{risk free rate of return} = \frac{1}{12 \cdot (\text{annual rate of a 3 month T-bill})}$$

$$\text{rate of return} = \frac{(\text{price at month end} + \text{dividend}) - (\text{price at month start})}{\text{price at month start}}$$

For market statistics, use the *Standard & Poors 500 Stock Index.*

Portfolio Beta

$$\text{Beta} = \sum_{\text{portfolio}} (\text{stock beta}) \cdot (\%\text{ of market value})$$

$$\%\text{ market value} = \frac{\text{market value of a stock}}{\text{total market value}}$$

market value of a stock = current price × no. of shares

Inflation Rate Effect. An oversimplified but often useful method of forecasting the effect of a given inflation rate on the stock market is as follows. First, assume that the cost of money is constant at 3 percent. Add to this value a 1 percent constant that will be assumed to be the risk factor for owning stocks instead of bonds. To this sum add the current inflation rate. Divide this final sum into 100; the result is the average stock market multiple of earnings. Now, multiply this result by the sum of the estimated yearly earnings of the 30 Dow Jones Industrial stocks. If the sum of the estimated earnings is not known, a simple computer program could determine earnings for the industrial stocks from the newspaper listings of price and price/earnings ratios (earnings = price/price-earnings ratio); a method of determining future earnings growth would have to be employed. The final product calculated is a projected Dow Jones industrial stock average.

The calculations would be as follows, assuming an inflation rate of 5 percent and estimated Dow industrial stock earnings of $110:

$$\frac{100}{(3\% + 1\% + 5\%)} \cdot 110. = 1222.$$

Calculation of the Future Value of an Investment. You can use the program in Listing 2-4 to calculate how much an investment will be worth in the future.

Listing 2-4. Future Value Program.

```
10    REM LISTING2.04 - The Future Value Program
110   FULLW 2:CLEARW 2:GOTOXY 1,1
120   DEFDBL F,D,E,B,C,A
130   INPUT "Enter the consumer price index for previous year ",F
140   INPUT "Enter the consumer price index for current year ",E
150   INPUT "Enter the present value of the investment (or product/
      salary) ",C
160   INPUT "Enter the number of periods to be calculated ",B
170   A=(100*(E-F)/F)/100
180   D=INT((C*(A+1)^B)*100+.5)/100
190   PRINT
200   PRINT "The future value is: $";D
210   PRINT:PRINT:INPUT A$
```

Investment Analysis Using Interest Rate Formulas. The set of interest rate formulae outlined below may be used to assess and compare the values of investments with respect to time and money, considering that money today is inherently worth more than the same money tomorrow. In an investment, money passes from and to the investor in the form of borrowed money, loaned money, dividends received, installment loan payments made, and so on; these are called *cash flows.* The resulting profit or loss can be measured as an interest rate, the rate being absolute throughout the whole period of investment or applying only to a specific time interval. A $30 profit on a $100 investment four years ago is a 30 percent profit in absolute terms, but when it is measured at an annual rate (using the equations below), the profit comes to 6.8 percent.

The interest equations below may be divided into two sets: equations 1, 4, 7, and 9 are used to measure investments in which transactions occur only twice—once at the beginning and once at the end of the investment period. The other eight equations apply to problems in which constant-dollar transactions occur at regular intervals. An installment loan is a good example of this kind of problem. If you borrow $4000 to buy a car and pay off the loan over 36 months at 12 percent interest, equation 11 may be used to compute the amount for each payment ($132.86).

It is important to note that there is no formula for solving for interest rates directly in the second set of equations, because i cannot be isolated on one side of the equation. The only method to solve for interest rates in this situation is to use a "brute-force" approach in which the computer tries values for i and solves for F or P until the right answer is found. The value for i would be successively approximated.

The formulae in Table 2-1 will be used throughout this chapter in discussing loans, mortgages, annuities, and real estate evaluation. The uses are as varied as the diversity of investments. The personal computer becomes useful in answering "what if?" questions involving changes in interest rates, time periods, and other variables with these equations or useful in solving equations 5 and 6 in Table 2-1, which require an iterative approach.

Financial Databases. The easiest way to enter information into stock-market programs is over the telephone. Various database services supply detailed financial information—both current and historical—which can be retrieved by any computer through a telephone modem. On-line services offer most, if not all, of the securities you are likely to be interested in. For instance, one of the popular personal computer networks (CompuServe) offers the following financial information for instant retrieval:

- Figures on more than 9,000 securities, updated throughout each trading day—no need to wait for day-old stock values in the newspaper.
- Detailed descriptive and financial information on thousands of major publicly-held companies.
- Current and historical information on more than 40,000 stocks, bonds, and options.
- Continually updated information on prices and basic news stories incorporating market commentary and statistics.
- Specialized reports on commodities, today's economy, and implications for the future.
- Financial commentary from the nation's leading news publications.

Alternatively, companies such as Standard & Poor offer market statistic updates sent periodically on floppy disk. The S&P package costs about $500 per year and provides monthly updates of some 100 types of basic financial data, ranging from sales to assets, for about 1,500 publicly traded companies.

Other databases specialize in business information and can supply text of leading industry newsletters, with extensive search and indexing capabilities. The NewsNet Network, 945 Haverford Road, Bryn Mawr, PA 19010, for instance, provides full text of over 125 business newsletters in the following areas:

advertising and marketing
aerospace
automobile industry

This table shows the appropriate formulae to use given three input parameters and a required output parameter.

GIVEN	no. of uniform periods	(n)	x	x	x	x	x	x			
	interest rate per period	(i)	x	x	x				x	x	x
	present value	(P)	x			x	x		x	x	
	future value	(F)		x		x		x	x		
	uniform payments	(R)			x		x	x		x	x
REQUIRED		n							1	2	3
		i				4	5	6			
		P		7	8						
		F	9		10						
		R	11	12							

1. $n = \dfrac{\log \dfrac{F}{P}}{\log (1 + i)}$

2. $n = \dfrac{\log \dfrac{1}{1 - iP/R}}{\log (1 + i)}$

3. $n = \dfrac{\log 1 + \dfrac{iF}{R}}{\log (1 + i)}$

4. $i = \sqrt[n]{\dfrac{F}{P}} - 1$

5. $i = \dfrac{R}{P}(1 - [1 - i]^{-n})$

6. $i = \dfrac{R}{F}([1 + i]^n - 1)$

7. $P = \dfrac{F}{(1 + i)^n}$

8. $P = R\dfrac{1 + (1 + i)^{-n}}{i}$

9. $F = P(1 + i)^n$

10. $F = R\dfrac{(1 + i)^n - 1}{i}$

11. $R = P\dfrac{i}{1 - (1 + i)^{-n}}$

12. $R = F\dfrac{i}{(1 + i)^n - 1}$

Table 2-1. Look-Up Table of Financial Formulas.

behavioral sciences and social services
corporate communications
education
electronics and computers
energy
entertainment and leisure
environment
farming and food
finance, accounting, and taxes
general business management
government regulations and law
international affairs
investments
labor
metals and mining
office automation
politics
publishing and broadcasting
real estate
politics
telecommunications
transportation

Interest Calculations. The microcomputer can be used to calculate simple, compound and true interest. A program could be written to calculate the exact number of days between two dates, and number of months, days, and years in the interest period: leap years would be accounted for. The following formula would be used:

$$i = \frac{cpd}{100\ 360}$$

where i = interest on the capital
c = capital, invested or borrowed
p = rate of interest
d = number of days

Compound Interest can also be calculated. Given three of the four variables F, P, i, and n, the fourth may be solved for using equations 1, 4, 7, or 9 in Table 2-1.

The true interest is calculated as follows:

$$R = \frac{24F_c}{mI_m\,(m + 1)}$$

where R = the true interest rate
F_c = finance charge
m = number of months
I_m = monthly installment

The BASIC program in Listing 2-5 computes the

Listing 2-5. True Annual Interest Rate Computation.

```
10      REM LISTING2.05 - True Annual Interest Rate Computation
20      REM for use with installment loans
25      FULLW 2:CLEARW 2:GOTOXY 1,1
30      INPUT "Enter the amount of the loan (without interest) ";B
40      INPUT "enter the amount of each payment ",A
50      INPUT "Enter the total number of payments ",C
60      INPUT "Enter the number of payments per year ",D
70      PRINT:PRINT
80      IF C=1 THEN 680
90      IF C*A>=B THEN 150
100     PRINT:PRINT
110     PRINT "The payments sum to less than the amount owed ";
130     PRINT
135     INPUT "Press RETURN when ready ",A$
140     GOTO 140
150     E=0:F=100
160     GOSUB 260
170     IF A=G THEN 360
180     IF A>G THEN 220 ELSE E=E-F:GOTO 230
220     E=E+F
230     F=F/2
240     IF F<.0001 THEN 360
250     GOTO 160
260     H=E/(100*D)
270     J=H+1
280     IF C*J<=75 THEN 10
290     G=B*H
300     RETURN
310     IF G>1 THEN G=B*J^C*H/(J^C-1) ELSE G=B/C
320     RETURN
360     E=.01*INT(.05+100*E)
370     IF E<199.5 THEN 430
380     PRINT
390     PRINT The interest rate is too high, re-enter ";
420     GOTO 10
430     PRINT:PRINT "True annual interest rate=";E;"%"
440     INPUT "Press RETURN when ready; enter QUIT to end: ",A$
460     IF A$="QUIT" THEN 710 ELSE GOTO 10
680     E=(A/B-1)*D
690     E=100*E
700     GOTO 360
710     END
```

true annual interest rate. An ideal application involves evaluation of installment loans.

Minimum Investment for Withdrawals. This formula may be used to determine the minimum investment required to allow regular withdrawals of a given amount over a given time period, assuming compounded interest with each withdrawal and an ending balance of $0. A retiree might use this formula to compute the amount to invest in a savings account at 6 percent interest to provide monthly withdrawals of $100.00 for 10 years.

$$P = \frac{R \bullet N}{i}\left(1 - \frac{1}{(1 + i/N)^{NY}}\right)$$

where P = initial investment
R = amount of regular withdrawal
i = nominal interest rate
N = number of withdrawals per year
Y = number of years

Mortgages

The computer can be very useful to the home buyer in simplifying the many financial options available. You can use your computer to determine mortgage payments based on the interest rates available, the length of the life of the mortgage, and the amount. With recent swings in interest rates, knowing what you will be paying at any given interest can be very important; a difference of a half or one percent can be substantial. This information is also important in budget planning—in determining how much of the family income must be allocated to mortgage or loan payments. You can do a "what if?" analysis; that is, if interest rates are predicted to decline by 3 percent next year, is it best to buy or wait? With your microcomputer and the financial formulae outlined in Table 2-1, the financial ramifications of home buying or other investments can be easily determined.

It may be worth your while to analyze a mortgage agreement on your computer before signing any contracts. A yearly amortization program could calculate a schedule of payments, the annual debt service, the mortgage constant, the remaining balance, the payment to principal, the payment to interest, the accumulated principal, and the accumulated interest for each year. A general amortization program could solve for the following additional factors: the number of payments to reach a certain balance, the payment amount, the annual percentage rate, and the principal amount. Listing 2-6 is a sample mortgage schedule program.

Listing 2-6. Mortgage Schedule Program.

```
10     REM LISTING2.06 - The Mortgage Schedule Program
90     FULLW 2:CLEARW 2:GOTOXY 1,1
120    DIM A(3),B(3)
130    B$="##     $######.##     $######.##        $######.##      $######
       #.##"
140    INPUT "Enter the number of years of the mortgage ",X
150    INPUT "Enter the yearly interest rate ",X1
160    INPUT "Enter the amount of the mortgage ",B
170    b1=12*x
180    X1=X1/1200
190    B2=B*X1/(1-(1/(1+X1))^B1)
200    T=0
210    B(2)=0:B(1)=0:B3=B2*B1-B:A(2)=0:A(3)=B:A(1)=0
220    PRINT USING "Monthly payment is $####.##";B2
230    PRINT
240    PRINT "YEAR PRINCIPAL PAID  PRINCIPAL LEFT   INTEREST PAID
       TOTAL PAID"
250    FOR I=1 TO X
260    FOR J=1 TO 12
```

```
270     T=T+B2
280     B(1)=A(3)*X1
290     A(1)=B2-B(1)
300     A(2)=A(2)+A(1)
310     A(3)=A(3)-A(1)
320     B(2)=B(2)+B(1)
330     B(3)=B(3)-B(1)
340     NEXT J
350     PRINT USING B$;I,A(2),A(3),B(2),T
360     NEXT I
370     PRINT
380     INPUT A$
```

Special programs could calculate the above values for wraparound mortgages and determine the price and yield of discounted mortgages.

An amortization schedule for a loan as well as the time required for repayment can be calculated by the loan amortization program in Listing 2-7.

Listing 2-7. Loan Amortization Calculator Program.

```
10      REM LISTING2.07 - Loan Amortization calculator
20      FULLW 2:CLEARW 2:GOTOXY 1,1
30      PRINT "LOANS":PRINT
40      PRINT "Select: 1) payment amount calculation"
50      INPUT "        2) time of payment calculation ",A
60      ON A GOTO 70,2000
65      GOTO 40
70      INPUT "Enter the amount of the loan ",AM
80      INPUT "Enter the number of payments (yrs. *12 usually) ",N
90      INPUT "Enter the annual interest rate ",I
100     B=I/1200
110     C=N
120     INPUT "Enter the month of the first payment (1-12) ",M
130     INPUT "Enter the year of the first payment ";Y
140     D=1:FOR X=1 TO C
150     D=(1+B)*D
160     NEXT X
170     D=1/D:F=B/(1-D)*AM
180     G=F:GOSUB 5000
190     F=G
200     H=Y:J=1:L=AM:K=M-1:E=0:P=0
210     CLEARW 2:GOTOXY 1,1
220     PRINT "AMORTIZATION TABLE"
230     PRINT "Monthly payment: $";F
240     PRINT "Amount of loan :$";TAB(18)AM;TAB(28)"Interest rate=";I;
260     IF S=0 THEN PRINT:GOTO 280
270     PRINT "Term+";TAB(55)N;TAB(59)"Months"
280     PRINT "No.";
290     PRINT TAB(8)"Date";TAB(19)"Interest";TAB(33)"Principal";TAB(50)
        "Balance"
300     FOR X=J TO J+9
310     K=K+1
320     IF K=13 THEN K=1:H=H+1
330     A2=L*B:G=A2
```

```
340   GOSUB 5000
350   A2=G:S=F-A2:G=S
360   GOSUB 5000
370   S=G
380   L=L-S:G=L
390   GOSUB 5000
400   L=G:P=A2:E=S+E
410   PRINT J;TAB(6)K;"-";H;TAB(19)A2;TAB(33)S;TAB(49)L
420   IF J=C-1 THEN 600
430   J=J+1
440   NEXT X
450   G=P
460   GOSUB 5000
470   P=G
480   PRINT "Total interest to date $";P;"  Total principal to date $";E
490   INPUT "Press RETURN to see next page ",A$
500   GOTO 210
600   A2=B*L
610   G=A2:GOSUB 5000
620   A2=G:S=L:A3=F:F=S+A2:K=K+1
630   IF K=12 THEN K=1:H=H+1
640   L=L-S:J=J+1:E=S+E:P=P+A2
650   PRINT J;TAB(6)K;"-";TAB(19)A2;TAB(33)S;TAB(49)L
660   PRINT "Total interest to date=$";P
670   PRINT "Total principal to date=";E
680   PRINT "Final payment=$";F
690   G=F:GOSUB 5000
700   F=G:F=A3
710   INPUT "Continue or end (C/E)";A4$
720   IF A4$="C" THEN 30 ELSE END
2000  CLEARW 2:GOTOXY 1,1
2010  INPUT "Enter the amount borrowed ",B1
2020  INPUT "Enter the interest rate/yr. ",B2
2030  INPUT "Enter the monthly payment ",E
2040  INPUT "Enter the month payments begin (1-12) ",M
2050  INPUT "Enter the year of the beginning payment ",Y
2060  B3=B1*B2/1200-E*(12-M)
2070  IF B3<=0 THEN 2130
2080  PRINT:PRINT:PRINT:PRINT
2090  PRINT "The minimum payment=$";B1*B2/1200
2100  GOTO 2010
2130  B=1-B2/1200*B1/E
2140  X=B:GOSUB 4000
2150  B=R
2160  F=1+B2/1200
2170  X=F:GOSUB 4000
2180  F=R
2190  J=-(B/F)
2200  PRINT
2210  IF B3=0 THEN PRINT "Payments cover interest only ":GOTO 2230
2220  PRINT "No. of months for payments=";J
2230  H=INT(J/12):N=J-H*12
2240  IF N>1 THEN N=N+1
2250  N=INT(N):C=12*H+N
2260  IF N>11 THEN H=H+1:N=N-12
2270  IF B3=0 THEN S=0:GOTO 2290
2280  PRINT "=";H;" years+ ";N;" months to pay loan"
2290  PRINT:PRINT:PRINT
```

```
2300 INPUT "Press RETURN to continue ",A4$
2310 J=N:B=B2/1200:F=E:N=N+12*H:AM=B1:R=B2
2320 F=F/B3
2325 F=E:I=B2
2330 GOTO 180
2350 AM=(X-1)/(X+1)
2360 C=AM*AM*AM
2370 R=2*(AM+1/3*C+1/5*AM*AM*C+A/7*C*C*AM+1/9*C*C*C+1/
     11*C*C*C*AM*AM)
4000 AM=(X-1)/(X+1)
4010 C=AM*AM*AM
4020 R=2*(AM+1/3*C+1/5*AM*AM*C+1/7*C*C*AM+1/9*C*C*C+1/
     11*C*C*C*AM*AM)
4030 RETURN
5000 G=INT((G=INT(G))*100+.50001)/100+INT(G)
5010 RETURN
```

Figure 2-2 is a sample run showing how this program functions.

Loan with Points. *Points* are a percentage of the value of a loan that is paid at the start of the loan period. Theoretically, the seller pays the points, but in practice it does not matter who pays—the price of the house increases with the addition of points.

One point represents 1 percent of the mortgage value. It must be paid at the beginning of the loan. The important question to consider is how does the addition of points affect the annual percentage rate

LOAN AMORTIZATION SCHEDULE

PRINCIPAL=$4800.00
#OF PERIODS=12
INTEREST RATE=5.6%

PAYMENT NUMBER	REMAINING PRINCIPAL	MONTHLY PAYMENT	PRINCIPAL PAYMENT	INTEREST PAYMENT
1	4410.16	412.24	389.84	22.40
2	4018.51	412.24	391.66	20.58
3	3625.02	412.24	393.48	18.75
4	3229.70	412.24	395.32	16.92
5	2832.54	412.24	397.16	15.07
6	2433.52	412.24	399.02	13.22
7	2032.64	412.24	400.88	11.36
8	1629.89	412.24	402.75	9.49
9	1225.26	412.24	404.63	7.61
10	818.74	412.24	406.52	5.72
11	410.32	412.24	408.42	3.82
12	0.00	412.24	410.32	1.91
OVERALL TOTALS		$4946.84	$4800.00	$146.84

Fig. 2-2. Loan amortization schedule produced by the program in Listing 2-7.

actually being paid for the loan? The program in Listing 2-8 will calculate this value given the number of points, amount of the loan, years, and annual percentage rate of the loan. It outputs the value for monthly payments and true annual percentage rate.

where
R = regular payment
i = annual interest rate
P = principal
N = number of payments per year
Y = number of years

Listing 2-8. The Loan-with-Points Program.

```
10    REM LISTING2.08 - The Loan with Points Program
15    FULLW 2:CLEARW 2:GOTOXY 1,1
20    INPUT "Enter loan amount, number of points ";L,R
30    INPUT "Enter annual percentage rate, years ";A,Y
40    P=P*.01:A=.01*A/12:Y=Y*12
50    R=L*((A*(A+1)^Y)/((A+1)^Y-1))
60    PRINT "Monthly payment--$";R
70    FOR D=1 TO 100
80    F=.0001*D+A:X=(1-P)*L*((F*(1+F)^Y)/((1+F)^Y-1))
90    IF X>R THEN 110
100   NEXT D:PRINT "Program unable to calculate value ":INPUT A$:END
110   PRINT "Actual annual percentage rate=";f*1200;"%.":INPUT A$:END
```

Direct Reduction Loan. The payment, present value, or number of time periods for a reduction loan may be calculated by using equations 2, 8 and 11 in Table 2-1.

Additional Loan Formulae. Here are some more formulae that you will find useful when you are dealing with loans.

- Principal on a loan

$$P = \frac{R \bullet N}{i} \bullet \left(1 - \frac{1}{(1 + i/N)^{N \bullet Y}}\right)$$

where P = principal
R = regular payment
i = annual interest rate
N = number of payments per year
Y = number of years

- Regular payment on a loan

$$R = \frac{i \bullet P/N}{1 - \left(\frac{i}{N} + 1\right)^{-N \bullet Y}}$$

- Term of a loan

$$Y = -\frac{\log\left(1 - \frac{P \bullet i}{N \bullet R}\right)}{\log\left(1 + \frac{i}{N}\right)} \bullet \frac{1}{N}$$

where
Y = term of payment in years
P = principal
i = annual interest rate
N = number of payments per year
R = amount of payments

Depreciation Calculations

Standard, composite, and excess depreciations may be calculated with the following methods:

1) Straight-line depreciation

$$D = PV/n$$
$$B_k = PV - kD$$

2) Sum-of-the-years-digits depreciation

$$B_k = \frac{S + (n-k)D_k}{2} \quad D_k = \frac{2(n-k+1)PV}{n(n+1)}$$

3) Variable rate declining balance depreciation

$$D_k = PV \frac{R}{n} (1 - R/n)^{k-1}$$

$$B_k = PV (1 - R/n)^k$$

In each of the above depreciation formulas,

- PV = original value of asset (less salvage value)
- n = lifetime number of periods of asset
- B_k = book value at time period K
- D = each year's depreciation
- k = the number of the time period (that is, 1, 2, 3, . . . n)
- S = salvage value
- R = depreciation rate
- D_k = depreciation at time period k

The program in Listing 2-9 can be used to compare depreciation methods.

Here are some sample results from the depreciation program.

YEAR NO.	STRAIGHT LINE	DOUBLE DECL.	SUM OF DIGITS
1	$ 1250.00	$ 2750.00	$ 2000.00
2	$ 1250.00	$ 1375.00	$ 1500.00
3	$ 1250.00	$ 687.50	$ 1000.00
4	$ 1250.00	$ 343.75	$ 500.00

The actual depreciation rate for an investment is computed with the formula

$$\text{depreciation rate} = 1 - \left(\frac{\text{resale price}}{\text{original price}}\right)^{1/\text{age}}$$

and may be used to answer queries such as "If a car was bought for $9000 and sold three years later for $5100, what was the depreciation rate?"

The *salvage value* of an item at the end of a given year may be calculated with the formula

$$S = P(1 - i)^Y$$

where S = salvage value
P = original price
i = depreciation rate
Y = age in years

Annuities

Given the values of the required variables as

Listing 2-9. Depreciation Method Comparison Program.

```
10    REM LISTING2.09 - The Depreciation Method Comparison Program
15    FULLW 2:CLEARW 2:GOTOXY 1,1
20    INPUT "Enter purchase cost ",C
30    INPUT "Enter life in years ",L
40    INPUT "Enter scrap life ",S
50    A$="##           $#####.##           $#####.##           $
      #####.##"
60    B=C-S:D1=B/L:M=((L+1)/2)*L:F=L
65    PRINT "Year no.     ","Straight line      Double decl.","Sum of
      digits"
70    FOR X=1 TO L:D2=B*(F/M):F=F-1
80    D3=2*C/L:C=C-D3
90    PRINT USING A$;X,D2,D3,C
100   NEXT X
110   INPUT A$
```

input data, an annuity program could calculate the remaining variable in any of the following situations:

- Sinking funds—a *sinking fund* is an annuity in which a future value is accumulated by making equal payments at equal intervals at a certain interest rate. The value can be computed using equation 10 in Table 2-1.
- Annuity due—the future or present value can be calculated using equations 8 and 10 in Table 2-1.
- Ordinary annuity—This value may or may not include a balloon payment. Again, use equations 2, 8, and 11 in Table 2-1.

Bonds and Warrants

A useful, simple program could be written to determine the value of both short- and long-term warrants. Given present value, coupon interest, yield to maturity, and maturity value or the number of periods (three values out of the four), a computer program can compute the remaining term. Taxes, commissions, and current yield could also be determined. The formula used to calculate the present value (cost) of a bond with annual coupons is as follows:

$$\text{Price} = \left[\left(\frac{1 - (1 + i/c)^{-n}}{ic}\right)\right]^{(1000\ Cr/2)} + [(1 + i/c)^{-n}(1000)]$$

where i = discount rate as a percentage
n = number of years to maturity, multiplied by 2
Cr = coupon rate of bond
c = number of compounding periods per year

The formula used to calculate the bond yield of annual coupon is as follows:

$$j = \frac{\dfrac{Fg - (B.V.)_1 - (B.V.)_n}{n}}{\dfrac{(B.V.)_1 + (B.V.)_n}{2}}$$

where j = nominal yield rate
$(B.V.)_1$ = original bond value
$(B.V.)_n$ = bond at n years
F = face value
g = nominal dividend rate
n = number of years

PERSONAL ACCOUNTING

There are a number of ways in which your personal computer can help you manage your personal finances more effectively. The computer can help you deal with everything from credit card payments to income tax calculations.

Personal Accounts Receivable/Payable

A personal AP/AR program similar to a business AP/AR program could manage a large portion of your financial affairs. The program could include the features described below.

A checking and savings account management program would enable you to maintain the current balance of your checking and savings accounts. Interest credits could be calculated and added. A file of each check (with its number, purpose, notes, amount, and payee) could be stored for later income tax preparation. Specialized reports could be generated from this check file including a check register for a specified time period, the distribution of expenditures, and statements of selected accounts. The ideal program would request all information concerning each check written, store this information, and print the check itself.

A budgeting program would keep you up to date on expenditures in various areas so that income can be allocated appropriately. A plan for family spending could take the following format:

Set-asides
    Emergencies and future goals ________
    Seasonal expenses ________
    Debt payments ________
Regular monthly expenses
    Rent or mortgage payment ________
    Utilities ________
    Installment payments ________

Other ________
Total ________
Day-to-day expenses
Food and beverages ________
Household maintenance ________
Furnishings, equipment ________
Clothing ________
Personal ________
Transportation ________
Medical care ________
Recreation, education ________
Gifts, contributions ________
Total ________
Total of all expenses ________

Alternatively, you could take realistic estimates for the upcoming year and enter these figures. A program could use this information in computing the percentage of gross income that each item requires. As a rule of thumb, housing should cost no more than one fourth of your gross income. (This is an example of one of the budgeting principles discussed in most references concerning family preparation.) The home computer removes the drudgery of manual calculations for those determined to stick to a well-planned budget.

On command, a budget program could print month-to-date figures and an end-of-month comparison of budget versus actual expenses. It can also show the amount of cash needed to meet budgeted expenses for the rest of the month. It could also maintain tax records, keep a running balance of cash on hand, keep an inventory of your possessions, and even help in planning weekly menus.

Table 2-2 shows a portion of a personal budget report that indicates where the money has been and will be spent in spreadsheet fashion. Such spreadsheets, besides being a personal planning benefit, are often useful when securing a personal loan.

A financial behavior determination program would help you analyze your expenditures and summarize your spending in various areas (the categories of the budget above) that would be useful in preparing a budget plan.

According to the experts at the U.S. Dept. of Labor, a family of four should typically allocate its spending as follows:

Housing	24 percent
Food	24 percent
Transportation	15 percent
Clothing, personal care	13 percent

Table 2-2. A Portion of a Personal Budget in Spreadsheet Form.

ACTUAL FOR
JOE SMITH
OCT. 8, 1982

EXPENSE	JAN	FEB	MAR	APR	MAY	JUN	JUL	AUG
RENT	650	0	0	0	0	0	0	0
FOOD	323	361	357	371	290	251	410	356
CLOTHES	154	0	54	0	0	0	0	68
UTILITIES	57	56	50	59	62	51	53	59
CREDIT CARD INTEREST	0	0	0	0	0	0	0	0
ENTERTAINMENT	143	100	58	13	24	45	125	54
GASOLINE	100	110	90	100	100	100	95	90
MORTGAGE INTEREST	0	0	0	0	0	0	0	0
MISCELLANEOUS EXPENSE	28	0	44	0	98	0	0	48
CAR EXPENSES	990	0	0	0	0	0	0	0
TOTAL EXPENSE	2445	627	653	543	574	447	683	675
NET INCOME	105	1623	1597	2091	1676	1803	1863	1825

Taxes 13 percent
Medical 7 percent
All other 4 percent

Families differ, but how do your own expenses correspond to these percentages?

A file of unfulfilled transactions, such as contracts, mail orders, etc., for which you have sent checks but have received no reply, would allow the removal of the appropriate accounts from the file as replies are received.

Daily Interest Passbook Savings Account

You can use the BASIC program in Listing 2-10 to maintain a savings account. The program has provisions for interest, withdrawals, and deposits.

Preparation of income tax forms is a task that lends itself well to computers because computers

Listing 2-10. Daily Interest Savings Program.

```
10      REM LISTING2.10 - The Daily Interest Savings Program

15      PRINT "Daily interest passbook savings computation ":PRINT
20      PRINT "Enter deposits as positive numbers, deductions as negati
        ve numbers
25      PRINT "Enter 0,0,0 at date prompt to end"
30      INPUT "Press RETURN to begin: ",A$
40      FULLW 2:CLEARW 2:GOTOXY 1,1
50      INPUT "Enter the annual interest in percent ",F
60      E=F/36000!
70      INPUT "Select: 1) use actual days in month 2) use 30 days for m
        onth ",D
80      G=0
90      INPUT "Enter the starting date numerically as month, day ",A,B
100     INPUT "Enter the starting balance ",C
110     IF D=1 THEN INPUT "Is this a leap year (1=YES, 2=NO)";H:GOSUB 3
        90
115     IF D<>1 THEN GOSUB 180
120     J=K:PRINT
130     PRINT "  #    DATE    WITHDRAWAL    DEPOSIT    BALANCE     INTERES
        T"
140     PRINT K;A;",";B;TAB(38);C
150     INPUT "Enter month, day, amount: ";A,B,L
160     IF D=2 THEN GOSUB 180 ELSE GOSUB 390
170     GOTO 250
180     M=B
190     IF (A=2) OR (A=4) OR (A=6) OR (A=9) OR (A=11) THEN 200 ELSE 230
200     IF (A=2) AND (B=28) THEN INPUT "Is this a leap year (1=YES, 2=N
        O) ";N:IF N=1 THEN RETURN ELSE 220
210     IF B>27 THEN B=31
220     IF B=30 THEN B=31
230     K=B+(A-1)*30
240     RETURN
250     O=K
260     IF J=K THEN 300
270     FOR P=J TO K-1
280     G=G+G*E+C*E
290     NEXT P
300     C=C+L
310     G=(INT((G-INT(G))*100+.5001))/100+INT(G)
320     PRINT K;A;",";M;
```

```
330    IF L<0 THEN PRINT TAB(13)L;:GOTO 350
340    PRINT TAB(24)L;
350    PRINT TAB(38)C;
360    PRINT TAB(50)G
370    J=0
380    GOTO 150
390    ON A GOTO 400,410,420,430,440,450,460,470,480,490,500,510
400    K=B:GOTO 520
410    K=B+31:GOTO 520
420    K=B+N+59:GOTO 520
430    K=B+N+90:GOTO 520
440    K=B+N+120:GOTO 520
450    K=B+N+151:GOTO 520
460    K=B+N+181:GOTO 520
470    K=B+N+212:GOTO 520
480    K=B+N+243:GOTO 520
490    K=B+N+273:GOTO 520
500    K=B+N+304:GOTO 520
510    K=B+N+334
520    RETURN
```

are great organizers and calculators, and they can save you time and money. Tax preparation programs range from simple arithmetic calculators to complete personal accounting programs. In the most popular approach, the computer requests answers to such questions as, "What are your federal withholding taxes?" You proceed to answer all the possible questions necessary to prepare a 1040 tax form (approximately 50), but unfortunately you must first do considerable accounting and calculating to answer some of the questions. The program completes the simple arithmetic for filling in the 1040 form and prints the proper values in the boxes on the form.

A more complex approach would involve the periodic storage of all elements of your finances on cassette or floppy disk (for example, each week you could store the names, addresses, purposes, numbers, and amount of all checks written or cashed). At year end, the computer would search and group all relevant data and do all of the necessary calculations. In this latter approach, a complete summary of all deductions, income, and so on could be printed categorically. References to the filed location of the original checks, bills, and receipts could be included for proof of the transactions. A warning could also be issued in the event that your deductions exceed 10 percent of your income (a tax audit would be likely). Provisions could be made to compare the taxes you would pay if you filed jointly with your spouse to what you would pay if you filed as an individual.

A tax planning program can help cut your tax liability in the years to come. Investment decisions, personal financial decisions, and business decisions with tax consequences can all be analyzed in planning a tax strategy. In a divorce, for example, the arrangement of a settlement can result in substantially less tax, depending upon how the money is allocated between property settlement, alimony, and child support. A tax planning program can be used to quickly answer "what if?" questions during the negotiation of a settlement. The ease of changing inputs and having the program recalculate the entire return can be a tremendous timesaver. Additionally, complex calculations such as income averaging on Form G can be done automatically, perhaps yielding a bigger refund for those who previously would not have attempted the calculations manually. A tax planning program in the form of a spreadsheet allows the simultaneous consideration of multiple cases covering different facts and years. The spreadsheet can include graphical representations showing the impact of adding or subtracting income, deductions, or credits, and varying tax computations over a several-year period—including regular tax, alternative minimum tax, add-on minimum tax, income averaging, and the consideration of limitations on the use of credits. For instance, you could xconsider the possibility of a second income versus staying at home by having your computer program figure the after-tax results of that extra income, which is often discouraging. As another example, assume that you own a business and want to know if you should pay your wife a salary. Depending upon your income level, this may or may not be advantageous; a tax planning program could determine the best option for your income bracket.

A recurring question among investors is, "What are the sources of tax-free income whose yields are equal to or greater than yields provided by taxable investments?" Should you invest in tax-free bonds and other tax-free securities, or place your money in a fully taxable bond, savings account, or treasury bill? (Remember, however, that you may wish to consider other factors, such as liquidity of assets.) The two formulas necessary to compute taxable and tax-free yields are given below. A simple BASIC program could compute these for a given situation and determine which alternative offers the better investment.

$$\text{taxable yield} = \frac{\text{tax-free yield}}{(1 - \text{FTB})}$$

$$\text{tax-free yield} = \text{taxable yield} \times (1 - \text{FTB})$$

$$\text{where FTB} = \text{Federal tax bracket}$$

For instance, if you are in the 35 percent federal income bracket, have invested in a money-market account at 8 percent, and are offered the opportunity to invest in a tax-free fund yielding 6.2 percent, which is the better investment? Using the second equation above, you find that the tax-free fund would be a better investment at 6.2 percent, versus 5.2 percent after taxes for the money-market account. A more sophisticated program could print a table of yields given the known tax-free or taxable yield starting value and the increment, and the starting value of the tax bracket and the increment. Investors in some states are allowed tax exemptions for qualifying tax-free investments. In this situation, simply add the exempted state tax rate to the federal tax rate when entering your tax bracket value.

Home Banking

You may soon be able to do your banking from home with a personal computer. Many banks are conducting pilot home-banking studies and are beginning to sell such services to depositors. These include the Central Trade Bank of Memphis (Memphis, Tenn.); Citibank (New York); First Tennessee Bank (Knoxville, Tenn.); Huntington National Bank (Columbus, Ohio); and Shawmut Bank of Boston (Boston, Mass.).

With most of these services, a customer dials the bank's central computer or uses one of the timesharing networks, such as CompuServe, through his modem. After providing a secret password, the customer can, for instance, ask for a list of recent deposits and pay bills directly by transferring money from his account to those of his creditors. Banks charge from $5 to $15 per month for this service.

Retirement Planner

The formulas given below, translated into BASIC statements, will calculate how much initial capital you need to financially survive a given number of retirement years at a given standard of living. Inflation and return on invested capital are accounted for. By using a BASIC program, you could quickly determine the effect of changes on these and other variables. You can use this information in deciding whether or not you can afford to retire. In BASIC notation, the formulae are:

```
S=(EXP(I*N))*(T+(F*(1-EXP(-J*N))/J)-(E*
   (EXP((I-J)*N)-1)/(I-J)))
```

```
T=(E*((EXP(I-J)*N)-1)/(I-J))-((F*(1-EXP
   (-J*N)))/J) for I not equal to J
```

T=(N*E)−(F*((1−EXP(−J*N))/J)) for I equal to J

where

- **N** = Number of years after retirement for which financial survival is planned
- **S** = Investment capital remaining after **N** years
- **T** = Initial capital
- **F** = Annual fixed (after tax) income
- **E** = Initial excess living expense
- **I** = Annual average inflation rate
- **J** = Annual after-tax return on investment

MONEY-MAKING APPLICATIONS

There are many ways to use your microcomputer to make money; you might consider starting a part-time or full-time business based on one of the following ideas.

Stock Market

One "hobbyist" is deriving his income from his stock prediction newsletter that is composed of market predictions determined using "twelve confidential indicators" on his home computer. In similar fashion, you could experiment with mathematical analysis of the stock market using the statistical methods outlined earlier in this chapter.

A personal computer could also serve to maintain stock portfolios and organize or correlate market predictions and stock recommendations to ease decision making. With the proliferation of financial databases available through the use of a modem, information on stock prices, market performance, and so on could be entered automatically to a stock analysis program designed to scan the entire market, stocks of a given industry group, or particular stocks. Financial databases may also be scanned to provide historical data or the latest news reports on selected corporations.

The home computer is certainly useful in mathematical analysis and data storage for other forms of financial investment, including stock options and commodities. An options analysis program was presented earlier in this chapter and should serve as a good starting point for newcomers in computer application to the options market. Again, use of financial databases accessible via modems permits the automatic input of data to your analysis program. The commodities trader will probably find the personal computer to be a boon in organizing and obtaining information in the fast-moving and volatile commodities market and in allowing trading from the home for the first time.

Services

The home computer owner is in the position to offer the following services.

Mailing Lists. A mailing list of people in your area could be used by local firms with direct mail campaigns. The mailing list could be compiled from area phone books, association directories, and so on, entered into your computer, and stored permanently on floppy disks. The list may be printed on adhesive labels and sold to local businesses. The advantage of being a local business serves to eliminate competition from large mailing list brokers in other cities.

Resumes. People in all metropolitan areas can use a resume preparation service to write, type, and mail resumes to potential employers. A computer word processing system could automate this business almost entirely.

Typesetting, Indexing, and Editing. All businesses and organizations can use a printing preparation enterprise for typesetting and editing promotional material. Small computers interfaced to IBM composers, executive typewriters, Diablo proportional printers, laser printers, or conventional typesetting equipment can produce excellent justified and camera-ready material for printing. The cost savings of using a computer will allow the entrepreneur to offer lower prices for such services and ensure greater accuracy. Additionally, an indexing service using a simple computer program to create book or magazine indexes could provide a valuable service to small publishing firms.

Home Swap and Rental Locator Services. The practice of swapping one's home with other people during vacation time is becoming popular. A service that used a computer to categorize homes available and homes wanted could profit by publishing a newsletter of listings.

A rental locator service categorizes homes and apartments for rent from classified newspaper ads or other sources. In metropolitan areas, where finding an ideal home to rent is a difficult task, a service to match people with the right living conditions at the right price would be useful. In a similar manner, a service company could match people with cars for sale by the owners.

One entrepreneur has developed a computerized bartering service for matching needs and services of those in high income tax brackets for the purpose of mutual tax write-offs. He charges a small fee for successful bartering arrangements.

Finder's Fees. A *finder's fee* is a sum of money paid to someone who finds something wanted by another person who is willing to offer an award for it, be it business opportunities, products, or rare items. Usually, finder's fees are expressed as a percentage of the amount of money involved in purchasing the item to be found. A few organizations publish newsletters listing finder's fee opportunities. A hobbyist could computerize hundreds of listings for future reference and could correlate the need of buyers with the offerings of sellers.

Telephone Answering Message Service and Newspaper Clippings Service. Telephone answering services of sufficient size can use a small computer to increase efficiency and lower costs. A newspaper clipping service, which clips articles of interest to paying clients, could use a computer to keep track of the varied categories to search for.

Computer Dating Service. Popular a few years ago, computer dating services could make a return appearance, especially in metropolitan areas.

Sports Predictions and Gambling. An enterprising hobbyist uses his computer to predict college football scores. The information produced is sold as "CLYDE the computer" sports forecasts to television stations for use on local news broadcasts. Other entrepreneurs have used computer predictions of sporting events to publish flyers that are sold at dog and horse races. It would be silly to deny that personal computers have also found widespread application in illegal gambling circles for the analysis of point spreads and historical performance, and for bookkeeping!

Employment Agency. The computer could be useful to an employment agency in matching the right people with the right jobs. The use of the computer may also serve to increase business in itself.

Small Business Systems and Software. Many hobbyists have turned personal computers into a profitable sideline business by selling packaged computer systems with accounting, word processing, and spreadsheet software to small business and offering technical support and training. You could also create personalized programs including databases and mailing lists on a freelance basis for firms with small computers.

Collection Service. A word processing computer system could automatically output personalized collection letters, which theoretically generate greater response. Thus, a low-cost collection service charging a flat rate or a percentage of the money collected would be an excellent sideline business for the computer hobbyist.

Word Processing. A word processing service can be employed by businesses to prepare typewritten personalized sales letters. Such a business would be almost totally automated by a small computer.

Bowling League Bookkeeping. A few hobbyists have sideline businesses that calculate bowling league scores and handicaps for 10 to 30 cents per player per week. This cost is usually less than the costs for hiring a person to do the bookkeeping.

Supermarket Comparison Service. A hobbyists turned businessman uses his personal computer to collect and compare price data for popular foods at local supermarkets and sells a listing of the most economical stores to shoppers.

Personalized Books. Children's books containing a child's name, address, and other personalized information can be printed by a small computer economically. Studies show that children prefer reading personalized books over any other type of book, and there is a considerable demand for them. An enterprising hobbyist could develop a large-scale business along these lines. Perhaps a humorous personalized book could be sold for adults as well.

Educational Programs. You could form a distributorship to bring educational computer materials to schools, bookstores, and other institutions. The market for educational computer programs is also growing. Popular tutorials could be developed concerning electronics, higher mathematics, business and investments, computers, and an unlimited variety of other topics.

Real Estate

Possible applications for personal computers in real estate include the following:

Residential Purchase Analysis. A useful program could calculate the total monthly payment, income tax deductions, and equity build-up resulting from the purchase of a home. An own versus rent analysis could also be useful.

General Real Estate Investment Analysis. By considering such factors as inflation and interest rates, mortgages, cash flow in percent growth return, taxable income (tax shelter), and financial feasibility can be calculated. Income property reports and closing statements may also be generated.

Rental Property Management. A program designed for management of rental properties could store the following types of information for each property or client: receipts, disbursements, gross income, calculated profit and loss, calculated return on investment, and calculated net income.

Appraisal Tabulator Program. A program designed for the appraiser could organize and tabulate variables and could determine an appraisal.

Real Estate Evaluation. The program in Listing 2-11 is designed for use by a potential investor in evaluating a piece of real estate, preferably an apartment building. The program estimates the total monthly income, annual rate of return, and tax deductions based on such input data as cost, down payment on mortgage, estimated overhead costs, and income.

Listing 2-11. Real Estate Purchase Evaluation Program.

```
10    REM LISTING2.11 - Real Estate Purchase Evaluation Program
20    REM Determines tax advantage and cash flow of
30    REM a prospective purchase
35    FULLW 2:CLEARW 2:GOTOXY 1,1
40    INPUT "Enter the purchase price of the real estate ",A
50    INPUT "Enter mortgage interest (%) ",B
55    INPUT "Enter mortgage down payment as a % of purchase cost ",C
60    B=B/100:C=C/100
70    INPUT "Enter number of years in the loan term ",D
80    INPUT "Enter the closing cost (% of purchase price) ",E
90    E=E/100
100   INPUT "Enter miscellaneous initial expenses as one sum ",G
110   INPUT "Enter the estimated income per month from the property "
      ,J
120   INPUT "Enter the real estate tax for one year ",K
130   INPUT "Enter the est. overhead costs (maint., utilities, insur.
      , etc.) ",L
132   INPUT "For tax deduction purposes, enter the est. property valu
      e ",M
134   INPUT "Enter your tax bracket as a % of your income ",R7
136   C$=" **$##,###.##-"
138   INPUT "Is the building on the property new or used (N or U)";B$
140   X=B/12+1
```

```
150   Y=X^(12*D)*(X-1)/(X^(12*D)-1)*(A-C*A)
160   N=L+K/12+Y
170   P=(A-C*A)*B
180   IF B$="N" THEN Q=2 ELSE Q=1.25
190   R=L+E*(A-C*A)/12
200   R1=(A-M)/20*Q
210   R2=K+R1+P+12*R-12*J
220   R3=R7/100*R2
230   R4=G+E*A+C*A-12*(J-N)
240   R5=INT(100*((J-N)*12+R3)/R4)
260   PRINT "Tax and cash flow analysis:"
270   PRINT "Monthly expenses     ";
280   PRINT USING C$;L
290   PRINT "Monthly taxes     ";
300   PRINT USING C$;K/12
310   PRINT "Monthly mortgage     ";
320   PRINT USING C$;Y
330   PRINT "Monthly income     ";
340   PRINT USING C$;J
350   PRINT"Monthly cash flow     ";
360   PRINT USING C$;J-N
370   PRINT:PRINT
380   PRINT "Tax hedge:"
390   PRINT"Expenses (yr. #1)     ";
400   PRINT USING C$;12*R
410   PRINT "Depreciation (yr. #1)     ";
420   PRINT USING C$;R1
430   PRINT "Deductable interest (yr. #1)     ";
440   PRINT USING C$;P
450   PRINT "Real estate tax (yearly) ";
460   PRINT USING C$;K
470   PRINT:PRINT "Total:yr. #1)     ";
480   PRINT USING C$;K+P+R1+R*12
490   PRINT "Total Income (yr. #1)      ";
500   PRINT USING C$;J*12
510   PRINT "Net deduction (yr. #1)     ";
520   PRINT USING C$;R2
530   PRINT "Tax advantage (yr. #1)     ";
540   PRINT USING C$;R3
550   PRINT:PRINT "Return on investment";
560   PRINT R5;"%"
570   PRINT:PRINT:INPUT A$
```

First, here's a sample run that will show you what information the program will request and what kinds of results it will produce:

ENTER THE PURCHASE PRICE OF THE REAL ESTATE? 75000
ENTER THE MORTGAGE INTEREST (%) ? 9.75
ENTER THE MORTGAGE DOWN PAYMENT AS A % OF PURCHASE COST? 10
ENTER THE NUMBER OF YEARS IN THE LOAN TERM? 25
ENTER THE CLOSING COST (% OF PURCHASE PRICE)? 2
ENTER MISCELLANEOUS INITIAL EXPENSES AS ONE SUM? 100
ENTER THE ESTIMATED INCOME PER MONTH FROM THE PROPERTY? 1125
ENTER THE REAL ESTATE TAX FOR ONE YEAR? 1300
ENTER THE ESTIMATED OVERHEAD COSTS (MAINT., UTILITIES, INSUR., ETC.)? 525

```
FOR TAX DEDUCTION PURPOSES, ENTER
    THE EST. PROPERTY VALUE? 15000
ENTER YOUR TAX BRACKET AS A% OF
    YOUR INCOME? 40
IS THE BUILDING ON THE PROPERTY NEW
    OR USED ("N" OR "U")? N


TAX AND CASH FLOW ANALYSIS

MONTHLY EXPENSES $525.00

MONTHLY TAXES $108.33
MONTHLY MORTGAGE $601.52
MONTHLY INCOME $1125.00

MONTHLY CASH FLOW $109.85-

TAX HEDGE:

EXPENSES (YR. #1) $7650.00
DEPRECIATION (YR. #1) $6000.00
DEDUCTIBLE INTEREST $6581.25
REAL ESTATE TAX (YEARLY) $1300.00

TOTAL: (YR. #) $21531.30
TOTAL INCOME (YR. #1) $13500.00
NET DEDUCTION (YR. #1) )8031.25

TAX ADVANTAGE (YR. #1) $3212.50

RETURN ON INVESTMENT 18%
```

Curve Fit. A program to fit such data as land prices or construction cost per square foot to a curve may be used to make more accurate forecasts, bids, and estimates.

Internal Rate of Return and Cash Flows. One purpose of an internal rate of return and cash flow programs such as the one in Listing 2-12 would be to calculate the net present value of a series of cash flows. In general, an investment, V_0, is made in some enterprise that is expected to bring periodic cash flows C_1, C_2, . . . C_n. Given a discount rate, i, the program will compute the net present value at period k, NPV_k for each cash flow. A negative value for NPV_k indicates that the enterprise has not been profitable. A positive value for NPV_k indicates that the enterprise has been profitable to the extent that a rate of return, i, on the original investment has been exceeded.

$$NPV_k = -V_0 + \sum_{j=1}^{k} \frac{C_j}{(1 + i)^j}$$

Listing 2-12. Internal Rate of Return Program.

```
10      REM LISTING2.12 - The Internal Rate of Return Program
150     FULLW 2:CLEARW 2:GOTOXY 1,1
160     DIM Y(10)
170     INPUT "Enter current cost of house ";HS
180     INPUT "Enter % rise ";PH
190     PH=PH/100
260     INPUT "Enter mortgage interest rate ";MR
270     MR=MR/100
290     INPUT "Enter mortgage duration in years ";NY
310     INPUT "Enter down payment ";DP
320     INPUT "Enter rate that could be earned on down payment ";IR
330     IR=IR/100
360     INPUT "Enter current income tax rate ";TR
370     TR=TR/100
380     INPUT "Enter % rise ";PT
400     PT=PT/100
410     INPUT "Enter transaction costs to buyer in %";BC
420     BC=BC/100
450     INPUT "Enter transaction costs to seller in %";SC
```

```
460    SC=SC/100
470    INPUT "Enter real estate taxes today ";RE
500    INPUT "Enter % rise ";PR
510    PR=PR/100
530    INPUT "Enter utility and maintenance costs ";HM
550    INPUT "Enter % rise ";PM
560    PM=PM/100
580    INPUT "Enter apartment rent today ";AR
590    INPUT "Enter % rise ";PA
600    PA=PA/100
630    INPUT "Enter apartment utilities ";AU
650    INPUT "Enter % rise ";PU
660    PU=PU/100
670    P1=(HS-DP)/((1-(1+MR)^-NY)/MR)
680    PRINT "YRS        INTERNAL RATE OF RETURN"
720    FOR I=1 TO 10
730    Y(0)=-DP-BC*HS
740    B1=HS-DP
750    FOR J=1 TO I
760    Y(J)=-(DP*TR)
770    Y(J)=Y(J)-P1
780    T1=TR+PT*(J-1)
790    Y(J)=Y(J)-RE*(1+PR)^(J-1)
800    Y(J)=Y(J)-HM*(1^PM)^(J-1)
810    Y(J)=Y(J)+AR*(1+PA)^(J-1)
820    Y(J)=Y(J)+AU*(1+PU)^(J-1)
830    Y(J)=Y(J)+((RE*(1+PR)^(J-1))+(B1*MR))*(TR+PT*(J-1))
840    B1=B1-(P1-(B1*MR))
850    NEXT
860    Y(I)=Y(I)+HS*(1+PH)^I-B1-HS*(1+PH)^I*SC
900    HIGH=1:LOW=-1
920    MEAN=(HIGH+LOW)/2
930    PV=0
940    FOR J=0 TO I
950    PV=PV+Y(J)/(1+MEAN)^J
960    NEXT J
970    IF (.05>PV) AND (-.05<PV) THEN 1000
980    IF PV>0 THEN LOW=MEAN ELSE HIGH=MEAN
990    GOTO 920
1000   A$="##      ###.#%"
1010   PRINT USING A$;I,MEAN*100
1020   NEXT I
1030   INPUT Q$
```

BUSINESS DECISION MAKING

The following computer applications can help you make the decisions that will optimize the way you run your business.

Spreadsheets

Most people have seen or worked with the traditional accounting ledger spreadsheet or worksheet. Typically there are descriptions along the left edge, month designations across the top of each column, and room for a totals column on the right. For budget preparation, each line could represent a budget category and have budgeted monthly amounts across the page. Each line and each month's column are totaled. A change to a single number involves replacing a figure with a new one, and reading the affected column and row. This is a tedious procedure, prone to error. Hence, you can understand the tremendous benefits of a totally electronic spreadsheet.

A spreadsheet program is a super calculator that provides you with a giant electronic grid that functions analogously to the traditional spreadsheet described above. When you change the values of numbers in the grid, the program automatically calculates what effect, if any, there is on all the other numbers. The spreadsheet can provide answers within seconds to all sorts of financial "what ifs." For example, to qualify for the mortgage you want, how much income must you have? Or how would your portfolio value change with a half-point advance in a stock?

The electronic spreadsheet may be as large as 2,048 rows long by 256 columns wide, depending on the program. Formulas, equations, and algorithms may be input to provide comparisons, ratios, totals, and other information.

Who uses a spreadsheet program? Anyone who works with numbers might find a use for such a program. Obviously accounting is a primary area of application, but scientists, engineers, managers, executives, and members of almost any discipline use spreadsheets. How useful a spreadsheet is in a particular situation depends on the degree to which it increases productivity. Frequently a spreadsheet user will get important answers that previously were not cost-effective to obtain. Anyone who needs more accurate and speedier calculations is a potential spreadsheet user.

Spreadsheet programs are being used in an endless variety of applications. Some use it for solving simple or complex equations, others for normal calculator functions, and others as a complete decision support tool. Specific uses include financial modeling, budgeting, doing cash flow analysis, planning, making projections, making business plans, creating sales reports, doing "what-if" analysis, pricing, making cost estimates, tax planning, improving time management, performing chemical formulation, doing regression analysis, and analyzing structural design. Anything that can be done using a calculator can be done more easily and more extensively through the use of a spreadsheet program.

Other Decision-Making Computer Applications

In addition to making the electronic spreadsheet available as a decision-making tool, the microcomputer enables you to use programs to guide you in making decisions in the following areas.

Long and Short Term Financing Requirements. A commercially available long-term financing requirement calculation program could compute the cost of capital for various forms of funding (for example, common stocks, preferred stocks, and bonds), select the cheapest form, and determine the amount needed to support operating plans. A short-term financing requirement calculation program could compute the amount and timing of short-term financing based on sales forecasts, inventory purchases, and collection and payment policies.

Breakeven Analysis. Programs can be used to compute breakeven points for projects or products based on fixed and variable costs and selling prices; learning curves may also be applied.

To break even, the following must hold true:

$$P \times K = FC + (VC \bullet Q)$$

where P = sales price of each unit
K = quantity of units sold
FC = fixed costs over the period in question
VC = variable costs per unit produced
Q = no. of units produced

Inventory Control. The generalized inventory model known as the *economic order quantity* (EOQ) is an important part of the management of inventory. The formulae below may be used to compute the EOQ, the minimum inventory costs for a specified time period, and the number of times to order replacement stock during a period.

$$EOQ = \sqrt{\frac{2KL}{M}} + S$$

$$C_{min} = \sqrt{2KLM}$$

$$N = \frac{L}{EOQ}$$

where EOQ = the economic order quantity in units

C_{min} = the minimum inventory costs for the time period.

N = the number of times replacement stock should be ordered during the period

K = the cost of placing and receiving each order

L = the total number of units used during the period

M = the cost of carrying one unit in inventory for the time period

S = the "safety" quantity of stock to be held in inventory, to minimize the risks or losses involved in running out of a crucial part or item.

Reorder Timing. Programs can be used to compute the reorder point based on inventory carrying costs, stockout costs, and demand variation.

Facility Scheduling. Programs can be used to compute job shop performance (average turnaround time, percent late, and so on) based on a variety of scheduling rules (for example, first in-first out, or most overdue items first) and on job processing times.

Demand Forecasting. Programs can be used to compute a forecast of future demand by exponentially smoothing past demand.

Market and Media Research. Programs can perform many aspects of this kind of research, including questionnaire analysis.

Purchasing. Program can analyze vendors (for example, order-filling speed, and previous complaints) to select the best over-all vendors.

Bid Preparation and Job Pricing. The salesman or contractor would find a bid preparation program useful in calculating variable sales prices, keeping running totals, and figuring markups or mark-downs. Preparation on the computer typically requires one fifth to one tenth the time required by manual methods and frees time for profitmaking.

GENERAL BUSINESS CALCULATIONS AND BUSINESS ACCOUNTING SYSTEMS

The computer can be used to keep track of accounts receivable, to prepare aged trial balances, monthly statements, follow-up sales letters, and collection letters, and to provide on-line account status inquiry handling.

Writing a Small Business Accounting System

The following is an outline of a small business accounting system designed for use on a small computer with a printer and floppy disks. The program is intended for use by an individual proprietorship or a small partnership. For such a business, tax returns are prepared (either form 1040 schedule C or form 1065), bookkeeping is done, and balance sheets are produced by the system described for management and banking purposes. Advantages of computerizing this information include savings in time and improved error detection.

The most desirable bookkeeping system is called the *double entry* system; each transaction is entered into two different accounts, and thus, the system is self-checking. With the double entry system, each transaction is first recorded as money coming from some account and then recorded as money going to some account. Debits, abbreviated as DR for computer use, represent an addition to your account or to an expense; credits, abbreviated CR represent a subtraction from an account or from an expense. To determine whether or not the bookkeeping has been done correctly, find out whether or not the debits always equal the credits. For example, if you paid a bill for $50 and received a check for $100 for services performed, the bookkeeping entries would be as follows:

a. Debit (subtract from what you owe) accounts payable for $50.

b. Credit (subtract from what you have) cash on hand for $50.
c. Debit (add to what you have) cash on hand for $100.
d. Credit (add to revenue) income or revenue for $100.

The continual upkeep of the status of each account for a business is the purpose of the bookkeeping program. An example of the account files along with a suggested computer abbreviation for each is listed here:

EXPENSES (debit to add, credit to subtract)

Return and allowances	RTN	(goods returned for refund)
Depreciation	DEP	(for equipment owned)
Business taxes	TAX	
Rent	RNT	
Repairs	RPR	
Bad debts	BDB	(for the charge-off accounting method)
Professional fees	PRF	
Amortization	AMT	(charge partial costs of organization expense, research and development, etc.)
Fuel	FUL	
Telephone	PON	
Electricity	PWR	
Salaries and wages	SAL	(does not include wages included in cost of goods sold)
Interest	INT	(interest paid, only)
Labor/production costs	LAB	
Purchases	PUR	
Insurance	INS	
Pension/profit sharing	PEN	
Depletion	DPL	(used for such assets as mines, oil fields, etc.)
Materials/supplies	MAT	
Cost of goods sold	CGS	(includes: purchases, materials, supplies, labor, production costs, other costs)

ASSETS (debit to add, credit to subtract)

Cash	CSH	(usually checking acct. balances)
Receivable	RBL	(amounts owned by customers on accounts)
Inventory	INV	
Prepaid expenses	PPD	
Supplies	SUP	
Equipment	EQT	
Investments	IVS	
Miscellaneous	ETC	

LIABILITIES AND EQUITY

Payables	PBL	(amounts owed on an account)
Notes	NOT	(borrowed money)
Long term payables	LTP	
Proprietor	PRP	(amount invested in business and net income
Drawing	DRW	(amount from which owner may use money for personal expenses)

Revenues (credit to add, debit to subtract)

Gross receipts	RCP
Other revenue	REV

The IRS requires reports in the following areas: depreciation, business taxes, repairs, and amortization.

The various reports that may be generated by the system include the balance sheet; a sample balance sheet is listed below:

ASSETS		LIABILITIES	
Equipment	5000.	Notes	2000.
Receivables	500.	Payables	3500.
Cash	3000.	Total	5500.
Total	8500.		

EQUITY

Proprietor 3000
Total (Liabilities + Equity) =
8500.

Assets represent what the businessman has, liabilities represent the amounts owned, and equities are amounts contributed or earned by the owners.

Another report that is a necessary part of a small business accounting system is termed the *income statement*. It displays the income and expense of the business during a certain length of time (a period); it may be used to fill out tax forms 1040C or 1065. To generate this report, total income is computed and total expenses are subtracted from this figure. Income for accounts may be stated on an accrual basis, which is to say that future expenses or revenues are included if the exact amount is known and certain (for example, the amounts customers owe may be stated on an accrual basis).

Business owners may prefer to prepare a tax return report on a cash basis in which the only revenue considered is to be cash in and the only expenses considered are cash out. To prepare such a report, you must eliminate payables, receivables, prepaid expenses, and supplies not yet part of the cost of goods sold; the revenue and expense accounts should be adjusted to reflect this change.

Another necessary report is the *ledger* of which may be two types: summary and detailed. The detailed ledger is a complete listing of each account transaction (name, amount, and so on) that has been input within a certain period of time (usually done on a weekly or monthly basis). The balances up to the time of the beginning of the report have been stored from prior ledgers and are read into the computer. Thus, a report listing each transaction and the remaining balance in each account is generated. The summary ledger report only lists the remaining balances after adding and subtracting all transactions for a given period of time.

The balance sheet is the final report necessary on a small accounting system. The sum of the liabilities is subtracted from the sum of the assets to determine the balance or net profit for the business owner. This balance is credited to the proprietor (PRP) account, and thus, the assets plus the net income will balance (equal) with the liabilities.

Additional functions of the accounting system could include forecasting income using trend-line analysis of previous balance sheets, forecasting other accounts using previous records, preparing amortization schedules, determining depreciation amounts and budgeting cash based on forecasted cash on hand and cash payable.

The accounting system flowchart is shown in Fig. 2-3.

Additional Applications for the Small Business Person or the Professional

The small business person or professional could use his or her microcomputer for the following additional purposes.

Order Processing. The computer could be used for order editing, freight cost computation, credit checks, stock availability checks, and order status checks. A billing/invoicing calculation program could provide the following information: net total, total tax, total tax plus freight, total profit, percent of net profit, total value of back-ordered items, total discount amount, total gross amount, and total cost amount.

Sales. The computer could prepare a breakdown of sales volume and profitability by product, customer, or salesman. Sales order processing software could print packing slips, deduct sold merchandise from inventory, verify orders, process returned goods, accumulate back orders, enter cash receipts, print invoices, print sales and credit journals, and maintain a customer master file.

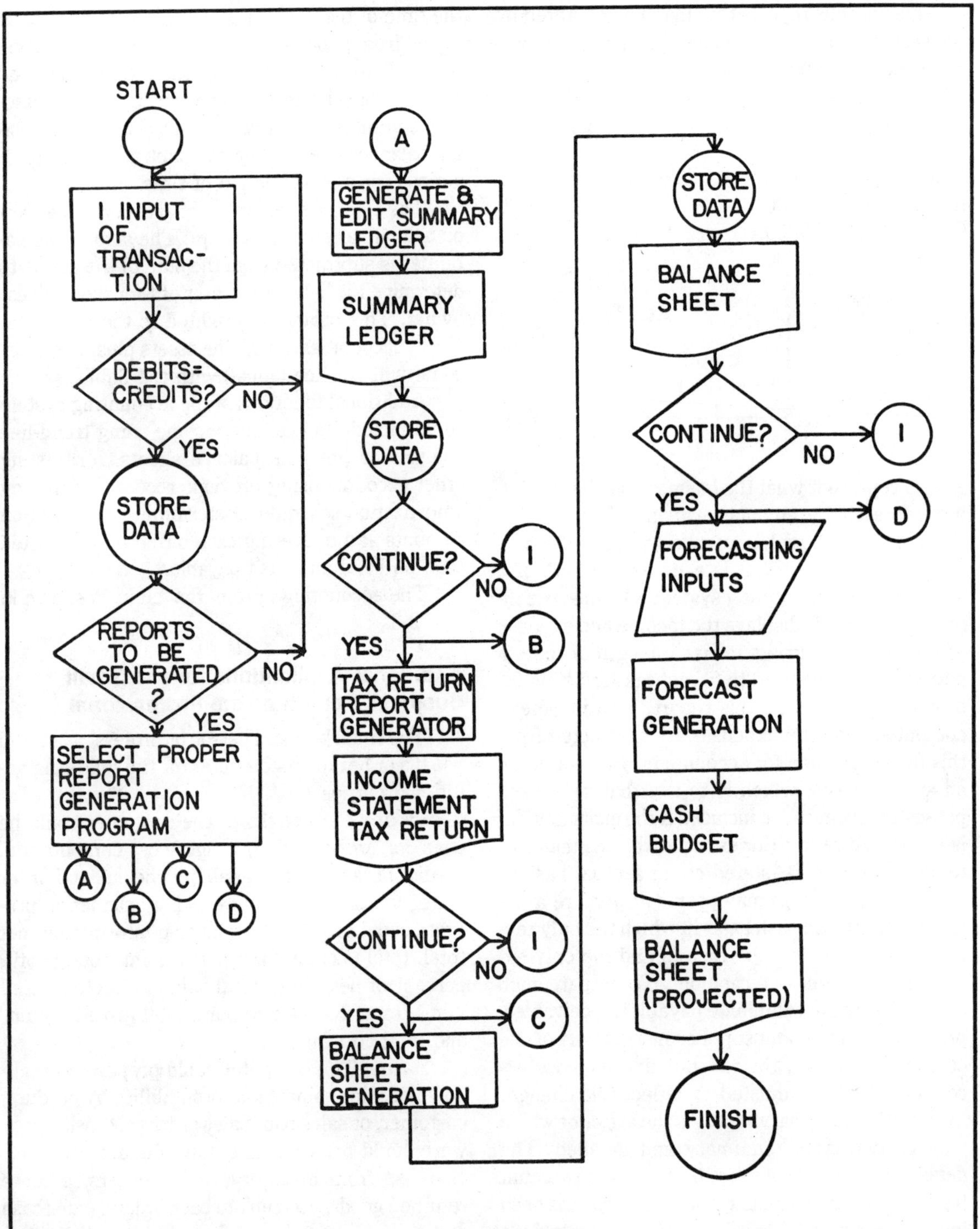

Fig. 2-3. A flowchart for an accounting system program.

General Accounting. General accounting functions include cost record keeping, budgeting, daily exception recordkeeping, and the issuing of profit and loss statements.

Mailing List. One of the prime assets of a small business is its mailing list, representing customers who are likely to be repeat purchasers. The personal computer simplifies mailing list maintenance and is capable of sorting names according to a variety of characteristics, depending upon how much information is stored by the program in addition to names and addresses. Consider the following promotional or money-saving activities that can easily be accomplished through the use of a full-featured mailing list program:

- Sort list by zip for bulk mail savings.
- Sort list alphabetically and printout as a customer reference.
- Mail pieces to residents of a certain town or zip for a special local promotion.
- Mailings to customers having an upcoming birthday.
- Mailings to all women announcing a special sale on dresses.
- Mailings to only the most active customers for a special "favored customer."

The ability of a mailing list program to sort customers by these and other criteria requires that special codes be input along with names and addresses. The coding used and its extent are at the user's discretion.

Customer File Management. By functioning in a manner similar to the way a mailing list program functions, a customer file management program could keep track of customers in a way that is useful to the business. The data stored could include customer name, address, phone, occupation, credit limit, current balance, brand preference, total purchases, sales representative, and date of last order. The business manager could then obtain lists of customers according to:

- Outstanding balance of 30+ days, for collection purposes.
- Brand preference, for research and promotional purposes.
- Sales representatives.
- Those who have not ordered within the last year, for consideration of removal from the active list or for a follow-up campaign.

A mailing list program could be combined with a customer maintenance program to provide a powerful tool—an accurate profile of your customer base, useful reports for the sales staff, and a means for direct-mail promotion.

Payroll. A complete payroll calculation program would include the following features: time card hours computation, check writing, and provisions for commissions, bonuses, piecework salaries, incentives. W-2 forms, and payroll summaries could also be output.

Inventory. A complete inventory management program should be able to output the following reports: detailed inventory, inventory status, on order, order exception, analysis by cost, list for use in physical inventory, period to date, year to date, minimum quantity search, and inventory projections. The following file update functions should also be provided: place an order, cancel an order, add a new inventory form, delete an existing inventory item, initiate a new period or year. The inventory program could also print purchase orders or reminders.

Contract Preparation. A word-processing system could print personalized contract forms. Cost estimation functions could also be integrated into the contract preparation program.

General Business Calculations. Consider the use of your personal computer or programmable calculator in performing the following general business computations, which previously may have been too awkward or time-consuming when done by manual methods: cash flow, breakeven point, government withholding calculations, selling price from cost and gross profit prorating, unit price comparisons, order quantity for optimum price break, moving average, seasonal average, cyclical analysis, histogram generation, worst-case analysis, universal rate of return, summation of ledger columns, optimum mark up or mark down, net present value, choice between debt and equity, lease versus buy determinations, funds statement preparation, perpetual sales quantity, and gross sales revenue.

Capital Equipment Investment Analysis. The simple BASIC program in Listing 2-13 computes the maximum purchase price for a piece of equipment based upon estimate profits.

Business Letters

Professionally prepared files of business letters are available for popular personal computers to save you time and enable you to produce better letters. Typically over 1,000 letters are available for review, modification, and output with the use of a word processing program.

The new U.S. Post Office E • COM (electronic computer-originated first class mail) system permits the transmission of business letters via modem to the E • COM network; the letter will be printed and mailed for delivery the next day anywhere in the U.S. The current rate is $0.26 each. The system may be used for anyone with a modem and a personal computer upon payment of a $50 annual accounting fee.

Listing 2-13. Capital Equipment Investment Analysis Program.

```
10     REM LISTING2.13 - The Capital Equipment Investment Analysis Pro
       gram
90     FULLW 2:CLEARW 2:GOTOXY 1,1
100    REM Capital equipment investment analysis
110    REM determines the maximum purchase price for equipment
120    REM based upon estimated profits
130    INPUT" Enter the est. no. of years of equipment life ",N
140    INPUT "Enter the interest rate in decimal ",I
150    FOR X=1 TO N
160    PRINT "Enter the projected earning for year: ";X
170    INPUT R(X)
180    NEXT X
190    FOR X=1 TO N
200    Q=Q+R(X)/I^X
210    NEXT X
220    PRINT "The recommended purchase price is: $";Q
230    INPUT Q$
```

Professional Practice Management

Professionals with large practices should consider using a personal computer system in:

- Maintaining appointments.
- Billing and collection.
- Generating appointment reminders.
- Accessing reference libraries and data resources for journal articles, diagnoses, case laws, standards, rules and regulations, codes, and drug information.
- Correspondence and document preparation
- Telecommunication with laboratories for diagnostic tests.
- Insurance form preparation or transmission.

Sales Device

The small computer may be used as a sales device in several ways. Now that telephone dialing interfaces are available, you can use the computer to call every possible telephone number in an exchange or from a customer file and deliver a tape-recorded retail sales message to anyone who answers. At expositions or retail sales outlets, a computer with a video display can continually list sales information. Crude question-answering capabilities could also be provided.

Use of the computer as a customer advisor can increase sales traffic as well. For example, a garden supply shop could provide customers with access to a computer programmed to answer gardening questions about specific plants (for example, questions about growing seasons and nutrient requirements), amount and type of fertilizer for a certain size lawn and type of grass, and possibly output a complete garden plan. A wine shop computer could recommend a type of wine to accompany a given meal, the glass and temperature to use, and the comparative prices of wines. The cosmetics department of a store could use the computer to suggest brand name cosmetics to use in achieving a certain complexion. A swimming pool maintenance company advertises that it offers a free computer analysis of anyone's swimming pool water. From water samples, the computer determines the type and amount of chemicals necessary to maintain a specific pool; these chemicals are then sold to the pool owner.

Time Calculations

Business people often need to know how much time (usually in terms of days) there is between two given dates. A program, such as the one in Listing 2-14 stores the number of days in each month and could serve to calculate this value. Additionally, time conversions between seconds, minutes, hours, days, weeks, months, and years could be performed.

Calculation of the difference in hours or days between two given times in another business application. The results can be used in determining hours worked for payroll purposes or in figuring accumulated interest. The program in Listing 2-15 calculates the difference between two times.

Time differences between major cities or time zones could be calculated by a program. A world map could also be displayed on a video screen with the appropriate times in major cities continuously updated. This application may be useful to those making long distance calls or flying into other time zones.

The Calculation of Reference Tables

Any mathematical function may be expressed as a table of values corresponding to the factors in the equation. Business people who need to calculate the value of a particular function could produce a table listing values at specified intervals for easy

Listing 2-14. Days-between-Dates Calculator Program.

```
10     REM LISTING2.14 - The calculation of the number of days between
       two dates program
15     FULLW 2:CLEARW 2:GOTOXY 1,1
20     DIM M(12)
30     FOR X=1 TO 12
40     READ M(X)
50     NEXT X
60     PRINT "Is this a leap year (1=YES, 2=NO) ";
70     INPUT A
80     IF A=2 THEN M(2)=28:GOTO 90
85     IF A<>1 THEN 60
90     INPUT "Input the first date numerically in this form: month,day
       ",M1,D1
92     IF M1>12 OR M1<1 THEN 90
94     IF D1>31 OR D1<1 THEN 90
110    INPUT "Enter the second date in the same form: ",M2,D2
115    IF M2>12 OR M2<1 THEN 110
117    IF D2>31 OR D2<1 THEN 110
125    IF M1=M2 THEN DA=D2-D1:GOTO 200
```

```
130    EM=M(M1)-D1
140    IF MA+1=M2 THEN 190
150    FOR X=M1+1 TO M2-1
160    DA=DA+M(X)
170    NEXT X
190    DA=DA+EM+D2
200    PRINT "The number of days=";DA
210    INPUT Q$
220    DATA 31,29,31,30,31,30,31,31,30,31,30,31
```

Listing 2-15. Time Difference Program.

```
10     REM LISTING2.15 - The Time Difference Program
15     FULLW 2:CLEARW 2:GOTOXY 1,1
20     PRINT "Time Difference Calculation"
30     PRINT "Compute difference in hours, minutes, and seconds"
40     PRINT "Enter the first time in 24 hr. clock format --"
50     PRINT "Hours, minutes, seconds."
60     INPUT H1,M1,S1
70     PRINT "Enter final time in 24 hr. format."
80     INPUT H2,M2,S2
90     NH=H2-H1
100    NM=M2-M1:IF NM<0 THEN NH=NH-1:NM=60+NM
110    NS=S2-S1:IF NS<0 THEN NM=NM-1:NS=60+NS
120    PRINT "The difference in hours, minutes, seconds is: ";NH,NM,NS

130    PRINT:INPUT Q$
140    END
```

reference. For example, a portion of a chart used in converting British pounds to American dollars is reproduced in Table 2-3. Note that the dollar equivalents are found in the interior of the chart. The conversion rate for this chart is 1.90 dollars per British pound. As an example of its use, the number of dollars that are equivalent to 4.90 pounds is given by the chart as 9.31. The BASIC program used to print the chart is shown in Listing 2-16 and can be used as a model for similar programs designed to calculate reference tables.

Your computer can be a timesaver by computing and outputting tables concerning areas such as

- Stock commissions.
- Values of an investment or savings account over periods of time.
- Unit prices after certain quantity purchases.
- Breakeven values for various prices and sales of a product.
- UPS/USPS rates to various cities for various weights.

THE COMPUTER AND THE PROFESSIONS

In this section a variety of ways in which the personal computer or programmable calculator can be used in the professions and in many blue-collar occupations are listed. This short listing is far from complete; uses of calculators and computers are so diverse that these descriptions can only be suggestive of a few of the many applications.

Accountants and tax specialists:	All aspects of work
Advertising:	Client fees
	Composition and printing costs
	Production (film and TV) costs
	Space and time buying
	Statistics in market research
Agriculture:	Yields per acre
	Livestock growth and feeding
	Livestock food supplements
	Crop mix and rotation
	Fertilizer ratios
Appraisers:	Comparative values
	Quantities
	Summations
Architects:	Strength of materials
	Loads, stresses, and strains
	Geometrical configurations
Artists and designers:	Supplies and materials
	Scale reductions and expansions
	Client fees by hours worked
Attorneys:	Terms of contracts
	Tax calculations
	Bankruptcy dispositions
Auto salesmen:	Optional equipment costs
	Discounts and prices
	Used car allowances
Auto service and repair:	Towing and road service costs
	Costs of materials and labor
	Estimates
Banking:	Interest, assets, annuities, insurance
	Foreign exchange
	Collateral
	Trust and pensions
Broadcasting:	Program scheduling
	Advertising rates
	Station logs
Building contractor:	Measuring land sites
	Amounts and costs of roofing, flooring, siding, etc.
	Electrical loads and needs
	Figuring gutters, windows, screen sizes
	Water pressures, plumbing
	Work schedules and transportation
Building maintenance:	Supplies and power
	Waste disposal
Buyer:	Comparative costs among suppliers
	Shipping charges
	Foreign size conversions
	Cost relative to markup at retail
	Profit potential
Chemists and lab technicians:	Quantitative measurements
	Composition of solutions and compounds
	Rates of reactions
	Volumetric and gravimetric analysis
Construction trades:	Calculations of materials, labor time, charges, and so on by bricklayers, masons, carpenters, plasterers, plumbers, etc.
Dieticians:	Food quantities and costs
	Nutritional and caloric

values

Educators, teachers:	Grading homework and examination papers Classroom games and instructions in arithmetic, English, etc.
Employment counselors:	Working conditions, wages, and salaries Fringe benefits Labor supply and openings
Engineers:	All phases of construction, including plant location studies, tax rates, labor and transportation charges, loads, amounts and costs of raw materials, excavation needs, fill, wood, wire and cement forms, steel reinforcement, strength of materials, electrical loads, chemical reactions, etc.
Geologists:	Land measurements Chemical analysis and assays Mineral depletion rates
Hotel and innkeepers:	Supplies and labor Occupancy rates Concession profits and activity Group discounts and catering
Independent businesses:	Balance sheet, profit and loss statements Purchases, returns, and allowances Cost of materials, labor, services, loans Figuring profit on investment and costs of expansion

Itemizing for tax deductions

Depreciation schedules

Insurance salesman:	Premiums, dividends on policies Annuities Alternative insurance packages Proper levels of coverage
Interior decorating:	Amounts and costs of fabrics, rugs, carpeting, drapes, wallpaper, etc. Discounts for quantity Shipping times and charges
Jewelers:	Pricing and costs Composition of precious metals Gem weights and sizes
Landscape architects and contractors:	Land areas, planting and fertilization schedules Land fill
Manufacturer's representative:	Cost of items less discounts Shipping and insurance costs Invoices prepared for suppliers and clients
Market research:	Statistics of opinion and field testing Extent and nature of competition
Medical, dental, and other health services:	Prescribing or utilizing medications, anesthetics, prosthetic devices, etc. Operational costs of services Supplies inventories and costs
Pattern makers:	Geometric configurations

	and prices
	Tips
	Measurements and conversions
	Alternative designs
Personnel administration:	Absenteeism rates, efficiency
	Vacations, illness rates
	Wage rate compliances and comparisons
	Employee benefits
	Hirings and severances
Pharmacists:	Pharmaceutical measurements
	Supplies inventory and costs
	Pricing
Photographers:	Composition of solutions
	Supplies comparisons
	Pricing
	Exposure times and shutter speeds
Pilots:	Passenger and freight loads
	Fuel consumption and capacities
	Navigation
Printers:	Paper stocks
	Scheduling printing runs
Psychologists:	Psychological testing
	Statistics of experiments
Publishing:	Composition and printing costs
	Postage and shipping costs
	Inventory control
	Distribution costs
	Discounts
Real estate:	Market and appraised value
	Development costs
	Taxes, insurance, water, and heating costs,
	Closing fees
	Commissions
Restaurants:	Food and liquor costs
Renting and leasing:	Interest charges and cash flow
	Inventory and usage rates
Sales, door to door:	Travel and other expenses
	Statements to suppliers
	Commissions
Sales, retail:	Taxes and commissions
	Inventory and turnover
	Pricing—markups and markdowns
Secretaries:	Petty cash, travel expenses
	Postage costs
	Budget, production, sales reports
	Employer's personal finances
	Correspondence and memo verification
Security analysts:	Profits, expenses, P/E ratios working capital, depreciation, growth rates, dividends, etc.
	Technical and fundamental analyses
Securities salesmen:	Margin costs and availability
	Dividend and interest yields
	Commissions earned
	Growth rates, price changes, balanced portfolios
Social services:	Welfare availability versus family needs
	Family budgeting
Surveyors:	Land measurements
Travel agents:	Discounts on fares, tours, hotels
	Commissions earned
	Distances and costs per
Trucking and shipping:	distance

	Converting foreign currencies, kilometer distances, etc.
	Billing airlines, steamship lines, bus companies, tours, hotels, etc.
	Load capacities by weight and volume
	Distances, time schedules, costs
	Equipment inventory and maintenance
	License fees and taxes
Typographers:	Printers' measurements
	Plates and etchings
Waiters and waitresses:	Tips
	Totaling checks
Wholesalers and manufacturers	Labor and overhead
	Loss on discounting customers' interest-bearing notes
	Interest on account balances
	Recording payments, promissory notes, partial payments
	Consignments and returns
	Shipping costs and taxes

Listing 2-16. The Reference Table Program.

```
10    REM LISTING2.16 - The Reference Table Program
15    FULLW 2:CLEARW 2:GOTOXY 1,1
20    PRINT "Convert dollars to foreign currency"
25    INPUT "Enter name of foreign currency to be converted: ",B$
30    PRINT "Enter dollar value of one unit of desired foreign curren
      cy "
35    INPUT "(I.E., 1.48 for Brittish pound) ",A
40    INPUT "Press RETURN to print chart. ",A$
50    A$="##.##  "
55    CLEARW 2:GOTOXY 1,1
60    PRINT TAB((60-LEN(B$))/2)B$:PRINT
70    PRINT "$      .00    .10    .20      .30      .40      .50      .60
      .70      .80      .90"
80    FOR X=1 TO 10
90    PRINT USING "$$X ";X
100   FOR B=0 TO 1 STEP .1
110   PRINT USING A$;A*(X+B),
120   NEXT B
130   PRINT
140   NEXT X
150   PRINT:INPUT Q$
160   END
```

Chapter 3

Mathematical and Statistical Applications

One of the biggest assets of the computer is its ability to perform complicated and tedious mathematical calculations with unerring diligence. Your personal computer may be programmed to emulate a simple adding machine or a complex scientific business calculator. It can perform statistical computations of use to those involved with businesses, investments, questionnaire analysis, the sciences, and other fields.

THE COMPUTER AS A SOPHISTICATED CALCULATOR

A program could be written to emulate the functions of an ordinary or an RPN calculator. The computer could be used as a simple business or scientific calculator for a variety of purposes. Additionally, functions not provided on an ordinary calculator could easily be included (for example, the ability to solve quadratic equations).

RPN stands for Reverse Polish Notation and is a system of representing mathematical equations. Some of the advanced scientific calculators use the RPN system because fewer keystrokes are required to do complex calculations with an RPN system than with the regular system. The RPN system is often easier to use after you have gained familiarity with it. The purpose of the program in Listing 3-1 is to emulate an RPN calculator, providing about 50 mathematical functions. This program is thus composed of 50 subroutines, identified by REM statements, that may be used as subroutines in other BASIC programs that require functions not provided by your version of BASIC.

In the RPN system there are no parentheses and no = (equals) key. Only two numbers are worked with at one time. A sample calculation would proceed as follows:

Step	Input	Display	Comments
①	2.5	2.5	Enter first number
		0	
		0	These are the four registers
		0	

Step	Input	Display	Comments
②	4	4 2.5 0 0	Enter second number as new numbers are input, preceding inputs are shifted through the registers.
③	*	10 4 2.5 0	* stands for multiplication. The answer to 2.5 × 4 was calculated and put in the first position in the display.
④	10.	10 10 4 2.5	enter third number
⑤	5	5 10 10 4	enter fourth number
⑥	/	2 5 5 10 10	/ stands for division. The following calculation was performed, and the answer was stored in the first display position: 10/5= 2
⑦	+	12 2 5 10	The + sign instructed that the two preceding results were to be added: 10+2=12; the answer was stored in the first position. The two preceding results were added because no new numbers were input for the computation.

Here are the functions available in this program:

function	description
*	multiplication
+	addition
/	division
–	subtraction
	powers (e.g., x y stands for X^y and x .5 stands for $\sqrt{x}$)
$\sqrt{\ }$	
INV	inverse (e.g., 1/x)
C	clear display/registers
SIN	compute the sine of x
ASIN	compute the arcsine of x
COS	compute the cosine of x
ACOS	compute the arccosine of x
TAN	compute the tangent of x
ATAN	compute the arctangent of x
SEC	compute the secant of x
ASEC	compute the arcsecant of x
COT	compute the cotangent of x
ACOT	compute the arccotangent of x
CSC	compute the cosecant of x
ACSC	compute the arccosecant of x
PI	place the value of π in the register
E	compute the exponential of x (i.e., e^x)
LOG	compute the logarithm of x
MEM+	add a number to the memory register
MEM–	delete a number from the memory register
%	change x to a percentage value
N!	compute the factorial of x
SD	compute the standard deviation for a set of scores
HYP	compute the value for the hypotenuse of a triangle

function	description
	given the two sides
SIDE	compute the value for a side of a triangle given the hypotenuse and another side
DEG	change x from radians to degrees
RAD	change x from degrees to radians
POLR	compute polar coordinates given rectangular coordinates
RECT	compute rectangular coordinates given polar coordinates
MET	compute metric conversions—a subprogram
HSIN	compute the hyperbolic sine of x
HCOS	compute the hyperbolic cosine of x
HTAN	compute the hyperbolic tangent of x
HSEC	compute the hyperbolic secant of x
HCSC	compute the hyperbolic cosecant of x
HCOT	compute the hyperbolic

function	description
	cotangent of x
#SIN	inverse hyperbolic sine of x
#COS	inverse hyperbolic cosine of x
#TAN	inverse hyperbolic tangent of x
#SEC	inverse hyperbolic cosecant of x
#CSC	inverse hyperbolic cotangent of x
#COT	inverse hyperbolic secant of x
SZ	switch the z registers
RZ	rotate the z registers
QUAD	compute solutions to quadratic equations with the quadratic equation
?	put computer in monitor mode so that ordinary calculations may be made in the form PRINT 5*1.6. Type CONT (in some BASICs) to continue with the program.

Listing 3-1. RPN Calculator Program.

```
10     REM LISTING3.01 The RPN Calculator Program
20     REM (c) 1978 Mark R. Sawchusch -- may not be sold
30     FULLW 2:CLEARW 2:GOTOXY 1,1
40     DIM A(100),M$(21),D$(50),K(25)
50     L=2
60     DEFDBL B,A,X,C,Z
70     PRINT "MAXI-CAL"
80     G=1:F=1
90     FOR D=1 TO 50:READ D$(D):NEXT D
100    PRINT "* + / MIN ^ INV C SIN ASIN COS TAN ATAN SEC ASEC COT ACO
       T CSC ACSC PI E LOG MEM+MEM- % N! SD HYP SIDE DEG RAD POLR RECT MET
       HSIN HTAN HSEC HCSC HCOT #SIN #CS #TAN #SEC #CSC #COT SZ RZ QUAD ?"
110    PRINT "Each command/function in line 60 must contain 4 letters
       and/or spaces for proper operation.  For explanation of the commands,
       see the text in the book accompanying this software"
115    PRINT:PRINT "Use END to return to menu"
```

```
120   D=1
130   REM Ask for command/values
140   REM
150   INPUT "Command ";C$
155   IF C$="END" THEN END
160   O=0
170   IF VAL(C$)=0 THEN 230 :REM is it a letter or number
180   A(G)=VAL(C$):A(G)=CDBL(A(G)):X=A(G):IF F(1)=2 THEN F(2)=2 ELSEF(1)=2
190   L=G
200   IF G=1 THEN G=2 ELSE G=1
210   GOTO 2200
220   GOTO 150
230   A(G)=L1:IF F(1)=1 THEN F(2)=1 ELSE F(1)=1
240   REM search to find the command
250   FOR I=1 TO 50
260   IF C$=D$(I) THEN 290
270   NEXT I
280   PRINT "ILLEGAL FUNCTION ":PRINT:GOTO 150
290   IF I<=44 THEN 310
300   IF I>=45 THEN I=I-44:GOTO 320
310   ON I GOTO 340,370,400,430,460,480,500,520,550,580,610,640,670,700,
      730,760,790,820,850,880,910,940,970,1040,1090,1120,1160,1320,1350,
      1370,1400,1430,1480,1490,1750,1780,1810,1840,1870,1900,1930,1960,
      1990,2020
320   ON I GOTO 2050,2080,2100,2110,2120,2160
330   REM CALCULATE *
340   IF F(1)=F(2) AND F(1)=1 THEN X=Z1*Z4 ELSE X=Z1*Z2
350   GOTO 2200
360   REM CALCULATE +
370   IF F(1)=F(2) AND F(1)=1 THEN X=Z1+Z4 ELSE X=Z1+Z2
380   GOTO 2200
390   REM CALCULATE /
400   IF F(1)=F(2) AND F(1)=1 THEN X=Z4/Z1 ELSE X=Z2/Z1
410   GOTO 2200
420   REM CALCULATE -
430   IF F(1)=F(2) AND F(1)=1 THEN X=Z4-Z1 ELSE X=Z2-Z1
440   GOTO 2200
450   REM CALCULATE POWERS
460   X=Z2^Z1:GOTO 2200
470   REM CALCULATE INVERSES
480   Z1=1/Z1:GOTO 2210
490   REM CLEAR REGISTERS
500   Z1=0:Z2=0:Z3=0:Z4=0:GOTO 2210
510   REM CALCULATE SIN
520   A(L)=SIN(A(L)*.0174533)
530   GOTO 2190
540   REM CALCULATE ARC SIN
550   A(L)=ATN(A(L)/SQR(-A(L)*A(L)+1))*57.29578#
560   GOTO 2190
570   REM CALCULATE COSINE
580   A(L)=COS(A(L)*.0174533)
590   GOTO 2190
600   REM CALCULATE ARC COSINE
610   A(L)=(-ATN(A(L)/SQR(-A(L)*A(L)+1))+1.5708)*57.29578#
620   GOTO 2190
630   REM CALCULATE TANGENT
640   A(L)=TAN(A(L)*.0174533)
650   GOTO 2190
660   REM CALCULATE ARC TANGENT
```

```
670   A(L)=ATN(A(L))*57.29578#
680   GOTO 2190
690   REM CALCULATE SECANT
700   A(L)=1/COS(A(L)*.0174533)
710   GOTO 2190
720   REM CALCULATE ARC SECANT
730   A(L)=(ATN(SQR(A(L)*A(L)-1))+(SGN(A(L)-1)*1.5708))*57.29578#
740   GOTO 2190
750   REM CALCULATE COTANGENT
760   A(L)=1/TAN(A(L)*.0174533)
770   GOTO 2190
780   REM CALCULATE ARC COTANGENT
790   A(L)=(-ATN(A(L)+1.5708))*57.29578#
800   GOTO 2190
810   REM CALCULATE COSECANT
820   A(L)=1/SIN(A(L)*.0174533)
830   GOTO 2190
840   REM CALCULATE ARC COSECANT
850   A(L)=(ATN(1/SQR(A(L)*A(L)-1))+(SGN(A(L)-1)*1.5708))*57.29578#
860   GOTO 2190
870   REM VALUE FOR PI
880   Z1=3.141592654#:GOTO 2210
890   GOTO 2190
900   REM CALCULATE NATURAL LOGARITHM
910   A(L)=EXP(A(L))
920   GOTO 2190
930   REM CALCULATE LOGARITHM
940   A(L)=LOG(A(L))
950   GOTO 2190
960   REM MEMORY ADDITION
970   DD=DD+1
980   INPUT "Which register ";D
990   IF D=1 THEN M$(DD)=STR$(Z1) ELSE IF D=2 THEN M$(DD)=STR$(Z2) ELSE
      IF D=3 THEN M$(DD)=STR$(Z3) ELSE M$(DD)=STR$(Z4)
1000  INPUT "Description:",C$
1010  M$(DD)=M$(DD)+" "+C$
1020  GOTO 150
1030  REM MEMORY LISTING
1040  FOR D=1 TO DD
1050  PRINT M$(D)
1060  NEXT D
1070  GOTO 150
1080  REM CONV. FOR %
1090  A(L)=A(L)*.01
1100  GOTO 2190
1110  REM COMPUTE FACTORIAL
1120  FOR YY=1 TO A(L)
1130  A(L)=A(L)*(A(L)-YY)
1140  NEXT YY:GOTO 2190
1150  REM STATISTICS
1160  PRINT "In statistical mode"
1170  PRINT
1180  PRINT "Enter values separately and enter 9999 when done"
1190  B=0:C=0:D=1
1200  INPUT K(D)
1210  IF K(D)=9999 THEN 1240
1220  B=B+K(D):C=C+K(D)^2:D=D+1
1230  GOTO 1200
1240  PRINT "Scores: ":FOR H=1 TO D-1
```

```
1250  PRINT K(H);
1260  NEXT H:PRINT
1270  PRINT "Sum of scores","Number of scores"
1280  PRINT B,D-1
1290  PRINT B/(D-1),C-(B/(D-1))^2
1300  PRINT "Standard deviation=";SQR(C-(B/(D-1))^2)
1310  REM COMPUTE HYPOTENUSE
1320  X=SQR(Z1^2+Z2^2)
1330  GOTO 2200
1340  REM COMPUTE SIDE OF TRIANGLE
1350  X=SQR(ABS(Z1^2-Z2^2)):GOTO 2200
1360  REM CONV. TO DEGREES
1370  A(L)=A(L)*57.2957791#
1380  GOTO 2190
1390  REM CONV. TO RADIANS
1400  A(L)=.017453292#*A(L)
1410  GOTO 2190
1420  REM RECT. TO POLAR CONV.
1430  Z1=SQR(Z1*Z1+Z2*Z2)
1440  A=Z2/Z1
1450  Z2=(ATN(A/SQR(-A*A+1)))*57.29578#
1460  GOTO 2210
1470  REM POLAR TO RECT. CONV.
1480  B=Z1*SIN(Z2*.0174533):Z2=Z1*COS(Z2*.0174533):Z1=B:GOTO 2210
1490  A(G)=Z1:PRINT "M E N U:"
1500  PRINT "Use the negative of the menu # to convert vice-versa)"
1510  PRINT "1) feet to meters"
1520  PRINT "2) inches to centimeters"
1530  PRINT "3) miles to kilometers"
1540  PRINT "4) gallons to liters"
1550  PRINT "5) fahrenheit to centigrade"
1560  PRINT "6) pounds to kilograms"
1570  PRINT "7) end conversions"
1580  INPUT "Select: ",H
1590  IF H<0 THEN 1610
1600  ON H GOTO 1620,1640,1660,1680,1700,1720,140
1610  ON -H GOTO 1630,1650,1670,1690,1710,1730
1620  X=.33047851#*A(G):GOTO 2270
1630  X=A(G)*3.28:GOTO 2270
1640  X=A(G)*2.54:GOTO 2270
1650  X=A(G)*.3937:GOTO 2270
1660  X=A(G)*1.609:GOTO 2270
1670  X=A(G)*.6215:GOTO 2270
1680  X=3.7853*A(G):GOTO 2270
1690  X=.2642*A(G):GOTO 2270
1700  X=.5555555#*(A(G)-32):GOTO 2270
1710  X=1.8*A(G):GOTO 2270
1720  X=.4536*A(G):GOTO 2270
1730  X=2.2046*A(G):GOTO 2270
1740  REM COMPUTE HYPERBOLIC SINE
1750  A(L)=(EXP(A(L))-EXP(-A(L)))/2
1760  GOTO 2190
1770  REM COMPUTE HYPERBOLIC COSINE
1780  A(L)=(EXP(A(L))+EXP(-A(L)))/2
1790  GOTO 2190
1800  REM COMPUTE HYPERBOLIC TANGENT
1810  A(L)=-EXP(-A(L))/EXP(A(L))+EXP(-A(L))*2+1
1820  GOTO 2190
1830  REM COMPUTE HYPERBOLIC SECANT
```

```
1840  A(L)=S/(EXP(A(L))+EXP(-A(L)))
1850  GOTO 2190
1860  REM COMPUTE HYPERBOLIC COSECANT
1870  A(L)=2/(EXP(A(L))-EXP(-A(L)))
1880  GOTO 2190
1890  REM COMPUTE HYPERBOLIC COTANGENT
1900  A(L)=EXP(-A(L))/(EXP(A(L))-EXP(-A(L)))*2+1
1910  GOTO 2190
1920  REM COMPUTE INV. HYPERBOLIC SINE
1930  A(L)=LOG(A(L)+SQR(A(L)*A(L)+1))
1940  GOTO 2190
1950  REM COMPUTE INV. HYPERBOLIC COSINE
1960  A(L)=LOG(A(L)+SQR(A(L)*A(L)-1))
1970  GOTO 2190
1980  REM COMPUTE INV. HYPERBOLIC TANGENT
1990  A(L)=LOG((1+A(L))/(1-A(L)))/2
2000  GOTO 2190
2010  REM COMPUTE INV. HYPERBOLIC SECANT
2020  A(L)=LOG((SQR(-A(L)*A(L)+1)+1)/A(L))
2030  GOTO 2190
2040  REM COMPUTE INV. HYPERBOLIC COSECANT
2050  A(L)=LOG((SGN(A(L))*SQR(A(L)*A(L)+1)+1)/A(L))
2060  GOTO 2190
2070  REM COMPUTE INV. HYPERBOLIC COTANGENT
2080  A(L)=LOG((A(L)+1)/(A(L)-1))/2
2090  GOTO 2190
2100  B=Z2:Z2=Z1:Z1=B:GOTO 2210
2110  B=Z4:Z4=Z3:Z2=Z1:Z1=B:GOTO 2210
2120  B=-Z2*Z2+SQR(Z2*Z2-4*Z3*Z1)/2*Z3
2130  Z1=-Z2*Z2-SQR(Z2*Z2-4*Z3*Z1)/2*Z3
2140  Z2=B
2150  GOTO 2210
2160  CLEARW 2:GOTOXY 1,1
2163  PRINT "Entering monitor mode; select CONTINUE from RUN MENU"
2165  PRINT "to continue..."
2170  STOP
2180  GOTO 150
2190  Z1=A(L):GOTO 2210
2200  Z4=Z3:Z3=Z2:Z2=Z1:Z1=X
2210  PRINT "Z1: ";1
2220  PRINT "Z2: ";Z2
2230  PRINT "Z3: ";Z3
2240  PRINT "Z4: ";Z4
2250  PRINT:PRINT
2260  GOTO 140
2270  PRINT "=";X:PRINT:PRINT:GOTO 1490
2280  DATA *,+,/,MIN,^,INV,C,SIN,ASIN,COS,ACOS,TAN,ATAN,SEC,ASEC,COT,
      ACOT,CSC
2290  DATA ACSC,PI,E,LOG,MEM+,MEM-,%,N!,SD,HYP,SIDE,DEG,RAD,POLR,RECT

2300  DATA MET,HSIN,HCOS,HTAN,HSEC,HCSC,HCOT,#SIN,#COS,#TAN,#SEC,#CSC,
      #COT,SZ,RZ
2310  DATA QUAD,?
```

STATISTICS

The microcomputer is well-suited for dealing with statistics. Basic statistics for one or two variables—the mean, variance, and standard deviation may be found for a set of observations on one variable. For paired variable sets, the above statistics could be determined for each, and the covariance and correlation coefficient calculated.

$$\text{Mean} \quad \overline{x} = \frac{\Sigma x}{n}$$

$$\text{Variance } \sigma^2_x = \frac{\Sigma(\text{deviation from true mean})^2}{n}$$

$$= \frac{\Sigma(x - \mu)^2}{n}$$

$$\text{Standard deviation } \sigma_x \sqrt{\text{variance}}$$

$$r = \frac{\Sigma XY - nXY}{\sqrt{(\Sigma X^2 - n\overline{X}^2)\,(\Sigma Y^2 - n\overline{Y}^2)}}$$

Means and Moments. For grouped or ungrouped data, the arithmetic, geometric, and harmonic means may be determined; the second, third, and fourth moments about the mean and the coefficients of skewness and kurtosis may also be calculated.

One- and Two-Way Analysis of Variance. The mean and variance for two treatment groups and for the entire sample may be calculated, and an F statistic can be applied to the differences between populations.

Contingency Table Analysis. The chi-square statistic may be used to test independence between row and column classifications of a contingency table.

Linear Regression. A set of observations may be fit to a straight line by linear regression; the coefficient of determination, the standard error of y on x, and the standard error for the coefficients may also be computed. Multiple linear regression fits, and polynomial regression could also be performed.

For the linear equation $y = a + bx$.

$$b = \frac{\Sigma XY - n\overline{XY}}{\Sigma X^2 - n\overline{X}^2}$$

$$a = \overline{Y} - b\overline{X}$$

where $X = (\Sigma\,\overline{X})/n$, $Y = (\Sigma\,\overline{Y})/n$

Survey Analysis. The following statistical parameters could be calculated by a complete survey analysis program: multivariate analysis, regression analysis, time-series analysis, variance determination, factor analysis, descriptions, and tabulations.

Generation of Frequency Tables. For a large sample, a sorting program could output a standard or relative frequency table.

Hypothesis Testing. A useful program could determine confidence intervals for a given sample, which may then be used in testing hypotheses. Statistical hypothesis testing is used to answer such questions as, "A businessman claimed that 20 percent of the public prefer his products; if 100 people were asked their opinion, what percentage would have to respond negatively for this claim to be refutable?"

Statistical Distributions. The approximations for normal and student's t-distributions given below are designed for easy translation into BASIC program statements and have wide applications in statistical analysis.

- Normal Distribution

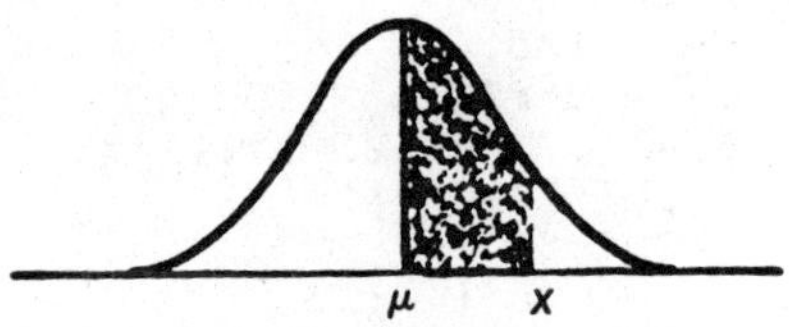

Standard Normal Distribution

$$u = \frac{(x - \mu)}{\sigma x}$$

The probability of x falling in the shaded area above is

$$1 - r(a_1 t + a_2 t^2 + a_3 t^3) + \epsilon(x)$$

where: $a_1 = 0.4361836$
$a_2 = -0.1201676$
$a_3 = 0.9372980$

$$r = (\epsilon^{-x/2})(2\pi)^{-1/2}$$
$$t = (1 + 0.3326x)^{-1}$$
$$|\epsilon(x)| < 10^{-5}$$

- Student's t-distribution

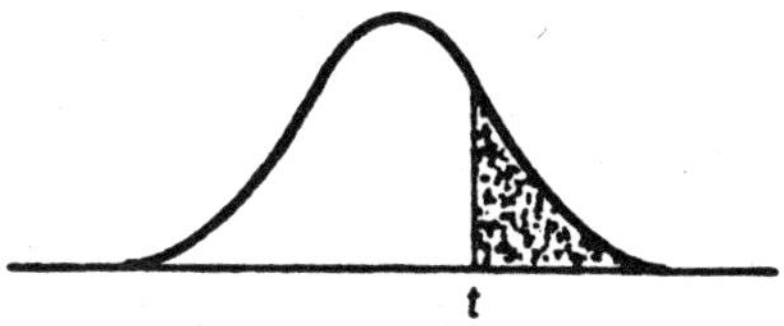

Student's *t*-distribution

area of right-tail = $1/4(1 + a_1x + a_2x^2 + a_3x^3 + a_4x^4)^{-4} + \epsilon(x)$

where: $a_1 = 0.196854$
$a_2 = 0.115194$
$a_3 = 0.000344$
$a_4 = 0.019527$
t = t-value
d = no. degrees of freedom

$$x = (t^{2/3}(1 - 2/9d) - 7/9)(2/9 + t^{2/3}\,2/9d)^{-1/2}$$
$$|\epsilon(x)| < 2.5 \bullet 10^{-4}$$

Similar approximations, available in statistical handbooks and the U.S. Bureau of Standards manuals of computer approximations, may be used to compute chi-square and F distributions.

The statistical analysis program in Listing 3-2 has a wide range of applications in business, stock analysis, and the sciences. The program consists of six subprograms including statistics with one variable, statistics with two variables, area under a curve computation, and exponential smoothing calculations.

Listing 3-2. Statistical Analysis Program.

```
10    REM LISTING3.02 - The Statistical Analysis Program
15    FULLW 2:CLEARW 2:GOTOXY 1,1
20    PRINT TAB(25)  "Statistical Analysis Program"
30    PRINT TAB(24) "for business and stock analysis"
40    DIM X(105),A(105),Y(105)
50    DIM Q(100,2),S(3,2)
60    PRINT:PRINT TAB(37)"MENU:"
70    PRINT TAB(25) "1) Statistics for 1 variable"
80    PRINT TAB(25) "2) Statistics for 2 variables"
90    PRINT TAB(25) "3) Area under a curve computation"
100   PRINT TAB(25) "4) Cumulative binomial probability calculation"
110   PRINT TAB(25) "5) Plot data"
120   PRINT TAB(25) "6) Exponential smoothing program"
130   PRINT TAB(25) "7)End"
140   INPUT A:IF A<1 OR A>7 THEN  60
150   ON A GOTO 160,1010,710,1800,1960,2060,2370
160   REM ONE VARIABLE CALCULATIONS
170   PRINT "Enter successive values separately, '9999' to end"
180   D=1:C=0:B=0:E=0
190   INPUT A(D)
200   GOTO 230
210   INPUT A(D)
220   IF A(D)=9999 THEN 270
230   B=B+A(D)
240   C=C+A(D)*A(D)
250   D=D+1
260   GOTO 210
270   D=D-1:M=B/D
280   CLEARW 2:GOTOXY 1,1
```

```
290   PRINT "NO. SCORES","SUM OF SCORES"
300   PRINT D,B
310   PRINT
320   FOR H=1 TO D
330   G=G+A(H)-M
340   SG=SG+(A(H)-M)*(A(H)-M)
350   NEXT H
360   SG=SG/(D-1):SG=SQR(SG)
370   PRINT "MEAN","VARIANCE","MEAN AVERAGE DEVIATION"
380   PRINT M,SG^2,SG,G
390   PRINT:PRINT "PROBABLE ERROR","COEFFICIEANT OF VARIATION"
400   PRINT .6745*SG,,D/M
410   PRINT
420   PRINT "STANDARD ERROR FOR THE MEAN=";SQR(SG*SG/D)
430   PRINT
440   FOR I=1 TO D-1
450   FOR J=1 TO D-1
460   X=A(J):Y=A(J+1)
470   IF A(J)<=A(J+1) THEN 490
480   A(J)=Y:A(J+1)=X
490   NEXT J,I
500   INPUT "Press RETURN to continue ",A$:CLEARW 2:GOTOXY 1,1
510   PRINT "# MEASURE FREQ REL FREQ DEV FROM AVE DEV SQUARED STD DEV
      "
520   J9=0
530   FOR J8=1 TO D
540   H=1
550   FR=1
560   J=1
570   IF A(J8)=A(J8+J) THEN FR=FR+1 ELSE 600
580   J=J+1
590   GOTO 570
600   J9=J9+1
610   A2$="## ####.## ######.##### ####.#### #######.### #####.#####"

620   PRINT USING A2$;J9;A(J8);FR;FR*1/D;M-A(J8);(M-A(J8))*(M-A(J8));
      (A(J8)-M)/SG
630   IF FR>1 THEN J8=J8+FR-1
640   RM=RM+FR*A(J8)*A(J8)
650   NEXT J8
660   PRINT "HIGHEST SCORE","LOWEST SCORE"
670   PRINT A(D),A(1)
680   PRINT "ROOT MEAN SQUARE= ";SQR(RM)
690   PRINT "THUS X=";M;" PLUS/MINUS ";SG/SQR(D)
700   INPUT "Press RETURN to continue ";A$:GOTO 60
710   REM AREA UNDER NORMAL CURVE
720   INPUT "Enter the standard Z value ",BE
740   PRINT
750   PRINT "X VALUE","AREA TO LEFT","AREA TO RIGHT"
760   A=BE
770   C=0:E=1:H=BE:D=0:G=BE*BE:F=.398942*EXP(-.5*G)
780   J=H/E
790   C=C+J:IF J/C<.000001 THEN 850
800   L=1:E=1:D=D+1:H=G*H
810   FOR K=1 TO D
820   E=E+2:L=L*E
830   NEXT K
840   E=L:GOTO 780
850   M=F*C+.5:N=1-M
```

```
860   PRINT A,M,N
870   GOTO 990
880   BE=BE/1.14142:O=BE*BE:P=EXP(-O)*.56419/BE:O=5.*O
890   P1=O*O:M=O*P:P2=0:P3=0
900   P5=1:P4=1
910   P2=P2+2
920   IF P3=P THEN 950 ELSE P3=P
930   P=P5:P4=O*P4*(P2-1)+P5:M=P2*M*P1*(P2+1)
940   GOTO 910
950   P6=P*.5:Q=1-P6
960   PRINT A,Q,P6
970   BE=A+10
980   GOTO 760
990   PRINT
1000  GOTO 60
1010  D=1:PRINT "REGRESSION AND CORRELATION ANALYSIS":PRINT
1020  PRINT "Enter X,Y values as pairs separated by commas"
1030  PRINT "Enter 9999,9999 when done"
1040  INPUT X(D),Y(D)
1050  IF X(D)=9999 AND Y(D)=9999 THEN 1100
1060  Q9=Q9+X(D):R9=R9+Y(D)
1070  Q8=Q8+X(D)*X(D):R8=R8+Y(D)*Y(D)
1080  R6=R6+X(D)*Y(D):D=D+1
1090  GOTO 1040
1100  D=D-1:N=D:Q7=Q9/D:R7=R9/D
1110  A9=Q8-Q9*Q7:A8=R8-R9*R7
1120  B9=R6-Q9*R7:B8=B9/A9:B7=R7-B8*G7
1130  A7=A8-B8*B9:A6=A7/(D-2)
1140  FOR I=1 TO N
1150  B(I)=Y(I):A(I)=X(I)
1160  NEXT I
1170  GOSUB 1640
1180  PRINT
1190  PRINT "AVE. OF X","AVE. OF Y"
1200  PRINT A1,A2
1210  PRINT "STD. DEV X","STD DEV Y"
1220  PRINT D1,D2
1230  PRINT "CORRELATION COEFFICIENT X-Y: ";C9
1240  PRINT:A9=A2
1250  INPUT "Press RETURN when ready ";Z9$
1260  PRINT "The following equations express the X,Y relationships"
1270  PRINT:PRINT "EQUATION 1"
1280  PRINT "Y=";S9;" X+";I9
1290  PRINT "% accuracy of Y variance description=";P9
1300  PRINT "Y-slope=";S9
1320  PRINT "F-ratio=";S9/(A6/(D-2))
1330  PRINT
1340  FOR I=1 TO D
1350  IF X(I)<=0 THEN 1420
1360  A(I)=LOG(X(I))
1370  NEXT I
1380  GOSUB 1640
1390  PRINT:PRINT "EQUATION 2"
1400  PRINT "Y=";S9;"*LOG X+";I9
1410  PRINT "% accuracy of description ";P9:PRINT
1420  FOR I=1 TO N
1430  A(I)=X(I):IF Y(I)<=0 THEN 1540
1440  B(I)=LOG(Y(I))
1450  NEXT I
```

```
1460  GOSUB 1640
1470  GOSUB 1730
1480  PRINT
1490  INPUT "Press RETURN when ready ",Z9$
1500  PRINT "EQUATION 3"
1510  PRINT "LOG Y=";S9;"*X+";I9:PRINT "OR"
1520  PRINT "Y=";EXP(S9);"^X+";EXP(I9)
1530  PRINT "% accuracy of description ";P9
1540  FOR I=1 TO N
1550  IF A(I)<=0 THEN 1780 ELSE A(I)=LOG(X(I))
1560  NEXT I
1570  GOSUB 1640
1580  GOSUB 1730
1590  PRINT "LOG Y=";S9;"*LOG X+";I9:PRINT "OR"
1610  PRINT "Y=";EXP(I9);"*X^";S9
1620  PRINT "% accuracy description ";P9
1630  GOTO 1780
1640  S1=0:S2=0:S3=0:S4=0:S5=0:FOR I=1 TO N
1650  S1=S1+A(I):S2=S2+B(I):S3=S3+A(I)*A(I)
1660  S4=S4+B(I)*B(I):S5=S5+A(I)*B(I)
1670  NEXT I
1680  A1=S1/N:A2=S2/N:V1=(S3-(D*A1(A1)))/(N-1)
1690  V2=(S4-(D*(A2*A2)))/(N-1):D1=SQR(V1)
1700  D2=SQR(ABS(V2)):D0=N*S3-S1*S1:I9=((S2*S3)-(S1*S5))/D0
1710  S9=((N*S5)-(S1*S2))/D0:P9=((S9*S9)*V1)/V2:C9=SQR(P9)
1720  P9=100*P9:RETURN
1730  S7=0:S8=0
1740  FOR I=1 TO N
1750  E=EXP(I9+S9*A(I)):S8=S8+(Y(I)-E)^2:S7=S7+(Y(I)-A9)^2
1760  NEXT I
1770  P9=100*(1-S8/S7):RETURN
1780  INPUT "Press RETURN when ready ",Z9$
1790  GOTO 60
1800  REM CUMULATIVE BINOMIAL PROBABILITIES
1810  F=0
1820  INPUT "Enter the # successes, # trials (f(y,n,p)), prob success
      /trial ";Y,N,P
1830  S1=1:FOR I=1 TO N
1840  S1=S1*I:NEXT I
1850  FOR X=0 TO Y
1860  S2=1:S3=1
1870  FOR I=1 TO X
1880  S2=S2*I:NEXT I
1890  FOR I=1 TO N-X
1900  S3=S3*I:NEXT I
1910  F=F+S1/(S2*S3)*P^X*(1-P)^(N-X)
1920  NEXT X
1930  PRINT "The cumulative binomial probability=";F
1940  PRINT "for F(Y;N,,P) where Y=";Y;", N=";N;" , P=";P
1950  GOTO 60
1960  CLEARW 2:GOTOXY 1,1
1970  PRINT "--------------------------------------------"
1980  DX=55/A(D)
1990  FOR X=D TO 1 STEP -1
2000  IF A(X)=A(X-1) THEN 2030
2010  A$="####.##":PRINT USING A$;A(X);:PRINT "I";
2020  PRINT STRING$(DX*A(X),"+")
2030  NEXT X
2040  PRINT "--------------------------------------------"
```

```
2050  GOTO 60
2060  REM EXPONENTIAL SMOOTHING
2070  DEFDBL Q,S
2080  GOSUB 2120
2090  GOSUB 2160
2100  GOSUB 2270
2110  GOTO 60
2120  INPUT "Enter smoothing constant(0-1)";A
2130  INPUT "Enter prediction period length ",T
2140  INPUT "Enter the first data set (9999 to end)",Q(1,1):Q(2,2)=Q(
      1,1)
2150  S(1,0)=Q(1,1):S(2,0)=Q(1,1):S(3,0)=Q(1,1):N=2:RETURN
2160  REM
2170  PRINT N;:INPUT Q(N,1)
2180  IF Q(N,1)=9999 THEN 2260
2190  S(1,1)=A*Q(N,1)+(1-A)*S(1,0):S(2,1)=(1-A)*S(2,0)+S(1,1)*A
2200  S(3,1)=(1-A)*S(3,0)+S(2,1)*A:P1=6*(1-A)*(1-A)+(6-5*A)*A*T+(A*T)
      *(A*T)
2210  P2=S(1,1)/(2*(1-A)*(1-A)):P3=6*(1-A)*(1-A)+2*(5-4*A)*A*T+2*(A*T
      )*(A*T)
2220  P4=S(2,1)/(2*(1-A)*(1-A))
2230  P5=2*(1-A)^2+(4-3*A)*A*T+(A*T)^2:P6=S(3,1)/(2*(1-A)*(1-A))
2240  Q(N+1,2)=P1*P2-P3*P4+P5*P6:S(1,0)=S(1,1):S(2,0)=S(2,1)
2250  S(3,0)=S(3,1):N=N+1:GOTO 2170
2260  RETURN
2270  PRINT:PRINT "PERIOD OBSERVATION PREDICTION ERROR"
2280  PRINT 1;Q(1,1)
2290  A$="####.##"
2300  FOR J=2 TO N-1
2310  PRINT USING A$;J;Q(J,1);Q(J,2);Q(J,2)-Q(J,1)
2320  IF J/12<>INT(J/12) THEN 2350
2330  PRINT:INPUT "Press RETURN to continue ",A$
2340  CLEARW 2:GOTOXY 1,1:PRINT "PERIOD OBSERVATION PREDICTION ERROR"

2350  NEXT J
2360  GOTO 60
2370  END
```

The first subprogram, statistics with one variable, is used to find basic descriptions for a set of data (that is, the mean and the standard deviation). The second subprogram determines the linear regression for a set of (*x*,*y*) pairs. For example, the relationship between the price of a stock (*x*) to the Dow Jones Industrial Average (*y*) could be determined by inputting corresponding pairs of values.

The third subprogram computes the area under a normal curve between two points. A normal curve is used to describe many phenomena; it is pictured and mathematically described above. The area under the curve is equal to 1; the average of a set of data (*x*) is the point at which the curve peaks. If two values on the *x* axis are picked, the area under the curve between these two points is equal to the probability of a value being between those points; this subprogram computes the area, or probability, between two given points.

The fourth subprogram computes the cumulative binomial probability for the occurrence of a given value. The fifth subprogram plots data described in subprogram one in simple bar graph format. This section could be improved to plot data on an *x*,*y* axis or to create a labeled histogram. The sixth subprogram exponentially smooths a set of data. Data values are entered, and an exponential function is used to predict future values. This smoothing constant should be adjusted so that the output error is minimized.

MATHEMATICS

Personal computers can be called upon to perform all of the following:

- Solution of quadratic and cubic equations: Given the coefficients of either a quadratic or cubic equation, a program could solve for both real and complex roots; equations of degrees could also be solved for.
- Roots of $f(x)$: A program could find the roots of a user-defined function using the bisection method or Newton's method.
- Vector operations: Given two vectors in two dimensions, a program could calculate their magnitudes, the angle between them, and their dot and cross products. The program in Listing 3-3 calculates the sum of two vectors.
- Curve solution (continued): area enclosed by these parts could also be calculated.
- Arithmetic, geometric, and harmonic progressions: A table of elements for the above three progressions could be generated. The element and the sum of the first n elements could also be determined.
- Factors of integers, GCD, LCM: The prime factors of an integer, the greatest common divisor (GCD), and the least common multiple (LCM) of two integers could be determined.
- Function value table: A useful program could print the values for a user-defined function over a specified interval.
- Prime number table: A table of prime numbers or a test for primes in a specified interval could be generated.

Listing 3-3. Vector Addition Program.

```
10     REM LISTING3.03 - The Vector Addition Program
20     FULLW 2:CLEARW 2:GOTOXY 1,1
30     PRINT "Enter the data for the first vector in this form:"
40     INPUT "magnitude,angle: ",M1,A1
50     X1=M1*COS(A1)
60     Y1=M1*SIN(A1)
70     INPUT "Enter the data for the second vector in the same format,
       ",M2,A2
80     X2=M2*COS(A2)
90     Y2=M2*SIN(A2)
100    X=X1+X2:Y=Y1+Y2
110    A=ATN(Y/X)
120    M=SQR(X*X+Y*Y)
130    PRINT "New vector magnitude=";M;" units"
140    PRINT "at an angle of ";A;" degrees."
150    PRINT "(X,Y) coordinate at endpoint=(";X;",";Y;")."
160    PRINT:INPUT Q$
170    END
```

- Triangle solution: For a triangle with three known "variables," the lengths of the sides, the angles between sides, and the area could be computed.
- Curve solution: The arc length, central angle, radius, chord length, and tangent length for a curve could be calculated given two known parts; the
- Partial sums and products: The partial sum or product of a user-defined function could be computed.
- Interpolation between known values: Lagrange polynomial interpolation, or the Newton divided difference method may be performed to interpolate values of a function.

- Gaussian integration: The integral of a user-defined function can be determined by Gaussian quadrature.
- Solutions of differential equations: First-order differential equations may be solved by a program using the Runge Kutta method; a step size may be determined to yield results within a specific error tolerance.
- Polynomial arithmetic: Addition, subtraction, multiplication, and division of polynomials may be accomplished.
- Polynomial evaluation: A polynomial $(P_x) = a_0 + a_1x + a_2x^2 + \ldots + a_nx^n$ may be evaluated at a point x with complex coefficients. The program in Listing 3-4 evaluates a polynomial expression at a given point and determines the first and second deviatives.
- Polynomial root finding: Barstow's method is well suited for computer evaluation of quadric factors for polynomials of degree n.
- Complex arithmetic: Addition, subtraction, multiplication, division, squares, inverses, and so on may be performed using complex numbers.
- Complex trigonometric functions: Common trigonometric functions may be evaluated using complex numbers.
- Base conversions: A useful program could transform numbers of any real base to another base.
- Graphing calculations: The intervals to use for proportional axes given the minimum/maximum values and number of major divisions could be calculated and used for plotting data manually or with a plotter/printer. Additionally, conversion routines between radians, quadrants, revolutions,

Listing 3-4. Polynomial Evaluation Program.

```
10      REM LISTING3.04 - The Polynomial Evaluation Program
100     FULLW 2:CLEARW 2:GOTOXY 1,1
110     REM computes value at a given pt. & 1st and 2nd derivatives
120     DIM B(50),Z(509),C(50,2)
130     E=0
140     INPUT "Enter the degree of the polynomial ";X
160     PRINT "Enter the coefficients separately ";
170     FOR D=0 TO X
180     INPUT B(D)
190     NEXT D
200     PRINT "Enter the no. of values to be evaluated"
210     INPUT N:N1=N
220     PRINT "Enter the points separately ";
230     FOR D=1 TO N
240     INPUT Z(D)
250     NEXT D
260     GOSUB 340
270     GOSUB 450
280     E=E+1
290     GOSUB 340
300     GOSUB 450
310     E=E+1
320     GOSUB 340
330     GOTO 500
340     FOR F=1 TO N1
350     N=Z(F)
360     GOSUB 400
370     C(E,F)=H
380     NEXT F
390     RETURN
400     H=0
```

```
410     FOR D=0 TO X
420     H=B(D)+N*H
430     NEXT D
440     RETURN
450     FOR D=0 TO X
460     B(D)=(X-D)*B(D)
470     NEXT D
480     X=X-1
490     RETURN
500     PRINT
510     PRINT "PT OF EVAL.","EVEL.","DER1","DER2"
520     PRINT
530     FOR F=1 TO N1
540     PRINT Z(F),C(F,0),C(F,1),C(F,2)
550     NEXT F
560     PRINT
570     INPUT Q$
```

and degrees could be provided.

- Coordinate conversion between rectangular and polar equivalents may be computed with these formulae:

$$r = \sqrt{x^2 + y^2}$$
$$\text{A} = \text{arctangent } (y/x)$$
$$x = r \text{ cosine (A)}$$
$$y = r \text{ sine (A)}$$

where: x = abscissa, y = ordinate } Cartesian coordinates

r = magnitude of ray, A = angle (in degrees) } Polar coordinates

The Solution of Simultaneous Equations

The small computer can be used to find the solution to a set of simultaneous equations. This mathematical operation has applications in many areas including business and science. An example of two equations to be solved simultaneously follows:

$$5X=4Y + 24$$
$$2.5Y=6X - 4$$

If the equations are solved simultaneously, a value will be found for X and Y such that both equations will be correct. The number of simultaneous equations that can be solved by the program in Listing 3-5 is limited only by the available memory in the computer.

Listing 3-5. The Simultaneous Equation Solver.

```
10      REM LISTING3.05 - The Simultaneous Equation Solver Program
100     REM no. of variables=no. of eqns.
110     REM there must be more than 1 equation
120     REM the arrays may be redimentioned to
130     REM accommodate any no. of equations
140     REM limited only by available memory
150     DIM M(30,30),P(30),L(30)
160     FULLW 2:CLEARW 2:GOTOXY 1,1
170     INPUT "Enter no. of variables ",Z
180     FOR E=1 TO Z:FOR D=1 TO Z
190     PRINT "Equation #";E;", variable #";D
```

```
200   INPUT M(E,D)
210   NEXT D:PRINT "Constant for equation #";E;
220   INPUT L(E):NEXT E
230   FOR E=1 TO Z-1
240   L=ABS(M(E,E)):B=E
250   FOR D=E+1 TO Z
260   IF ABS(M(D,E))<L THEN 280
270   B=D:L=ABS(M(D,E))
280   NEXT D
290   IF L=0 THEN 550
300   IF B=E THEN 390
310   FOR D=1 TO Z
320   G=M(B,D)
330   M(B,D)=M(E,D)
340   M(E,D)=G
350   NEXT D
360   V=L(B)
370   L(B)=L(E)
380   L(E)=V
390   FOR D=E+1 TO Z
400   T=M(D,E)/M(E,E)
410   FOR C=E+1 TO Z
420   M(D,C)=M(D,C)-T*M(E,C)
430   NEXT C
440   L(D)=L(D)-T*L(E)
450   NEXT D
460   NEXT E
470   IF M(Z,Z)=0 THEN 550
480   E=Z-1:P(Z)=L(Z)/M(Z,Z)
490   U=0:FOR D=E+1 TO Z
500   U=U+M(E,D)*P(D)
510   NEXT D
520   P(E)=(L(E)-U)/M(E,E)
530   E=E-1:IF E>0 THEN 490
540   GOTO 570
550   PRINT:PRINT "EQNS ARE UNSOLVABLE"
560   GOTO 610
570   PRINT:PRINT
580   FOR E=1 TO Z
590   PRINT "VARIABLE #";E;"=";P(E)
600   NEXT E:PRINT
610   INPUT "TRY AGAIN (1=YES, 2=NO) ";N
620   PRINT:PRINT
630   IF N=1 THEN PRINT:GOTO 170 ELSE END
```

Integral Evaluation

Among the many methods used for computer evaluation of integrals in Simpson's Rule:

$$\int_a^b f(x)dx \sim h/3[f(a) + 4f(a + h) + 2f(a + 2h) + 4f(a + 3h) + \ldots + 2f(a + (n - 2)h) + 4f(a + (n - 1)h) + f(b)]$$

where $h = \dfrac{b - a}{n}$ and n = number of iterations (as n increases, accuracy increases)

The trapezoidal approximation is another algorithm used with computers.

Plotting Mathematical Functions

With a little ingenuity, the TAB function may be used to produce crude plots of trigonometric and other functions. Try this "one-liner":

```
10 FOR X=0 TO 6.28 STEP .25:PRINT TAB
   (SIN(X)*30+30);"*":NEXT X
```

The Plotter Program. The program in Listing 3-6 is a general-purpose plotting routine designed for use with a printer. Three types of plots may be made: two-dimensional, three-dimensional, and simultaneous plots. Lines 40-80 explain how functions to be plotted are to be entered into the program.

Listing 3-6. The Plotter Program.

```
10      REM LISTING3.06 - The Plotter Program
20      REM Plot functions in 2D, 3D, or simultaneously.
30      REM rotate output 90 degrees for actual plot
35      FULLW 2:CLEARW 2:GOTOXY 1,1
40      PRINT "If the functions defined in lines 690, 710,730 are to"
50      PRINT "be changed, stop the program and enter in this format:"
60      PRINT "FUNCT. #1- 690 Y=SIN(X) (Y IN TERMS OF X)"
70      PRINT "FUNCT. #2- 710 Y1=COS(X) (Y1 IN TERMS OF X)"
80      PRINT "FUNCT. #3- 730 Z=EXP(Z) (Z IN TERMS OF Z- FOR 3D PLOTS"
90      FULLW 2:CLEARW 2:GOTOXY 1,1
100     PRINT
110     PRINT
120     INPUT "SELECT: 1) 2D PLOT, 2) 3D PLOT, 3) END ";A
130     ON A GOTO 160, 420, 150
140     GOTO 120
150     END
160     PRINT "SELECT: 1) PLOT 1 FUNCTION":PRINT"             2) PLOT 2 FUNC
        TIONS SIMULTANEOUSLY"
170     INPUT A
175     IF A<1 OR A>2 THEN 160
180     F1=A
190     PRINT "Enter min. X value, max. X value, X increment (separated
        by commas)";
200     INPUT E,F,D
210     PRINT "Enter min. Y value, max. Y value ";
220     INPUT H,G
225     IF H=G THEN 210: REM causes divide by 0 error
230     Y1=40/(G-H)
240     PRINT "Y MIN: ";H;" Y MAX: ";G;" INCREMENT: ";Y1
250     PRINT
260     PRINT TAB(5)H;TAB(56);G
270     FOR B=1 TO 58
280     PRINT "+";
290     NEXT B
300     PRINT
310     A$="####.##"
320     FOR X=E TO F STEP D
330     PRINT USING A$;X;:PRINT ":";
340     GOSUB 690
350     IF F1=1 THEN 390
360     GOSUB 710
370     IF Y>Y1 THEN PRINT TAB(9+(INT(10*Y1*Y1)))"*";TAB(9+(INT(10*Y*Y1
        )))"#" ELSE PRINT TAB(9+(INT(10*Y*Y1)));"#";TAB(9+(INT(10*Y1*Y1)))"*"
380     GOTO 400
390     PRINT TAB(9+INT(10*Y*Y1));"*"
400     NEXT X
```

```
410     GOTO 120
420     REM 3D PLOT ROUTINE
430     A$="*"
440     E=5
450     V=25
460     G=.707106
470     C=961
480     INPUT "Enter X increment ";IN
500     FOR X=-31 TO 31 STEP IN
510     A=0
520     B=1
530     D1=E*INT(SQR(C-X*X)/E)
540     FOR Y=D1 TO -D1 STEP -E
550     Z=SQR(X*X+Y*Y)
560     GOSUB 730
570     Z=INT(V+Z-G*Y)
580     IF A$="*" THEN A$="+" ELSE A$="*"
590     IF Z<=A THEN 650
600     A=Z
610     IF Z=F THEN IF A$="*" THEN A$="+" ELSE A$="*"
620     PRINT TAB(Z)A$;
630     IF B=0 THEN F=Z
640     B=0
650     NEXT Y
660     PRINT ""
670     NEXT X
680     GOTO 120
690     Y=ABS(SIN(X))
700     RETURN
710     Y1=ABS(COS(X))
720     RETURN
730     Z=30*(EXP(-Z*Z/100)):RETURN
740     RETURN
```

Determining the Equation of a Line

The program in Listing 3-7 accepts (*x,y*) data points and uses linear regression to determine the equation of the line that best fits (describes) the data. Applications are numerous. For instance, if you were on a weight-loss plan and inputted values for your weight versus amount of exercise or calorie intake, the program could find the equation of a line that best fits this data. Thus, you could input a value for one variable (for example, calorie intake) and receive a corresponding value (for example, weight) for the other variable. Other areas that could be analyzed include stock price versus Dow Index, miles traveled versus gallons used, distance versus time, and heating costs versus outside temperature. This program uses the *least squares*

Listing 3-7. Line Equation Calculator Program.

```
10      REM LISTING3.07 - The Line Equation Calculator Program
20      REM may be used to describe a set of data
30      REM and determine a corresponding point for
40      REM any entered point
45      FULLW 2:CLEARW 2:GOTOXY 1,1
50      INPUT "Enter a name for the first set of data ",A$
60      INPUT "Enter a name for the second set of data ",B$
```

```
70    PRINT "Enter X,Y pairs successively, separated by commas"
75    PRINT "Enter 0,0 to end"
76    N=1
80    INPUT X,Y
90    IF (X=0) AND (Y=0) THEN 200
110   N=N+1
120   PRINT "SET NO.: ";N
130   A=A+X
140   B=B+X*X
150   C=C+Y*Y
160   D=D+Y
170   E=E+X*Y
180   GOTO 80
200   N=N-1:M=(E*N-D*A)/(B*N-A*A)
210   V=(D*B-E*A)/(B*N-A*A)
220   FULLW 2:CLEARW 2:GOTOXY 1,1
230   PRINT "Y=";M;" X+";V
240   PRINT "Enter a value for ";A$;" to receive a corresponding"
250   PRINT "value for ";B$
260   INPUT "Enter 9999 if you want vice-versa, '0' to end ",A
265   IF A=0 THEN END
270   IF A=9999 THEN 350
280   PRINT
290   PRINT "Y=";M*A+V
300   GOTO 240
350   REM
390   FULLW 2:CLEARW 2:GOTOXY 1,1
400   PRINT:PRINT "X=";-1/M;"*Y";V/M
410   PRINT "Enter a value for ";B$;" to receive a corresponding"
420   PRINT "value for ";A$
430   PRINT "Enter 9999 for vice-versa"
440   INPUT A
460   IF A=9999 THEN 350
470   PRINT "The value for X="; (A-V)/M
475   IF A=0 THEN END
480   PRINT
490   GOTO 410
```

method of linear regression.

Solving for Corresponding Values

Given two points of a line, linear interpolation can be used to solve for y values corresponding to a given x value. Although this method is not as accurate as the least squares linear regression method, it can be used in situations in which the correlation coefficient is high.

$$y = y_1 + \frac{(y_2 - y_1) \bullet (x - x_1)}{(x_2 - x_1)}$$

where: x_1,y_1 = coordinates of first point on the line

x_2,y_2 = coordinates of second point on the line

x = abscissa of point to be interpolated

y = ordinate of the point on the line with x

Computer Calculus

Long perceived as merely number crunchers, computers are now moving into the realm of elegant mathematics. Computer algebra programs are now available for personal computers. These programs can manipulate abstract symbolic mathematical expressions and have the ability to do virtually everything taught in the first two years of university mathematics. They can factor polynomials, simplify expressions, differentiate functions, solve equations, expand functions into a Taylor series, invert matrices, and even integrate functions as a *coup de grace*. An outgrowth of the MACSYMA program developed on large mainframe computers, muMath is a rewritten version capable of running on virtually any Z80 or 8080 microcomputer. A simplified version (called Picomath) has also been written in BASIC to run on just about any personal computer. Both programs are marketed by Microsoft Corporation, 10700 Northup Way, Bellevue, WA 98004, and should be seriously considered for purchase by professionals who must have reliable solutions to mathematical problems and by students of mathematics. Examples of symbolic computer algebra produced by the muMath program appear below, and demonstrate that their programs are approaching true artificial intelligence capabilities:

Factor $x^{25} + 1$:

$(x - 1)(x^4 - x^3 + x^2 - x + 1)(x^{20} - x^{15} + x^{10} - x^5 + 1)$

Integrate $\dfrac{2x}{x^3 + 1}$:

$$2\,\frac{\log(x^2 - x + 1)}{6} - \frac{\log(\text{abs}(x + a))}{3}$$

$$\frac{\text{atan } 2x - 1}{(\sqrt{3})}$$

Expand $x \prod_{n=1}^{\infty} (1 - x^n)^{24}$

$x - 24x^2 + 252x^3 - 1472x^4 + 4730x^5 + \ldots$

Determinant of $\begin{bmatrix} x^3 & x^2 & x & 1 \\ y^3 & y^2 & y & 1 \\ z^3 & z^2 & z & 1 \\ w^3 & w^2 & w & 1 \end{bmatrix}$

$-(k - w)(y - w)(y - x)(z - w)(z - x)(z - y)$

Calculate 30!

265252859812191058636308480000000

MATHEMATICAL RECREATIONS AND PROGRAMMING CHALLENGES

Interesting mathematical problems and ideas to implement on your computer include the following:

Using Probability to Forecast the Outcome of a Sporting Event. For example, an equation expressing the probability that a stronger team will win in a seven-game series is

$$p^4 + 4p^4q + 10p^3q^2x + 10\,p^2q^2(1 - x)p$$

where p = probability that stronger team will win ($\geq .5$)

q = probability that weaker team will win ($= 1 - p$)

x = conditional probability particular to a sport (for example, for basketball this value has been calculated to be = .408.)

For further information see *Mathematics Magazine*, Sept.-Oct. 1975, pp. 187-192.

The program in Listing 3-8 can help in predicting the outcome of the World Series (or other seven-game series) if you can estimate (that is, guess) the probability of a given team winning each of the seven games based upon such factors as game location, opposing pitchers, and other rational or irrational hunches. For further discussion consult "The World Series Competition," *Journal of the American Statistical Association* 47, Sept. 1952, pp. 335-80.

Solving Mathematical Puzzles. Puzzles such as the following can probably be solved with the use of brute force, trial-and-error computer techniques only—if they can be solved at all:

- Find three distinct right triangles with the following properties:

  A. Are pythagorean (all three sides are integers)

  B. The perimeters of the three triangles are equivalent

  C. The areas of the triangles are in arithmetic progression

Listing 3-8. World Series Predictor.

```
10      REM LISTING3.08 - World Series Predictor
13      FULLW 2:CLEARW 2:GOTOXY 1,1
15      RANDOMIZE 0
20      DIM P(20),F(20),T(20),G(20)
30      PRINT "Enter the game probabilities for all seven games"
40      PRINT "in decimal form (E.G. use .40 for 40%)"
50      PRINT "Note that the user must determine individual game probab
        ilities"
55      PRINT " (National versus American League)"
60      PRINT " on the basis of pitchers, hunches, where played, etc."
65      PRINT " program determines outcome of a 1000 game series to"
66      PRINT " predict the series outcome"
70      FOR X=1 TO 7:INPUT P(X):NEXT X
74      PRINT "Wait while I play 1000 games."
75      PRINT
80      N=0:A=0:FOR X=1 TO 7:IF RND(1)<P(X) THEN 100
90      A=A+1:IF A=4 THEN 140 ELSE 110
100     N=N+1:IF N=4 THEN 170
110     NEXT X
140     A1=A1+1:G(N+A)=G(N+A)+1:GOTO 190
170     N1=N1+1:F(N+A)=F(N+A)+1
190     T(N+A)=T(N+A)+1
200     IF N1+A1<1000 THEN 80
210     PRINT "SERIES #","TOTAL","NATIONAL","AMERICAN"
220     FOR X=4 TO 7:PRINT X,T(X),F(X),G(X)
230     NEXT X:PRINT,"------","------","------"
240     PRINT "TOTALS:","1000",N1,A1:PRINT
245     PRINT "Simulated 1000 game results above"
250     PRINT "Average length of series is ";(4*T(4)+5*T(5)+6*T(6)+7*T(
        7))/1000
260     INPUT Q$
```

- Find the smallest solution in positive integers x and y of $x^2 - n \bullet y^2 = 1$ where $n = 61$.
- Find how many ways the integer 10,000 can be expressed as a sum of distinct positive integers (ignoring permutations).
- Find the minimum value of the gamma function. gamma (n) = (n − 1)! for an integer n in the range $1 < n < 2$.

Puzzles that are simpler to solve include such popular logic games as

- Instant Insanity™ blocks: five blocks with different colors on each side must be arranged so that all five blocks in a row have the same colors on each side. The computer could determine all possible solutions. (7,962,624 possible combinations exist and there are 192 solutions.)
- The High IQ. Game consists of a board in the shape of a cross with markers in every hole except the center hole. The player jumps markers with adjacent markers as in checkers and then removes the one jumped over. Markers may not be moved unless a jump is possible. The object of the game is to jump all the markers on the board, leaving only one final marker; this is difficult to accomplish. The computer could determine the strategy for winning the game and the number of different ways possible to win (is there only one method?). A mathematical analysis of this game appeared in *The Journal of Recreational Mathematics,* Vol. 5, No. 2, pp. 133ff. The trian-

gular version was discussed in *The Mathematics Teacher,* January 1979, pp.53ff.

Computing pi, *e*, Solutions for High-Degree Equations, and Mathematical Oddities. Many mathematicians take delight in computing values for irrational expressions, determining equations for special mathematical circumstances, and discovering unusual properties of specific numbers. The computer is, of course, useful in such computations.

Calculation of the value of π to any number of decimal places can be accomplished by the BASIC program in Listing 3-9.

Listing 3-9. The Pi Calculator Program.

```
10      REM LISTING3.09 - The Pi Calculation Program
15      FULLW 2:CLEARW 2:GOTOXY 1,1
20      PRINT "PI CALCULATION PROGRAM"
25      PRINT "Demonstrates iterative techniques (requires 30,000"
30      PRINT "loops to calculate to five decimal places.)"
40      DEFINT D
50      PRINT "to stop the program before PI calculation is complete"
60      PRINT "select STOP from the control menu."
70      INPUT "Press RETURN to begin ",A$
80      S=0:V=-1:R=1
90      FOR D=1 TO 10000
100     L=10000
110     T=2*R-1
120     V=-1*V
130     S=S+V/T
140     N=N+1:R=R+1
150     L=L+10000:IF L>110000! THEN 110
160     PRINT N,4*S
170     NEXT D
180     INPUT Q$
```

The value of π can be calculated using this successive approximation:

$$\pi = 4 - 4/3 + 4/5 - 4/7 + 4/9 - 4/11 + \ldots$$

Similarly, the value of the natural log e may be calculated using this successive approximation:

$$e^x = 1 + x + \frac{x^2}{2!} + \frac{x^3}{3!} + \frac{x^4}{4!} + \ldots$$

Programs to compute a Fibonacci sequence are also popular. The sequence is created by adding each previous term to the term before that:

1,1, 2, 3, 5, 8, 13 . . .

Sunflower and daisy florets, pine cones, pineapples, the shells of some mollusks, and even patterns of paving stones and the mating habits of bees and rabbits exhibit properties given by the Fibonacci sequence. For instance, the seeds of sunflowers and daisies form a pattern of two sets of spirals, one clockwise and the other counterclockwise. The numbers of spirals in the two sets are usually consecutive Fibonacci numbers (for example, 34 and 55).

Playing Games. Interesting mathematical games for your computer include the following:

- The four color map problem: A recreation that has interested mathematicians for many years is to prove that only four colors are needed to copy any map in such a manner that no bordering countries are of the same color. The proof was accomplished by a large-scale, brute-force computer program.

A game based on this fact could involve two players who attempt to force each other to color two bordering countries the same color. In each turn, a player would choose any color to apply to any country on a map with random boundaries. Proper logic will ensure that one player will lose. The computer could serve as one of the opponents.

- Magic squares game: The magic squares game pits the computer against a human in an attempt to complete a magic square while blocking an opponent. A magic square is composed of smaller squares, each with a separate number inside. The numbers in the smaller squares in horizontal, vertical, and diagonal rows sum to the same amount. Opposing players could attempt to complete a magic square in opposing directions.
- Maze games: Maze games involve a randomly generated maze and a computer-controlled mouse that learns to find its way through the maze.
- Exacto: This game for young people involves two five-digit numbers that have been randomly selected by the computer. Players are instructed to transform the first number into the second through multiplication, division, addition, or subtraction of any other number within a specified range. The computer would keep track of all computations at each stage. The players are scored according to speed or number of operations required to finish.
- Euclid: In this game (p,q) represents a pair of positive numbers such that p is greater than q; A and B signify the two players. Players alternate turns. Each turn consists of replacing the larger of the two numbers given to a player by any positive number obtained by subtracting a positive multiple of the smaller number from the larger number. (All numbers are integers). The first player to obtain zero for the (new) smaller number is declared the winner.
A sample game is shown below; (51,30) is the starting pair of numbers.

A:(30,21) B:(21,9) A:(9,3) B:(3.0)
B wins

or the game could have been

A:(30,21) B:(21,9) A:(12,9) B:(9.3) A:(3,9)
A wins

- The Two-Move Game: In the first half of this game, the two players secretly enter four nonnegative numbers totaling the same number into the cells of a 2 × 2 matrix:

$$\begin{array}{cccc} x1 & x2 & y1 & y2 \\ x3 & x4 & y3 & y4 \end{array}$$

The entries are then exposed and a third 2 × 2 matrix is developed in which the entries are $x_i y_i$. This final matrix is then analyzed by the first player who chooses a column and tries to maximize. The second player then chooses a row and tries to maximize. The player with the greatest variation wins. A mathematical strategy exists to win this game; can you find it?
- Sim: The game of Sim involves a game board like this:

x x

x x

x x

The players take alternate turns drawing lines between two points. The first player to draw an equilateral triangle or square loses. A mathematical strategy exists to win this game.
- Life: This popular computer recreation was devised by John Conway, a mathematician at Cambridge University. It simulates an ecological system and illustrates the rise, fall, and changes of a society of living organisms as they interact with their environment and each other. The game begins with a small population of organisms; as time progresses (measured in terms of

generations), the population experiences one of three fates: it dies out due to over or underpopulation, it becomes stable, or it oscillates in a repeating pattern. Each member of the population has one of three fates during each generation. It can die from "starvation," give birth to another organism, or survive in a stable form.

The game board is a grid of arbitrary size, often larger than 20 × 20. Each square on the grid may be occupied by one organism or empty. Thus, each organism always has eight surrounding squares. It will die if it touches fewer than two or more than three occupied squares. If three occupied squares touch an empty square, a new occupant is born to fill that square. Births and deaths are evaluated simultaneously.

When the game of Life is written in machine language, it will progress at speeds faster than one generation per second and can create a fascinating display of computer graphics. The course of a population through the first few generations is shown in Fig. 3-1.

Computing Probabilities. You could use your computer to calculate the following probabilities.

- Poker Probabilities: You could compute the probability that $m * n$ cards held by a defender in a bridge hand will be split m and n, or the probabilities for obtaining a certain hand in poker after certain cards have been played.
- Birthdays: In a classroom of 24 students, how many would you estimate have the same birthday? The chances are slightly better than even than two or more students will have birthdays on the same date, counter to our intuition! For a given number of people, x, the percent chance that two or more will have the same birthday is given by

$$\% \text{ chance} = 100 - 100 \bullet \left(\frac{365 - x}{365} \right)$$

Write a BASIC program to calculate the percent chance of coincident birthdays for any input of x, the number of people in the group considered.

- An Apocalyptic Possibility: An equation expressing the probability of an accidental nuclear missile launch by the United States or the Soviet Union falsely triggering World War III is as follows:

$$PA = 1-(1-P)^{(N(U+S)}$$

where
PA = Probability of the Apocalypse (for

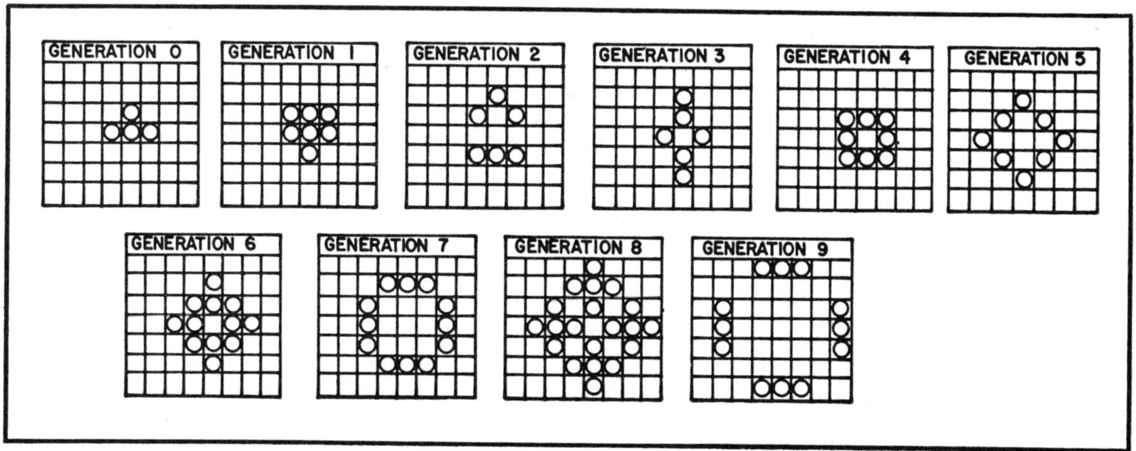

Fig. 3-1. The course of a Life population through nine generations.

percent chance, multiply PA • 100)

U = Total number of strategic missiles in the U.S. arsenal (2000 est.)

S = Total number of strategic missiles in the Soviet arsenal (2300 est.)

P = Probability of accidental launching of a nuclear missile by either side during a 24-hr. period (1F-8 estimated)

N = Number of days under consideration (20 years = 7,300 days)

Write a BASIC program to consider different values for U, S, P, and N.

Calculating Useful Information. You can use your computer to figure out practical information such as the following:

- Easter: A program to calculate the date of Easter for any year would make use of the fact that Easter falls on the first Sunday following the arbitrary Paschal Full Moon, which does not necessarily coincide with a real or astronomical moon. The Paschal Full Moon is calculated by adding 1 to the remainder obtained by dividing the year by 19 and applying the information given in Table 3-1.

  Thus, for the year 2000, the key is 6, or April 18. A program to calculate the day of the week (see the "Business and Financial Applications" chapter) could then indicate that April 18, 2000 is a Tuesday. Note: If the Paschal Full Moon falls on a Sunday, Easter is the following Sunday. The earliest Easter can fall is March 23rd and the latest is April 25th.
- Horizons: The distance to the horizon in miles is approximately = $\sqrt{1.5h}$, where h = elevation above sea level in feet. Write a BASIC program to draw a mountain and print the miles to the horizon for viewers located at 100-foot intervals.

Table 3-1. The Paschal Full Moon Date.

1-Apr 14	6-Apr 18	11-Mar 25	16-Mar 30
2-Apr 3	7-Apr 8	12-Apr 13	17-Apr 17
3-Mar 23	8-Mar 28	13-Apr 2	18-Apr 7
4-Apr 11	9-Apr 16	14-Mar 22	19-Mar 27
5-Mar 31	10-Apr 5	15-Apr 10	

Creating Artistic Patterns. You can use your microcomputer to generate interesting, artistic patterns such as *Pascal's triangle*. As described in the December 1966 issue of *Scientific American*, Pascal's triangle may be used to generate artistic geometric patterns. A sample Pascal triangle is shown below; each number in the successive rows is generated by adding the two numbers above and to the immediate left and right of the number in question.

```
        1
       1 1
      1 2 1
     1 3 3 1
    1 4 6 4 1
  1 5 10 10 5 1
```

To write a BASIC program to generate patterns using the triangle you could, for instance, represent all odd numbers by an X and all even numbers by a space. Print the results on a line printer; a variety of interesting geometrical patterns involving triangles will be formed.

Chapter 4

Technical/Scientific Applications

Personal computers, rather than their large-scale counterparts, are increasingly being used by technicians and scientists for problem solving. They offer the advantages of ease of use, low cost, and greater probability. Although many large-scale scientific problems are best left to supercomputers, the personal computer has become an asset in its own right in all types of laboratories.

In this chapter I will examine the ways personal computers have been put to scientific and technical use. The personal computer can help to rid the professional or amateur scientist of the mathematical drudgery that is so much a part of the discovery process. It can rapidly and accurately solve problems, many of which previously would not have been undertaken because of their sheer magnitude.

Many of these applications are specialized; the purpose of this chapter is to touch upon just a few of the most commonly used scientific applications, provide sources for further information, and demonstrate some solutions in BASIC. Due to space restrictions, formulas and in-depth coverage of each application is impossible, but this information should be readily available in standard reference manuals.

WEATHER FORECASTING

Forecasting the weather is usually thought to be a task for large computers only. However, local weather forecasting can be accomplished with surprising accuracy by taking note of wind direction and barometric changes. A chart in use by local weather bureaus has been based upon these two parameters and could easily be computerized. This data could be input automatically by the use of electronic barometers and wind direction instruments.

Wind change	Barometric condition	Forecast code
From	*To*	
S	SW	7 L
S	SE	3 E
		4 F
		9 M

Wind change	Barometric condition	Forecast code
NE	SE	3 G
		4 H
		5 J
		6 K
		9 M
N	E	3 I
		4 A
		9 N
		8 O
NW	SW	1 C
		2 B
		3 D
		7 L

If a forecast is not listed for the proper barometric condition, enumerated below, other factors must be used to provide the forecast.

Barometric Conditions
(In inches Hg)

1. 30.1 or more and steady
2. 30.1-30.2 rising rapidly
3. 30.1 or more falling slowly
4. 30.1 or more falling rapidly
5. 30.0 or less falling slowly
6. 30.0 or less falling rapidly
7. 30.0 or less rising slowly
8. 29.8 or less rising rapidly
9. 29.8 or less falling rapidly

A rapid change is considered to be over .06 inches per hour, where 3 inches Hg = 760 mm Hg.

Forecasts

A. Summer rain probable/12-24 hours. Winter rain or snow, increasing wind; bad weather often sets in when barometer begins to fall and winds set in from the N.E.
B. Fair, followed within two days by rain.
C. Continued fair, no decided temperature change.
D. Fair for two days with slowly rising temperatures.
E. Rain within 24 hours.
F. Wind increasing, rain within 24 hours.
G. Rain within 12-18 hours.
H. Wind increasing, rain within 12 hours.
I. Summer light winds, rain may not fall for several days. Winter rain within 24 hours.
J. Rain will continue for 1 to 2 days.
K. Rain, with high wind, followed within 36 hours by clearing, and in winter by colder temperatures.
L. Clearing within a few hours, fair for several days.
M. Severe storm imminent, followed within 24 hours by clearing, and in winter by colder temperatures
N. Severe northeast gale and heavy precipitation, in winter, heavy snow followed by a cold wave.
Clearing and colder.

A cloud chart with forecasts included is also useful. The forecast data for the various types of clouds could be stored and a comparison made between the forecast and a forecast from the above chart.

Other suggestions for applying a personal computer to weather calculations include the following.

1. Pressure/height conversions to allow an aneroid barometer to serve as an altimeter.
2. Dew point temperature and relative humidity from wet and dry bulb readings.
3. Normal maximum, mean, and minimum temperature degrees days for a given date and location.
4. Estimates of cloud base heights from dew point and surface temperature observations.
5. Almanac data for a given time and date (for example, declination of the sun, distance of the sun from the earth, phase of the moon, and positions of the planets) stored for ready access.
6. Analysis and display of hourly weather data derived from a phone line connected with a weather data channel.

7. Temperature humidity index and relative humidity calculations. The program in Listing 4-1 determines the effective temperature given the relative humidity and the actual temperature.
8. Wind chill factor calculations. To calculate the wind chill factor, use the following formula:

$$H = (.14 + .47\ V)\ (36.5 - T)$$

where H = chill in calories lost per square centimeter of skin per second
V = wind velocity (m/sec.)
T = Temperature (°C)

The program in Listing 4-2 converts dry bulb temperature in °F and wind speed in mph to apparent wind chill temperature.

THE SUNDIAL DESIGN PROGRAM

Use the program in Listing 4-3 to compute the correct angles to use in constructing a sundial for your latitude.

The vertical member (called the *style* or *gnomon*) should be set so that it lies in a north-south direction as shown in Fig. 4-1. The top edge points to the North Star, equal to the latitude in degrees above the horizon. The program gives you the angles to use in graduating the scale for each hour.

ENERGY EFFICIENCY COMPUTATION

You can use your small computer to make the following studies.

Listing 4-1. Temperature-Humidity Index Program.

```
10      REM LISTING4.01 - The Temperature Humidity Index Program.
15      FULLW 2:CLEARW 2:GOTOXY 1,1
20      PRINT "Temperature Humidity Index calculator"
25      PRINT "determines the effective temperature ."
30      INPUT "Enter the relative humidity ";H
40      IF H>94 THEN A=0 ELSE IF H>89 AND H<95 THEN A=2
50      IF H>79 AND H<90 THEN A=4 ELSE IF H>69 AND H<80 THEN A=6
60      IF H>59 AND H<70 THEN A=10 ELSE A=14
70      INPUT "Enter the temperature (in degrees F) ",T
80      TH=.8*T+15-A
90      PRINT "The temperature humidity index=";TH
95      INPUT "Calculate another? (Y/N) ";A$:IF A$<>"N" THEN CLEARW 2:G
        OTOXY 1,1:GOTO 30
100     END
```

Listing 4-2. Wind Chill Calculator

```
10      REM LISTING4.02 - The Wind Chill Calculator Program
15      FULLW 2:CLEARW 2:GOTOXY 1,1
20      INPUT "Enter temperature in fahrenheit ";T
30      INPUT "Enter wind speed in M.P.H.";V
40      T1=T:V=(V*1609.35)/3600:TC=33-((T-32)*(5/9))
50      H=(10.45+(SQR(V)*10)-V)*TC:X=H-506.784
60      IF X<0 THEN X1=T1:GOTO 80
70      X1=50-(X/12.3):X1=INT(((X1*10)+5)/10)
80      PRINT:PRINT "WIND CHILL TEMP=";X1;" DEGREES FAHRENHEIT"
90      INPUT Q$
```

Listing 4-3. The Sundial Design Program.

```
10      REM LISTING4.03 - The Sundial Design Program
90      FULLW 2:CLEARW 2:GOTOXY 1,1
100     PRINT "SUNDIAL DESIGN PROGRAM"
110     PRINT "computes necessary angles for your latitude"
120     INPUT "Enter your latitude ";A
140     PRINT "Cut out a style such that the upper edge makes an angle"
150     PRINT "of ";A;" degrees with the base."
160     S=SIN(A)
170     X=1
180     FOR B=15 TO 90 STEP 15
190     T=TAN(B)
200     C=S*T
210     X=X+1
220     PRINT "At ";X;" o'clock, the angle should be ";ATN(C)*57.29578#
230     REM in statement 220 the constant 57.29578 is used to convert
240     REM from radians to degrees
250     NEXT B
260     INPUT Q$
```

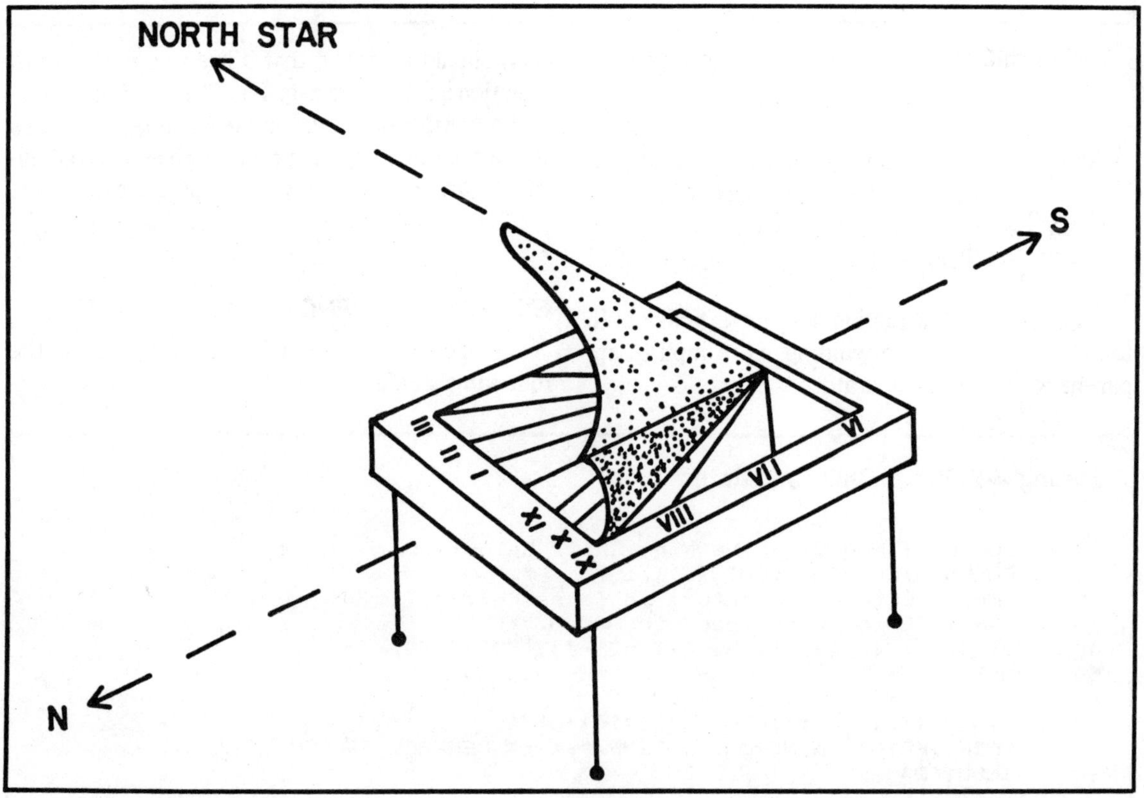

Fig. 4-1. The Moorish sundial.

- A computerized statistical comparison between the water temperature in a solar energy system and the outside temperature, the angle of the sun, and so on could serve to evaluate the efficiency of a home solar energy system. Analog-to-digital converters could be used to gather the information automatically.
- Those of you considering the installation of a solar heating system might want to do another statistical analysis of the heating requirements for your home based on Btu/hr times the number of hours that your furnace operates during the heating season. The size of a solar system necessary to heat your house can then be calculated using this data and the manufacturer's efficiency data.

In the central United States on June 21, the maximum solar energy striking the Earth is 290 Btu/square foot (approximately 15 hours in the day). On December 21, the solar energy is a maximum of 220 Btu/square foot (approximately 9 hours in the day). Thus, you can compute average values for the variables in the formula below.

$$\text{Solar collector Btu output} = \frac{B \times h \times s \times m}{2}$$

where

B = Btu/sq. ft.
h = hrs./day
s = sq. ft. of collector
m = max. efficiency

at ground temperature (40 °F) to 100 °F and that the desired water temperature for home use is 120 °F.

- The answer to "How much fuel can be saved by turning the thermostat down from 70 °F to 60 °F at night?" may be determined using this equation:

$$A = \frac{.0625\ (n-1)W}{z}$$

Where

A = amount of heat (Btu)
W = the normal heat loss/hr. (Btu)
n = the number of hours of discontinued heating
z = the number of hours from the beginning of reheating until the house is at an acceptable temperature

- To find the heat loss of your home, use the formula

$$H = \frac{kA(t-t^1)T}{d}$$

where

H = heat transmission (Btu)
k = coefficient of thermal conduction (Values for the type of construction used in your home may be found in builder's manuals)
A = exposed area
$(t-t^1)$ = temperature difference between inside and outside (°F)
T = duration of exposure (hours)
d = thickness of walls (inches)

- To calculate fuel requirements use the formula

$$C = \frac{H(t_a-t_b)\ N \times S \times q}{100{,}000 \times (t_i-t_o)}$$

Where

C = fuel cost
H = heat loss/hr.
t_o = outside temperature
t_i = inside temperature
t_a = average inside temperature
t_b = average outside temperature
N = number of hours of heating required
S = number of units of fuel
q = cost per unit of fuel

The program in Listing 4-4 calculates estimated costs for heating your home with gas, oil, and electricity. Be sure to enter your heat loss in British thermal units, not degrees.

Listing 4-4. The Home Heating Program.

```
10    REM LISTING4.04 The House Heating Program
20    FULLW 2:CLEARW 2:GOTOXY 1,1
30    Q$="####.##"
40    PRINT "HOUSE HEATING EVALUATION PROGRAM"
50    PRINT:PRINT "The purpose of this program is to compute the"
60    PRINT "relative efficiency of heating a home with"
70    PRINT "electricity, natural gas, or oil.  It will be
80    PRINT "necessary to contact your local distributors of"
90    PRINT "the above fuels to make a cost comparison."
100   PRINT "There are other factors to consider when evaluating"
110   PRINT "the cost for heating (I.E. the amount of insulation"
120   PRINT "you have), but the ratios between different"
130   PRINT "fuels should be consistent."
140   PRINT "Use the cost efficiencies the program outputs along with
      "
150   PRINT "the cost of the heating system to determine which you"
160   PRINT "should choose."
170   INPUT "Enter estimated heat loss per hour: ",H
180   REM this may be approximated using formula in text or with buil
      ders manuals
190   PRINT "If you know the efficiency of the oil burning system"
200   PRINT "Please enter the value, ";
210   INPUT "otherwise enter 'O' ";B
220   IF B=0 THEN B=.8 ELSE B=B*.01
230   INPUT "Enter the ave. no. of months of cold season per year ",C

240   C=C*720
250   INPUT "At what temperature will you set the thermostat ";D
260   INPUT "What is the average winter temperature ";E
270   REM compute heat loss per hour
280   X=((D-E)/70)*((H*C)/(140000!*B))
290   PRINT "What is the ave. price of oil in your area per gallon-"
300   INPUT "If not known type 'O'",F

310   IF F=0 THEN F=.5
320   PRINT "You will require an estimated ";X;" gallons of oil--cost
      ="X*F
330   INPUT "Enter the cost per kilowatt hr. in your area in dollars
      ";G
340   PRINT "Electricity to run the oil pump may cost up to ";206*G;"
      dollars."
350   PRINT "If you know the efficiency of the natural gas heater ple
      ase"
360   INPUT "enter, otherwise enter 'O' ",B
370   IF B=0 THEN B=.8 ELSE B=B*.01
380   Y=((D-E)/70)*((H*C)/(100000!*B))
390   INPUT "What is the cost per therm in your area ",I
400   PRINT "You will require an estimated ";Y;" therms to heat"
410   PRINT "Cost=$";:PRINT USING Q$;I*Y
420   Z=((D-E)/70)*(H*C)/3405
430   PRINT "and an estimated ";Z;" KWH will be required to heat with
      "
```

```
440    PRINT "Electricity--cost=$";:PRINT USING Q$;Z*G
450    INPUT "Press RETURN to continue ",A$:CLEARW 2:GOTOXY 1,1
460    PRINT "SUMMARY:"
470    PRINT "MEDIUM","AMOUNT","COST"
480    PRINT "OIL";:PRINT USING Q$;X,X*F
490    PRINT "NATURAL GAS";:PRINT USING Q$;Y,I*Y
500    PRINT "ELECTRICITY";:PRINT USING Q$;Z,Z*G
510    PRINT "Remember that these values are only estimates"
520    PRINT "and will differ according to the insulation, building"
530    PRINT "material, furnishings, and climate."
540    PRINT "The values given are most useful in determining the"
550    PRINT "most inexpensive method of heating your home."
560    PRINT "Thus, the procurement costs for the various systems"
570    PRINT "should be analyzed along with the above costs to"
580    PRINT "arrive at a final figure."
590    REM A complete program could be written without much difficulty

600    REM to consider the above factors...
610    INPUT Q$
```

- To calculate the Btu rating for an air conditioner for your home, use the program in Listing 4-5.
- Use the simple program in Listing 4-6 to track the yearly cost of operation for electrical appliances and determine where cuts in electric bills would best be made.
- You can use additional formulas available in building manuals to compute the savings of installing insulation or the area of a solar collector necessary to heat a house of certain dimensions and construction.

TECHNICAL AND SCIENTIFIC CALCULATIONS

The computer can be used to perform calculations needed by those involved in many fields from navigation to chemistry.

Aviation

The private or business pilot will find the following calculations useful. Some are designed for portable programmable calculators so that pro-

Listing 4-5. The Air Conditioning Program.

```
10     REM LISTING4.05 - The Air Conditioning Program
15     FULLW 2:CLEARW 2:GOTOXY 1,1
20     PRINT "AIR CONDITIONING REQUIREMENT CALCULATION"
30     PRINT "determines the BTU rating for an air cond./heater for yo
       ur home"
40     PRINT "Enter the estimated total square feet of exterior wall a
       rea"
50     INPUT "      for your house ",W
60     INPUT "Enter the estimated total glass area for your house ",G
70     INPUT "Enter the estimated total area within the roof cross-sec
       tion ",R
80     INPUT "Enter the number of occupants ",N
90     BTU=W*5+G*35+R*12+N*100+2000
100    PRINT "The estimated BTU necessary to air condition your home="
       ;BTU
110    PRINT
120    INPUT Q$
```

Listing 4-6. Electricity Cost Analysis Program.

```
10     REM LISTING4.06 - The Electric Cost Analysis Program
15     FULLW 2:CLEARW 2:GOTOXY 1,1
20     INPUT "Enter cost per K.W.H. in $";C
30     INPUT "for next appliance, select 1) watts, 2) volts + amps ";X

40     ON X GOTO 50,70
45     GOTO 30
50     INPUT "Watts ";W
60     GOTO 90
70     INPUT "Volts, Amps ";V,A
80     W=V*A
90     INPUT "Enter approximate no. hours per day this appliance is us
       ed ";H
100    KWH=(H*360*W)/1000
110    PRINT "This appliance uses approximately ";KWH;" kilowatt hours
       "
120    PRINT "per year, at an annual cost of $";KWH*C
130    PRINT:GOTO 30
```

grams may be used while in flight.

1. Flight plan with wind allowances: calculation of the heading, speed, fuel, ETA, and so on for a trip of multiple legs could be done.
2. Long-range flight plan: calculations could be done for great circle routes and could include distance, time, fuel, and source.
3. Atmosphere, speed, temperature, and altitude: from pressure altitude, a program could calculate the speed of sound, temperature, pressure and density relative to standard sea level.
4. Prediction of freezing level and lowest usable flight level.
5. Wind components and average vector: crosswind and tail or head wind components of a single wind vector could be calculated.
6. Dead reckoning of position.
7. Great circle flying navigation.
8. Course correction to fly correct path.
9. Rhumb line navigation.
10. Unit conversions: length, volume, weight, English and metric temperature conversions.

$$°F = (9/5)(°C + 32°)$$
$$°C = (5/9)(°F - 32°)$$

Several BASIC programs and additional information on aviation calculations may be found in *Computers for Sea and Sky* by Steven J. Rogowski, Creative Computing Press, Morristown, NJ 07960.

Marine Navigation

Some of the following applications are designed for use with programmable calculators as well as pocket or lap computers so that they can be used aboard a small vessel.

1. Time-speed-distance with current sailing: A useful program could solve time-speed-distance equations and could consider the current in determining the proper course to steer and the speed through the water necessary to reach a given destination in a specified length of time.
2. Distance short of, beyond, or to a horizon: A program could calculate the distance to the apparent horizon as well as the distance to and visibility of an object of known height.
3. Velocity, VMG, and current vectors: Given any two of drift and set of the current, speed and course through the water, and speed and course made good, a program could calculate the unknown value.

4. Running fix from two objects: A program could calculate a fix of a vessel from bearings of two objects.
5. Planet location. A program could estimate the altitude and azimuth of the four navigational planets. The UCT (Universal Coordinated Time, formerly Greenwich Mean Time or GMT) of twilight could also be calculated or manually input.
6. Rhumb line and great circle navigation calculation.
7. Sight reduction calculation.
8. Length conversions (for example, nautical miles to statute miles).
9. Vector addition.
10. Estimated time of arrival.
11. Conversion of compass points to degrees.
12. Area navigation by VOR (very-high-frequency omnirange).
13. Rhumb line navigation.
14. Dead reckoning of position.
15. Great circle computations.
16. Distance from VOR/OMNI.
17. Course correction.
18. Distance by two bearings.
19. Conversions between knots, miles, statue miles, kilometers.
20. Speed computation given distance covered and time.

Many of the above navigation calculations are explained in *Computers for Sea and Sky*, by Steven J. Rogowski, Creative Computing Press, Morristown, NJ 07960.

The program in Listing 4-7 computes the distance in nautical miles and bearing between two points on Earth. Enter starting and ending latitudes and longitudes as decimal degrees.

Medical Calculations

Doctors, nurses, technicians and other medical personnel may find the following calculations useful.

1. Conversions of weight, length, and volume to other units, or English to metric conversion.
2. Lung diffusion calculations.
3. Blood acid-base status determination.
4. Beer's law calculation.
5. Protein electrophoresis: given integration counts of a number of protein fractions, the percentage of each may be found.
6. Body surface area estimation.
7. Oxygen saturation and content. Oxygen content and saturation in the blood may be found given pO_2, pCO_2, pH, and body temperature.

Publications containing computer programs and applications of use to the health professional include:

Computer in Biology and Medicine
Computers in Medicine
Medical Computer Journal 42 East High St., East Hampton, CT 06424
Physicians Microcomputer Report, P.O. Box 6483, Lawrenceville, NJ 08648

Surveying Calculations

Those involved in surveying could utilize the following calculations.

1. Azimuth/bearing traverse: given reference coordinates, leg length, azimuth or bearing, and quadrant, the endpoint coordinates, departure, latitude, and total distance may be computed.

Listing 4-7. Great Circle Navigation Program.

```
10    REM LISTING4.07 - The Great Circle Navigation Program
15    REM enter southern latitudes and eastern longitudes as negative
      numbers
20    FULLW 2:CLEARW 2:GOTOXY 1,1
```

```
30      INPUT "Enter latitude and longitude of starting point ";U,W
40      INPUT "Enter latitude and longitude of ending point ";Z,R
50      PRINT:M=.01745329#
60      A=SIN(U*M)*SIN(Z*M)+COS(Z*M)*COS((R-W)*M)
70      D=60*(-ATN(A/SQR(-A*A+1))+1.5708)*57.29579#
80      C=(SIN(Z*M)-(SIN(U*M)*COS(D/60*M)))/(SIN(D/60*M)*COS(U*M))
90      H=(-ATN(C/SQR(-C*C+1))+1.5708)*57.29579#
100     F=SIN(R-W)
110     IF F>=0 THEN H=360-H
120     PRINT "The distance is ";D;" nautical miles "
130     PRINT "at a bearing of ";INT(h);" degrees."
140     INPUT Q$
```

2. Slope reduction determinations.
3. Point of intersection calculation.

Chemistry

Chemists and chemistry students may find the following calculations useful.

1. Calculation of requirements to produce a given solution. The program in Listing 4-8 will do the calculations for you.
2. Calculations of the following parameters, given adequate inputs: pH, molality, total atomic weights, gas density and pressure, electron energies, gravimetric factors, liquid pressure, degree of saturation, gram equivalent weight, normality, percent composition, mole fraction, mole percent, and ionic strength dilution factor.
3. Plotting/simulation of reaction rates, electron distribution, and so on.

Physics

Those involved with physics will also find the computer's capacity for performing calculations useful. Potential uses include the following.

1. Plotting of potential energy functions, lab data, and so on.
2. Conversions of units.
3. Solutions to elementary equations: velocity, acceleration, momentum, work, power, etc.
4. Statistical analysis and data compilation.

An article discussing the use of personal computers to physicists appeared in *Physics Today*, De-

Listing 4-8. Stock Solution Computation Program.

```
10      REM LISTING4.08 - The Stock Solution Computation Program
20      REM computes the amount of stock solution and water necessary t
o
30      REM produce a given solution
35      FULLW 2:CLEARW 2:GOTOXY 1,1
40      PRINT "Enter these values: concentration of working solution, "

50      PRINT "concentration of stock solution,"
55      INPUT "Total amount of solution, ",PW,PS,QT
60      OS=(PW*QT)/PS
70      W=QT-OS
80      PRINT "The quantity of stock solution=";OS
90      PRINT "The quantity of water to add=";W
100     PRINT:PRINT
110     INPUT Q$
```

cember 1983, pp., 25-28. The author states, "It is very likely that most calculations in physics will be performed by the home computer in the future," because of the benefit of independence from large computer organizations, bureaucracies, and economic constraints. He describes a Monte Carlo simulation that ran for about a week on his personal computer and estimated that the same job would have cost $2000 if run on his university CPU.

General-Purpose Experimental Applications

Scientists in many fields can use their home computers to perform the following types of calculations.

1. Statistical analysis of data: useful statistical applications include curve fitting and plotting, Chi-square tests, analysis of variance and standard deviation, solutions to equations, and correlation coefficients.
2. Calculation of tables for a specific application: functions that are commonly referred to, yet do not have reference tables, could be calculated for a number of values, and the results displayed in table form for easy reference.

In addition to using computers for calculations, scientists can interface microcomputers to lab instrumentation and develop automatic data log and acquisition systems. They can also develop voice input interfaces that could accept data called out by a lab technician too busy to manually record data.

ENGINEERING APPLICATIONS

Professionals and hobbyists will have use for computer programs in the following engineering fields.

Electrical Engineering

Computers can help those who deal with electricity by performing calculations and analyses, and by facilitating design work.

Active High- and Low-Pass Filter Design. High- and low-pass filters may be designed for given center frequency, gain, and Q values for the resistors and capacitors in the infinite-gain multiple-feedback circuit. Listing 4-9 shows a program that performs these functions.

This program may be modified and extended for use in designing simple filters by the use of the schematics and formula in Fig. 4-2.

Active Bandpass Filter Design. Second-order active bandpass filters may be designed using a multiple-feedback network. Both high-Q and low-Q circuits could be designed. Standard values may be selected for easy implementation.

Listing 4-9. Low-Pass Filter Design Program.

```
10    REM LISTING4.09 - The Low-Pass Filter Design Program
90    FULLW 2:CLEARW 2:GOTOXY 1,1
100   PRINT "LOW PASS FILTER DESIGN PROGRAM"
110   PRINT "Shunt M-derived filter"
120   INPUT "Enter the cutoff frequency ",F1
130   INPUT "Enter the frequency of remote cutoff ",F2
140   INPUT "Enter the terminating resistance ",R
150   L=SQR(1-(F1*F1/(F2*F2)))*R/(3.14159*F1)
160   C1=(1-(SQR(1-(F1*F1/(F2*F2))))-2)/(4*3.14159*SQR(1-F1*F1/(F2*F2
      ))*F1*R)
170   C2=SQR(1-(F1*F1/(F2*F2)))/(3.14159*R*F2)
180   PRINT "The value for L=";L
190   PRINT "The value for C1=";C1
200   PRINT "The value for C2=";C2
210   INPUT Q$
```

SIMPLE filters:

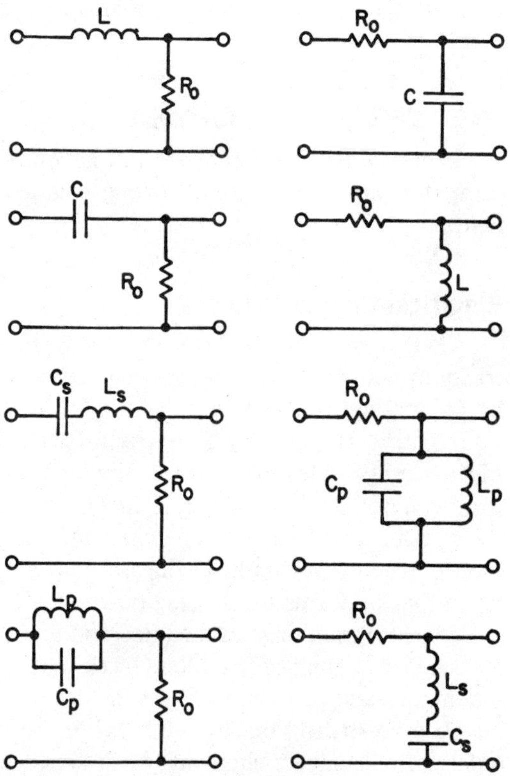

Normalized to design impedance R_o,
ω_o = cut-off angular frequency (low-pass or high pass)

ω_o = center frequency (band-pass or band stop)
ω_2 = upper cut-off frequency (band-pass or band stop)
ω_1 = lower cut-off frequency (band-pass or band stop)

$$\omega_o = \sqrt{\omega_1 \omega_2}$$

$$n = \frac{\omega_2 - \omega_1}{\omega_o}$$

Definition:

x = normalized frequency parameter = $\frac{\omega}{\omega_o}$

v = deviation parameter = x (low pass) = $-\frac{1}{x}$ (high pass)

$$v = \frac{x - \frac{1}{x}}{n} \text{ (band pass)} = \frac{n}{\frac{1}{x} - x} \text{ (band stop)}$$

Design:

Low-pass and high pass:

$$L = \frac{R_o}{\omega_o} \qquad C = \frac{1}{\omega_o R_o}$$

Band-pass and band stop:

$$\omega_o\sqrt{L_p C_p} = \omega_o\sqrt{L_s C_s} = 1$$

$$L_s = \frac{L}{n},\ C_s = nC \quad L_p = nL,\ C_p = \frac{C}{n}$$

Performance:

A = attenuation (dB) = $-8{\cdot}68589 \ln\sqrt{1+v^2}$

ϕ = phase = $-\arctan v$

Fig. 4-2. Schematics and formulas for simple filters.

Chebyshev and Butterworth Filter Design. Chebyshev and Butterworth low-pass filters may be designed for specified filter order, termination resistance, and corner frequency.

Resonant Circuits. The impedance and resonant frequency could be calculated by a program for series or parallel resonant circuits whose component values are specified.

Attenuators. Component values for T and Pi impedance matching circuits may be found for specified input/output impedances and desired loss. Minimum-loss pad matching may be performed for given impedances.

T to Pi Transformations. T(Pi) networks may be transformed to Pi(T) networks having the same characteristics. A T network design program is shown in Listing 4-10.

Ladder Network Analysis. The input impedance for a ladder network could be calculated; the network may be composed of any combination of resistors, capacitors, and inductors.

Coil Properties. The inductance or number of turns for a single or multilayer coil may be found given wire diameter and dimensions of the coil. The inductance of two parallel, round wires, one forming a return circuit is given by

$$L = .0041\,[2.303 \log_{10}(2\,D/d - D/l)]$$

Listing 4-10. Network Design Program.

```
10     REM LISTING4.10 - The Network Design Program
20     FULLW 2:CLEARW 2:GOTOXY 1,1
100    PRINT "T-NETWORK DESIGN PROGRAM"
105    PRINT "provides a graphic representation of the circuit"
110    INPUT "Enter the resistance of the circuit with output terminal
       s unloaded ",RI
120    INPUT "Enter the output resistance with the input terminals unl
       oaded ",RO
130    INPUT "Enter the resistance with the output terminals shortcirc
       uited ",RN
140    A=-1
150    B=RO+1
160    C=RO*RN-RI
170    Q1=(-B+SQR(B*B-4*A*C))/(2*A)
180    Q2=(-B-SQR(B*B-4*A*C))/(2*A)
190    IF Q1>=0 THEN R3=Q1 ELSE R3=Q2
200    R2=RO-R3
210    RI=RI-R3
220    PRINT:PRINT:PRINT
230    PRINT"T-NETWORK CIRCUIT"
240    PRINT:PRINT "        R1        R2"
250    PRINT "---------    ----       ---------------"
260    FOR X=1 TO 3
270    PRINT "!            !          !"
280    NEXT X
290    PRINT "R-IN------------------     ---------------R OUT"
300    PRINT "---------------------  -------------------";R3;"OHM"
310    PRINT "--------------------------"
320    FOR X=1 TO 3
330    PRINT "!             !          !"
340    NEXT X:PRINT"---------------------------------------------"
350    PRINT:PRINT
360    INPUT Q$
```

where L = inductance (μH)

D = distance in cm between centers of wires

d = diameter of wire (cm)

l = length of conductor (cm)

Power Transformer Design. Core weight may be calculated for a specified power requirement. For a specified core, area flux density, and frequency, the number of primary and secondary turns is found. A BASIC program to design power transformers may be found in *Electronic Design News*, October 27, 1983, p. 346.

Rectifier Circuits. Full-wave or half-wave rectifier circuits may be evaluated for given component values, input voltage, and frequency. The dc output voltage and peak-to-peak ripple may also be calculated.

S and Y Parameter Transformations. A set of S(Y) parameters expressed as magnitudes and angles may be transformed to a set of Y(S) parameters.

Phase-Locked Loops. Natural frequency, damping factor, and loop noise bandwidth may be found for either passive or active phase-locked loops. Loop gain and component values for the circuits are required for input.

Transistor Amplifier Design. Collector current and sensitivity factors can be computed for transistor circuits for specified current gain, supply voltage, and resistor values.

Fourier Series. Fourier coefficients may be computed for discrete values for a periodic function. Sine and cosine coefficients may be found and could be used to calculate new values of the function.

Reactive L-Network Impedance Matching. Networks that will match any two complex impedances may be determined.

Bilateral Design, Stability Factor, Maximum Gain, and Optimum Matching. A program could compute the maximum gain available and the load and source reflection coefficients that yield the maximum gain.

Frequency Conversion Program. A BASIC program to interconvert velocity, period, wavelength, and frequency values could make use of these commonly-used formulas:

$$T = 1/f$$
$$\omega = 2\pi f$$
$$\lambda = v/f$$
$$f = 1/T$$
$$f = \omega/2\pi$$
$$f = v/\lambda$$

where T = period
f = frequency
ω = radian frequency
λ = wavelength
V = propagation velocity

Similarly, frequency and reactance conversions may be accomplished with these formulae:

$$X_c = \frac{1}{2\pi fC} = \frac{1}{\omega C}$$

$$X_L = 2\pi fL = \omega L$$

$$C = \frac{1}{2\pi fX_c} = \frac{1}{\omega X_c}$$

$$L = \frac{X_L}{2\pi f} = \frac{X_L}{\omega}$$

$$f = \frac{1}{2\pi CX_c}$$

$$f = \frac{X_L}{2\pi L}$$

555 Timer Circuit Design. Given the frequency duty cycle and either the timing capacitor or resistor, a program could calculate the other timing component, charge time, discharge time, and period of the commonly used 555 stable multivibrator circuit.

Resonance Calculations. Resonant frequency of inductance-capacitance circuit is given by:

$$f_r = \frac{L - R_L^2 C}{2\pi \sqrt{LC\,(L - R_C^2 C)}}$$

where L = $1/(4\pi^2 f^2 C)$
C = $1/(4\pi^2 f^2 L)$
R_L = series resistance of inductor
R_C = effective series resistance of capacitor
f_r = resonant frequency

Antenna Design. A given frequency could be inputted to a program that would calculate the antenna dimensions for a dipole, yagi, or cubical quad antenna. The program in Listing 4-11 can be used to calculate the dimensions for a yagi antenna to receive television, radio, or amateur radio broadcasts; the antenna is designed for a specific frequency. Such an antenna can often receive signals from distances not previously approached. If the mathematical specifications of the antenna design are unclear, refer to an electronic manual for a picture. Construction of the antenna is not difficult and should cost no more than $20.

Decibel Conversion and Voltage to dBm Conversion. Voltage ratio in decibels is given by

$$N_{dB} = 20 \log_{10} (E_{OUT}/E_{IN})$$

Listing 4-11. Yagi Antenna Design Program.

```
10    REM LISTING LISTING4.11 - The Yagi Antenna Design Program
15    FULLW 2:CLEARW 2:GOTOXY 1,1
20    PRINT "YAGI ANTENNA DESIGN PROGRAM"
25    PRINT "Enter the frequency for which the antenna is to be desig
      ned"
30    INPUT "     in megahertz: ",F
35    PRINT:PRINT
40    PRINT "For ";F;" megahertz the lengths of the element are:"
50    PRINT "ELEMENT NUMBER","LENGTH IN INCHES"
51    A=466.667/F:D=A*.05*A:B=11.52*A
53    W=6*A:X=4.32*A:E=11.28*A
55    Y=4.8*A:G=3.6*A:L=4.8*A
57    C=11.4*A:Z=11.46*A
59    R=5*W+X+G+Y+L+.333
60    PRINT "1",D
70    PRINT "2",B
80    PRINT "The boom"
90    PRINT "4",E
100   PRINT "5",E
110   PRINT "6",A
120   PRINT "7",Z
130   PRINT "8",E
140   PRINT "9",E
150   PRINT "10",E
160   INPUT "Press RETURN to continue ",A$
165   PRINT:PRINT
170   PRINT "ELEMENT SPACING:"
180   PRINT "ELEMENT NUMBER:","SPACING IN INCHES:"
190   PRINT "1-2",L
200   PRINT "2-3",X
210   PRINT "3-4",W
220   PRINT "4-5",W
230   PRINT "5-6",W
240   PRINT "6-7",Y
250   PRINT "7-8",Y
260   PRINT "8-9",W
270   PRINT "9-10",W
280   PRINT "The boom is ";C;" inches long (";C/12;" feet long)"
290   INPUT Q$
```

where E_{OUT} = output voltage
E_{IN} = input voltage

Such computations would be helpful to the serious audiophile. Also of interest to the audiophile would be a formula used to compute the inductance of a straight-wound speaker wire:

$$L = .0021\,[2.303 \log_{10} (41/d) - .75]$$

where L = inductance (μH)
d = diameter of wire (cm)
l = length of conductor (cm)

Evaluation Routine for a Program of Boolean Function. AND, OR, NOT, and the other logic statements could be evaluated as a program; the circuit status at each step would be output.

Ohm's Law Calculation. A computer can

be used to determine the unknown value.

$$E = IR$$

where R = resistance (ohms)
E = voltage
I = current

Resistor or Capacitor Color Codes. An ideal program for the novice in electronics would output the value for a resistor or capacitor given the color from a component.

Inductance Bridge Calculation. Given this

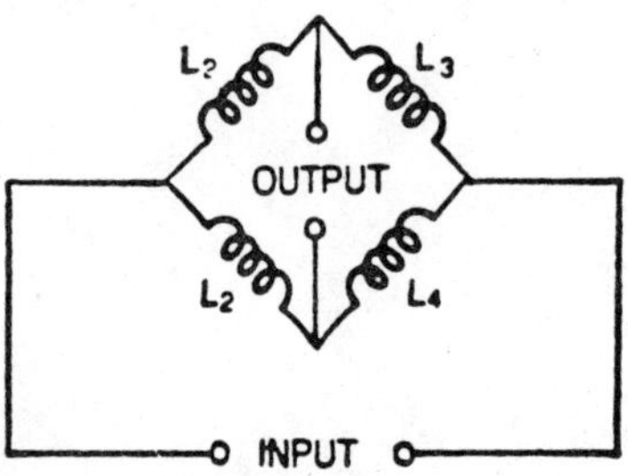

design, if any three values are known the fourth may be calculated:

$$L_1 = L_2L_3/L_2$$
$$L_2 = L_1L_4/L_3$$
$$L_3 = L_1L_4/L_2$$
$$L_4 = L_2L_3/L_1$$

RL Equivalent Impedance Calculation. The program in Listing 4-12 will calculate equivalent impedances.

Voltage Divider Calculation (ac). The program in Listing 4-13 will calculate the modules and phase of the angular frequencies you enter.

Logic Circuit Analysis. The purpose of the program in Listing 4-14 is to simulate the operation of a simple logic circuit. The circuitry (gates and connecting lines or *nodes*) is described to the computer along with the input states to the circuit (on and off are represented as 1 and 0 respectively). Next, the program determines what the resultant states of nodes will be throughout the circuit fol-

Listing 4-12. Resistance-Inductance Equivalent Impedance Program.

```
10      REM LISTING4.12 - The RL Equivalent Impedance Program
90      FULLW 2:CLEARW 2:GOTOXY 1,1
100     PRINT "RL EQUIVALENT IMPEDANCE"
110     PRINT "Answers a question such as 'What is the equivalent imped
        ance of a"
120     PRINT "300 OHM resistor and a 30 millihenry inductor at a frequ
        ency of"
130     PRINT "2000 hertz?'"
140     INPUT "Enter resistance in OHMs ",R
150     INPUT "Enter inductance in millihenries ",IND
160     INPUT "Enter frequency ",FREQ
170     equ=(2*3.141582#*FREQ*IND*.001)*(1/(SIN(ATN((2*3.141592#*FREQ*I
        ND*.001)/R))))
180     PRINT "The equivalent impedance=";EQU
190     INPUT Q$
```

Listing 4-13. Alternating Current Voltage Divider Program.

```
10      REM LISTING4.13 - The A/C Voltage Divider Program
90      FULLW 2:CLEARW 2:GOTOXY 1,1
100     PRINT "A/C VOLTAGE DIVIDER CALCULATIONS"
```

```
110    PRINT "determines the modulus and phase"
120    INPUT "Enter the angular frequency ",A
130    R1=1000000!:R2=0:I1=0:I2=1/(A*.000001)
140    R=(R2*(R1+R2)+I2*(I1+I2)/(R1+R2)*(R1+R2)+(I1+I2)*(I1+I2))
150    I=(-R2*(I1+I2)+(R1+R1)*I2)/((R1+R1)*(R1+R1)+(I1+I2)*(I1+I2))
160    C=SQR(R*R+I*I)
170    D=180*ATN(I/R)/3.14159
180    PRINT "ANGULAR FREQUENCY","MODULUS","PHASE"
190    PRINT A,,C,D
200    PRINT
210    INPUT "Calculate another (Y/N) ";A$:IF A$="Y" OR A$="y" THEN 12
       0
220    END
```

Listing 4-14. Logic Circuit Analysis Program.

```
10     REM LISTING4.14 - The Logic Circuit Analysis Program
20     FULLW 2:CLEARW 2:GOTOXY 1,1
25     PRINT "LOGIC CIRCUIT ANALYSIS PROGRAM"
30     DIM F(3000)
40     FOR X=1 TO 7
50     READ X(X)
60     NEXT X:READ A1,A2
65     A(9)=25
70     B$="AND OR  INV NAND NOR XOR XNOR"
80     PRINT
90     PRINT "SELECT: 1) ENTER A CIRCUIT"
100    PRINT "         2) ENTER SPECIFIED STATES FOR NODES"
110    PRINT "         3) ANALYZE CIRCUIT OPERATION"
120    PRINT "         4) OUTPUT THE STATES OF NODES"
130    PRINT "         5) OUTPUT THE CIRCUIT"
135    INPUT "         6) END PROGRAM ",A3
140    ON A3 GOTO 150,350,500,1300,1500,1720
145    GOTO 80
150    INPUT "SELECT: 1) NEW CIRCUIT, 2) OLD CIRCUIT ",X
155    IF X=2 THEN 190
160    FOR A4=8 TO 511
170    F(A2+A4)=0
180    NEXT A4
190    PRINT
200    INPUT "Enter the label ",A5:A5=8*A5
205    IF A5<=0 THEN 80
210    FOR A4=0 TO 7
220    F(A5+A4+A2)=0
230    NEXT A4:A6=0
240    INPUT "Enter the gate ",W$
250    IF W$="REDO" THEN 190
260    IF W$="AND" THEN A6=1
261    IF W$="OR" THEN A6=2
262    IF W$="INV" THEN A6=3
263    IF W$="NAND" THEN A6=4
264    IF W$="NOR" THEN A6=5
265    IF W$="XOR" THEN A6=6
266    IF W$="XNOR" THEN A6=7
270    IF A6=0 THEN 240
```

```
300   F(A2+A5)=A6:A5=A5+1
310   INPUT "Enter the node ",A6
320   IF A6<>0 THEN 300 ELSE 200
350   INPUT "SELECT: 1) REDO OR BEGIN, 2) CONTINUE ",X
360   IF X=2 THEN 400
365   IF X<>1 THEN 350
370   PRINT : FOR A4=1 TO 255
380   F(A1+A4)=255
390   NEXT A4
400   INPUT "Enter the node ",A6
405   IF A6<=0 THEN 80
410   INPUT "Enter the state ",A7
420   F(A1+A6)=A7
430   GOTO 400
500   A8=0
520   A8=A8+1:PRINT "NO. ";A8
525   A9=0
530   FOR A4=1 TO 63
540   A6=F(A4*8+A2)
545   IF A6=0 THEN 950
550   ON A6 GOTO 600,650,700,750,800,850,900
600   B=0:GOSUB 1180
610   GOTO 920
650   B=1:GOSUB 1180
660   GOTO 920
700   B1=F(A1+F(A2+2+8*A4))
710   GOSUB 980
720   GOTO 920
750   B=0:GOSUB 1180
760   GOSUB 980
770   GOTO 920
800   B=1:GOSUB 1180
810   GOSUB 980
820   GOTO 920
850   GOSUB 1110
860   GOTO 920
900   GOSUB 1110
910   GOSUB 980
920   IF B1=F(A1+F(8*A4+1+A2)) THEN 950
930   A9=1
940   F(A1+F(A2+8*A4+1))=B1
950   NEXT A4
960   IF A9=1 THEN 520
970   GOTO 80
980   IF B1>1 THEN 1000
990   B1=1-B1:RETURN
1000  B1=257-B1:RETURN
1110  B2=F(A1+F(8*A4+2+A2))
1120  B3=F(A1+F(8*A4+3+A2))
1130  IF B2<>0 AND B<>0 THEN 1140 ELSE B1=B2+B3:RETURN
1140  IF B2-1<>0 AND B3-1<>0 THEN 1150 ELSE B1=B3*B2:GOSUB 980
1145  RETURN
1150  B1=1
1160  IF B3=B2 THEN B1=0
1170  RETURN
1180  B1=1-B
1190  FOR B4=2 TO 7
1200  B2=F(8*A4+B4+A2)
1210  IF B2=0 THEN 1260
```

```
1220  B5=F(B2+A1)
1230  IF B5<>B THEN 1240 ELSE B1=B:RETURN
1240  IF B1+B5<>257 THEN 1250 ELSE B1=B:RETURN
1250  IF B5=1-B THEN 1260 ELSE B1=B5
1260  NEXT B4
1270  RETURN
1300  A9=1
1310  FOR A4=1 TO 255
1320  IF F(A4+A1)>1 THEN 1400
1330  PRINT A4;":  ";F(A4+A1)
1400  NEXT A4
1410  PRINT
1420  GOTO 90
1500  FOR A4=1 TO 63
1510  A6=F(8*A4+A2)
1520  IF A6=0 THEN 1700
1530  PRINT A4;TAB(4);
1540  A9=10:PRINT MID$(B$,A6*4-3,4);
1550  FOR B4=1 TO 7
1560  A6=F(8*A4+A2+B4)
1570  IF A6=0 THEN 1610
1580  PRINT TAB(A9);A6;
1590  A9=4+A9
1600  NEXT B4
1610  PRINT
1700  NEXT A4
1710  GOTO 90
1720  INPUT Q$:END
2000  DATA 1,4,6,9,13,16,19,23
2001  DATA 768,1025
```

lowing all logic "decisions." Essentially, this program allows you to design and test a logic circuit without breadboarding it.

The program recognizes the following gates: AND, OR, INV, NAND, exclusive OR (abbreviated XOR), and exclusive NOR (abbreviated XNOR); up to 64 gates and 255 nodes may be used in one circuit. To begin, the program will allow you to input a circuit; answer 1 for a new circuit to the first question. Next, the program will request a *label* for the first gate, which may be any gate in the circuit. This label is simply a distinguishing number (any number) you want for the gate. Now, input the gate type AND, OR, etc.), and then input the identifying nodes connected to the gate (first the output node and then the input nodes). For example, to describe the illustrated circuit, the following sequence could be used:

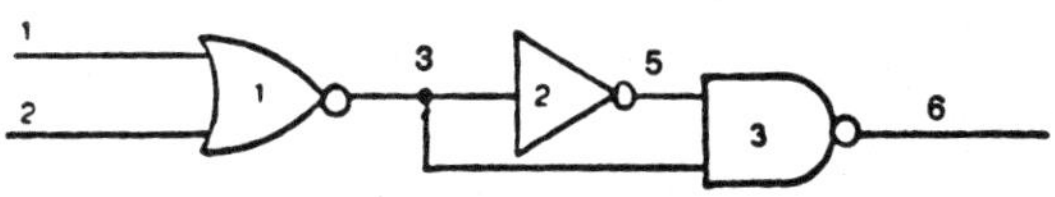


```
SELECT:  1) NEW CIRCUIT
         2) OLD CIRCUIT?1

ENTER THE LABEL?1
ENTER THE GATE? NOR
ENTER THE NODE?3
ENTER THE NODE?1
ENTER THE NODE?2
ENTER THE NODE?0
```

(0 is used here to mean go to next gate)

```
ENTER THE LABEL?2
```

```
ENTER THE GATE?INV
ENTER THE NODE?5
ENTER THE NODE?5
ENTER THE NODE?3
ENTER THE NODE?0

ENTER THE LABEL?3
ENTER THE GATE?NAND
ENTER THE NODE?6
ENTER THE NODE?5
ENTER THE NODE?3
ENTER THE NODE?0
```

Remember to enter the output node for each gate first, followed by the input nodes.

After describing the circuit, the logic states of various nodes will be described. Simply type the number of the node and its initial state (1 or 0). Usually, only the input nodes are described.

Finally, the program analyses the operation of the circuit, outputting the state of each node after the circuit has been completed. The circuit is analyzed according to standard logic tables. In this manner, the professional or hobbyist can test circuit operation without breadboarding.

Additional Applications for Electrical Engineers. The following list includes a number of other areas in which the microcomputer can make the lives of those who work with electricity easier.

- Transistor configuration conversion
- Resistive attenuator design
- Smith chart conversions
- Phase shift oscillator design
- Dc bias analysis
- Waveform limits determination
- Plotting of waveforms
- Plate resistance/ transconductance calculations
- Gauss calculations
- Reactance chart calculations
- Design of controlled rectifier circuits
- Integrated circuit current-source design
- Solution of resistive networks
- Rf amplifier analysis
- Bipolar junction transistor analysis
- Complex matrix calculations as used in electrical engineering
- Wheatstone bridge design

Civil Engineering

Civil engineers will find small computers useful for performing the following functions.

- Moment of inertia calculation
- Vector statics
- Section properties
- Stress on an element or beam
- Static equilibrium about a point

Chemical Engineering

Chemical engineers can use small computers for the following:

- Ideal gas equation of state
- Conservation of energy calculations
- Heat exchanger analysis
- Curve fitting
- Hydrocarbon combustion calculations

Machine Design

Machine designers can use computers to do the following:

- Constant acceleration calculations, relation to time and velocity
- Kinetic energy determination
- Critical shaft speed calculation
- Cam design functions
- Gear and spring calculations/design
- RPM/torque/power computation
- Tachometer/dwell meter calculation: Your oscilloscope can be converted into a tachometer and dwell meter in conjunction with your computer. The following information must be input to the computer to determine engine RPM and dwell angle:

  a. Number of cylinders in the engine
  b. Interval in milliseconds for open ignition points

c. Interval in milliseconds for closed ignition points

Factors b and c are determined using the oscilloscope. (RPM may also be calculated using the factors of tire diameter, gear ratio, and vehicle speed.)

$$\text{ignition pulse frequency} = \frac{\text{RPM} \times \text{No. Cylinders}}{120}$$

Chapter 5

Educational Applications

One of the most important uses for a personal computer is certainly education. The acronym *CAI*, which stands for Computer Assisted Instruction, is often used. Not only can the computer serve as a drill and practice machine for teaching subjects ranging from the alphabet to Schrödinger wave equations, but it can teach the fundamentals of computer programming and prepare the learner for a career and for the computerized future.

Needless to say, we all have memories of learning addition and subtraction, repeating spelling words until we spelled them correctly, and memorizing dates of important historical events. Most of us considered this to be one of the boring essentials of elementary education, and our attention span was accordingly short.

With the addition of the computer to education, this is no longer the case. Although the subject matter has not changed, the method of drill and practice has become much more entertaining with the computer. Countless studies have shown that computerized education makes learning more interesting and is more effective. The task of learning school subjects has become colorful, individualized, and in some cases exciting. The students have instant feedback from the computer so that they know whether their answers are right or wrong and can build from that point; this kind of immediate feedback has been shown to be an effective learning tool.

Computer programs designed for drill and practice are usually capable of providing questions at various levels of difficulty. With simple multiplication, for example, problems with single-digit, double-digit, or even triple-digit (or more) multiplication can be provided. In this way, the student learns his basic multiplication tables before tackling 472 × 952. The computer can either randomly generate these problems or choose them from a large collection stored in memory. As the student masters a certain number of problems at the beginning level, he can advance at his own pace to succeeding levels. If he encounters difficulty at a particular level, the computer provides more of the same kinds of problems or offers help. The computer can even be programmed to remember what level a student has achieved and can begin from that point the next time he uses the program.

Each time the student answers a question, the computer informs him whether the answer is right or wrong. If the answer is correct, the student can be awarded with a picture of a smiling face, a colorful, animated display, or an encouraging message. If the student responds incorrectly, the computer offers a gentle correction, which may be humorous to keep the learning experience enjoyable rather than painful.

Computer drill and practice systems have been applied to every educational area from preschool to college level. Some programs make use of computer graphics for those situations in which "a picture is worth a thousand words." Newer systems make use of random access video disk players in which short video segments can be selected by the computer.

Certainly one of the best ways to learn about computer operation and programming is to purchase a personal computer. Not only can a child learn how to program computers to do simple (or even complex!) tasks, but he can also learn how to think logically and how to draw conclusions based on fact and analysis rather than on guesswork or emotions. To be able to define and analyze a problem, and develop a set of computer instructions to solve it is a considerable accomplishment and is certainly applicable in many areas other than computer programming. Children and adults also need to become familiar with computer operation, capabilities, and programming in preparation for our increasingly computerized world.

Caveat emptor. Software publishers have discovered that there's no surer way to a parent's pocketbook than to sell the notion that using a personal computer will improve a child's mind. If you intend to purchase a "professionally" prepared program, ask for a demonstration before spending that $30. Beware of flim-flam floppies, snake oil, and superhype. You may want to consult *Software Reports*, which evaluates 382 educational programs in 20 subject areas in terms of content, ease of use, entertainment, and other criteria. It's available from many computer stores and by mail from Allenbach Industries, 2101 Las Palmas Dr., Carlsbad, CA 92008. Additionally, many of the popular home computing magazines carry regular reviews of educational software.

APPLICATION IDEAS

The educational uses for personal computers are unlimited; a few of the possible ways of using the computer to instruct yourself, your children, or your friends include the following. You may wish to incorporate these ideas in programs that you can sell to others.

- Create a program describing how to program computers in BASIC or another language such as assembly language or Fortran, etc. with step-by-step examples.
- Create a story-building program for youngsters in which the computer randomly selects individual story parts and combines them to produce a different story each time. Questions could be asked to test reading comprehension, grammar, and writing skills. For example, the program could produce a personalized story for a child using his or her name. Occasionally, questions such as this should be displayed:

Johnny, should I write the next sentence as
1. "Johnny and I went to the park."
or
2. "I and Johnny went to the park."

  If the child answers correctly, the computer reply could be "O.K., that's correct." A wrong answer could be explained—"No that's wrong. The person who is talking should place the 'I' last, after the names of other people."
- Create an IQ builder program to familiarize people with the types of questions and problem solving methods used on tests such as the Scholastic Aptitude Test, Civil Service tests, and the American College Assessment test. Research has shown that familiarization with the tests can improve performance considerably. Sample questions are readily available in test-preparation books.
- Create a future-potential evaluation program designed to quiz high school or college students

about their talents, interests, and abilities. The program could direct them toward promising occupational careers based upon this information.

- Computerize psychological questionnaires, which are often found in popular magazines and books for recreational and education use. Tests particularly suited for computerization are those requiring tedious calculation to analyze. For instance, this quiz is designed to test your "happiness quotient" and could be easily computerized:

Answer each question as true or false.

1. My work is usually fulfilling or interesting.
2. I have a good ability to relax.
3. I can enjoy happiness in little things easily.
4. I seldom envy other people.
5. My moods have great fluctuation.
6. I have a great desire to change either my location, family situation, or job.
7. I usually sleep well and don't feel tired in the morning.
8. I periodically "blow my top" without knowing the real reason.
9. I am usually a pessimistic person.
10. I cannot have happiness without others being around me.

Scoring:

Start with zero, add one point for each true answer to questions 1, 2, 3, 4, 7 and add one point for each false answer to questions 5, 6, 8, 9, 10. Multiply the total by 10 to determine percentage happiness (average score is approximately 50).

An ambitious programmer could program the computer to print out an analysis of the subject based on his answers. Such a program would make use of stock phrases to be used for many possible combinations of answers and could read like this:

If you don't derive much pleasure from little things or if you regularly lose your temper (3 and 8), you should give some attention to your attitudes. Is your social situation the cause of the trouble (6) or is it your job situation (1)? Often, the simple recognition of this difficulty will serve to clear up the situation. The person who is truly happy can find happiness while alone (10) and isn't envious (4). The moody person (5 and 9) can often benefit from the advice of a counselor.

- Create a spelling program that would allow you to input and store words. Words would be randomly selected and flash on the screen from .1 to 10 seconds. The player must then type in the word from memory.

COMPUTER ASSISTED INSTRUCTION

Computer assisted instruction (CAI) refers to the use of a computer as a teaching device. Graphics, text, or questions can be presented on the screen. The simple program presented is designed to ask a question of any subject, wait for a response in Listing 5-1, determine whether or not the answer was correct, and keep track of progress. Two incorrect answers are allowed before the correct answer is given; change line 100 if this is not desired.

Sample data for a quiz about computers could be as follows:

```
300 DATA IS YOUR COMPUTER CONSIDERED A MICROCOMPUTER OR A MINICOMPUTER, MICROCOMPUTER
310 DATA WHAT DOES CPU STAND FOR, CENTRAL PROCESSING UNIT
```

The question comes first in the DATA statements and is immediately followed by a comma and the answer.

COMPUTER TUTOR

You can use your computer to assist you in the memorization of lists, vocabulary words, and other types of abstract information. For instance, the computer could quiz you in flashcard fashion from a list of vocabulary words, displaying each randomly selected word individually. Once you have glanced at a word, and attempted to recite the definition to yourself (or to the computer), press the

Listing 5-1. General CAI Program.

```
10    REM LISTINGS5.01 - General CAI Program
15    FULLW 2:CLEARW 2:GOTOXY 1,1
20    PRINT "GENERAL COMPUTER-ASSISTED INSTRUCTION PROGRAM-"
25    PRINT "Questions and answers are contained in the data
      statements."
30    PRINT "CAI - to stop at any point type STOP as an answer"
50    Y=0:Z=0:N=3:REM N=the number of questions in the data
      statements
60    INPUT "Press RETURN to begin",A$:CLEARW 2:GOTOXY 1,1
70    FOR A=0 TO N-1:Y=1
80    READ A$,B$
90    PRINT A$
100   INPUT C$:IF C$="STOP" THEN 180
110   IF C$=B$ THEN 170 ELSE 130
120   GOTO 180
130   IF Y=2 THEN 160
140   PRINT "Incorrect answer...please try again":Y=Y+1
150   GOTO 100
160   PRINT "The answer was: ":PRINT B$:Z=Z+1
170   NEXT A
180   PRINT "You answered ";A-Z;" or ";(A-Z)/N*100;"% questions
      correctly"
190   PRINT "and ";Z;" questions were answered incorrectly."
200   INPUT "Try again (Y/N)";A$
210   IF A$="Y" THEN 50
220   END
230   DATA HOW MANY BYTES IN A KILOBYTE,1024
240   DATA IS YOUR COMPUTER CONSIDERED A MICROCOMPUTER OR MINI
      COMPUTER,MICROCOMPUTER
250   DATA WHAT DOES CPU STAND FOR, CENTRAL PROCESSING UNIT
```

enter or return key. The definition could be automatically displayed afterwards at this point. If you did not know the correct definition, you could type "w" (wrong) to indicate this mistake, and the word and definition could be stored for review. If you were right, you would simply press the enter or return key and the next word would be displayed. Additionally, the number and percentage of correct answers could be maintained.

The high school or college student should find computerized quizzes helpful in memorizing such information as

1. Historical names, dates, and places—presidents, authors, inventors . . .
2. Parts and functions of the anatomy
3. Mathematical or chemical formulae
4. Verses in literature
5. Spellings or definitions of difficult words
6. Trigonometric identities
7. Geography—states, capitals, countries
8. Technical and scientific terminology
9. Anglo/metric unit conversions

EDUCATIONAL SIMULATIONS

Because of the ability of the computer to perform calculations rapidly, they are well-suited to be used for educational and mathematical simulations. Simulations for educating young people include the following:

The Manhattan Indian Problem. This simulation teaches the principle of compounded interest. As the story goes, the new world settlers paid the Indians $24 for the entire island of Manhattan in 1626. Today, this property is worth millions of dollars. But, what would have happened if the settlers had deposited the $24 in a savings account at 6 percent interest compounded daily? How much would that account be worth today? A computer generated chart listing the value of the account after each decade would serve to illustrate the geometrical growth rate involved and the surprising answer to the Manhattan Indian Problem. Use the formula $A_1 = A(1+r)^n$ where A_1 = value acquired (capital + interest), A = original investment, v = interest rate, and n = number of years.

The Growth of an Amoeba Colony. This simulation simulates the growth of a colony of amoebas (one-celled organisms) in a jar with a limited food supply. The reproduction rate will cause the colony population to double per unit time. The formula for geometric progressions is

$$S = a \times \frac{q^n - 1}{q - 1}$$

where S = sum, a = the first term (in this case = 1), q = the ratio for successive values (in this case = 2 because the colony doubles with each generation). However, pollution and limited food supply will decrease colony size at an increasing rate. Otherwise, within one month's time, a single bacterium (about one-tenth of a millimeter in diameter) dividing at a rate of five times a day would produce a volume of organisms equal to *one million times the volume of the sun*, provided food and space were available! A numerical listing or plot of the population versus time could be generated by the computer. Will the colony reach equilibrium (a stable state)? Along parallel lines, simulations of a large-scale (for example, ecological balance in a forest) could be undertaken.

The Laws of Physics. The demonstration of some laws of physics could take the form of graphic illustrations of planetary orbits, acceleration due to gravity, motion of a pendulum, and so on.

A popular physics demonstration program called "The Lunar Landing Simulation" is presented in Listing 5-2. In this simulation, the

Listing 5-2. Lunar Lander Simulation Program.

```
10      REM LISTINGS5.02 - The Lunar Landing Simulation Program
15      FULLW 2:CLEARW 2:GOTOXY 1,1
20      PRINT "LUNAR LANDING SIMULATION"
30      PRINT "------------------------"
40      PRINT
50      INPUT "Do you want instructions (Y/N)";A$
60      IF A$="N" THEN 310
70      IF A$<>"Y" THEN 50
80      PRINT
90      PRINT "You are landing on the moon and have taken over manual"
100     PRINT "control 500 feet above a good landing spot.  You have a"
110     PRINT "downward velocity of 50 ft/sec."
120     PRINT "120 units of fuel remain."
130     PRINT :FOR X=1 TO 10000:NEXT
140     PRINT "Here are the rules that govern your space vehicle:"
150     PRINT "(1) after each second, the height, velocity and
        remaining"
160     PRINT "fuel will be reported:"
170     PRINT "(2) after the report, a '?' will appear.  Enter the"
180     PRINT "number of units of fuel you wish to burn during the"
190     PRINT "next second.  Each unit of fuel will slow your descent"
200     PRINT "by 1 ft/sec."
```

```
205   FOR X=1 TO 10000:NEXT X
210   PRINT "(3) The maximum thrust of your engine is 30 ft/sec/sec
      or"
220   PRINT "30 units of fuel per second."
230   PRINT "(4) When you contact the lunar surface, your descent"
240   PRINT "engine will automatically cut off and you will be"
250   PRINT "given a report of your landing speed and remaining"
260   PRINT "fuel."
265   FOR X=1 TO 10000:NEXT X
270   PRINT "(5) If you run out of fuel, the '?' will no longer
      appear,"
280   PRINT "but your second by second report will continue until"
290   PRINT "you contact the lunar surface."
300   PRINT
310   PRINT "BEGIN LANDING PROCEDURE........."
320   PRINT "G O O D  L U C K"
330   PRINT
340   PRINT "SEC FEET    SPEED   FUEL","PLOT OF DISTANCE"
350   PRINT
360   T=0
370   H=500
380   V=50
390   F=120
400   IF B=0 THEN 430
410   PRINT T;TAB(4)H;TAB(12)V;TAB(20)F;TAB(29)"I";TAB(H/12+28);"**"
420   GOTO 440
430   PRINT T;TAB(4)H;TAB(12)V;TAB(20)F;TAB(29)"I";TAB(H/12+29)"**"
440   INPUT B
450   IF B<0 THEN 600
460   IF B>30 THEN 600
470   IF B>F THEN 490
480   GOTO 500
490   B=F
500   V1=V-B+5
510   F=F-B
520   H=H-.5*(V+V1)
530   IF H<=0 THEN 620
540   T=T+1
550   V=V1
560   IF F>0 THEN 400
570   IF B=0 THEN 590
580   PRINT "*** OUT OF FUEL ***"
590   PRINT T;TAB(4)H;TAB(12)V;TAB(20)F;TAB(29)"I";TAB(H/12+29)"**"
600   B=0
610   GOTO 500
620   PRINT "*** CONTACT ***"
630   H=H+.5*(V+V1)
640   IF B=5 THEN 670
650   D=(-V+SQR(V*V+H*(10-2*B)))/(5-B)
660   GOTO 680
670   D=H/V
680   V1=V+(5-B)*D
690   PRINT "TOUCHDOWN AT ";T+D;" SECONDS."
700   PRINT "LANDING VELOCITY=";V1;" FT/SEC."
710   PRINT F;" units of fuel remaining."
720   IF V1<>0 THEN 750
730   PRINT "CONGRATULATIONS  A PERFECT LANDING"
740   PRINT "YOUR LICENSE WILL BE RENEWED...LATER"
750   IF ABS(V1)<5 THEN 780
```

```
760   PRINT "*** SORRY, BUT YOU BLEW IT ***"
770   PRINT "APPROPRIATE CONDOLENCES WILL BE SENT TO YOUR NEXT OF
      KIN."
780   INPUT "Another mission (Y/N) ";A$
790   IF A$="Y" THEN 310
800   IF A$<>"N" THEN 780
810   PRINT
820   PRINT "CONTROL OUT."
830   PRINT
840   END
```

learner must control the flight of an Apollo moon lander under the influence of gravity. Limits on oxygen, food, and fuel supply must be contended with also. Similar programs have been written to graphically simulate the piloting of an airplane.

Simulations on a large scale that require extensive preparation have also been accomplished on personal computer. These include the following.

The Acoustics of a Room. The acoustics of a room could be mathematically simulated if such parameters as the dampening effects of the walls, the shape of the room and its contents, the location of the sound source were provided; this could be useful to the architect or stereo-listening perfectionist. For example, in designing a small stereo listening room or studio, concentrations of standing waves cause unequal resonances in different spots within the room. To reduce the nonuniformity of standing waves at lower frequencies, room proportions must be carefully controlled to insure optimum diffusion of sound. Standing waves in a rectangular room are governed by a simple equation that could be modeled on your personal computer:

$$f(n_l, n_w, h_h) = (c/2)\,[(n_l/l)^2 + (n_w w)^2 + (n_h/h)]^{1/2}$$

where c = velocity of sound, and l = length, w = width, h = height of the room; the n's are the mode numbers; the lowest mode number ($n = 1$) represents the lowest frequency resonance appearing, governed by the dimension, and higher n's represent higher frequency resonances. To calculate the frequency of a standing wave along one axis of the room, you set the n values for the other two axes equal to zero. For example, if $n_1 = 1$ and the others equal zero, the formula will give the lowest frequency standing wave along the length of the room. When two terms are nonzero, the standing waves are tangential. To obtain uniformity, the tangential waves are most desirable, the oblique waves are next, and the axial waves are least desirable. Thus, by using this equation, you can adjust room dimensions to provide the most even spacing of axial standing waves together with a preference for tangential waves, thereby allowing the greatest uniformity in frequency.

A Simulation of World Dynamics. This simulation, which is similar to Jay Forrester's Limits to Growth computer simulation, could be accomplished on a small scale. World dynamics involves the interaction of population, pollution, resources, and so on to predict future outcomes.

A Simulation of Astronomical and Physical Theories. This kind of simulation could possibly be accomplished with a personal computer system. Of course, the memory requirements would be very large, and simulation time could be hundreds of hours. See the article "Doing Physics with Microcomputers" in *Physics Today*, December 1983, pp. 25-28. The author describes a Monte Carlo simulation of the three dimensional Ising model for study of phase transitions.

A Simulation of Automotive Fuel Economy. This simulation could include such factors as fuel injection, fuel additives, pollution monitors, etc.

A Simulation That Stages Your Own World Series or Super Bowl. You could use statistical techniques to simulate a game or series of games using stars whose performances are based on their career averages.

ADDITIONAL CAI IDEAS

Examples of teaching programs for a variety of levels are listed below.

Elementary Math Flashcards. Programs designed to increase speed and efficiency in basic mathematics (for example, addition and multiplication) in which a time limit would be set for answering a question.

Word Problems. A program designed to output "random" word problems in mathematics for practice.

Rhymes and Riddles. In this learning game, young children could try to unscramble words to form a line from a nursery rhyme or an answer to a riddle.

Fractions. A drill program in recognizing common denominators and adding and multiplying fractions.

Spell. A program that teaches the student to recognize commonly misspelled words.

Roots. A guessing/learning game in which the student must guess the square or cube root of a random number.

Kinema. A program in physics that helps the student learn to calculate the path of a projectile.

Gasvol. A plotting/calculating program that draws pressure/volume diagrams of a gas (chemistry and physics use).

Logic Reasoning. This program tests the student on conditional statements, hypotheses, conclusions, deductions, fallacies, and definitions.

Balance. A drill program on balancing chemical equations.

Metric. An exercise in converting between the English and metric systems of units.

Bases. A demonstration program in teaching how to do conversions from one numerical base system to another.

Listing 5-3. Multiplication Drill Program.

```
10      REM LISTING5.03 - The Multiplication Drill Program
20      FULLW 2:CLEARW 2:GOTOXY 1,1
30      RANDOMIZE 0
40      INPUT "MULTIPLICATION DRILL-- Would you like instructions
        (Y/N) ";Z$
50      IF Z$="N" THEN 110
60      IF Z$<>"Y" THEN 40
70      PRINT "I'm going to see how well you can multiply.  When I show
        you"
80      PRINT "a problem, type in the answer and then press RETURN."
90      PRINT "I'll tell you if you are right and will give you a score
        after"
100     INPUT "ten questions. O.K. ";Z$
110     A$="#########.":B$="########."
120     REM
130     FOR X=1 TO 10:X1=X1+1
140     A=INT(RND*10+1):B=INT(RND*10+1)
150     PRINT
160     E=0:PRINT "PROBLEM #";X1
170     GOSUB 190:NEXT X
180     GOTO 480
190     PRINT USING A$;A
200     PRINT "X";:PRINT USING B$;B
210     C=A*B
220     PRINT "-------------------------------"
230     INPUT "=      ";D
240     IF D=C THEN 360
```

```
250   E=E+1
260   IF E=2 THEN M=M+1:PRINT "The answer was: ";C:GOTO 300
270   PRINT "You goofed...try again."
280   GOTO 190
300   F=F+1
310   A(F)=A
320   B(F)=B
330   RETURN
340   REM
360   X2=X2+1:R=INT(RND*5+1)
370   ON R GOTO 380,400,420,440,460
380   PRINT "RIGHT ON!!!"
390   RETURN
400   PRINT "FINE..."
410   RETURN
420   PRINT "GOOD WORD!!!"
430   RETURN
440   PRINT "KEEP IT UP!"
450   RETURN
460   PRINT "EXCELLENT!"
470   RETURN
480   PRINT "Your score is now ";X2;" correct and ";M;" errors.(";INT
      (100-(M/X1)*100);"%)"
490   INPUT "Do you want to continue (Y/N)";Z$
500   IF Z$="Y" THEN 530
505   IF Z$<>"N" THEN 490
510   PRINT "Thanks for playing with me..."
520   END
530   G=0:FOR X=1 TO 10
540   IF (A(X)>0) OR (B(X)>0) THEN G=G+1
550   NEXT X
560   IF G=0 THEN 130
570   PRINT "I didn't forget you missed these:"
580   FOR X=1 TO G
590   A=A(X):B=B(X)
600   GOSUB 190
610   NEXT X
620   GOTO 130
```

Multiplication Drill. The program in Listing 5-3 randomly generates single-digit multiplication problems for practice in memorizing the multiplication tables. It has a variety of randomly selected responses to right and wrong answers and also keeps score. Problems that are answered incorrectly are stored and asked again at the end of the quiz.

Speed Reading/Tachistoscope. A program, such as the one in Listing 5-4, that helps you learn to read faster could be easily implemented by using a timing loop. Lines from a piece of literature could be stored in data statements and flashed momentarily on the screen; only one line at one time should be displayed. The timing loop is simply a FOR-NEXT loop that will require a specified amount of time to be executed (for example, FOR X = 1 TO 500: NEXT X requires approximately 1 second to execute with some forms of BASIC). The amount of time you are given to read each line should be gradually decreased until a speed of several hundred words (for example, 500) per minute is obtained.

A tachistoscope can be used to improve your perception and short-term memory. Psychologist G. Miller reports that anyone should be able to see from five to nine letters in any given brief exposure, whether 1/100 of a second long or 1/2 a second, which shows the limitation in our ability to perceive visual information in brief exposures. In addition,

Listing 5-4. Speed Reading Program.

```
10     REM LISTINGS5.04 - The Speed Reading Program
15     FULLW 2:CLEARW 2:GOTOXY 1,1
20     PRINT "SPEED READING PRACTICE PROGRAM"
30     N=1000:REM set the initial timing per line
40     INPUT "Press RETURN to begin";A$:CLEARW 2:GOTOXY 1,1
50     PRINT "The home computer revolution has arrived...over 50,000
       hobbyists"
60     GOSUB 210
70     PRINT "now own a microcomputer system for personal computing"
80     GOSUB 210
90     PRINT "applications.  Experts predict that the market will
       grow."
100    GOSUB 210
110    PRINT "rapidly until everyone has a computer.  Recently, a
       book "
120    GOSUB 210
130    PRINT "titled THE PERSONAL COMPUTER APPLICATIONS HANDBOOK was"
140    GOSUB 210
150    PRINT "published; the book is filled with potentials ranging"
160    GOSUB 210
170    PRINT "from games to business.
180    GOSUB 210
190    N=N-50
200    INPUT "Try again (Y/N)";A$:IF A$="Y" THEN 20
205    IF A$<>"N" THEN 200 ELSE END
210    FOR X=1 TO N
220    NEXT X:REM timing loop
230    CLEARW 2:GOTOXY 1,1
240    RETURN
```

we are able to see many more letters displayed by the tachistoscope if they form a familiar word instead of an unfamiliar or foreign word. A tachistoscope program could be written for personal confirmation or as a science fair project. The program could offer adjustable speeds, familiar and unfamiliar words, and display of words for confirmation.

Chapter 6

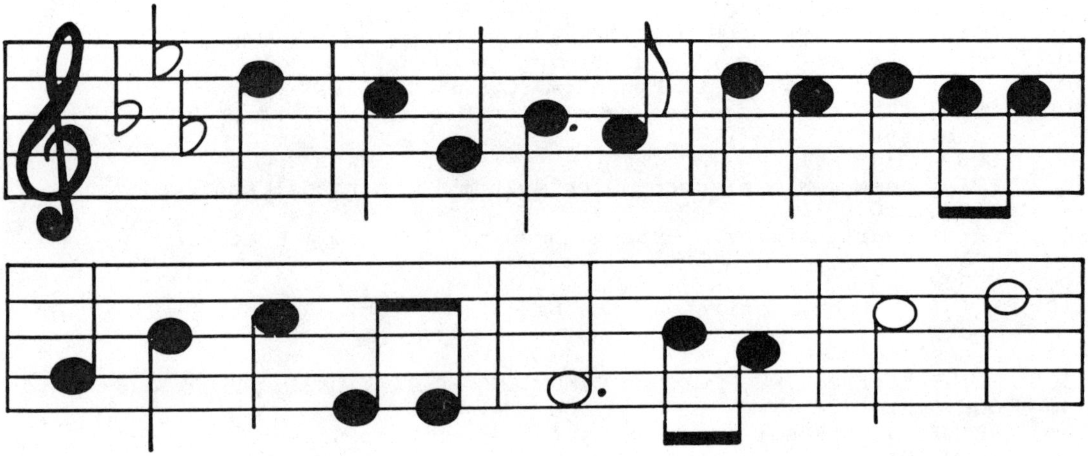

Hobby Applications

Your personal computer can make hobbies, from arts and crafts to photography easier, quicker, and more creative.

THE ARTS

It does not seem possible that a computer can create original art work until you consider the mathematical basis as well as randomness of some art forms. Art is an area in which the personal computer can be used in many different ways—and many of these ways are yet undiscovered.

The Visual Arts

The computer can serve both as a source of inspiration and as a tool for the artist or craftsperson. Below are some of the areas in which a computer can be used.

Mathematical Functions. Plotting or graphing a mathematical function can often produce interesting geometrical designs. Color terminals equipped to plot a grid in full color, each color indicative of the value of the function at each individual point, produce fantastic geometrics. The designs generated can be used in knitting or embroidering, or for producing a geometrical painting. A plotter or graphic pointer may be used for output. A standard printer may be used with the demonstration program in Listing 6-1, which creates plots with a three-dimensional appearance. Figure 6-1 shows some sample output from the three-dimensional plotter program.

Alteration of a Design. A given design (for example, a drawing of a human face or an American flag,) transformed into a series of points on a grid can be manipulated using a mathematical algorithm to produce "modern art" effects. Additionally, one design may be gradually transformed into another, through a series of plots, producing a fascinating result reminiscent of animation.

Kaleidoscope. A kaleidoscopic pattern may be produced by plotting a continuous set of points that wander randomly horizontally and vertically in one of four corners on the screen. The other three

Listing 6-1. Three-Dimensional Plotter Program.

```
10      REM LISTING6.01 - The Three Dimensional Plotter Program
20      REM other functions to try include: S*(COS(Z/16))^2
30      REM the symbol ^ means exponentiation
35      FULLW 2:CLEARW 2:GOTOXY 1,1
40      DEF FNA(Z)=S*EXP(Z*-Z/100)
50      INPUT "Enter scale factor (try 30) ";S
60      INPUT "Ready printer; press RETURN when ready to proceed";A$
65      FOR X=-S TO S STEP S/20:L=0
70      Y1=5*INT(SQR(S^2-X*X)/5)
80      FOR Y=Y1 TO -Y1 STEP -S/6
90      Z=INT(S-5+FNA(SQR(X*X+Y*Y))-.7*Y)
100     IF Z>L THEN L=Z:LPRINT TAB(Z)"+";
110     NEXT Y
120     LPRINT " ":NEXT X:END
```

corners are plotted by "reflecting" the wandering line, drawing in mirror-fashion. An example is shown in Fig. 6-2.

Random Art Patterns. For the ultimate in simplicity, a program could generate random numbers that in turn would cause graphics characters on the screen to turn on or off or would control a pen plotter in "random-walk" fashion. This, however, may exceed the confines of what is considered art. One hobbyist reports using his computer to randomly combine picture elements and then print "landscapes" using a plotter. Figure 6-3 shows an image produced using randomly determined elements.

A/D Converters. Use of an analog/digital converter to digitize and transform real-world events can produce interesting results. For example, one hobbyist interfaced a human dancer to his

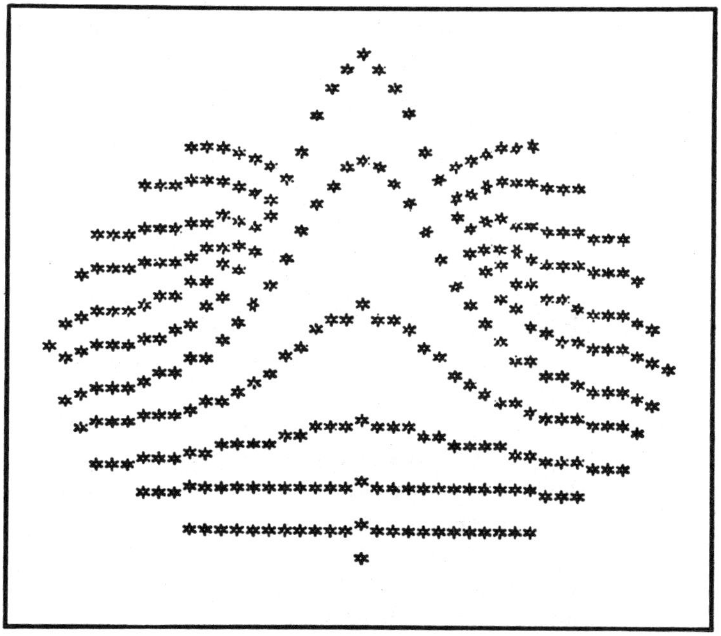

Fig. 6-1. Sample output from the three-dimensional plotter program.

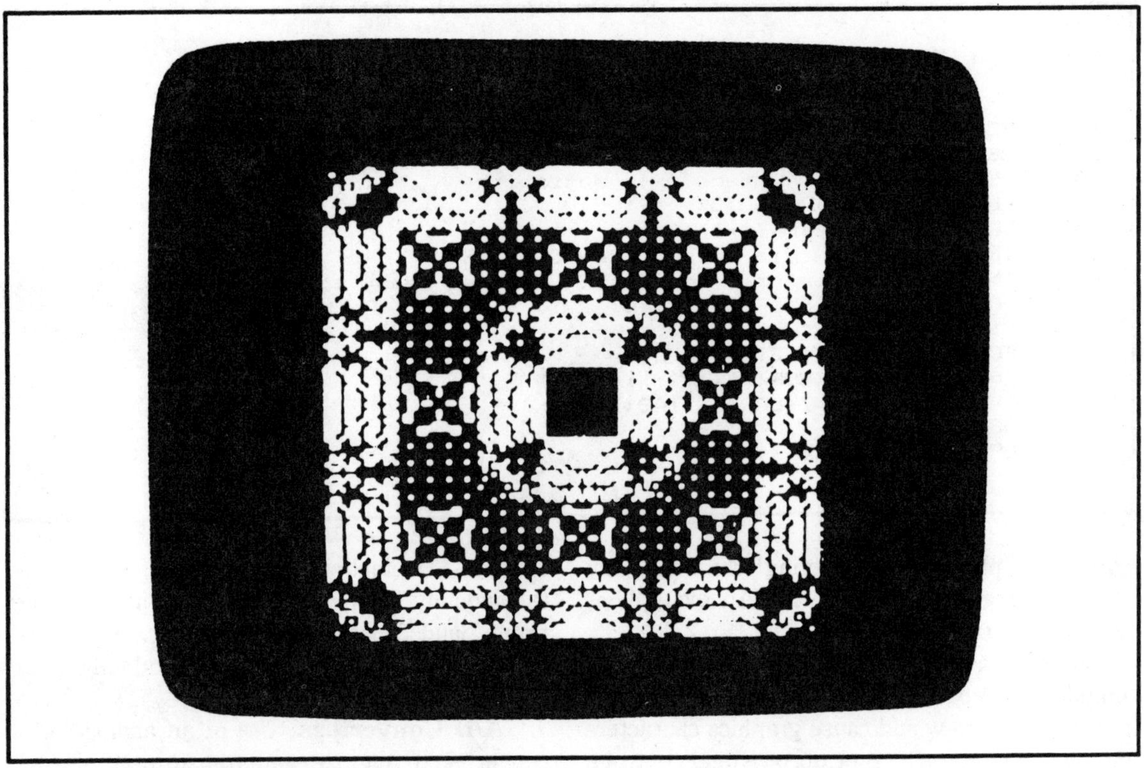

Fig. 6-2. A kaleidoscope pattern.

computer by applying a dozen mercury switches to the dancer's body. The dancer's movements caused the switches to open and close, producing digital signals for the computer. The computer, in turn, created "choreographed music" from the signals.

Anamorphic Art. Anamorphic images are those that appear distorted, but when viewed with a special device or from a unique perspective appear normal. An example of such a special device is a cylindrical mirror placed in the center of the image. The computer may be used to transform a set of points describing a "normal" image into an anamorphic equivalent. For examples of anamorphic art, see Leeman, Fred. *Hidden Images: Games of Perception, Anamorphic Art, Illusion*. New York: Harry N. Abrams, Inc., 1975. Figure 6-4 shows the results of such a program.

Crossword Poetry. An interesting "crossword" of the words from a poem or piece of literature may be created by the computer. A program to create such "art" would scan each word and determine how that word could fit in crossword form with adjacent words:

```
      B U T
W H O     W H E N T H E L E A V E S
  A       A       R
  S E E N N       E
          G       M
                  B
                  L
T H E             I
                  N
                  G
    W I N D ?
        E           T H E     W I N D
        I                       S
        T
        H
        E
    N O R     I     P A S S I N G
                      T H R O U G H
            Y O U
```

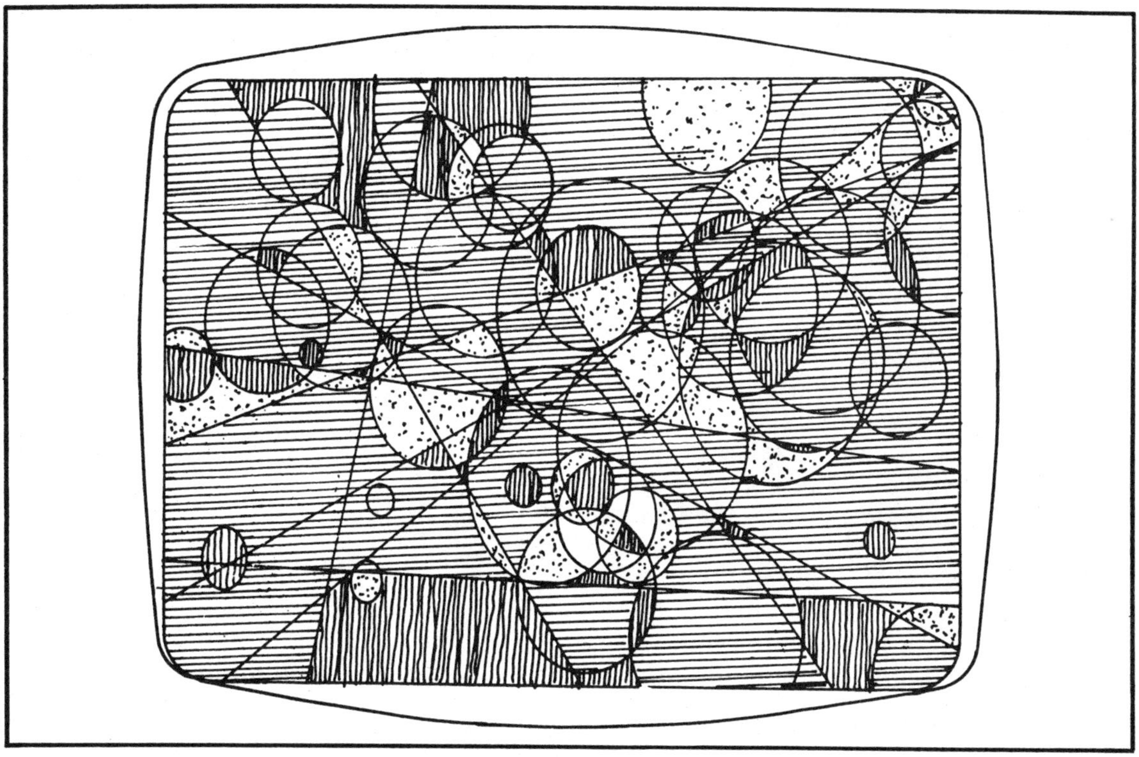

Fig. 6-3. A video image created by a program that randomly placed lines and circles of various sizes on the screen and filled in each area with a random color or texture.

Fig. 6-4. "Computer Curvilinear Projection—Complex and Concave" by Ramon Masters. See *Computer Graphics and Art,* (February, 1978) for a detailed explanation of how these and similar images can be created.

READ AS"Who has seen the wind?
Neither I nor you.
But when the leaves hang trembling,
The wind is passing through."

Textile Patterns. By combining the video graphics characters found on many personal computers into patterns, a textile appearance may be created. This may be considered art in itself or used as a model for a tapestry design. A simple program could select five graphics characters at random and then printout a full line of each graphic character. This pattern would then be repeated; surprisingly good results may be obtained. A more sophisticated program could combine different graphics characters within the line in symmetric fashion. Similarly, new quilting patterns could be designed mathematically. A sample textile pattern program is presented in Listing 6-2.

Perspective Drawing Aid. Given a set of points describing the (x, y, z) dimensions of objects in a picture, the computer could use matrix manipulations to produce a new set of points describing the picture from another perspective or viewpoint. Figure 6-5 shows an example. Additionally, if video graphics or plotting capabilities are available, the new picture could be plotted. Perspective transformations are useful in technical illustration and other art forms as well.

As an example of the perspective transformations that can be accomplished using a large array of points, let (x,y) be a coordinate pair under the "old" coordinate system. Let (x_θ, y_θ) be the center coordinates of the new system rotated through angle θ in relation to the old system. The new coordinates (x', y') may be calculated with these equations:

$$x' = (x - x_\theta) \cos\theta + (y - y_\theta) \sin\theta$$
$$y' = -(x - x_\theta) \sin\theta + (y - y_\theta) \cos\theta$$

A dimension-scaling program would request

Listing 6-2. Textile Pattern Generator Program.

```
10      REM LISTING6.02 - The Textile Generator Program
20      FULLW 2:CLEARW 2:GOTOXY 1,1
30      RANDOMIZE 0
40      PRINT "COMPUTER TEXTILE GENERATOR"
50      PRINT "creates random 'textile' patterns"
60      PRINT "for output on a video screen or"
70      PRINT "graphics printer.  Requires a TVT"
90      PRINT "accessable using 'CHR$(X)'"
100     INPUT "Press RETURN to begin, enter END to finish:";A$
110     IF A$="END" OR A$="end" THEN END
150     N=RND*9+1
160     FOR X=1 TO N
170     A$(X)=CHR$(INT(RND*54+163))
180     NEXT X
190     CLEARW 2:GOTOXY 1,1
200     FOR M=1 TO 6
220     FOR X=1 TO N
240     FOR Y=1 TO 80
260     PRINT A$(X);
270     NEXT Y
275     PRINT ""
280     NEXT X
290     NEXT M
295     PRINT ""
300     GOTO 100
```

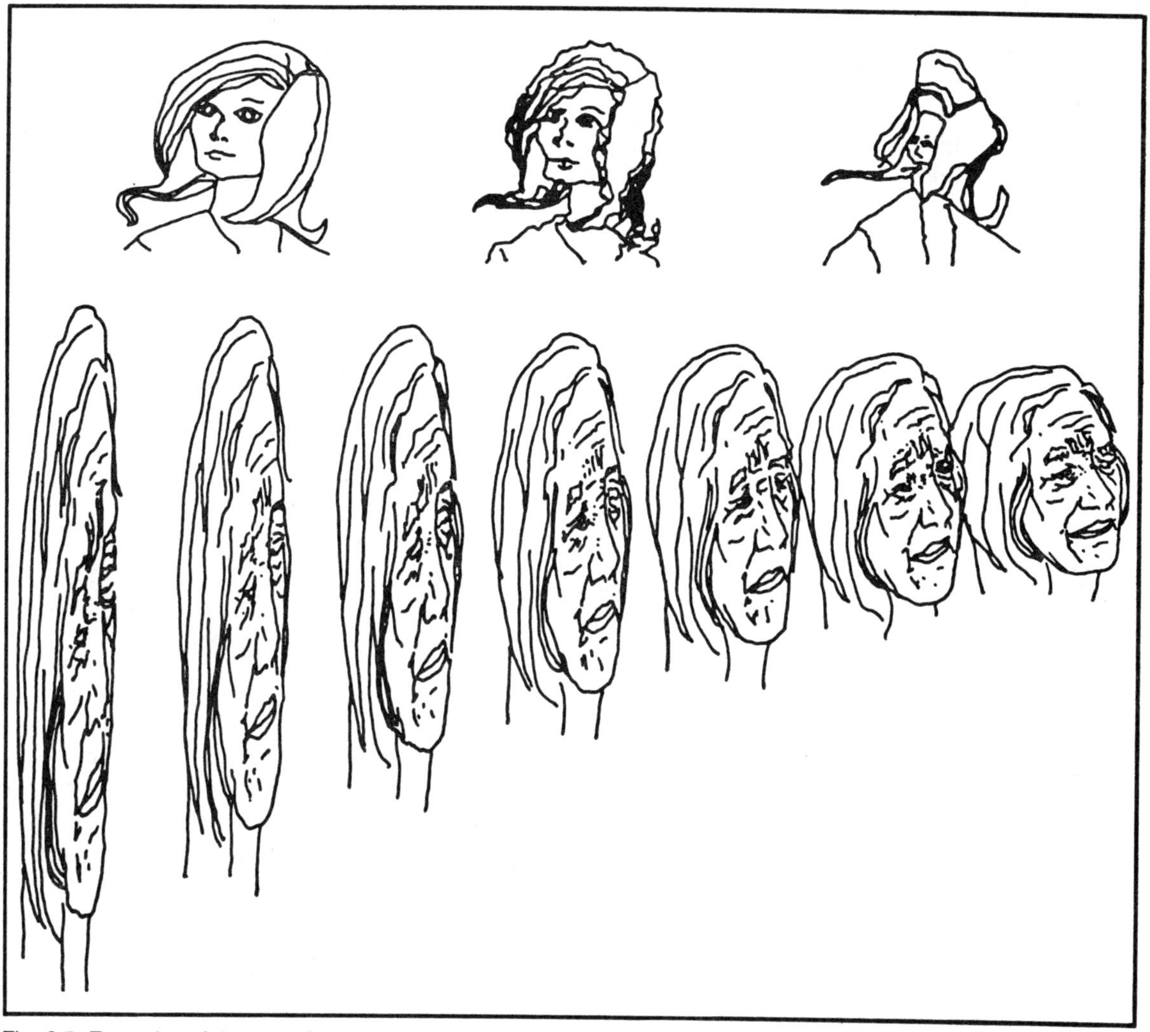

Fig. 6-5. Examples of the use of mathematical algorithms to alter drawings.

the largest dimension of the object and the largest dimension of the drawing of the object; the scaling factor is the ratio of these values. The program would eliminate the headaches of creating a scale drawing by multiplying the input dimensions of the object by the scaling factor to arrive at the scaled down dimensions for the drawing.

Computer as Sculptor. One hobbyist has created a computer-controlled router that can sculpt material in accordance with a set of programmed points (*x*, *y*, *z*). The computer controls the rotation of the sculpturing material (*y* axis) and the horizontal/vertical (*x* and *z* axes) motion of the router by means of servomechanisms. Eliminating one axis, the computer could also control a lathe to produce sculptured furniture legs of exacting proportions, for example.

Computer Painting. A commercial computer-controlled airbrush system is being used to create murals from photos or other graphic images. The image is digitized (through the use of a TV camera and A/D converter) and then painted with much larger proportions by the use of a special (*x*, *y*) "plotting" system, which uses an airbrush in lieu of a pen. An enterprising hobbyist could construct such a system.

Computer Posters. Everyone has seen the "computer portraits" popular at carnivals and shopping malls, in which a television picture of a subject is digitized and output on a line printer. One hobbyist has circumvented the expense of a television digitizer by taking an ordinary photograph and placing a fine grid over it; he assigns each square in the grid a brightness level and inputs this information. The computer prints dark characters or blocks for the squares with a low brightness level and vice versa for squares with a high brightness. Through this tedious and time-consuming process he creates computer posters and portraits without the expense of a television camera and video image digitizer.

A simple silhoutte poster may be created by specifying the number of "X" and space characters to print on each line in DATA statements. For example, to print two spaces, one "X," one space, and one "X" on line number one, you could create a DATA statement that read DATA L1, S2, X1, S1, X1 and use the LEFT$ function to read the first character in each data item. The computer would then print the decoded representation and continue with the next line. The advantage to this method is that it requires less than the use of verbatim PRINT statements would.

The Verbal Arts

What usefulness could there be in creating poems by computer? Unlike humans, computers have the capability of being "completely" random. They are free from the "inspirational" selection of words when composing a poem; "completely" is in quotes because there will always be some bias introduced by the programmer. A computer-generated poem can serve as a stimulus for the human poet. He can elaborate on the poem and extract inspirational clues in composing his own poetic works.

One crude method for generating computer poetry makes use of the following format in randomly selecting words from large lists of nouns, verbs, adjectives, definite articles, prepositions, conjunctions, and adverbs:

TITLE:	Adjective + Noun
FIRST LINE:	Adjective + Noun (plural) + Adverb + Verb (plural, present tense) + Adjective + Noun (plural)
SECOND LINE:	Adjective + Noun (plural) + Verb (plural, present tense) + Adverb + Adjective + Noun (plural)
THIRD LINE:	Article (definite, such as *the*) + Noun (singular) + verb (singular, present tense) + Preposition + Article (definite) + Adjective + Noun (singular)
FOURTH LINE:	Noun (plural) + Verb (plural, present tense) + Conjunction + Article (definite) + Noun (singular)

To ensure some continuity, the second adjective and noun of the first line may be repeated as the first adjective and noun of the second line. One computer-generated poem based on this structure read:

Clear Spirits
Warped trunks frailly dwell delicate leaves
Delicate leaves shudder cunningly intricate lines
The image vanishes to the sharp second
Bee fly against the cloud.

Computers have poetic license too!

Along similar lines, an aphorism generator could create aphorisms *ad infinitum* using the form

"_________ is the_________ of _________"

replacing each blank with a randomly selected noun. The underlying philosophical truism is up to the reader. The program in Listing 6-3 is an outline for an aphorism generator; you supply your own list of nouns.

Listing 6-3. Aphorism Generator Program.

```
10    REM LISTING6.03 - The Aphorism Generator Program
20    DIM A$(50):REM adjust the dimension equal to the number of word
      s in the data datements
25    FULLW 2:CLEARW 2:GOTOXY 1,1
30    FOR X=1 TO 50:READ A$(X):NEXT
40    PRINT A$(INT(RND(1)*50)+1);" IS THE ";A$(INT(RND(1)*50)+1);" OF
      ";A$(INT(RND(1)*50)+1)
50    GOTO 40
60    REM add 40 nouns of your choice to the data statement below
70    DATA SUCCESS, AGONY, MONEY, DEATH, LOVE
80    DATA REWARD, NAIVETTE, FATHER, BEAUTY, SEX
```

The Musical Arts

Within the field of music, the personal computer can be used in a number of different areas. Some of these are listed below.

Music Education. Possible music education applications include the following:

1. A graphic, flashcard-style quiz that could display notes and other musical notation on the scale for identification as practice reading music.
2. A quiz on pronunciations and definitions of music terminology (for example, *andante, diatonic,* and *staccato*).
3. A musical staff drill. A graphic keyboard and staff could be presented, and the computer could select the note on the staff corresponding to the key that is "pressed." Key signature drills could be done in a similar manner.
4. A basic ear-training skills program. A computer capable of producing musical tones could quiz students on recognition of pitches, intervals, chords (major, augmented, diminished, and minor), and scales (major, natural minor, harmonic minor, and melodic minor) and scales (major, natural minor, harmonic minor, melodic minor, whole-tone, and chromatic).
5. A name the tune game. A computer-produced familiar tune can teach identification by sound of the degrees of the scale, using *solfeggio* syllables or scale degree numbers.
6. A wrong-note program. Pitch error-detection can be practiced within various combinations of four-voiced chord types. Following the selection of a chord type, the computer can visually represent the chord and play the sound with one incorrect note. The student must identify the wrong voice and its corresponding pitch.
7. Harmony drills. Computer-produced aural diatonic chord progressions may be taught on various levels of difficulty.
8. Write that tune game. The computer plays a random or preprogrammed series of notes that the student must then reproduce on a video staff or on an interfaced musical keyboard.
9. Chord progressions practice. Students may predict chord progressions and receive feedback from the computer and subsequent visual and/or aural output.
10. Guitar chords practice. Students can practice finger placement required to produce guitar chords, with visual/aural feedback.
11. Famous composers and their music quiz. A quiz-style program could teach famous composer's names, pronunciations, and compositions with the aural output of excerpts from those works.
12. Transposition practice. The student is presented with a short melody to transpose to a randomly selected key. The computer verifies correct transposition.
13. Tuner program. Two computer-produced tones

(separated by less than one half-step) are tuned to match each other by the student, who may select an increase or decrease in one of the tones.

14. Rhythm practice. The student could practice playing rhythm patterns on a keyboard. The computer can analyze them for accuracy, play the passage the way it should be played, and even demonstrate how the student's response differed from the expected response.
15. Composition packages. This program, given the notes of a composition, can display the piece in standard musical notation and actually play it. The student can experiment with tempo, timbre, and musical envelopes. Having control of timbre and musical envelope allows composition of a piece performed by three voices resembling the clarinet, flute, and oboe and demonstrates the interaction between voices.

Music Composition. In the past, computer programs designed to compose music were based more upon random numbers than musical principles. Thus, the songs that were produced could only be compared to a child randomly hitting piano keys. Lately, progress has been made in developing more complex programs that adhere to the "rules of thumb" for composing particular types of music. One program, which used the following rules, was somewhat successful in composing "pop" music.

Basic melody requirements:

1. The first note must be other than a fourth, a flatted fifth, a minor second, or a ninth.
2. An ascending minor second progresses to a second, and a descending minor second progresses to the tonic; an ascending flatted fifth progresses to a fifth, and a descending fifth progresses to a fourth.
3. Not more than five notes in descension or ascension are allowed without a complementary movement.
4. The melody should consist of 35 to 60 notes.
5. The release begins on a subdominant major note.
6. Melodic leaps must not be larger than a major tenth.
7. A melodic leap may not be followed by another melodic leap larger than a major sixth.
8. No more than three consecutive melodic leaps are allowed.
9. No ascending or descending passage may contain more than one melodic leap.

One of the songs composed is represented as

/C/F*DA/G8C:8CF"G/C*AF8G8/G***/DEF"G/
ABC:B8C:8/C*B8C:8/D*C/F*DA/G8C:8C:F"G/
G*AF8G8/G***/DEF"G/ABC:B8C;8/C:*A*/F***
/A**C8CD/FE*/B**C:8EF"/G***

The corresponding music is shown in Fig. 6-6.

Rather than subjecting purely random notes to these compositional rules, a probability distribution used in conjunction with a random number generator could help to produce notes that would more likely fit the rules. The chart in Table 6-1 illustrates how this might be done. The name for each interval is given along with the corresponding number of notes on a keyboard. The next column gives a probability for selection of that interval, which may be changed according to the composer's wishes. The following two columns give the range of numbers, generated by a random number generator, that corresponds to the probability of selecting a given + or − interval. In this way a random number generator selecting numbers from 1-100 can provide a given probability distribution of notes.

To further ensure the choice of "good" notes, second or third-order probability distributions could be specified; that is, for each possible preceding interval (10), a probability distribution would exist for the purpose of choosing a particular value for the next interval. For instance, in traditional music, a tritone is usually followed by a stepwise interval (whole or half step); thus, the second-order probability distribution for a tritone would be heavily weighted toward a stepwise interval in selecting the next note of the composition.

The music demonstration program in Listing 6-4 may be used to transpose from any key to any

Fig. 6-6. An example of music generated by a computer.

other key. It also serves to compose a four part harmony for any song written in the key of C. For the transposing subprogram, notes may be entered in the following format: C is C, C sharp is C#, C flat is C′ and so on for A through G. For the harmonizer subroutine, notes are input in a numerical format;

Table 6-1. Probability Distribution for the Random Selection of Notes.

INTERVAL	NO. OF NOTES AWAY FROM LAST NOTE	PROBABILITY OF SELECTION	RANDOM NUMBER RANGE IN + DIRECTION	IN − DIRECTION
Unison	0	4%	49-52	49-52
Half Step	±1	14%	53-59	42-48
Whole Step	±2	12%	60-65	36-41
Minor Third	±3	10%	66-70	31-35
Major Third	±4	8%	71-74	27-30
Perfect Fourth	±5	12%	75-80	21-26
Tritone	±6	2%	81	20
Perfect Fifth	±7	14%	82-88	13-19
Minor Sixth	±8	6%	89-91	10-12
Major Sixth	±9	6%	92-94	7-9
Minor Seventh	±10	4%	95-96	5-6
Major Seventh	±11	2%	97	4
Octave	±12	6%	98-100	1-3

Listing 6-4. A Music Program.

```
10      REM LISTING6.04 - The Music Program
15      FULLW 2:CLEARW 2:GOTOXY 1,1
20      PRINT" MUSIC PROGRAM:"
25      PRINT "HARMONIZES AND TRANSPOSES":PRINT
30      INPUT "SELECT: 1) TRANSPOSER,  2) HARMONIZER,  3) END";A
40      ON A GOTO 3000,100,780
50      GOTO 30
100     REM harmony composing program
110     REM a four part harmony is produced from a given melody in the
        key of C
120     DIM B(5,100),Y(6,6),V(100):RESTORE
130     J$=" ##  +##     +##      +##     +##"
140     FOR T1=1 TO 6:FOR T2=1 TO 6:READ Y(T1,T2)
150     NEXT T2,T1:R1=1
160     DATA 5,4,1,6,2,3,6,4,2,1,5,3,6,4,3,1,2,5,1,5,4,6,3,2,2,6,5
170     DATA 4,1,3,1,5,3,6,2,4,1,0,-3,-5,-7
180     INPUT "Enter the number of notes in the melody ",W9
190     FOR E=0 TO 4:READ B(E,W9):NEXT E
195     REM INPUTTED MELODIES MUST BE IN THE KEY OF C
200     PRINT "Enter notes individually in the following format:"
210     PRINT "MIDDLE C=0"
220     PRINT "Notes above middle C are +1,+2,+3...corresponding"
230     PRINT "to D, E, F..."
240     PRINT "notes below middle C are -1,-2,-3...corresponding"
250     PRINT "to B, A, G..."
260     FOR T1=1 TO W9:INPUT V(T1):NEXT T1
270     PRINT:PRINT " #  SOPRANO  ALTO    TENOR  BASS"
280     L2=1
290     FOR W=W9 TO 1 STEP -1
300     IF W=W9 THEN 760 ELSE R1=1
310     FOR R=R1 TO 6
320     B=V(W):B(1,W)=B:L2=Y(L1,R):B(0,W)=L2
330     M=B(4,1+W):M(1)=L2-8:M(2)=L2-15
340     FOR S=1 TO 2
350     IF ABS(M(S)-M)>5 THEN A=M(3-S):GOTO 370
355     NEXT S
360     IF B>B(1,W+1) THEN A=M(2) ELSE A=M(1)
370     S=1:B(4,W)=A
380     FOR T=0 TO 4 STEP 2
390     G=B-(T+A):GOSUB 790:IF G=0 THEN 410
400     K(S)=A+T:S=S+1
410     NEXT T
420     IF S>3 THEN 690
425     FOR U=0 TO 6
430     F(3,U)=K(1):F(0,U)=0:F(2,U)=K(2)
440     K=K(2):J=K(1):K(2)=J+7:K(1)=K
450     NEXT U
460     FOR U=0 TO 6
470     FOR E=2 TO 3
480     K=F(E,U)
490     IF (5-E*4>K) OR (17-E*4<K) OR (ABS(K-B(E,W+1))>5) THEN 610
500     B(E,W)=K:IF B(2*E-3,W)<=B(2*E-2,W) THEN 610
505     NEXT E
510     IF L1=L2 THEN 570
515     FOR E1=1 TO 4
```

```
520   FOR E2=E1+1 TO 4
530   M=B(E1,W+1)-B(E2,W+1)
540   G=M:GOSUB 790:IF (G=0) OR (G=4) THEN 550 ELSE 560
550   IF B(E2,W)-B(E2,W+1)=B(E1,W)-B(E1,W+1) THEN 610
560   NEXT E2,E1
570   FOR E=2 TO 3
580   M(E)=ABS(B(E,W)-B(E,W+1))
590   NEXT E
600   F(0,U)=M(2)+M(3):GOTO 620
610   F(0,U)=88
620   NEXT U
630   V=88:FOR U=0 TO 6
640   V1=F(X1,U)
650   IF V1>V THEN 660 ELSE V=V1:U9=U
660   NEXT U
670   IF V=88 THEN 690
680   B(3,W)=F(3,U9):B(2,W)=F(2,U9):GOTO 760
690   NEXT R
700   W=W+1:IF W9<>W THEN 710 ELSE PRINT "Program cannot continue"
705   INPUT "Try again (Y/N) ";A$:IF A$="Y" THEN 30
707   IF A$="N" THEN 780 ELSE 705
710   L1=B(0,W+1):L2=B(0,W)
720   FOR R=1 TO 6
730   IF L2=Y(L1,R) THEN 750
740   NEXT R
750   R1=R+1:GOTO 310
760   PRINT USING J$;W,B(1,W),B(2,W),B(3,W),B(4,W)
770   L1=L2:NEXT W
780   INPUT Q$:END
790   G=G-INT(G/7)*7:RETURN
3000  REM TRANSPOSER
3010  REM READ HARMONY PROG. DATA FIRST
3020  FOR X=1 TO 36
3030  READ A:NEXT A
3040  DIM A$(18,18),W$(100)
3050  FOR B=1 TO 17
3060  FOR C=1 TO 17
3070  READ A$(B,C)
3080  NEXT C,B
3090  INPUT "Enter the key the song is in (E.G. C#)";B$
3100  FOR X=1 TO 17
3110  IF B$=A$(1,X) THEN 3120
3115  NEXT X
3120  INPUT "Enter the key to transpose to ",C$
3130  FOR T=1 TO 17
3140  IF C$=A$(1,T) THEN 3150
3145  NEXT T
3150  PRINT "Enter the notes of the song separately"
3160  PRINT "Enter END to end":R=1
3170  INPUT W$(R)
3180  IF W$(R)="END" THEN 3190 ELSE R=R+1:GOTO 3170
3190  R=R-1
3200  FOR Z=1 TO R
3210  FOR P=1 TO 17
3220  IF W$(Z)=A$(P,X) THEN 3230
3225  NEXT P
3230  PRINT A$(P,T);" ";
3240  NEXT Z
3250  DATA C,C#,D-,D,D#,E-,E,F,F#,G-,G,G#,A-,A,A#,B-,B,C#,D
```

```
3260  DATA D,D#,E,E,R,G-,G,G,G#,A,A,A#,B,B,C,D-,D,D,D#,E,E,F
3270  DATA G-,G,G,G#,A,A,A#,B,B,C,D,D#,E-,E,F,F,F#,G,G#,A-,A,A#
3280  DATA B-,B,C,C,C#,D#,E,E,F,F#,G-,G,A-,A,A,A#,B,B,C,C#,D-,D
3290  DATA E-,E,E,F,F#,G-,G,A-,A,A,A#,B,B,C,C#,D-,D,E,F,F,F#,G,G
3300  DATA G#,A,A#,B-,B,C,C,C#,D,D,D#,F,F#,G-,G,G#,A-,A,B-,B,B,C
3310  DATA C#,D-,D,D#,E-,E,F#,G,G,G#,A,A,A#,B,C,C,C#,D,D,D#,E,E,F
3320  DATA G-,G,G,G#,A,A,A#,B,C,C,C#,D,D,D#,E,E,F,G,G#,A-,A,A#,B-
3330  DATA B,C,C#,D-,D,D#,E-,E,F,F,F#,G#,A,A,A#,B,B,C,D-,D,D,D#,E
3340  DATA E,F,F#,G-,G,A-,A,A,A#,B,B,C,D-,D,D,D#,E,E,F,F#,G-,G
3350  DATA A,A#,B-,B,C,C,C#,D,D#,E-,E,F,F,F#,G,G,G#,A#,B,B,C,C#,D-
3360  DATA D,E-,E,E,F,F#,G-,G,G#,A-,A,B-,B,B,C,C#,D-,D,E-,E,E,F,F#
3370  DATA G-,G,G#,A-,A,B,C,C,C#,D,D,D#,E,F,F,F#,G,G,G#,A,A,A#
3380  GOTO 30
```

middle C is 0, the higher frequency notes D, E, F . . . are +1, +2, +3 . . ., and the lower frequency notes B, A, G . . . are −1, −2, −3 . . . Because the song input must be in the key of C, sharps and flats are not absolutely necessary and are not provided for by the program. The addition of sharps and flats would be one improvement to experiment with. Of course, the transposing program may be adapted to use numerical notation instead of alphanumeric notation and then be used in conjunction with the transposing subprogram. Figure 6-7 shows the numerical system.

Additional possibilities for using your personal computer in music composition include the following:

1. Produce a stricter set of rules for composition than those given above; rely less upon randomness.
2. Develop programs to compose in assorted musical styles including classical, rock and roll, and children's music. Computer musicians have applied statistical analysis to various styles and composers to determine characteris-

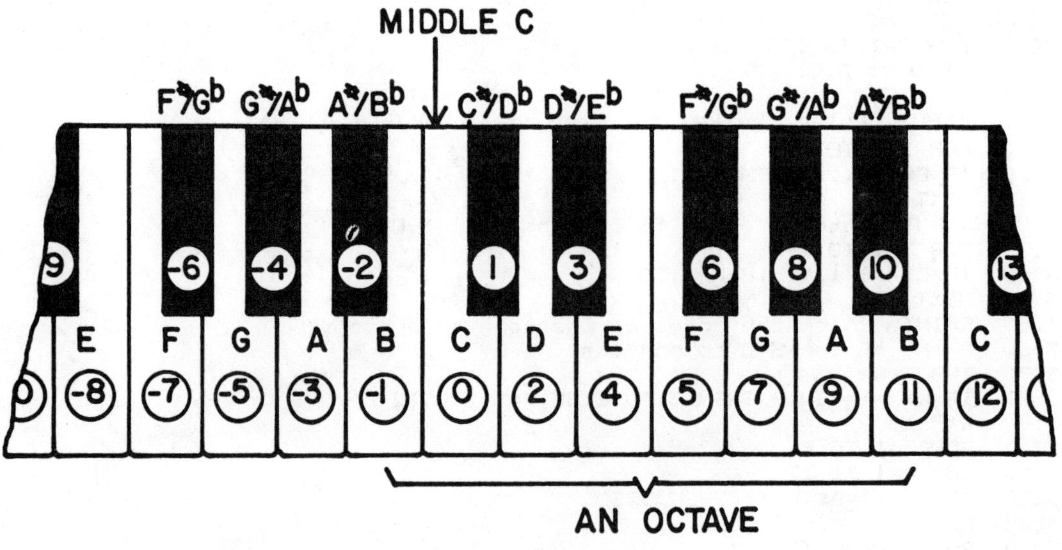

Fig. 6-7. A numbering system for harmonization and other music composition programs.

tic probability distributions. Random numbers subjected to these probability criteria can produce music reminiscent of the original style.

3. Develop programs to compose songs for given lyrics by using the timing of each syllable to time the duration of the notes accordingly. The ambitious programmer might try to link a lyric-producing program with a music composition program; some unusual results would undoubtedly be produced.
4. A popular melody could be mathematically transformed to produce a new melody, and this new melody would likely be more tuneful than compositions based on random number generators, fractals, or probability distributions. The original melody would be numerically encoded such that each note and note duration has a unique number. With the melody so coded, an algorithm could be applied to each note, translating that note into another. The simplest such algorithm could reflect each note around a central value, transforming high notes into low ones and vice versa. It could also be a mathematical formula, but extensive experimentation would be necessary.

The following formula is useful as a part of a musical tone generation program based upon the numbering notes according to octave (V), where middle C is in the fourth octave, and according to position within the octave where C = 1, C# = 2 . . . B = 12.

$$\log_2 \frac{f}{55} = V + \frac{P-22}{12}$$

where f = frequency in Hz.

A program that performs a simple song transformation is presented in Listing 6-5.

5. Given the score of a music piece written for a solo instrument (for example, the piano), the computer could transpose and analyze melodies, bass, and counter rhythms to produce sheet music versions for other instruments.
6. A microcomputer connected to a player piano via a solenoid interface could digitally record songs you play or song notes you input. The song could be stored on cassette or floppy disk and recalled to be played at normal speed, faster, slower, backwards, with staccato, and so on.
7. A microcomputer interfaced with a monophonic electronic synthesizer could theoretically produce a polyphonic effect, add a continuous bass or beat pattern, and perform

Listing 6-5. Simple Song Transformation Program.

```
10    REM LISTING6.05 - Simple Song Transformation Program
20    REM reflects notes around a central value
30    READ N:REM set N-number of notes in the song
35    DIM M(N)
40    FULLW2:CLEARW 2:GOTOXY 1,1
45    FOR X=1 TO N
50    READ M(X)
60    M(X)=10+(10-M(X)):REM reflect around note #10
70    NEXT X
80    FOR X=1 TO N
90    PRINT M(X);"   ";
100   NEXT X
110   INPUT Q$:END
120   REM first data point is # of notes in song
130   REM followed by notes of song
140   DATA 10
150   DATA 4,2,5,7,5,5,13,1,12,3
```

a sequence of switching or mixing for live performances.

8. From a given composition, a simplified version could be extracted by the computer (the melody is usually carried by the highest notes, the bass by the lowest) and printed in standard musical notation. Also, a given piece could be arranged so that all chords are broken up into varying arpeggios.
9. Given a melody, the computer could be programmed to compose a bass countermelody.

Computer-controlled Synthesizers. In 1982, a group of synthesizer manufacturers developed a standardized interface, called MIDI (Musical Instrument Digital Interface), to enable communication between synthesizers and computers. Each key is encoded in a fashion similar to a computer (ASCII) keyboard. For each key struck, a series of codes are sent: a NOTE ON signal, a PITCH signal, a VELOCITY signal, and (depending on the machine) other signals specifying pitch blends, patch changes, key release, after touch pressure, and front panel changes. This information can be sent to any other MIDI synthesizer so that two or more keyboards can perform in exact synchronization, although the patches are different on each machine. Special codes can indicate that only specified synthesizers are to respond to the following code. Through a serial interface, this information can also be sent to a computer, which may serve as a polyphonic sequencer or imitator of a multitrack tape machine. The computer may record, edit, store, and play back your music or play music entered through the ASCII keyboard. A composer can quickly change tempo, pitch, instruments, accents, and so on with the aid of such a system, which is capable of producing a flawless rendition.

The *Computer Music Journal* (P.O. Box E, Menlo Park, CA 94025) is a good source of information on composing, scoring, and playing music on computers, for the professional or amateur.

HOBBIES

The microcomputer can perform invaluable services for those involved in almost all hobbies.

Photography

The serious photographer should investigate the use of the computer to obtain more precise values for such things as development times, light exposures, and filters through the use of mathematical formulae. For example, the standard exposure meter assumes the following: 1) for any emulsion, the curve of the density versus the log of the exposure yields a straight line and is characterized by a single factor—speed; 2) time and intensity of light are interchangeable to provide a certain exposure (reciprocity). Actually, these assumptions are only approximations of true values. In extreme cases, reciprocity does not work; the density versus log of exposure curve is not linear, and emulsions have differing contrasts and latitudes. A reference manual describing the mathematical calculations of photography should describe the formulae used to take these factors into account.

Other ways in which photographers can use microcomputers include the following areas.

1. Exposure compensation is useful in the darkroom to calculate the exposure required to compensate for a change in photo enlargement magnification. Using the inverse square law, if you have data on a "perfect" print expressed as enlarger head height above the easel (H_O) and time of exposure (T_O), the formula for computing the new time of exposure (T_N) at the new height (HJ_N) with the same aperture is

$$T_N = \left(\frac{H_N}{H_O}\right)^2 \times T_O$$

   A useful program could calculate exposure times for a range of specified heights at all available f-stops to permit easy enlargement of a negative to a given size.
2. Fill-in flash computation is used to determine the correct lens f-stop when a flash is used in the presence of strong ambient light to fill in undersired shadows.

3. If you intended to do specialized photography requiring homebuilt equipment, the computer could be useful in optical and dimension calculations.
4. Automated control of darkroom equipment (including such features as temperature correction for chemicals, timer, development calculator) could expedite the development process. Alternatively, the computer could serve as a timer and reminder for steps to be taken in the development process.
5. An inventory of slides or photographs could be stored on disks or tapes, and topics could be indexed and cross-referenced. Thus, to create a slide show of a particular topic, you can use the computer to determine all relevant slides and output a listing of each along with its location and remarks.
6. A simple switching interface to a cassette recorder and slide projector could automate a complete audio-visual slide presentation. An exotic audio-visual light show could be controlled in a similar manner.
7. Focal length conversions from one camera to another, based on the diagonal or horizontal angle of view, could be done.
8. A program could be written to calculate film speed (ASA), flash ECPS value, or flash guide number, given the other two values. Once the flash guide number is known, the maximum f-stop for the distance from the flash to subject, may be calculated.

$$\text{f-stop} = \frac{\text{Guide number}}{\text{distance}}$$

   The published flash guide number is for one speed of film only . If you use a different film with a different speed, the new guide number may be found using the formula

$$\text{New Guide No.} = \frac{\text{New Film Speed}}{\text{Old Guide No.} \times \text{Published Film Speed}}$$

9. Close-up photography values for subject distance, required lens focus setting, or field of coverage could be calculated given the other three values.
10. The depth of field indicates the distance from some point in front of the subject to some point in back of the subject for which a given photograph will be acceptably sharp. A computer program could mathematically determine how the desired near and far distances can be obtained, in terms of the f-stop and distance settings to use. The *hyperfocal* distance, or the nearest distance for which a lens can be focused to give satisfactory definition of infinity, is given by

$$H = \frac{F^2}{f \times d}$$

    where H = hyperfocal distance
    F = focal length of lens
    f = f/number
    d = diameter of circle of confusion.

11. A photograph of your video screen displaying alphanumerics or graphics could be used to title home slide shows or movies. A recommended procedure is to darken the room completely, use a tripod, and shoot with ASA 125 Plus-X at f/1.4, 1/8 second.

For serious hobbyists or professionals, a BASIC program for microcomputers to design and evaluate lenses was described in *Photonics Spectra*, December 1983, pp. 58-62.

Animated Films. Although most microcomputers are not fast enough to display high-resolution real-time animation, a time-lapse film could be made with the end result being equivalent to real-time graphics. The graphic resolution should be a minimum of 200 by 200 individually definable blocks. Much better, although much more expensive, would be a system equipped with a plotter to draw all of the figures necessary to produce an animated film sequence. The three dimensional rotation of an object is a popular film subject due to the *relative* ease in programming.

Amateur Radio

The ham radio or citizen's band radio enthusiast could use a personal computer to assist with his hobby in these ways:

Morse Code Tutor. Computerists interested in passing the Morse code test to become amateur radio operators could use their machines to quiz themselves both visually and audibly. The visual representation of Morse code is, of course, a series of dots and dashes: - -.-.- - -. . . . Those of you who are using a computer without a built-in speaker can use one of the following methods to obtain the audible representation of the code.

1. Use an interfaced tone output speaker
2. Use timing loops to generate tones of a certain duration on an AM radio placed next to the CPU.

The standard method of learning Morse code is first to study the visual representations, and second, to transcribe an audio transmission at a gradually increasing rate. A program similar to the general CAI program described in Chapter 5 could be used to requiz you on the codes you have missed.

Message Displayer. By using a Morse code decoder/sender interface between the radio and your computer, received and sent messages could be displayed on a video monitor in English, allowing the computer to "translate" Morse code (or some other code) to English and vice versa.

Message Monitor. The computer could monitor a specified frequency for a particular audio signal or coded message. Transmissions immediately following this signal would be recorded digitally or on cassette tape. Thus, you need not attend to the radio constantly to receive a message. Received messages could also be forwarded automatically on another frequency to another station in a network.

Message Relay. A stored message could be sent at the proper time if the station operator was unable to send it personally.

Controller. Add intelligence to your test equipment or radio with a controlling microprocessor. Test sequences could be done automatically.

Station Log Maintainer. Maintain your station log automatically—all entries could be stored, and classified, and special reports generated (for example, how many countries have been contacted? Have there been any repeat contacts?). If you hear someone and you're not sure whether or not you talked with him 6 months ago, you could type in his name or call letters and find out the last contact from a computer database of log entries.

Error Correcting Code Senders. Error correcting codes could be automatically generated to improve communications.

Contest Record Keeper. Several ham radio contests have utilized small computers to keep track of all contacts.

Collections

Whether it be books, magazines, coins, stamps, antiques, or matchbook covers, most everyone collects something. The microcomputer can help you organize and present your collection.

Collection Inventory. If your collection involves many items, such as hundreds or even thousands of stamps, it is certainly a good idea to catalog each item. A computer database program, as described in the first chapter, is ideal for maintaining large collections of any kind.

In addition to storing an individual record specifying all pertinent information on each item, the computer would also be able to categorize, cross-index, and generate special lists of items. A special list could include all items that have a particular characteristic, for instance, a list of all British stamps or all stamps issued in 1979.

The fields to use in setting up a stamp collection database might look like this:

1. CATALOG NUMBER
2. NAME OR IDENTIFYING TITLE
3. DENOMINATION
4. SUBJECT
5. ORIGINAL COST
6. CONDITION
7. DATE ISSUED
8. QUALITY
9. CURRENT VALUE
10. COUNTRY OF ORIGIN

11. DESCRIPTIVE INFORMATION AND HISTORY
12. WHERE PURCHASED
13. MISCELLANEOUS COMMENTS

Using the database program, you could request the sum of field 5 or 9 for all records to determine the original cost and current value for the entire collection.

Collection management on your personal computer allows more time for the fun of collecting without the bother of record-keeping. Additionally, a cassette or floppy disk copy of the inventory could be stored in a safe location in the event an insured collection is destroyed.

Collection Narrator. Hobbyists with collections will find that their personal computer with video display makes an excellent visual narrator of a collection. For example, a stamp collector created a file on his entire collection, with information on each item randomly accessible. His narrations were similar to this:

Decade of Space Achievement Issue
Issued: August 2, 1969 Purchased: September 1, 1969
Purchase price: .16 Value: .60

This stamp pair depicts the ascent of man upon the surface of the moon.

Interested persons can be instructed how to obtain information on a particular item, or else the computer can present a continuous display of each item in sequence; this technique can save you from monotonous repetition of information to visitors at an exhibition. Businessmen at expositions could put their personal computer to similar use in explaining products.

Astronomy

Potential applications for your personal computer in amateur astronomy include the following:

1. Locate and identify stars—Calculation of declination, sidereal hour angle from observed altitude, azimuth, and time.
2. Make records of observations efficiently in computer format for quick retrieval.
3. Interface telescope drive mechanics to a microprocessor controller for automatic photographic observations. For more information see *InfoWorld*, Volume 5, Number 47 (12/83) pp. 45-46; and *Sky and Telescope*, January 1981, p. 71.
4. Interconvert astronomical units, kilometers, light years, and parsecs.
5. Calculate and plot orbits of satellites and planets.

The astronomy demonstration program in Listing 6-6 calculates the relative position of Venus in degrees and hours from the sun for a given date.

Listing 6-6. The Astronomy Demo Program.

```
10      REM LISTING 6.06 - The Astronomy Demo Program
15      FULLW 2:CLEARW 2:GOTOXY 1,1
20      PRINT "ASTRONOMY DEMO PROGRAM"
30      PRINT "calculates the relative position of venus and the sun;"
40      PRINT "calculates the number of days since 12/31/49"
50      INPUT "Enter this year as two digits (E.G. '84' for 1984) ";Y
60      PRINT "Enter number of days since December 31 of last year "
70      INPUT "for example, Feb. 5 would be 36 days: ",D
80      CLEARW 2:GOTOXY 20,5:PRINT "PLEASE WAIT--CALCULATING"
90      X=364*INT((Y-50)/4)+365*((Y-50)-INT((Y-50)/4))+DA
100     PI=3.131592#:A=P1/180:C=A*.9856:B=180/PI:D=99.2*A:E=D+C*X
110     IF E<PI*2 THEN 128
120     E=E-PI*2:GOTO 110
```

```
128   PRINT TAB(15)"It makes me nervous to have you watch me
      think."
129   PRINT TAB(10)"I'll call you when I'm finished!"
130   E=SIN(E-A*105)*1.9*A+E:F=A*1.602:G=A*80.85:H=G+F*X
140   IF H<PI*2 THEN 150 ELSE H=H-PI*2:GOTO 140
150   H=H+SIN(H-A*135)*.8*A
160   J=SIN(H-A*232)*.0055+.7233
170   K=H-E:I=SIN(E-A*195)*.016+1:M=-PI/2
180   L=SQR(J*J+I*I-2*J*I*COS(K))
190   N=SIN(K)*(J/L)+SIN(M)
200   IF N<0 THEN M=PI/3600+M:GOTO 190
202   R=M*12/PI
205   PRINT CHR$(7),CHR$(7)
210   CLEARW 2:GOTOXY 1,1
215   PRINT "The relative location of Venus is ";M*B;" degrees from
      the sun."
220   PRINT "=to ";R;" hours from the sun."
225   FOR X=1 TO 5000:NEXT X:GOTOXY 25,7:PRINT "WHEW!!!"
230   INPUT Q$:END
```

A series of BASIC astronomical calculation programs for ephemeris of comets and minor planets, locations of celestial objects, and altitude and azimuth of the sun appeared in *80 Microcomputing*, October 1983.

Gardening

Writing a garden analysis program for one-time use would not be a practical idea, but your friends and neighbors could use such a program, and you may be able to sell the completed software to a local garden supply store. A complete analysis program is more complicated than it appears on the surface, no pun intended. These are some of the factors to consider:

1. pH, water, soil density, and sunshine levels of the plot.
2. Desired pH, water, soil density, and sunshine levels for the plants to be planted.
3. Nitrogen, phosphorus, and potassium contents in the soil compared to plant requirements.
4. The size of the garden.

Proper planning will allow you to position certain vegetables that ward off insects next to others that need this protection. The space needed between adjacent plants should also be considered. Specific plant requirements and the harvest times of the vegetables could be printed, along with a graphic presentation of the garden plot:

```
BEETS ..................................................
CORN -----------------------------------------------
RADISHES ::::::::::::::::::::::::::::::::::::::::::::::
TOMATOES ----------------------------------------
```

Additional outputs could explain how to form a compost heap and how to use fertilizer. One gardener uses his personal computer to track insecticide and herbicide application, precipitation dates and amounts, temperature, and chores to be done. Tables of times to plant, spray, and prune can also be stored for ready reference and to simplify planning.

Sports

A file of team and player statistics, player's names and numbers, and other sports information could be stored on the computer (preferably on floppy disk) for quick retrieval by the television sports fan. Sports statistics could be compiled, graphed, and analyzed. Probability forecasting of score and point spread based upon past performance of opposing teams could be accomplished. The computer could also "learn" from its mistakes, retaining the outcomes of many games in memory.

At local sporting events a microcomputer could

be useful in maintaining scores, team records, and player records or statistics as the game progresses (for use by the announcer or for permanent records).

A series of elapsed-time computations could be accomplished efficiently with the proper program. A programmable calculator could serve as a digital stopwatch as well.

Bowling, golf, and other sports involving the tedious calculation of averages and other statistics for a league are well-suited for computer bookkeeping. Sell such a computer service or offer it gratuitously to your local bowling alley or golf course.

Gambling

Your computer could become a helpful advisor for those who play poker and various other card games. All information available (for example the cards in your hand and the amount of the bet) would be input before each round, and an analysis based upon the laws of probability could determine your best move. (Perhaps your opponents would object to this advantage!) For example, these are the probabilities for obtaining particular poker and bridge hands:

Royal flush	649,739 to 1
Straight flush	72,192 to 1
Full house	693 to 1
Flush	508 to 1
One pair	1.37 to 1
Straight	254 to 1
13-card suit	158,753,389,899 to 1
12-card suit	367,484,698 to 1
Nine honors	104 to 1
Yarborough—no honors	1,827 to 1
Four aces/four of a kind	378 to 1
Three of a kind	47 to 1
Two pair	21 to 1
One pair	2 to 1
Nothing of interest	2 to 1

These probabilities were in part computed by the use of the formulas for combinations and permutations. The number of combinations of n things taken r at a time is designated by

$$_nC_r = \frac{n!}{(n - r)!(r!)}$$

and the number of permutations of n objects taken r at a time, $_nP_r$ is

$$_nP_r = \frac{n!}{(n - r)!}$$

The mathematical concept of *expectation* is very useful in determining when to drop out of a poker hand or other gambling operation.

Expectation = probability times winnings

For example, suppose a poker player plans to call a bet of $2, which would increase the pot (potential winnings) to $14. If he can see from the exposed cards that his probability of winning is .4, his expectation is .4 × $14 = $5.60, for which he must pay $2. Since the expectation is worth more than the purchase price, he should call the bet. This is but one concept to incorporate with a better analysis program.

Other forms of gambling (for example, football betting and jai-alai) may be computer-analyzed based upon past performances of the opponents and a confidence level established to conservatively pick the winner/point spread. Statistics to be incorporated in a database could include each time's win/loss record, the coach, the location (home or away), the playing surface, and each team's record against the point spread. A complete computer analysis of hundreds of games played from any one sport could yield a system for predicting future outcomes through the use of statistical cross-correlation between all variables.

Fishing

Potential applications for serious fishermen include the following:

1. The analysis of weather patterns and times in order to forecast the ideal time to fish.
2. The recording of weight and species of catch, locations fished, weather, tides, depth and temperature. Use this statistically correlated data for future reference. A portable microcomputer with an A/D converter could gather some of this data automatically. One lobster fisherman has statistically analyzed his placement of lobster traps on his microcomputer to optimize his catch.
3. The computation of high and low tide times and time of sunrise/sunset.

The Computation of Times of Sunrise/Sunset and High and Low Tides. Pilots as well as fishermen will find a sunrise/set calculating program useful. To keep such a program as simple as possible, tide or sunrise data from previous days could be entered to eliminate highly technical calculations. The times for future sunrises or sunsets may then be projected by linear regression or moving average calculation.

For those inclined to astronomical calculations, no pun intended, the time of sunrise/sunset may be more accurately calculated by consideration of the changing inclination to the sun and time of rotation for the earth.

Biorhythms, Astrology, and ESP

Those involved in exploring the more controversial aspects of human existence will also find the microcomputer useful.

Biorhythms. Biorhythms are supposedly the cycles in emotional, physical, and intellectual states governing everyone's behavior. Dozens of computer programs have been written to generate personalized biorhythm charts, yet interesting additions could be included. Potential innovations include the following:

1. Plotting or numerically comparing the biorhythms of two or more friends or a family.
2. Computing the average of all three biorhythmic cycles.
3. Generating a biorhythm chart in the form of a standard calendar.
4. Judging the reliability of biorhythms by objectively analyzing your three states at the end of each day and making a statistical comparison, and plotting this data versus your biorhythm.
5. Investigating the use of histograms and other means of presenting data to output biorhythms in a more favorable format, including artistic designs.
6. Comparing the reliability of your standard biorhythm to one beginning with your estimated date of conception.

Astrology. The determination of the alignments of the planets and the sorting of astrological data are best done with a computer. Horoscopes, interpolation midpoints, aspects, and Placidus house and astropoints calculation may be done. Tarot, I-Ching, and numerology may be accomplished in a similar manner.

The Psychic. Purely for entertainment, "psychic" and "ESP" programs have been written using random number generators; can you predict the computer's choice of a card or number?

Additional Hobby Application

Hobbyists will find microcomputers useful in all of the following areas:

Designing Recreational Vehicles. A hang glider or ultralight enthusiast considering designing a new aerofoil could find a detailed computer-simulated wind tunnel test beneficial. The proposed design could be mathematically described to the computer, and an aerodynamic simulation of this magnitude could only be done by someone with a good background in aerodynamics. Similar simulations could be applied to boats and other recreational vehicles.

Model Building. A simple, time-saving program could calculate the scaling factor for model builders by dividing the length of the model by the length of the object to be modeled. Next, each dimension of the object would be input, and the corresponding dimension for the model would be calculated by multiplying the original dimension by the scaling factor.

Model Railroading. Model railroading enthusiasts with large layouts may wish to automate the trains, lights, switches, and so on with a controlling microprocessor. One hobbyist went so far as to print train schedules and tickets, and analyze freight businesses on his personal computer. For more information on real-time computer control of model railroads, see the ongoing series by Bruce Chubb that began in the February, 1985, issue of *Model Railroader.*

Scuba Diving Plan. A simple program could calculate one of these four parameters, given the other three:

1. Time underwater in minutes = TUW
2. Surface air consumption rate in cubic ft/min =S
3. Depth in feet = D
4. Total air volume of tank in cubic feet = TAV

$$\frac{33 \cdot TAV}{D \cdot S} = TUW$$

Geneological Storehouse. A few hobbyists have obtained a sufficient amount of geneological information such that a personal computer is necessary to file and update the information. In addition, having specified characteristics of each family member instantly available eases the task of further geneological research.

Aquarium Maintenance. One hobbyist uses his computer to compute amounts of chemicals necessary to maintain a seawater aquarium environment. Complex calculations are necessary to obtain exact values over a range of temperatures and conditions.

Chapter 7

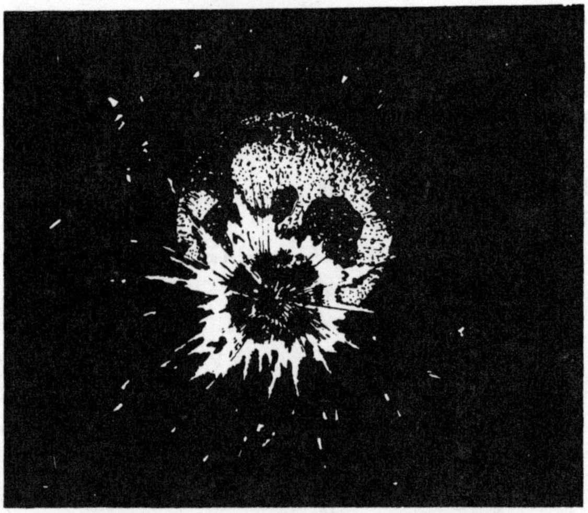

Games and Recreational Applications

According to polls, the most popular use for personal computers is games, with over 60 percent of owners claiming this to be their primary application. Although this percentage may decline with the advent of inexpensive, easy-to-use software for other purposes and the burgeoning computer networks, games will continue to be one of the most popular applications.

Games are not only fun, but they often have the added benefit of being educational. The child (or adult!) can hone his skills of eye-hand coordination and develop abilities to react creatively, solve problems logically, and make decisions. Games are often the best learn-to-program challenges for the beginner, yet the professional programmer may even find himself defeated in attempting to write complex game programs (for example, chess or Go). Games encourage imaginative and constructive programming and responses.

There are at least eight major categories of games that have been adapted to the computer:

1. Fantasy and adventure games: Stemming from the popular college game, *Dungeons and Dragons*, fantasy and adventure games lead you step by step through an imaginary world to find a special treasure, to solve a mystery, or to outfox an evil wizard. However, you must figure out how to overcome or go through the many obstacles designed to prevent your success in this elaborate puzzle. You can type simple commands in English, such as "go east," and the computer will describe where you are and what the situation is after each command. The more elaborate adventure games may use vivid graphics to draw the scene and even use voice output. Another series of programs called *interactive fiction* allows you to interact with the characters and situations in a story.
2. "Video" games: Games of this kind usually involve a live action, shoot-em-up approach, pitting you, for example, as the sole champion of a ship or planet versus the rest of the universe, which is invariably out to get you. If you begin to be successful, of course the battle conditions deteriorate and the battlefield fills with increas-

ingly difficult targets to hit. This genre is the most popular form of computer game and a challenge to your eye-hand coordination; all manner of competitions are available.

3. Strategy and battle games: For those who prefer a more enlightened approach to gaming, strategy games offer complex rules and tactics to employ in fighting battles against a computer or a human opponent. They often make use of excellent computer graphics displaying a battlefield and tokens representing forces on each side.
4. Card games: Care to play bridge with three computerized opponents? The computer has also been programmed to play poker, gin, Kalah, Tripoli, solitaire and many other card games. Card tricks, bridge tutors, and poker betting systems have also been programmed.
5. Board and word games: Included in this group are the old favorites of chess, backgammon, and checkers and the new-fangled Clue™, Monopoly™, Boggle™, and Scrabble™. Some of the word games may be equipped with vocabularies of up to 90,000 words. Chess, checkers, and backgammon programs already can compete at the master level, and it is only a matter of time before they become reigning world champions.
6. Gambling games: All the games in Vegas, from one-armed bandits to roulette, have been adapted to the personal computer. For those who take gambling seriously, programs are available to perform complex handicapping analysis for horse racing and football games, and to do the calculations necessary for the prediction of other sporting events.
7. Sports games: Football, baseball, auto racing, skiing, and numerous other sports have been computerized and often include live action with complex graphics.
8. Party games: Many popular party games, from charades to spin the bottle, have been programmed. For those willing to take the advice of a computerized sex analyst, several commercial programs will ask you and your mate a series of questions and then determine the optimum "interlude," for which it provides explicit instructions.

BOARD AND STRATEGY GAMES YOU CAN PROGRAM

Although most of the popular live-action or real-time games on the market required hundreds to thousands of man-hours to develop, many nonanimated games can be written by the beginner and are sometimes just as entertaining as the more complex games. A sampling of game ideas to tackle in BASIC follows; some would require less than 30 program lines, and others are more difficult, possibly requiring hundreds of lines.

Many popular board and logic games take on an added dimension when computerized, especially if the computer is programmed to be the opponent. Some of the many possibilities include the following games:

Tricolor. Tricolor is a game played on a hex board with hexagonal cells colored red, white, and blue (or different shades). An actual playing board should be used in the computerized version, because creating a board display on a video screen would be difficult.

Each player begins with 18 pieces. Those of one player are white; those of the other are black. At the start of the game, white places his pieces on hexes 1-18, and black on hexes 44-61, as shown in Fig.7-1.

The pieces are called *stacks* because you can place more than one piece together to form a stack. The range of a stack, that is, the maximum number of cells it can traverse in any one direction in a single move, is determined by the number of pieces in the stack; one cell for a single piece, two cells for a stack of two pieces; and three cells for any larger stack.

The combat strength of a stack depends upon both the number of pieces it contains and the color (or shade) of the cell on which it rests. Taking the strength of a single white piece on a white cell as the unit, the strength of a stack of two pieces on a white cell is two units, and the strength of any larger stack on a white cell is three units. The strength of a stack on a black cell is twice what it

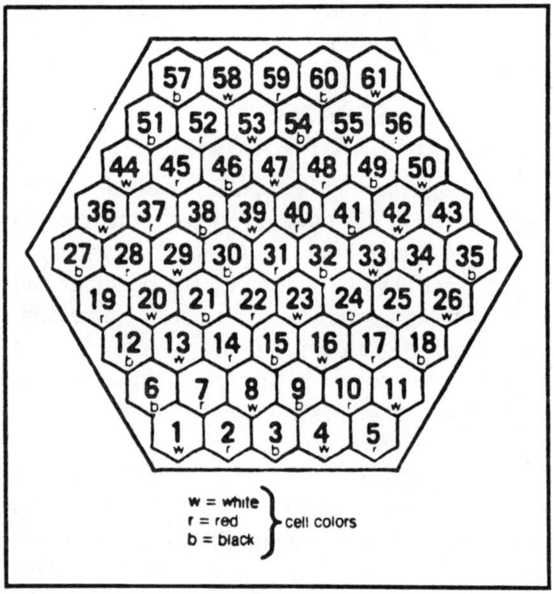

Fig. 7-1. The Tricolor game board.

would be on a white cell, and a stack on a red cell is worth three times as much as it would be on a white cell.

Players take alternate turns, each moving a single stack along a diagonal or horizontal line as far as he wishes, within the range of the stack. The entire stack or only a portion of it can be moved; the number of pieces in the part moved determines the strength of the stack. Occupied cells may not be jumped, but a player may move his stack to a cell occupied by another stack owned by himself or by the opponent. If the stack is his own, the stacks are merged. If the opponent owns the other stack, an "attack" has been initiated, and the disposition of pieces is as follows: A stack may attack an opposing stack only if it is stronger (contains more pieces). If it is more than twice as strong, the opposing stack is "killed," and all hostile pieces in the stack are removed from play; friendly pieces are added to the winning stack. If the attacking stack is not more than twice as strong, it "captures" the opposing stack by combining it with itself. If a capture or kill can be made in a player's turn, it must be made. The game ends with the capture or killing of all of one player's pieces.

Black Sheep. Black sheep is played on a chessboard between two players, one "white" and the other "black." White begins the game with four white checkers that are placed on the four black squares on one side of the chessboard. Black uses one black checker and places it on either of the middle black squares on the opposite side of the board. The white pieces may only move forward to the opposite side; black may move forward or backward. Both colors may only move one square at a time and only on the diagonal.

Black moves first and then moves alternate. The object for black is to reach the opposite side of the board without being "trapped" (surrounded by white pieces in such a way that there is no adjacent diagonal unoccupied square to move to). The objective for white is to trap black before it reaches the other side of the board. Apparently, no one has determined a winning strategy for this game; thus it would be challenging to develop a heuristic strategy for the computer to play either side.

Jam. In this simple, yet challenging game, the small circles in the diagram in Fig. 7-2 represent cities; the lines represent roads. Each road has a designated number. Players alternate turns choosing one of the nine roads as their own property. The

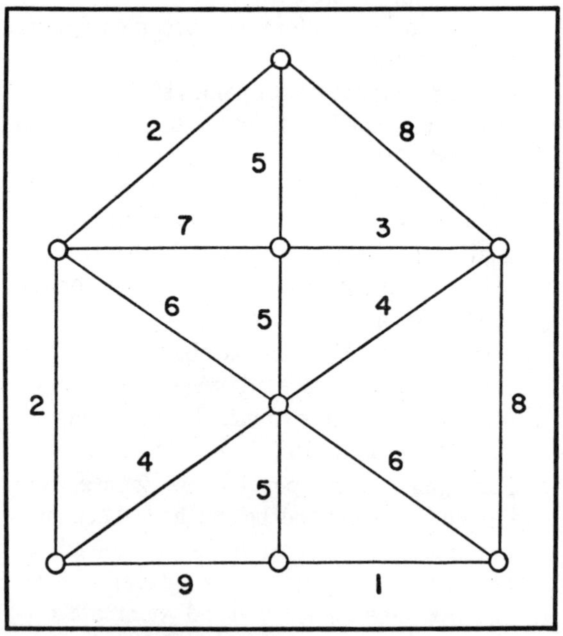

Fig. 7-2. The Jam game board.

winner is the first to own three roads that connect directly with any one city. The game may be won with a mathematical strategy similar to that used in tic-tac-toe.

Hot. "Hot" is a clever variation of tic-tac-toe. The following words are listed on a computer screen: TANK, WOES, SHIP, WASP, HOT, BRIM, HEAR, FORM, TIED. Players take alternate turns picking one word from the list; words are removed from the list as they are chosen. The first player to pick three words that contain the same single letter is the winner.

The game may be analyzed by the computer in the same manner as tic-tac-toe, if the words are arranged on the board as in this diagram:

SHIP	BRIM	TIED
WASP	HEAR	TANK
WOES	FORM	HOT

By choosing three words in a row horizontally, vertically, or diagonally, a player can win the game. Thus, the strategy for play is the same as in tic-tac-toe, except the player that does not know these congruencies is at a disadvantage.

Bridge-It. In the game of Bridge-it, the first player is designated as O and the second player as X. Using the grid shown in Fig. 7-3, putting a connecting line between two horizontally or vertically adjacent markers of the player's symbol. The O player attempts to form a connected "bridge" from the top to bottom of the board, while the X player attempts to form a bridge from the left to right side of the board. The first to form a bridge wins the game.

A winning strategy exists for this game as illustrated in Fig. 7-4. For the O player to win, he should put his first line between the Os at positions 9, 2, and 11, 2 as shown in Fig.7-5. The game may be won by the O player if the following strategy is

	1	2	3	4	5	6	7	8	9	10	11
1		O		O		O		O		O	
2	X		X		X		X		X		X
3		O		O		O		O		O	
4	X		X		X		X		X		X
5		O		O		O		O		O	
6	X		X		X		X		X		X
7		O		O		O		O		O	
8	X		X		X		X		X		X
9		O		O		O		O		O	
10	X		X		X		X		X		X
11		O		O		O		O		O	

Fig. 7-3. The Bridge-It game board.

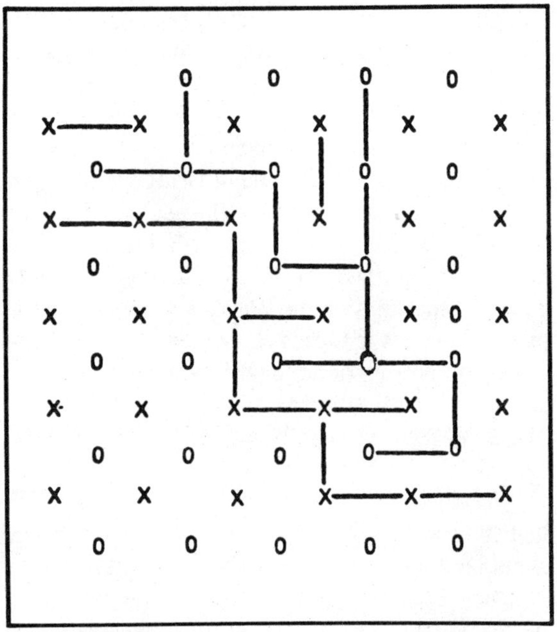

Fig. 7-4. The Bridge-It game board showing a win by X.

used. Whenever X joins a connecting line, the line will touch one of the dotted lines or semicircles in Fig. 7-5. O should draw a connecting line between two O markers such that the line will touch the end of the dotted line just touched by the line drawn by X following each X turn. In this manner, O will inevitably win.

Hex. Hex is a game similar to Bridge-it, but the game has not been solved such that a win is always certain. For this reason, hex would probably be more interesting to play against a computer. A heuristic strategy similar to that used in Bridge-it could be employed.

One game of Hex is played on a board composed of hexagons, with eleven hexagons on each side (although other sizes have been used). Two opposite sides of the board are named black, while the other two are named white, as shown in Fig. 7-6. The hexes at the four junctions between sides are neutral. One player has black pieces, the other player has white. Alternate turns are taken, with each player placing one of his pieces on any unoccupied hexagon. The object for both players is to complete a continuous chain of his pieces between the two sides labeled by his color. The game is mathematically solvable on boards with certain dimensions. For an interesting discussion of winning strategy and Hex variants, the reader is referred to *The Journal of Recreational Mathematics*, Vol 8(2), 1975-1976, p. 120.

Cross Capture. Cross Capture is played on a chessboard. At the start of the game, a set of randomly distributed letters or numbers is put on the board (video display), with no more than one character per square. Most of the board remains empty. A sample board is shown in Fig. 7-7. Players take turns choosing one of the letters, and all other letters on the board that fall in a given category become property of that player. One category may be defined as all the letters in the same horizontal, diagonal, or vertical row as the chosen letter or as all the letters within a certain proximity to the chosen letter (for example, one space away). The player who possesses the most letters at the end of the game is declared the winner.

Tic-Tac-Toe Variation. An interesting tic-tac-toe variation is played as follows. Each player puts his three pieces on a tic-tac-toe board such that piece ownership alternates around the periphery of the board. Following this setup, each player is al-

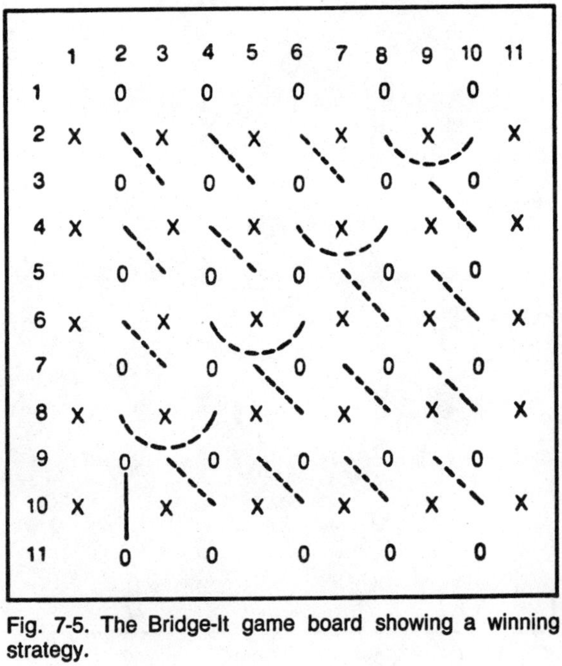

Fig. 7-5. The Bridge-It game board showing a winning strategy.

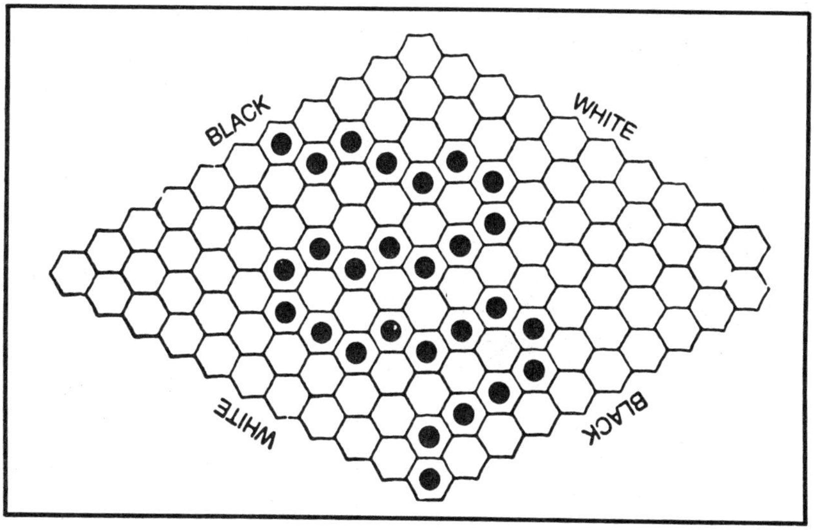

Fig. 7-6. The Hex game board.

lowed to move one of his pieces to an adjacent square. The winner of the game is the first to make three-in-a-row.

Tuknanavuhpi. Tuknanavuhpi is a Hopi chase game played on a 4 × 4 board with diagonals drawn in each of the 16 squares. Pieces move on the points where lines meet on the board, not on the squares. There are two players; each one has 20 pieces placed on the board as indicated in the diagram in Fig. 7-8. The middle of the board is initially empty.

Players take alternate turns moving their pieces in any direction along the lines on the board, from one intersection to another adjacent intersection. As in checkers pieces are captured by jumping over any of the opponent's pieces. The winner is the player who has captured all of his opponent's pieces.

Many other games popular in other cultures but undiscovered in the United States are well-suited to be computer games. These include Teekso, Hasami Shogi, Dreidel, Bell and Hammer, Asalto, Yofe, Ur, and Alquerque, which are referenced in game encyclopedias.

Nim. The game of Nim has become a very popular computer game. The rules are simple.

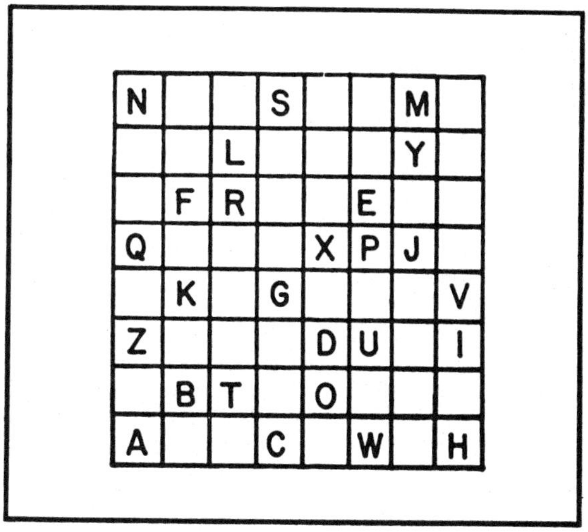

Fig. 7-7. A sample Cross Capture game board at the start of a game.

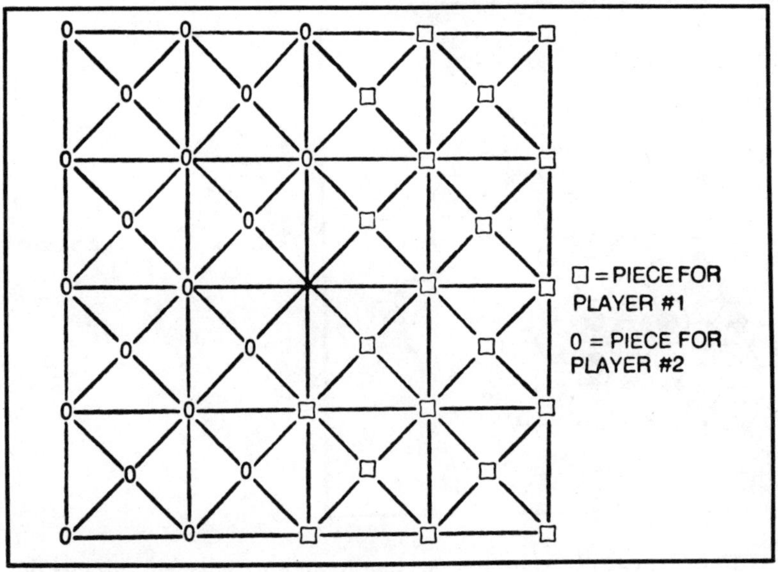

Fig. 7-8. The Tuknanavupi game board.

From a pile of any number of items (13 is the usual number), players take turns picking one, two, or three items. The player forced to pick up the last item loses the game. A winning strategy for the second player is to ensure that with every move you leave the pile with the number of objects equal to 9, 5, or 1. The program in Listing 7-1 plays and explains a variant of Nim. You can adapt it to play

Listing 7-1. The Nim Program.

```
10    REM LISTING7.01 - The Nim Program
20    FULLW 2:CLEARW 2:GOTOXY 1,1
30    RANDOMIZE 0
100   PRINT "This program plays the game of Nim.  Assume"
110   PRINT "that there are 25 sticks in a pile.  The players take"
120   PRINT "turns removing 1,2,3, or 4 sticks from the plie.  The"
130   PRINT "player who is forced to take the last stick loses."
140   DIM C$(5),L$(5),W$(5)
150   FOR X=1 TO 5:READ C$(X):NEXT X:FOR X=1 TO 5:READ L$(X):NEXT X
160   FOR X=1 TO 5:READ W$(X):NEXT X
170   PRINT
190   INPUT "Do you want to go first (Y/N) ";Q$
200   PRINT
210   X=25
220   IF Q$="Y" THEN 300
230   IF Q$<>"N" THEN 190
250   PRINT "I choose 4 sticks."
260   PRINT "There are now 21 sticks left."
270   X=21
280   PRINT
300   FOR I=1 TO 10
310   GOSUB 380
320   IF X=1 THEN 650
330   IF X<1 THEN 760
340   GOSUB 490
350   IF X=1 THEN 760
```

```
360    NEXT I
370    REM----------------NUMBER OF STICKS OPPONENT TAKES--------------
380    INPUT "How many sticks do you want ";N
400    IF N<>INT(N) THEN 450
410    IF N<1 THEN 450
420    IF N>4 THEN 450
430    X=X-N
440    RETURN
450    PRINT C$(INT(RND*5+1))
460    PRINT
470    GOTO 380
480    REM----------------NUMBER OF STICKS I TAKE-------------------
490    N=X-5*INT((X-1)/5)-1
500    IF INT((X-1)/5)<>(X-1)/5 THEN 520
510    N=INT(RND*4+1)
520    X=X-N
530    IF N>1 THEN 560
540    PRINT "I choose 1 stick."
550    GOTO 600
560    PRINT "I choose ";N;" sticks."
570    IF X>1 THEN 600
580    PRINT "There is 1 stick left."
590    GOTO 610
600    PRINT "There are now ";X;" sticks left."
610    PRINT
630    RETURN
640    REM---------------HE WINS---------------------------------------
650    PRINT L$(INT(RND*5+1))
660    PRINT
670    PRINT
700    PRINT "Let us play another game."
710    PRINT "Since you went first last time, I will go first."
720    PRINT
740    GOTO 250
750    REM----------------I WIN----------------------------------------
760    PRINT W$(INT(RND*5+1))
770    F=F+1
780    IF F>5 THEN 950
790    PRINT
810    INPUT "Do you want to play another game (Y/N) ";R$
820    IF R$="Y" THEN RESTORE:GOTO 160
830    IF R$<>"N" THEN 810
840    REM--REMARKS IF OPPONENT TAKES ILLEGAL NUMBER OF STICKS------
850    DATA I THINK YOU ARE TRYING TO CHEAT!
860    DATA I CANNOT ALLOW THAT.,DID YOU READ THE DIRECTIONS?
870    DATA DO NOT TRY THAT AGAIN, WHY NOT GIVE UP?
880    REM------------REMARKS IF OPPONENT WINS------------------------
890    DATA HOW LUCKY CAN YOU GET, YOU ARE BETTER THAN I EXPECTED
900    DATA I WAS NOT PAYING ATTENTION
910    DATA I CAN BEAT YOU--WATCH THIS,NOBODY IS PERFECT
920    REM----------------REMARKS IF I WIN---------------------------
930    DATA THE GOOD GUYS WIN AGAIN, I GUESS I WON, YOU LOSE
940    DATA I MUST BE SUPERIOR, NOW DO NOT GET ANGRY
950    END
```

the Nim variations explained below.

Nim Variations. Here are a few games that can be mathematically analyzed in a manner similar to the way Nim has been analyzed

• Rectangular Dominoes: Players take turns plac-

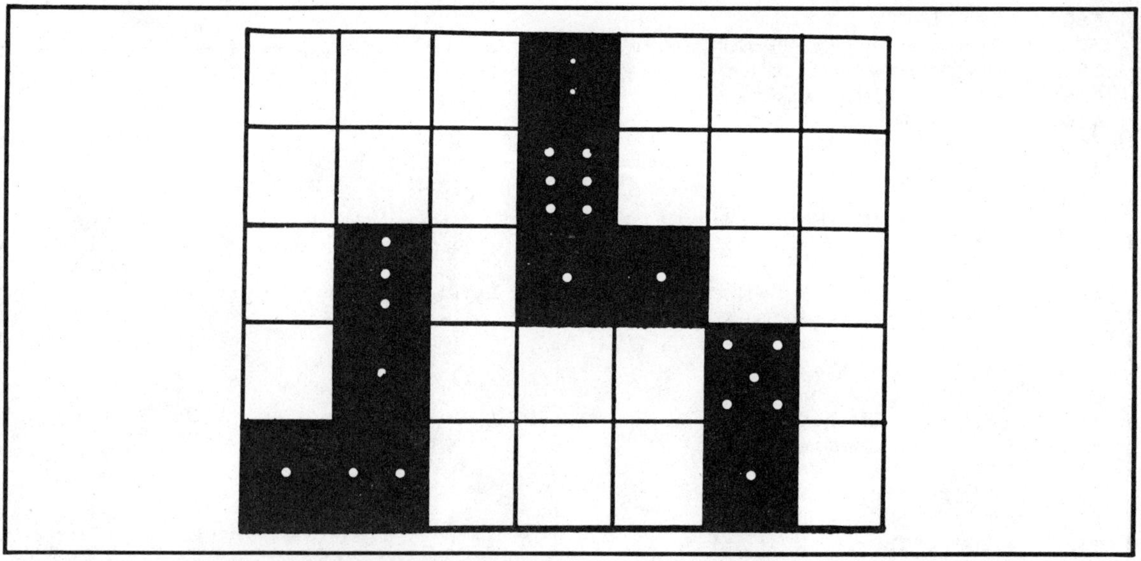

Fig. 7-9. A sample Rectangular Dominoes game.

ing dominoes on a chess-type board or a board of arbitrary size (8 × 8 is fine). The board is of a size such that a domino placed horizontally or vertically on it will cover up exactly two squares. The first player places his dominoes horizontally, the second player places his vertically; dominoes may not overlap. The winner of the game is the player who makes the last possible move. Figure 7-9 shows a sample game.

- Welter: The board for this game consists of an arbitrary number of squares in one line (usually about 20). An arbitrary number of tokens are randomly placed in the squares, with only one token in each square (there are usually about five tokens). A sample game is shown in Fig. 7-10. Players take turns moving a single token to any unoccupied square to the left, jumping over other tokens if desired. The player who makes the last move wins the game.
- Traffic Jam: The game board in Fig. 7-11, represents one-way roads between towns. An arbitrary number of vehicles are placed on the board to set up the game. Players take turns moving one of the vehicles in the proper direction from one town to an adjacent town. The game continues until a traffic jam develops, in which no further moves are possible; the player who makes the final move is declared the winner.
- Innocent Marble game: In this game, either zero, two, or four markers may be placed in the circles on the game board shown in Fig. 7-12; only one marker may be in any one circle. Players take turns moving any one marker from one circle to an adjacent one, in the directions of the arrows. Whenever a marker is moved to a circle that is already occupied, both markers are removed from play. The winner is the player making the last possible move.
- Tsyanshidzi: This is the Chinese national game in which players may select from two piles of objects either an arbitrary number of objects from one pile or the same number of objects from each pile, but no fewer than one object from each pile. As always, the player taking all remaining objects wins. This game requires a more complex analysis than the simple game of Nim does.
- Acey-deucey: In this game the computer "shuffles" a card deck and deals two cards. The player

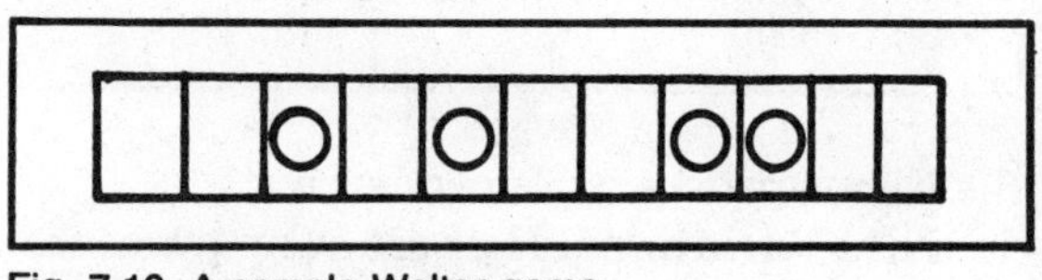

Fig. 7-10. A sample Welter game.

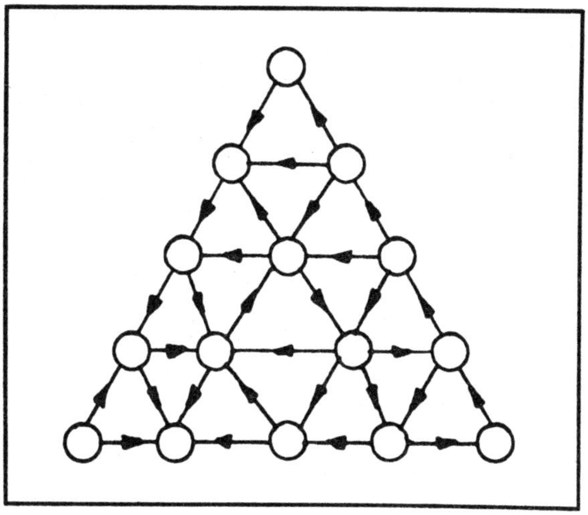

Fig. 7-11. The Traffic Jam game board.

then bets against the computer, wagering that the next card dealt will fill in between the first two cards in rank. Can you determine the mathematical strategy behind a winning program?

Neutron. Neutron is a two-player game played on a 5 × 5 grid, as shown in Fig. 7-13. At the start of the game, White owns the five pawns at the top, and Black the five pawns at the bottom. The neutron (n) begins at the center and is neutral. Each turn has two parts: first, the player must move the neutron in any one direction, and then the player must move one of his pawns in any direc-

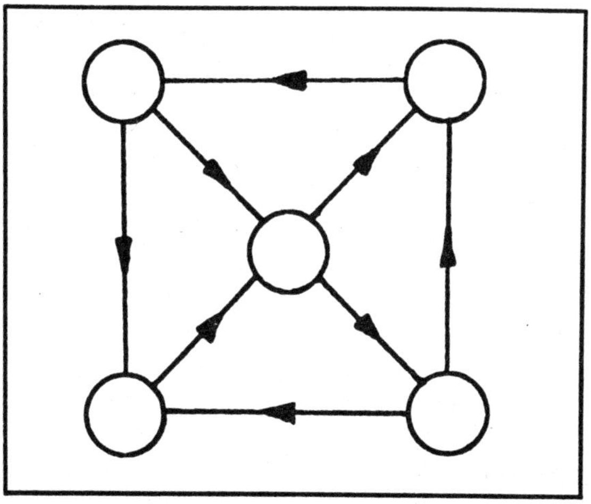

Fig. 7-12. The Innocent Marble game board.

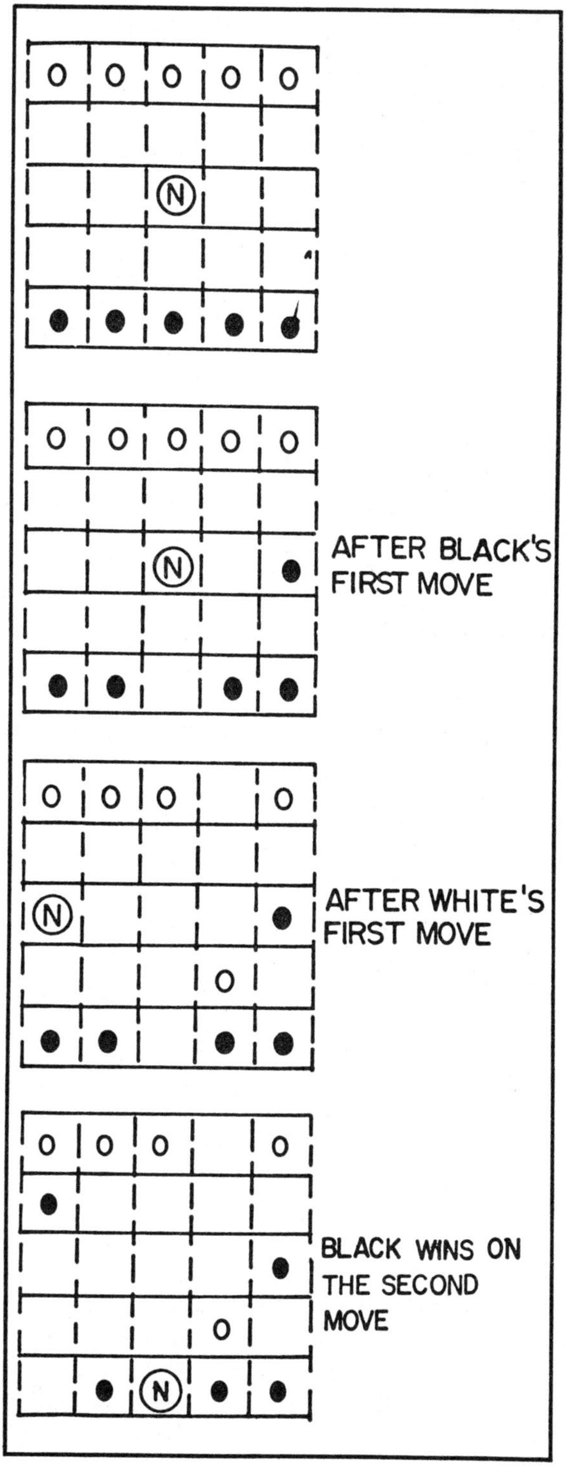

Fig. 7-13. The Neutron game board.

tion. The winner is the first to maneuver the neutron to his back row, whether moved by himself or by forcing the opponent to do so. You can also win by stalemating an opponent—that is, by trapping him so that he cannot complete his turn. For instance, if Black can completely surround the neutron with his pawns so that White cannot complete his turn, Black wins. There is another thing to remember: Any time a pawn or neutron is moved, it *must* be moved as far as it can go in a straight line (within the game board confines). A piece stops just before it reaches another piece of wall. Also, to even things out, White moves first but does not move the neutron on this first turn. A program to play Neutron would be based on tree-searching principles, as described in most artificial intelligence books and in the *Etudes for Programmers* (Wetherell, Prentice-Hall, 1978). This would be an ideal prelude in programming for those interested in computer chess.

Hexpawn. This game was first introduced by Martin Gardner in *Scientific American* (Volume 200, No. 3). The game is played on a 3 × 3 grid as in tic-tac-toe. The two players each place their three pieces as shown in the first diagram in Fig. 7-14. The pieces move in a manner similar to the way pawns move in chess, that is, they move one space diagonally to capture and remove an opponent's piece. Players alternate turns, and the winner is the first player to reach the opponent's side of the board with a piece or the remaining player when the opponent has no legal move.

Hexpawn presents an excellent opportunity to write a program that learns as it plays, because the number of different ways to play is small. Consider the game shown in the third diagram in Fig. 7-14. The computer must choose between one of the four moves indicated. If number 4 is chosen and leads to defeat, this information is stored and the mistake is not repeated in the future. The computer continues to randomly select legal moves, provided these moves have not proven fatal in previous games, until it becomes a perfect player.

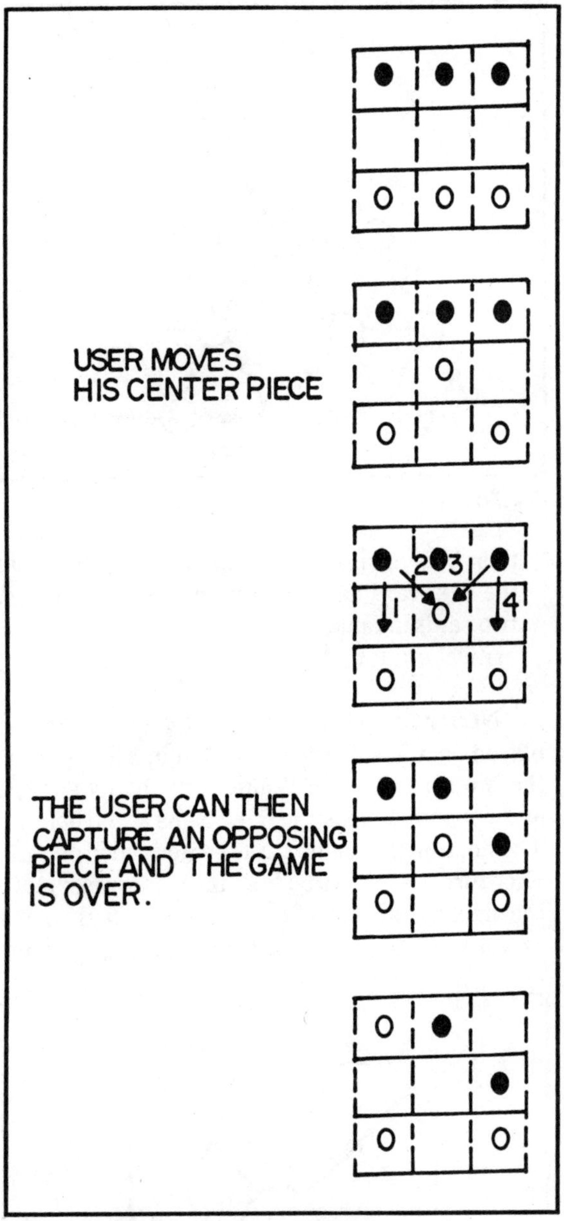

Fig. 7-14. The Hexpawn game board.

Countdown. How's your sense of timing? One or two players can test their skill with the computer serving as timekeeper and scorekeeper. First, the computer chooses and displays a random amount of time (say, from 5 to 60 seconds). Each player then presses a key when he or she thinks that amount of time has elapsed. The person who is closer is declared winner. Computers can execute a FOR-NEXT loop while the time is elapsing and from the number of executions multiplied by a time factor, determine the time elapsed. A variation of this game could test reaction time of two players; as soon as the word GO is displayed, the two players race to push their own keys, and the computer determines who reacted faster.

Mill. Mill is a two player game using the board shown in Fig. 7-15. Players alternate turns, placing one of their nine pieces on any of the corners or intersections of lines on the board. The moment one player gets three pieces in line, he may remove an opposing piece, provided that piece is not part of three in a row already.

After each player's nine pieces are placed, they may be moved one at a time to a vacant and adjacent corner or intersection. If any other lines of three are formed, another opposing piece may be removed. If a player has only three pieces on the board, he may move any one piece to any corner or intersection during his turn. The first player to be left with only two pieces is the loser.

Marked Square Game. In this simple game, the game board is a 9 × 9 grid. Players alternately mark one square with their initials. At the end of the game when all squares are filled, players receive 1, 2, or 3 points (respectively) for 3, 6, or 9 squares with their initials in a row; the player with the most points wins. The computer could serve as scorekeeper or opponent.

COMPUTER QUIZZES

Computer quiz games can be instructive as well as fun if clever programming techniques are used. Examples of these techniques include the following:

- Having a large database of questions from which a few are randomly selected to produce a new set of questions for each quiz
- Automatically recording the score and rewarding the player with graphic or musical interludes for good scores; new scores may be compared

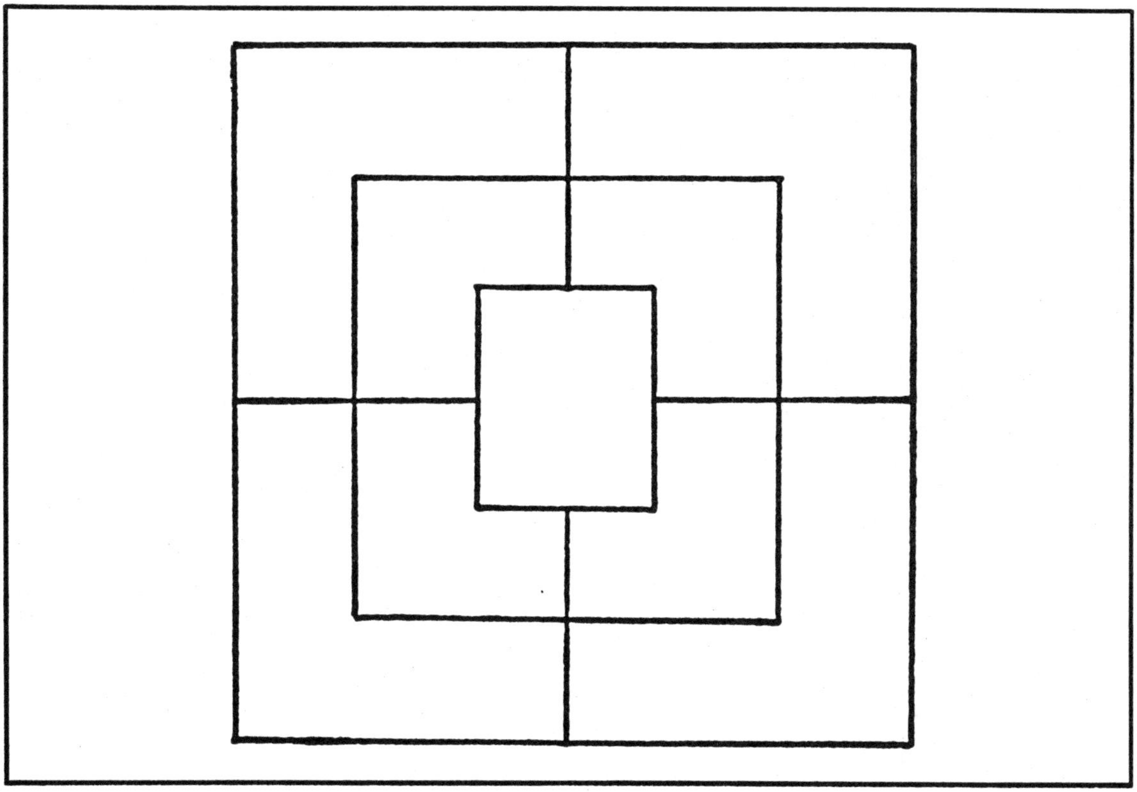

Fig. 7-15. The Mill game board.

with old scores or with those of other players

- Providing explanations of missed answers
- Allowing for the selection of questions according to the player's level of ability or providing for an automatically-adjusting level of difficulty based upon performance.

Assorted suggestions concerning topics for quiz games include the following:

- Names and capitals of states or countries, possibly using computer graphics to draw maps
- Vocabulary words
- IQ tests
- Personality and aptitude tests
- Foreign language vocabulary or grammar
- Preschool skills including comparing and counting random shapes, words, and numbers, and copying letters, words, and numbers
- Practice questions for examinations such as the SAT, GMAT, MCAT, LSAT, and ACT.
- Analogies
- Spelling bees
- Verses from literature or the Bible
- Trivia questions for trivia lovers, on science fiction, movies, and history
- Basic math skills
- Chemical equation balancing
- English grammar
- History of the United States, the Renaissance period, or World War I
- Constellations or planets

GAMES THAT USE WORDS

You can program a wide variety of games and activities based on words including the following:

- *Cryptograms*, or coded messages, could be displayed for you to decode; simple clues could be provided.
- *Anagrams*, or jumbled words, are a popular recreation. The program in Listing 7-2 randomly chooses one of many words stored in the DATA

Listing 7-2. The Anagram Creator Program.

```
10     REM LISTING7.02 - The Anagram Creator Program
20     RANDOMIZE 0
30     FULLW 2:CLEARW 2:GOTOXY 1,1
40     PRINT "ANAGRAM CREATOR"
50     PRINT "Scrambles words for entertainment"
60     N=6 :REM number of words in data statements
70     DIM M(N),W$(N),A(20)
80     FOR I=1 TO N
90     M(I)=I
100    NEXT I
110    FOR I=1 TO N-1
120    R=(N+1-I)*RND
130    R=INT(R)+I
140    T=M(R)
150    M(R)=M(I)
160    M(I)=T
170    NEXT I
180    FOR I=1 TO N
190    READ W$(M(I))
200    NEXT I
210    FOR I=1 TO N
220    A$=""
230    A=LEN(W$(I))
240    FOR B=1 TO A
250    A(B)=B
260    NEXT B
```

```
270    FOR B=1 TO A-1
280    S=(A+1-B)*RND
290    S=INT(S)+B
300    C=A(S):A(S)=A(B):A(B)=C
310    NEXT B
320    FOR B=1 TO A
330    A$=A$+MID$(W$(I),A(B),1)
340    NEXT B
350    PRINT A$
360    INPUT C$
370    IF C$=W$(I) THEN PRINT "RIGHT!" ELSE PRINT "WRONG, THE ANSWER W
       AS: ";W$(I)
380    NEXT I
390    INPUT "PLAY AGAIN (Y/N) ";A$:IF A$="Y" THEN RESTORE:GOTO 80
395    INPUT "THANKS FOR PLAYING ",Q$
400    REM DATA STATEMENTS CONTAIN WORDS HERE....
410    DATA COMPUTER,TELEVISION,GAME,INSTRUMENT,WRITE,BASIC
```

statements beginning with line 500. The program scrambles the letters in the word and prints it on the video screen for you to unscramble and input.

- The game of Hangman, in which one has 10 guesses to determine the letters in a randomly chosen word, serves to familiarize the player with vocabulary terms.
- Word search puzzles *ad infinitum* may be computer generated, either from a word list or as a random matrix similar to the popular Boggle™ game. A program to determine the locations of all words in the puzzle could also be implemented. You could also have the computer assist in creation of a crossword puzzle. Choose a topic and enter words; the computer will automatically fit the common letters together to form a crossword grid. Next, enter an obscure or humorous clue for each word. The completed crossword can be saved for later use or printed and sent to friends.
- Word guessing games, similar to Twenty Questions, can be computerized. In these games, the player asks the computer questions to determine what word has been randomly selected. Replies for the many possible questions a human could pose must be stored; thus, there are difficult programming challenges. The dialogue with one such program went like this:

(c = computer, h = human)

h: Does it grow?
c: To answer that question might be misleading.
h: Can I eat it?
c: Only as food for thought.
h: Do computers have it?
c: Strictly speaking, no.
c: The word is "Knowledge."

- A word game similar to the popular Mastermind™ game would involve the computer selecting a three-letter word from a large list. The player would guess by entering a three-letter word and would be told whether or not the computer's word contained any of the letters in the word the player guessed and whether or not those letters were in the correct position. The object is to guess the computer's word in the fewest number of tries.
- In the game of Confound, the computer outputs 15 letters (consonants and vowels). The players must form the longest word possible using these letters. The computer serves to keep score and check to ensure that no letters were used improperly, that is, used more often than they appear in the list.

Using the combination of a random number generator, a list of words, and simple rules for English grammar, a microcomputer can compose original stories *ad infinitum*; the results are often amusing. Here are some story writing suggestions:

- Use a standard story line in which blanks are left to be filled in with inputted words, which could consist of personalized information, or arbitrary nouns, adjectives, and adverbs, as done in the Mad Libs™ party games. For example, a story could begin

> Space, the *(adjective)* frontier.
> These are the voyages of the starship *(noun)*,
> It's a five-year mission:
> To seek out new *(noun)* and new *(noun)* . . .

The operator is requested to provide one adjective and three nouns to fill in the four blanks above, but is unaware of the story line until later, when these words are incorporated and the story is printed out. Here is a sample result.

> Space, the *nauseating* frontier.
> These are the voyages of the starship *lemon*
> Its five-year mission:
> To seek out new *games* and new *computers* . . .

Also included in this category are "Me Books" for young children. The computer fills the blanks in a story with a child's name, address, and other personalized information. The resulting personalized story often increases a child's interest in reading.

- A much more difficult approach to story writing involves the random selection of words or phrases to compose a series of sentences that follow standard rules of grammar. A program written in 1960 (before high-level languages were in widespread use) called SAGA was designed to produce short scripts for movie westerns. Here's a sample of the output:

Sheriff:

> The Sheriff is at the window
> Sheriff sees robber
> Robber sees Sheriff
> go to door
> wait
> open door
> Sheriff sees robber
> go through door
> robber see Sheriff
> go to window

Robber:

> take gun from holster with right hand
> aim
> fire
> Sheriff nicked

Sheriff:

> take gun from holster with right hand
> aim
> fire
> robber hit
> blow out barrel
> put gun down at door
> go to table
> pick up glass with right hand . . .

Writing a program to accomplish the above is more complex than it would seem on first examination; the program was considered quite an achievement in 1960. Random numbers were used to determine the sequence of events; the events were selected from a wide range of preprogrammed possibilities. The program had to guard against a character firing a gun without first withdrawing it from his holster and similar situations. Also, a routine was necessary to compose "sentences" using the rules of grammar (for example, "gun takes robber from holster with right hand" would not be allowed, but "robber takes gun from holster with right hand" would be allowed). The use of programmed phrases instead of individual words to select from would simplify this task considerably. In like manner, a science fiction spoof or soap opera dialogue could be written. A professional software house sells a program to produce random, technical double-talk to "fill out business reports that are too short." A sample line produced by the program reads, "The product configuration requires considerable analysis and trade-off studies to arrive at the total system rationale."

MAGIC

Magic tricks performed by your computer would make an interesting demonstration for your guests. Here are some suggestions:

Micro Mentalist. The computer becomes a mind reader in this trick. The performer, who is the computer operator, is given an item from the audience. The performer enters a question such as, "What is the item given to me by the audience?" After a brief delay, the computer displays the name of the item.

The trick is based on a code programmed into the computer that allows the performer to indicate inconspicuously to the computer which of approximately 20 items he has been given. The code is contained within the input sentence; different sentences stand for different objects. For example, "What do I have now?" could indicate a watch, and "What am I holding?" could indicate a match folder. The computer merely matches the input question to the item list stored in its memory.

Age Determination. The performer hands a member of the audience a pocket calculator and tells him to enter his age and then subtract his favorite one-digit number. Next, the guest multiplies this result by nine and adds his age to the product. The final result is called out and is input to the computer. The determination of the guest's age is accomplished by adding the first two digits in the result to the last digit (for example, if the result were 176, adding 17 and 6 gives you 23, the guest's age).

The Break in the Chain. This trick is performed with a complete set of dominoes (usually 28 pieces). Beforehand, the performer removes one of the dominoes (it may not be a double) and inputs the two numbers on the domino to be stored in the computer. The guests are given the remaining set and are asked to complete a single domino chain as in regular play. Once completed, the numbers on the two ends of the chain are noted, and the performer inputs a question such as, "What are the two numbers?" The computer replies correctly by displaying the two previously stored numbers. The trick is automatic and will work with any domino chosen, excluding doubles.

COMPUTER-INTELLIGENCE GAMES

Programs can be written to make a computer "learn" from its mistakes, entering the realm of artificial intelligence. A checker-playing program that stores the results of all previous moves has been written. Although the time necessary to decide on a move increases as the game progresses, the computer's moves are much better than they were at the beginning of the game. Here are some games that the computer can "learn" to play.

- Nim, described earlier in this chapter, is a popular computer game in which a player may take one, two, or three items from a pile of 20 in an attempt to force an opponent to take the last item. Although this game is completely solvable, a Nim program could be written as a demonstration of computer "learning."
- A BASIC game called *Animal*, in which the computer plays the game of Twenty Questions with a human, has been written. The computer asks such questions as "Does it swim?" to try to determine what animal the human is thinking of. If that animal is not in the computer's file, the human is requested to provide information so that a file on the new animal can be created. Thus, the computer "learns." Of course, it may be interesting to use a subject other than animals; for example, you could use places instead of animals to help young people learn geography.
- A crude "mind reading" program based upon probability could be created. The human would be instructed to choose one of two words. Then the computer will output the word it "believes" was chosen. After a number of trials, the computer should be able to formulate a strategy for guessing which word will be chosen next, because humans can never be random and tend to guess in patterns; theoretically, the computer should be able to achieve better than 50 percent correct responses.

Other applications of personal computers in the area of artificial intelligence include programs that can tutor humans to play complex games such as chess, in which moves can be analyzed and changed, and suggestions or tips given.

PROGRAMS FOR YOUNG CHILDREN

Programs that make liberal use of graphics and are designed to be foolproof may serve as educational tools for young children. They can familiarize children with using a keyboard, cursors, and computer graphics, and can provide learning experiences. Suggestions include the following:

- Matching Games: Children can match letters, words, and shapes.
- Drawing Machine: A joystick controller or arrow keys permit drawing on a video screen. A library of shapes including squares, triangles, and circles can also be used to construct pictures.
- Face Maker: Children can create their own funny face on a video screen by selecting eyes, ears, a nose, hair, and a mouth from a collection of possibilities.
- Storybook: Using the keyboard, children can write their own stories, which the computer then interprets and animates on the screen. Stories can involve stored images such as houses, trees, people, and cars, which may then be animated to illustrate a sentence such as, "The girls walked from home to school."

THE COMPUTER AS BOARD DISPLAY DEVICE, BOOKKEEPER, AND GAME ADVISOR

Certain games are designed in such a way that the computer cannot be programmed to be a formidable opponent. You can use the computer with these games in other ways, including the following:

- Board display and bookkeeping for complex board games such as Risk™, Stratego™, Go, Metagames, and Avalon-Hill games can be accomplished with high-resolution graphics. In addition to displaying the board, the computer could
  - —Generate random numbers to replace spinners, dice, cards
  - —Record each move for later review
  - —Compute the game status at the end of each turn
  - —Compute energy, arsenal, moves, positions, money and statistics for each player.
- Advising and bookkeeping for such games as checkers and chess can be accomplished. The computer could store each move, advise against potential checks, skewers, and forks, alert the players to discoveries, and print a listing of the game, move by move, at the finish. Advising for gambling games such as blackjack could take the form of the creation of an odds table for the high cards remaining in the deck, the computation of whether to stay or hit, and the calculation of the safest amount to bet.

DRAWING AND KALEIDOSCOPE PROGRAMS

Most picture drawing programs utilize the arrow (cursor positioning) keys on the video terminal keyboard to direct a cursor point that leaves a line. Several additions could be made to these programs, including animation routines, special standard designs that may be called to the screen, provisions for storing a design on cassette or floppy disk, and for using light pens and joysticks. The *kaleidoscope effect* refers to a computer algorithm used to alter a design in kaleidoscope fashion (that is, the design is multiply reflected as its mirror image) in real time. Fascinating "modern art" designs can be made with programs that use random numbers with the DRAW, LINE, CIRCLE, FULL, and PAINT commands found in some BASIC interpreters. Random lines and circles of various sizes fill the screen, and each area defined by lines is filled in with various colors.

SIMULATION AND ADVENTURE GAMES

Simulations of real-world situations need not be outputted as complex numerical listings; they may be transformed into games suited for people young and old. Some of the many possibilities include the following:

Pool Table. A pool playing game displayed using video graphics could serve to teach the principles of elastic collisions and angular geometry.

Motorcycle Jump. A simulation in which a motorcycle must leap a certain distance to land safely could illustrate projectile motion. The ramp angle and initial motorcycle velocity would be determined by the person playing the game.

Projectile motion formulae are provided below for those with faint recollections of high school physics:

1. Position relative to point of projection after time t:

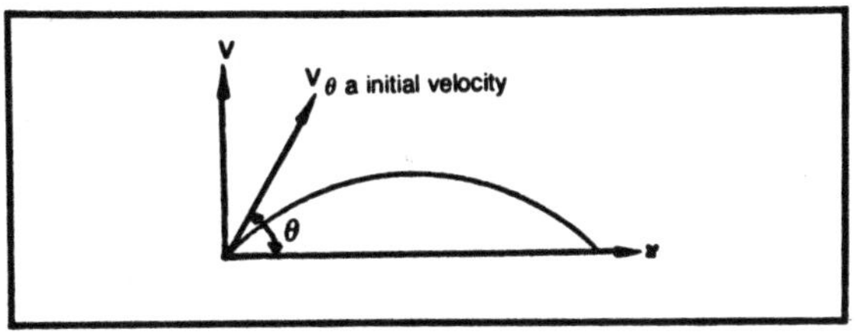

$$x = v_0 t \cos\theta$$

$$y = v_0 t \sin\theta - \frac{gt^2}{2}$$

2. Range, maximum height and time of flight:

$$T = \frac{2v_0}{g}\sin\theta$$

$$R = \frac{2v_0^2}{g}\sin\theta\cos\theta$$

$$H = \frac{v_0^2}{2g}\sin^2\theta$$

3. Necessary angle of projection for given range with given speed of projection:

$\sin 2\alpha = \frac{R_g}{v^2}$ Rg giving two possible

angles, α_1, and α_2.

Navigation. A simulation in which the participant must find his way to an island, using a radio direction finder in his sailboat, could teach principles of geometry as well as sailboat handling for example.

Detective. The participant would assume the role of a detective in this simulation. A valuable gem has been stolen from a museum and five persons are suspected. The use of deductive reasoning is the only way the detective can solve this crime.

MX Missile. In this grid search game, one player hides MX missiles among several possible silos and may shuffle missiles while the other player shoots at them trying to hit silos containing missiles.

World Race. Using a combination of race and rally tactics, players compete to be the first to motor from England to New York and back to New York, navigating their way through Europe, Asia, the Far East, and South America. Strategy plays a large part, because players have to motor through towns in every country in order to pick up points. Out-of-the-way towns score higher than those along main routes. The winner is the player who reaches New York in the least time and with the most points. Rabies in Europe, tropical rains in South America, drought in Africa, and so on deter everyone's progress. The game serves to teach geography.

Wall Street. A stock market simulation, preferably multiplayer, would allow players to buy and sell stocks according to market conditions. A computer determines the outcome of each round and the price for each stock and serves a bookkeeper.

World Conflict. This multiplayer simulation would place each player as the head of a nation. Players must decide whether they should go to war, form cartels, or make concessions and compromises. The computer could select the conflicting situations (for example, oil embargoes, assassinations, nuclear threats, Communist expansion).

Decision. A simulation of corporate management and big business could place each player as a top-level executive. Each executive has the authority to produce the product of his choice and sell the product at the best market price. Throughout the game, prices fluctuate according to the law of supply and demand.

Fire. The object of this simulation is to subdue a raging forest fire with chemicals, backfires, and other fire-fighting methods. The success of the player depends upon quick decisions concerning how to control a geometrically increasing fire.

Atomic Fission. This simulation demonstrates geometric progressions by simulating a nuclear reaction in which each split atom releases enough energy to split two or more other atoms, and so on.

Auction. Principles of bidding at an auction could be simulated in a one- (or more) player game involving the auction of art. Players must be careful of forgeries.

Adventure. The object of this simulation is survival in a desperate attempt to locate buried treasure on an island. How does one obtain fresh water on an island surrounded by salt water?

Ethics. This simulation, involving the conflict between morals and greed, uses the computer as the judge of ethics. Conflicting situations in which players must decide the outcome are provided. If a preprogrammed decision does not match with a player's, that player accumulates "morality deductions." The winner is the player with the most money and fewest deductions.

Careers. This simulation game places the player in new occupations to enable him or her to experience decision making, conflicts, opportunities, and financial stress from different viewpoints in a variety of careers.

Artillery. This is a simulation in which a gun in a fixed emplacement must fire a projectile at such a velocity and angle that it will hit a target. The distance the projectile lands from the target could be displayed as the integer of the log to the base 2 of the absolute value of the distance; several other possibilities exist for teaching mathematical principles.

Grid Search Simulations. A search game, for example, one that pitted a destroyer against a submarine, could be programmed. The game would use a 10 × 10 grid that must be selectively searched by the ship or the submarine in its efforts to find and attack the other vessel. Similarly, a game played on the same grid could involve a spy searching for hidden documents with hidden enemy agents to watch for as well.

Rat Race. A video graphics program that draws a maze and animates a mouse could be created. The programming involved in enabling the mouse to "learn" to solve the maze could demonstrate rudimentary artificial intelligence principles.

Computer. Based on a large-scale computing system, the object of this simulation is to process two complete programs before your opponents can. Players who make the best decisions can avoid the jeopardies of power failures, restricted use of I/O channels, bugs, and priority interrupts.

Laser Tank. The player and the opponent (the computer) each have a laser-firing tank and a base. The object is to be the first to destroy the opponent's base while avoiding his fire. Obstacles litter the battlefield, and laser fire is destructive only at a limited range.

Robotwar. The purpose of this simulation is to teach computer programming. Two opposing players are instructed to secretly design programs, written in a custom language, that would create and control robots designed to annihilate any other robots. The programs would be entered, and a video display of the combat field would be updated in real time. The objective could be to hit the opposing robot five times to win.

Robotwar II. The program in Listing 7-3, Robotwar II, is a challenging game to play against your computer. In the game, you are represented by an *, while the computer controls annihilating robots represented by +. An electrified, lethal fence defines the playing field.

The computer's robots will destroy you if they come close. However, the robots will destroy themselves if they run into the fence. Your objective is to evade the robots until all have been destroyed by the fence. To move in a desired direction, use the chart in Fig. 7-16, which indicates the number to input.

Listing 7-3. The Robotwar II Program.

```
10      REM LISTING7.03 - The Robotwar II Program
100     RANDOMIZE 0
150     FULLW 2:CLEARW 2:GOTOXY 1,1
160     PRINT TAB(20)"---------------ROBOTWAR II-----------------
170     PRINT
180     INPUT "Instructions (Y/N) ";Y$:IF Y$="Y" THEN GOSUB 1800
185     IF Y$<>"N" THEN 180
190     CLEARW 2:GOTOXY 1,1
195     REM SET UP THE GAME
200     DIM A(10,20),E(21),F(21)
210     G=0:Z7=1
220     FOR B=1 TO 10
230     FOR C=1 TO 20
240     A(B,C)=0
250     IF B<>1 THEN 260
251     A(B,C)=1
260     IF B<>10 THEN 270
261     A(B,C)=1
270     IF C<>1 THEN 280
271     A(B,C)=1
280     IF C<>20 THEN 290
281     A(B,C)=1
290     NEXT C
300     NEXT B
310     FOR D=1 TO 21
320     B=INT(RND*8+2)
330     C=INT(RND*8+2)
340     IF A(B,C)<>0 THEN 320
350     A(B,C)=1
360     IF D>=6 THEN 370
361     A(B,C)=2
370     IF D<>6 THEN 380
371     A(B,C)=3
380     E(D)=B
390     F(D)=C
400     NEXT D
490     GOSUB 1900
499     REM PRINT PATTERN
500     FOR B=1 TO 10
510     FOR C=1 TO 20
520     IF A(B,C)<>0 THEN 530
521     PRINT " ";
530     IF A(B,C)<>1 THEN 540
531     PRINT " ";
540     IF A(B,C)<>2 THEN 550
541     PRINT "$";
550     IF A(B,C)<>3 THEN 560
551     PRINT "O";
560     NEXT C
570     PRINT
580     NEXT B
590     REM MAKE MOVE
600     B=E(6)
610     C=F(6)
620     A(B,C)=0
```

```
630   INPUT Y
640   IF Y=0 THEN 800
650   ON Y GOTO 660,660,660,690,680,680,680,690,1400
660   B=B-1
670   GOTO 690
680   B=B+1
690   ON Y GOTO 700,800,720,720,720,800,700,700
700   C=C-1
710   GOTO 800
720   C=C+1
790   REM CALCULATE THE RESULTS
800   IF A(B,C)=1 THEN 1500
810   IF A(B,C)=2 THEN 1600
820   A(B,C)=3
830   E(6)=B
840   F(6)=C
850   FOR D=1 TO 5
860   IF A(E(D),F(D))<>2 THEN 960
870   A(E(D),F(D))=0
880   IF E(D)=B THEN 890
881   E(D)=E(D)+1
890   IF E(D)<=B THEN 900
891   E(D)=E(D)-1
900   IF F(D)>=C THEN 910
901   F(D)=F(D)+1
910   IF F(D)<=C THEN 920
911   F(D)=F(D)-1
920   IF A(E(D),F(D))=3 THEN 1600
930   IF A(E(D),F(D))=0 THEN 940
931   G=G+1
940   IF A(E(D),F(D))<>0 THEN 950
941   A(E(D),F(D))=2
950   IF G=5 THEN 1700
960   NEXT D
970   INPUT "MAP (Y/N) ";Y$
980   IF Y$="Y" THEN CLEARW 2:GOTOXY 1,1:GOTO 490
990   IF Y$<>"N" THEN 970
1000  GOTO 600
1400  PRINT "SORRY TO SEE YOU QUIT"
1401  Z9=Z9+1
1410  GOTO 1710
1500  PRINT "YOU TOUCHED THE FENCE"
1501  Z9=Z9+1
1510  GOTO 1710
1600  PRINT "YOU HAVE BEEN DESTROYED BY A LUCKY COMPUTER"
1601  Z9=Z9+1
1610  GOTO 1710
1700  PRINT " ** YOU DESTROYED THE ENEMY **"
1701  Z8=Z8+1
1710  INPUT "DO YOU WANT TO PLAY AAIN (Y/N) ";Y$
1720  IF Y$="Y" THEN Z7=Z7+1:CLEARW 2:GOTOXY 1,1:GOTO 210
1730  IF Y$<>"N" THEN 1710
1731  PRINT "COMPUTER WON: ";Z9" ","THE HUMAN WON: ";Z8
1732  PRINT "COMPUTER'S AVERAGE: ";100*(Z9/(Z8+Z9));"%; THE HUMAN'S
      AVERAGE: ";100*(Z8/(Z8+Z9));"%"
1733  PRINT
1740  PRINT "HOPE YOU DON'T FEEL FENCED IN
1750  PRINT "TRY AGAIN SOMETIME."
1760  FOR X=1 TO 200:NEXT:END
```

```
1800  PRINT "YOU--'O'; ROBOTS--'4'"
1810  PRINT "FENCE--'X'. FENCE IS LETHAL!"
1820  PRINT "ROBOTS WILL DESTROY YOU IF THEY COME CLOSE.  THE FENCE
      WILL DESTROY"
1830  PRINT "ANYTHING THAT TOUCHES IT--INCLUDING YOU.  EVADE THE
      ROBOTS UNTIL"
1840  PRINT "THE FENCE HAS DESTROYED THEM ALL.  TO MOVE, INPUT A
      NUMBER FROM"
1850  PRINT "THE CHART WHICH APPEARS NEXT TO THE GAME GRID."
1860  INPUT "PRESS 'RETURN' TO START ";Y$:CLEARW 2:GOTOXY 1,1:RETURN
1900  REM MOVES CHART
1920  GOTOXY 20,1:PRINT TAB(50)"2"
1930  GOTOXY 1,2:PRINT TAB(50)"!"
1940  GOTOXY 1,3:PRINT TAB(45)"1";TAB(50)"!";TAB(55)"3"
1950  GOTOXY 1,4:PRINT TAB(46)"!";TAB(54)"!";TAB(65)"0=NOMOVE"
1960  GOTOXY 1,5:PRINT TAB(47)"!";TAB(53)"!"
1970  GOTOXY 1,6:PRINT TAB(40)"8----";TAB(50)"0";TAB(56)"----4"
1980  GOTOXY 1,7:PRINT TAB(47)"!";TAB(53)"!"
1990  GOTOXY 1,8:PRINT TAB(46)"!";TAB(54)"!"TAB(65)"9=END GAME"
2000  GOTOXY 1,9:PRINT TAB(45)"7";TAB(50)"!";TAB(55)"5"
2010  GOTOXY 1,10:PRINT TAB(50)"!"
2020  GOTOXY 1,11:PRINT TAB(50)"6"
2030  RETURN
```

VIDEO GAMES

A personal computer with a memory-mapped video display and high-resolution graphics could emulate the popular video games. Although programs written in BASIC do not execute as fast as the real video games do, programs written in assembly language do run as fast. Here are some ideas you might want to try:

Maxwell's Demon. Semi-floating molecules are trapped in one chamber of a two-chamber box. A gate connects the two compartments. The molecules are constantly bombarding each other and bouncing off walls; the object is to open and close the gate at the right times so that all molecules will be trapped in the other compartment.

Hockey and Tennis-Type Games. These computer games could be controlled with joysticks, simple potentiometers, or keyboard switches, just as their video game counterparts are.

Tanks. In a projectile-shooting battle between two tanks, the computer could act as the opponent. Similarly, a battle could be designed for jet fighters, biplanes, or ships instead of tanks.

Pinball. A moving set of paddles could replay a "ball" to hit targets and score points.

Lunar Lander. This game involves a lunar-landing module that is governed by rocket propulsion, fuel supply, and gravity. It must land at a low velocity so that no damage is done and must land on a plateau, avoiding lunar mountains and craters. The lunar lander program could be made more complex by requiring that you take off from the lunar surface, navigate over an obstacle of random size, and land again accurately.

Football, Baseball, and Basketball. An animated display of players, ball positions, and the playing field could be used to display the action in these sports.

Racetrack. The object of this game is to finish the race in the least time. Hazards include at-

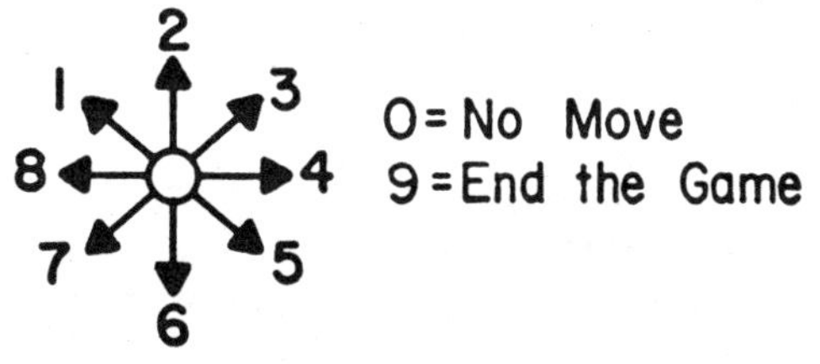

Fig. 7-16. The numbers corresponding to the directions in the Robot II game.

taining too much speed to slow down before a curve, oil slicks, and other cars. Hazards cause you to lose time.

Skydiver. The player in this game must control chute opening and jump time for a parachutist who must land at a precise point. A wind of randomly selected direction and velocity presents a challenge to overcome.

Robot Bowl. The player controls a bowling robot in an attempt to knock down as many pins as possible. The time of release, angle of approach, and weight of the ball are selected by the player.

Shooting Gallery. Several moving targets of different point values and a directional "gun" could comprise a video version of the popular shooting gallery.

Golf. A golf game with a set of graphic holes (or design-your-own-hole provisions) would let the players choose the clubs they will use for each shot and the angle at which the ball will be hit. Hazards include sand traps, water, "dog-legs," and strong winds.

RECREATIONS INVOLVING THE ATARI ITSELF

A hobby computer magazine once listed some suggestions on "busting your computer" to determine the limitations of your BASIC (or other high-level language). The results may surprise you. Here are a few ideas:

- Determine the maximum number of parentheses that can be used in one statement. (Don't be surprised if over 100 are allowed!)
- Determine the maximum dimension allowed for an array.
- Determine the maximum number of nested FOR-NEXT loops allowed.

Other challenges include writing a "self-duplicating" program that is not simply composed of verbatim PRINT statements, yet prints a duplicate of itself. If you are ambitious, you might attempt to break the record for carrying out π to the most decimal places (500,000).

COMPUTERS AND CHESS

Chess is one of the most popular computer recreations for several reasons. First, it requires an advanced level of computer programming, described by some as "artificial intelligence," that enables a computer to emulate human thought. Second, it may be difficult to find chess opponents at your level of ability. The computer, as your opponent, solves that problem by having adjustable skill levels, making it possible to find an opponent of your own strength. Third, many chess programs can serve as chess tutors by suggesting moves, demonstrating piece movements, allowing the rearrangement of boards, and even stepping you through a collection of games from masters-level tournaments. Many of today's chess programs are rated in the middle 1200s or above and can serve as a formidable opponent for novice to intermediate level players.

Chess-playing programs are almost always written in assembly language for the purpose of speed; they may analyze from a few thousand to several million possibilities before making a move. A large-scale computer chess program is described below for those interested in the inner workings of the game. The discussion can, perhaps, provide added insights for your game and can assist those who are interested in writing their own chess programs. A warning, however: most credible chess programs have required thousands of man-hours in development time and are truly a programmer's ultimate challenge.

The program described here is name OSTRICH; it competed in the First World Computer Chess Tournament. The OSTRICH program is composed of three modules: BOOK, which provides standard book opening moves for up to the first five moves, CHESS, which is the main program used during most of the game, and END GAME, which takes over in rook/king or queen and king/king end games. CHESS, the main module, is comprised of approximately 9000 instructions, which are divided into five subprograms:

1. A subroutine for the control of input and out-

put and for the control of the size of the search tree. The *search tree* refers to the branching search for all move possibilities that the computer performs before making each move. The size of the tree indicates the depth or number of moves ahead that will be considered for each move.

2. A subprogram to generate all move possibilities or search the tree.
3. A subprogram to arrange each possible move on a hierarchical scale according to its plausibility (each move is given a plausibility score). Following this initial ordering, another set of routines is called upon to improve the ordering.
4. A subprogram to calculate a terminal score or to evaluate the chess board at each terminal or branching point in the tree.
5. A subroutine to update all arrays, lists, and pointers used by the remainder of the program.
6. The lists of the locations of each chess piece: An 8 × 8 array holds an identification number for each of the pieces on the board, in a corresponding memory location. The white pieces are identified as follows: King = 6, Queen = 5, Rook = 4, Bishop = 3, Knight = 2, and Pawn = 1. The black pieces are identified as the negative of the corresponding white piece number. The boards position array is updated after each move.
7. The piece location arrays: Two separate arrays are generated at the beginning of each tree search. The list contains the names and corresponding locations of the white pieces; the other does the same for the black pieces.
8. The possible moves list: A list of possible moves for *ply* 1 (ply refers to the depth searched), ply 2, and ply 3, corresponding to each initial move, is generated. Additionally, memory is reserved to indicate which moves will result in a capture.
9. The control piece array: This array stores the squares that each piece "controls" as well as the pieces that control a particular square. Thus, it is possible to determine the power of each piece along with what pieces are in control of the specific square in question.
10. The change array: All changes made at a node in the search tree are stored in this array when control advances to a new node. The purpose of the list is to expedite the restoring of positions.
11. The pinned pieces list: A listing of all pinned pieces is maintained in this array.
12. The *en prise* pieces list: A separate list of *en prise* pieces at each search node is maintained.
13. The Alpha and Beta cut-offs lists: Two lists, one of the last eight moves resulting in alpha refutations and the other of beta refutations, are maintained.
14. The ply 3 plausibility list: CHESS maintains a list of the best ply 3 move for each possible ply 2 opponent's move for each ply 1 move investigated.
15. The principal variations list: Each principal variation originating in the tree search is stored in this list.
16. The position records list: This listing of all moves since a recent capture or pawn move is used to determine whether a draw should be made because of repetition.

Tree Size

Tree size is automatically controlled by the program so that decisions will not exceed a predetermined time limit. Conditions that warrant an extension of the tree size include potential checks, captures, pawn promotions, pawns on the seventh rank, and the presence of *en prise* pieces.

The flowchart in Fig. 7-17 illustrates the processing that occurs each time a new node is reached. The node is determined to be either "terminal" or "nonterminal." A terminal node can be declared by a subroutine known as the gamma algorithm, by the fact that the node is past the tree length or by the fact that the node is past the minimum ply, but the board has no special features. All other nodes are classified as nonterminal.

Nonterminal Node Processing

The One Move Generator subroutine is the first processing done at a nonterminal node. This

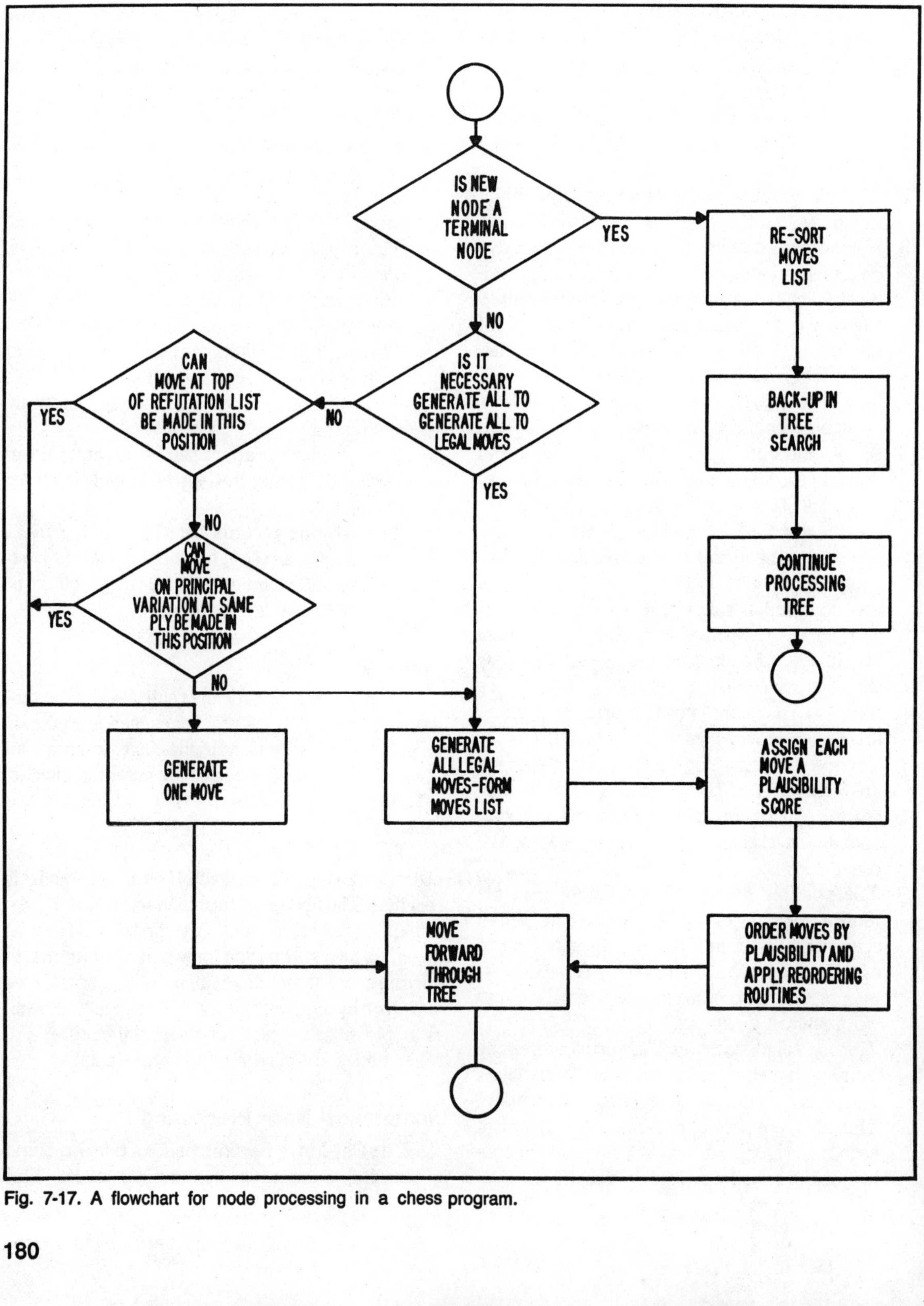

Fig. 7-17. A flowchart for node processing in a chess program.

subroutine determines whether one move is sufficient or all legal moves must be generated; if the first move could cause a refutation, the program continues; otherwise, the Move Generator determines all legal moves. Following move generation, a plausibility score is assigned to each move, and moves are sorted according to decreasing plausibility. The list is then resorted by special routines.

Plausibility Scoring

All possible moves are assigned a plausibility score that is based on the following parameters:

1. Captures: The score given for each capture is 2400 points plus the results of this formula:

   additional points = (point value of captures − piece point value of capturing piece)/10

   where the points for the chess pieces are pawn = 600, knight = bishop = 1800, rook = 3000, queen = 5400, king = 300,000.
2. Castling: The point value for castling is 10,000 points.
3. Randomizer: This routine adds a random number of points to each move such that no piece will have excessive moves on the moves list. Up to ten points may be added.
4. Advance: Any move which retreats a queen, knight, or bishop receives a penalty of 20 points.
5. Pawn attack: Any move which places a queen, rook, bishop, or knight where it can be captured on the next move by a pawn receives a penalty of 200 points.
6. Pawn scoring: A pawn move past the fourth rank is awarded 300 additional points, and a move past the sixth rank is given 1000 additional points. A move of the king's or queen's pawn is awarded 21 additional points, and a move of the bishop's pawn is given 15 additional points.
7. Rook scoring: Moves for rooks past the sixth rank are given 200 additional points. Moves for rooks on the first rank to another square on the first rank that has no pawns on the second and third ranks is awarded 40 points.
8. Refutation moves: Any move on either the alpha or beta refutation lists is given an additional 300 points.
9. *En prise* moves: Any move that defends an *en prise* piece is given a bonus of 300 points. Moves of *en prise* pieces are awarded 300 points if the move is to a safe square and are penalized 20 points if the move is an unsafe square.
10. Attack moves: If a move will place a piece where it can attack more pieces than before the move, additional points are awarded according to the pieces which may be attacked (and other factors).

Reordering the Moves List

Following the plausibility score analysis, special reordering routines are used to generate a final listing of moves in the order of their advantages. The three reordering routines used by OSTRICH are as follows:

1. Capture reordering: The plausibility analysis arbitrarily places capturing moves at the top of the moves list; however, a capture is usually not the best move in most positions. This routine generally places captures by non-pawns on the opponent's side behind the non-capturing moves next on the list. No capture is moved to a point on the list where it will not be considered in the final analysis, however. Captures of pieces moved at the last ply are placed at the top of other captures, except at ply one, where this is done only under the condition that the following move will be a recapture.
2. Special reordering: A move called "Second Best" is generated after each move; it is the second to last move that the search evaluated as it searched the first ply move list. This move is matched with the same move on the moves list, if it is there. Any such move is placed on the top of the moves list, if it is legal.
3. Midsearch reordering: A midsearch reorder is done to the ply one moves list when the third move at ply one is to be considered. A match

is sought between the moves remaining on the ply one list, and the move at the third ply is retrieved from the present principal continuation. If a match is found, that move is placed at the top of the moves list; if no match is found, matches are sought between this move and the most recent refutations.

Processing at Terminal Nodes

A scoring routine is applied to each terminal node, once it has been determined to be a terminal node. The seventeen scoring functions are as follows:

1. Board material: Credit is awarded for the number and types of pieces that will remain on the board. The values given to each piece are pawn = 1, bishop = knight = 3, rook = 5, queen = 9, king = 300.
2. Material ratio: The material ratio routine scores favorably for trading pieces when you are ahead in material and penalizes for trading when you are behind: 100 points are awarded to the side that is ahead.
3. Castling: A king-side castling is given 600 points, while a queen-side castling is given 300 points.
4. Board control: Points are awarded in the following manner for control (ability to capture) of certain squares on the board: 12 points for each of the four center squares, 7 points for control of any square in the ring surrounding the four center squares, and 12 points for squares surrounding the opponent's king.
5. Tempo: 200 points are deducted from the score of either side for wasting time in one of the following ways: moving one piece twice in the opening, moving king or rook prior to castling, moving a piece to its last previous position, using more than one move to move a piece to a position it could have reached in one move.
6. Opening queen moves: Moves of the queen before the eighth move are penalized 400 points.
7. Blocking unadvanced pawns: 470 points are deducted for moves that block unadvanced king's or queen's pawns.
8. Minor piece development: A penalty of 140 points is given for each unmoved center pawn, bishop, or knight.
9. Center pawns: An additional 50 points are awarded for all pawns on K4 or Q4; 70 points are awarded for a pawn on K5 or Q5.
10. Pawn structure: Isolated pawns are penalized 400 points; doubled pawns are penalized 20 points; advancing pawns are awarded 10 points.
11. Passed pawns: Passed pawns on the seventh rank are worth 700 points; on the sixth, 400 points; on the fifth, 340 points; on the fourth, 40 points; on the third, 100 points; on the second, 40 points. If pawns and kings are the only pieces left, the point values are doubled.
12. King defense: If there are more non-pawn opposing pieces in the king's sector than defending pieces, a penalty of 75 points is assessed.
13. Doubled rooks, bishop pairs: If the two rooks are on the same column, 150 points are awarded; if one side has two bishops and the other side does not, 150 points are awarded.
14. Trades: If the piece that moved at the last ply is under attack, the score is adjusted as follows: the score is reduced by the value of the attacked piece if the number of defenders is zero. Otherwise, a sequence of trades is performed on the square, and the score is changed based on the pieces exchanged.
15. King vs pawns: If, after move 30, the king is within one square of an opposing pawn, 200 points are awarded.
16. Knight position: Any knight on column 9 or 7 is penalized 40 points.
17. Attacks: Ply one moves that place an opposing piece *en prise* are awarded 40 points.

The Gamma Algorithm

The gamma algorithm was mentioned earlier during the discussion concerning how to determine whether a node is terminal or nonterminal. Although the algorithm is complex, the logic behind its decision-making is that "if the situation is becoming progressively worse and better moves are available, classify this node as terminal."

Possibilities for Chess-Related Programs

1. Chess end-game program: Of course, computer analysis becomes much simpler at the end of a chess game, when only a few pieces are left. The beginning programmer might wish to write a chess program to play end games between a few selected pieces only. The program would provide any initial setup of pieces before the game. The strategy is shown in Fig. 7-18.

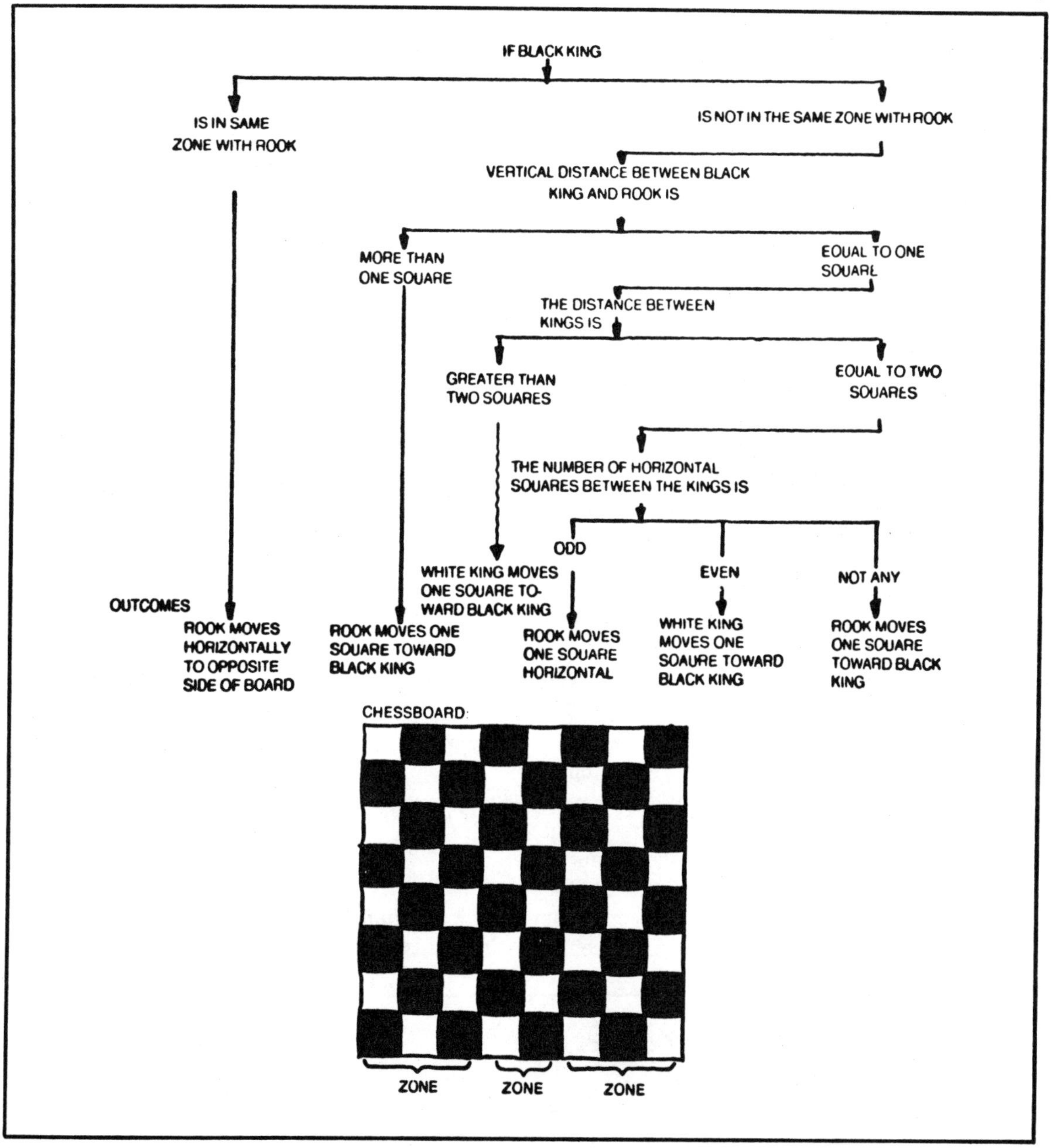

Fig. 7-18. A mechanical chess playing machine used this strategy to win in an end game. The machine possessed a white king and rook, while the human opponent possessed only a king.

2. Chess variations: Perhaps computers would be able to compete better in playing one of these chess variations:

    - Marseille game—each player moves two pieces in succession.
    - Legal game—white uses eight extra pawns instead of a queen.
    - Marked pawn—the first player to make a capture wins this chess variation.
    - Chancellor—the knight and rook have the same combined move capabilities as each one has individually.
    - Grasshopper—pieces may leap over others; captures are as usual.

3. Advisor: A computer program updated with each move you make could advise you of situations you might miss. It would be interesting to compare the move you intend to make with the computer's suggestion.
4. Check: Write a program that will determine whether Black or White is in check given a particular board setup.
5. Take the queen: Write a program that can determine whether a black rook can take the white queen in no more than four moves if neither white pieces nor any other black pieces are allowed to move in between the successive moves of the black rook.
6. Eight queens: This chess recreation was devised in the seventeenth century. The challenge is to discover how many ways it is possible to place eight queens on a chessboard in such a manner that no one queen can be taken by another. There are 92 solutions to the problem, which may be found by a computer program using this strategy: Place a queen in the first column and row of the board and a second queen in an uncapturable or conflict-free row of column 2, and so on until a solution is generated or a conflict arises. When a conflict arises, backtrack to the column immediately before and place the queen in a new conflict-free position, and then continue on. If no other conflict-free position exists, backtrack to the next previous column and place that queen in a new conflict-free position, and so on.
7. Five queens: Write a program to determine how five queens may be placed on the board in such a manner that every square is dominated by at least one of the queens.
8. Twelve knights or eight bishops: Write a program to place 12 knights or 8 bishops on the board in such a manner that all other squares are dominated.
9. Knights's tour: This program would find the path a knight must take if he is placed on any square, and in 64 moves, he must land on each square once and only once. This problem may be solved by use of heuristic strategy: For any square x on the chessboard, let $p_i(x)$ ($i=1, 2, 3\ldots$) be the number of squares accessible from x in i moves, not counting squares already visited. The knight always moves to a square x for which $p_i(x)$ exist, choose an x such that $p_2(x)$ is also as small as possible.

ADDITIONAL GAME PROGRAMS

Below are three listings that you can type into your computer and use.

Card Shuffler

You can incorporate the handy shuffling routine in Listing 7-4 into computer card games. The

Listing 7-4. A Card Shuffling Routine.

```
10     REM LISTING7.04 - The Card Shuffling Routine
20     RANDOMIZE 0
100    FULLW 2:CLEARW 2:GOTOXY 1,1
105    PRINT "CARD SHUFFLING ROUTINE"
```

```
110    DIM M(52)
120    N=52:FOR I=1 TO N
130    M(I)=I:NEXT I
140    FOR I=1 TO N-1
150    R=(N+1-I)*RND
160    R=INT(R)+1
170    T=M(R)
180    M(R)=M(I)
190    M(I)=T
200    NEXT I
210    FOR I=1 TO N
220    PRINT M(I);" ";
230    NEXT I
240    INPUT Q$
```

cards of the deck are numbered from 1 to 52 and are stored in the array M(x). A separate subroutine would convert these numbers into corresponding spot or face cards and suits.

William Tell Game

The program in Listing 7-5 presents a puzzle that will challenge those of all ages. The program describes "William Tell," and it's your job to de-

Listing 7-5. The William Tell Program.

```
10     REM LISTING7.05 - The William Tell Program
110    FULLW 2:CLEARW 2:GOTOXY 1,1
130    RANDOMIZE 0
140    PRINT TAB(10)"WILLIAM TELL"
170    DIM A$(20),B$(20)
190    PRINT "William Tell is a game of logic in which the computer"
200    PRINT "gives you examples of what William Tell is and you have"
210    PRINT "to guess the secret behind the words that characterize"
220    PRINT "William Tell.  The computer will provide you with examples"
230    PRINT "as a hint.  You must then guess what William Tell is and"
240    PRINT "is not by typing in new words you think may characterize"
250    PRINT "William Tell.  If you haven't figured it out after 20"
260    PRINT "tries you can ask for the answer or try the same set"
270    PRINT "again.  Here is your first example and chance to guess:"
290    PRINT : FOR X=1 TO 20
300    READ A$(X),B$(X)
310    NEXT X
330    REM THIS LIST OF EXAMPLES MAY BE EXPANDED
340    DATA BRILLIANCE,GLORY,GLASSES,SPECTACLES,MELLOW,INTOXICATED
350    DATA DULL,STUPID,COMMODITY,OBJECT,SHEEN,BRIGHT,UNDRESSED
360    DATA NUDE,MISSION,OBJECTIVE,SPEECH,PROSE,PASSIVE,INERT
370    DATA SUGGESTION,ADVICE,SYMMETRICAL,REGULAR,JITTERY,NERVOUS
380    DATA IMPRESSIVE,MAGNIFICENT,ERRONEOUS,FAULTY,FEEBLE,LAME
390    DATA CALLOUS,INSENSITIVE,SOOTHING,SERENE,SHALLOW
400    DATA SUPERFICIAL,NAMELESS,ANONYMOUS
410    FOR Y=1 TO 20
420    PRINT "WILLIAM TELL IS ";A$(Y);" BUT NOT ";B$(Y)
```

```
430    INPUT "WILLIAM TELL IS...";C$
440    GOSUB 730
470    IF F=1 THEN GOSUB 560:GOTO 530
480    INPUT "BUT, WILLIAM TELL IS NOT...";C$
490    GOSUB 780
500    IF F=1 THEN PRINT "WILLIAM TELL IS ";C$;"!!!"
510    GOSUB 790
530    PRINT
540    NEXT Y
550    GOTO 640
560    INPUT "BUT, WILLIAM TELL IS NOT ";C$
570    GOSUB 730
580    IF (F=1) AND (G=1) THEN PRINT "WHOOPS, I THOUGHT YOU GOT IT":
       PRINT "LET'S TRY SOME MORE...":G=0:PRINT
590    IF (F=0) AND (G=1) THEN 630
600    IF (F=0) THEN PRINT:PRINT "BY GOLLY, MAYBE YOU HAVE IT!":PRINT
       "LET'S TRY ONCE MORE...":PRINT :G=1
610    IF F=1 THEN PRINT "WILLIAM TELL IS ";C$;"!!!":PRINT
620    RETURN
630    PRINT "RIGHT!!!!!"
640    INPUT "WOULD YOU LIKE TO TRY AGAIN (A) OR HEAR THE ANSWER (H) "
       ;A$
650    IF A$="H" THEN 670
655    IF A$<>"A" THEN 640 ELSE 370
660    REM ENCODED ANSWER FOR WILLIAM TELL
670    PRINT "THE SECRET IS:"
680    A$="UGJJ?K/RCJJ/GQ/?LW/UMPB/AMLR?GLGLE/RUM/AMLQCASRGTC*/GBCLRGA
       ?J/JCRRCPQ,"
690    FOR X=1 TO LEN(A$)
700    IF MID$(A$,X,1)="/" THEN PRINT " "; ELSE PRINT CHR$(ASC(MID$(A$
       ,X,1))+2);
710    NEXT X
720    INPUT Q$:END
730    F=0:REM ANSWER EVALUATION
750    FOR X=1 TO LEN(C$)
760    IF MID$(C$,X,1)=MID$(C$,X+1,1) THEN F=1
765    NEXT X
770    RETURN
780    REM WRONG ANSWER CHOICES
790    ON INT(RND*5+1) GOTO 800,810,820,830,840
800    PRINT "NOPE...GIVE IT ANOTHER TRY:":RETURN
810    PRINT "SORRY, NOT EVEN CLOSE.":RETURN
820    PRINT "THAT DOES NOT COMPUTE (IT'S WRONG)":RETURN
830    PRINT "YOU'RE STILL COLD...TRY AGAIN:":RETURN
840    PRINT "THAT ONE ALMOST BLEW MY CIRCUIT../.HERE'S ANOTHER HINT:"
       :RETURN
```

termine what else characterizes William Tell. The solution is encoded so that typing in the program does not reveal the secret.

Personality Test

The program in Listing 7-6 will be interesting to guests. A series of verses is printed, and the player is asked to provide an interpretation. Although this program is based upon psychological research, don't take it too seriously. However, it is interesting to note that the day of the computer psychologist is near; computers have already been used to question patients and provide an overall psychological analysis on the basis of standard psychological tests.

Listing 7-6. The Personality Test Program.

```
10    REM LISTING7.06 - The Personality Test Program
20    FULLW 2:CLEARW 2:GOTOXY 1,1
30    PRINT "The following personality test in not comprehensive, but
      has"
40    PRINT "been used to determine general characteristics."
50    PRINT
60    PRINT "Instructions:  Three verses will be printed.  Following"

70    PRINT "each verse will be a list of interpretations.  Enter"
80    PRINT "the corresponding number for the interpretation you"
90    INPUT "believe is the best.  Press RETURN when ready. ",A$
100   CLEARW 2:GOTOXY 1,1
110   PRINT "A book of verse underneath the bough,"
120   PRINT "A jug of wine, a loaf of bread--and thou"
130   PRINT "Beside me singing in the wilderness--"
140   PRINT "Oh, wilderness were paradise enow!"
150   PRINT
160   PRINT "1)  Happiness or contentment can be found without much p
      lanning"
170   PRINT "2)  Happiness is in accepting and enjoying simple things
      "
180   PRINT "3)  Happiness is always present if we take the time to l
      ook"
190   PRINT "4)  If you set your mind to it, happiness can be found"
200   PRINT "5)  Happiness is where we find it"
210   INPUT X1
220   CLEARW 2:GOTOXY 1,1
230   PRINT "There is a time in the affairs of men,"
240   PRINT "Which, taken at the flood, leads on to fortune;"
250   PRINT "Omitted, all the voyage of their life"
260   PRINT "Is bound in shallows and in miseries."
270   PRINT
280   PRINT "1)  Make the most of your chance when you get it"
290   PRINT "2)  In many cases of failure, people were affected by ci
      rcumstances"
300   PRINT "    over which they had little control."
310   PRINT "3)  One who plans well will survive well under the laws
      of nature"
320   PRINT "4)  Life is such that it pays to watch what you do befor
      e you run into trouble"
330   PRINT "5)  One should be on the watch for opportunity to knock,
      otherwise he"
340   PRINT "    will miss out on going places."
350   INPUT X2
360   CLEARW 2:GOTOXY 1,1
370   PRINT "No man is an island, entire of itself."
380   PRINT
390   PRINT "1)  Everyone should consider the needs and wants of othe
      rs"
400   PRINT "2)  Use other's influence to help you plan your life."
410   PRINT "3)  One who acts without regard for others does not real
      ize that"
420   PRINT "    he is a social animal."
430   PRINT "4)  To get where you want to be in life you must realize
      the need"
```

```
440   PRINT "    for help from others."
450   PRINT "5)  Although I am the captain of my soul, I must make my
      way"
460   PRINT "    in life among many other captains."
470   INPUT X3
480   CLEARW 2:GOTOXY 1,1
490   PRINT "The test indicates that you posses these traits:"
500   IF X1=1 THEN PRINT "IRRESPONSIBLE" ELSE IF X1=2 THEN PRINT "CON
      VENTIONAL AND MORALISTIC" ELSE IF X1=3 THEN PRINT "MORALISTIC"
      ELSE IF X 1=4 THEN PRINT "FORMAL" ELSE PRINT "PRACTICAL"
510   IF X2=1 THEN PRINT "PRACTICAL AND LOGICAL" ELSE IF X2=2 THEN PR
      INT "MORALISTIC" ELSE IF X2=3 THEN PRINT "CONVENTIONAL" ELSE IF
      X2=4 THEN PRINT "HUMOROUS AND SENSIBLE" ELSE PRINT "EGO-CENTRIC"
520   IF X3=1 THEN PRINT "CONVENTIONAL" ELSE IF X3=2 THEN PRINT "PRAC
      TICAL AND LOGICAL" ELSE IF X3=3 THEN PRINT "OBJECTIVE" ELSE IF
      X3=4 THEN PRINT "EGO-CENTRIC" ELSE PRINT "MORALISTIC"
530   PRINT "If the same trait is listed twice then it is all the "
540   PRINT "more indicative of you."
550   INPUT Q$:END
```

Chapter 8

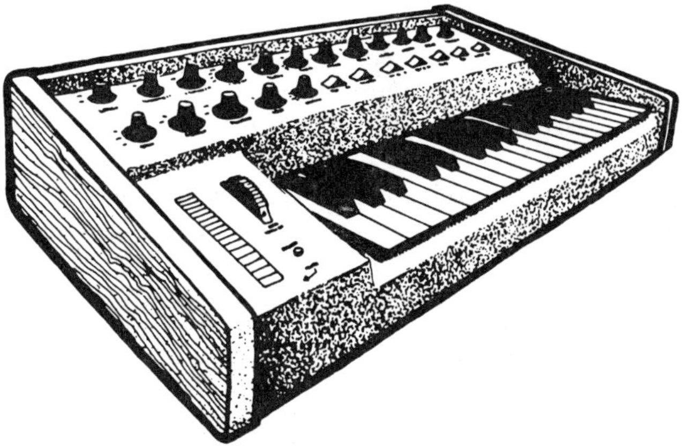

Control and Peripheral Applications

The potentials for computer control and monitoring of the home are endless; only a few of the possible applications have been put into practice with the incorporation of microprocessors in household appliances. Several industry demonstration homes have been built to exhibit microprocessor control of the home. The following suggestions have been included in these homes or have been suggested by leading industry forecasters and futurists:

- Climate control is just one of the many functions provided by the home computer system. The rate of temperature change and humidity is noted, and the air conditioner or heater is turned off before the house is at a preset level; the temperature will "coast" to the desired level. The system also times the thermostat. In winter it turns down the temperature at night, turns it up again in the morning, and then turns it back down while you go off to work; in the summer it controls the air conditioner in the same manner. To conserve energy, the hot water heater is also turned down during certain hours when hot water isn't needed.
- A vocal input interface to the home computer is continuously active, waiting for a command by one of the occupants. All appliances and lights controlled by the system can be switched on and off by voice command, or can be programmed to start and stop at selected times.
- An intelligent alarm system will turn off all electricity and gas and call the fire department in case of fire. A burglar detection system calls the police if an intruder is detected ultrasonically or by other sensors.
- Interfaces to stereo, televisions, and telephones are also interesting. The telephone controller acts as a phone message recorder with additional features. If a message is taken, the unit can be instructed to call someone at another number and deliver the message. A telephone call to the machine itself can allow you to change the recorded message, play back messages, or control any of the devices connected with the home computer.

A telephone file of commonly used numbers is stored in the computer. Additionally, you can dial numbers by simply calling them out vocally; if a busy signal is encountered, the computer continually redials the number until the line is free.

- The stereo interface transforms an ordinary stereo into a "jukebox" from which recordings may be selected and played at the touch of a button. A special device can monitor radio broadcasts and record all music; commercials and news are not recorded (voice patterns can be distinguished from music.) You can preprogram the volume level and the type of music you want to have recorded for special purposes such as musical interludes and background music for dinner. A given song can be played a selected number of times, or the computer may be programmed to skip to the next song on a record or cassette.
- The television interface will turn on the set at selected times or record shows on video tape; a directional antenna or satellite dish is automatically turned for the best reception.
- Even the bar is automated. Drinks of your choice are mixed automatically (bottles of ingredients are connected by hoses to the special machine).
- You can use a voice synthesizer to audibly awake you in the morning with "Good Morning Mr. T. It's 8 A.M.," and then summarize your itinerary for the day.
- An automatic system can release fresh food and water for pets left at home for a long period, can sense when the animal has not eaten the food, and can notify the veterinarian to check the home.

Some other applications currently being used by hobbyists include the following:

- Voice or sound synthesizers are incorporated into games to provide dialogue or sound effects.
- Voice input computers are used for recording information called out by an operator. One hobbyist uses such a system tomake simple calculations in his home workshop while his hands are full. Although such systems are usually limited to a vocabulary of about 30 words, some hobbyists have managed to develop automatic "dictation-taking" typewriters for limited purposes (a word capacity of 100 is considered maximum).
- A hobbyist has used his small computer to replace over 7000 mechanical relays necessary to control a pipe organ in his home. Similarly, computers could be used to light the keys on an organ to help you learn to play a song. Although a commercial player piano has been developed to digitally record music and play it back later, the cost is high. If you were to implement such a system with your computer, additional features could be added; speed, sustain, attack, and other features could all be varied.
- One hobbyist is using a microprocessor to create intelligent test equipment that can automatically perform a set of test routines on a given circuit. This is an interesting application for amateur radio operators. A calculating oscilloscope is able to compute exact items for rises, perform integrals and differentials, compute peak areas, RMS values, and peak-to-peak distances, and do n-point averaging; all data can be stored.
- With the addition of silver contacts and a small amplifier, your computer could serve as a biofeedback monitor or lie detector. Galvanic skin resistance, temperature, or heatbeat could all be measured with the use of the proper instruments. This information could be sent through a joystick port or other A/D port and analyzed or displayed by the computer. An article describing the construction and operation of a computer biofeedback monitor appeared in *80 Microcomputing*, October 1983, pp. 176-192.

The capabilities of a computer allow sophisticated analysis and conversion of waveforms not obtainable with standard biofeedback equipment. An assembly language program could be written to convert alpha brain wave signals, which are in the range of 8-12 Hz, to audible sound by raising all the frequencycomponents of the brain wave signal to the audible range while preserving the ratios between frequencies. Such a program could be used for a variety of unique applications—for example, for converting your voice from a very deep level to a "Mickey Mouse" level or for dealing with any situation requiring the conversion of analog signals. You can envision future digital music players that have the added capability of altering songs through the use of hardwired computer circuits.

- A New Hampshire resident uses his home computer to control his wood stove; he reports a 10-to 30-percent improvement in efficiency.
- A digital/audio file, in which a standard cassette interface is used to record digital information between songs (audio), could be used to index songs, prompt a vocal announcement by a voice synthesizer, or control volumes, speakers, times, or mixing.
- Hobbyists have connected computers to exercise equipment, such as jogging pads or exercise bikes, to keep track of energy expended, speed, or time. These special input devices could also be used as controllers for special video games.
- Special software and hardware configurations could permit two or more opposing players to use separate but interconnected computers in such a manner that they cannot see each other's game field. Games of this type (*multiplayer* games) are gaining in popularity on computer networks.
- Chess fanatics who also happen to be gadget fanatics would take delight in a computer-interfaced chessboard capable of sensing the movement of pieces. A robotic arm, of course, would move pieces for the computer.
- Personal computers can be used to generate titles for home video or film movies that can involve animated color graphics. Titles for slide shows could also be made by photographing the screen.
- Along similar lines, your computer could flash subliminal messages over television programs for behavior modification. These would last 1/30 of a second and assail your subconscious with messages to help you control your weight, deal with stress, smoking, or alcoholism, or become motivated toward success. Messages such as "I exercise" and "I am successful" could be repeated every minute.
- Radio scanner buffs can interface their computer to a scanner via CompuScan™, a Bearcat product, allowing them to monitor up to 200 channels. The computer can display the frequency and the description of the channel received on a video monitor.
- Weather sensors such as electronic anemometers, thermometers and barometers can be interfaced with a computer to provide automatic weather monitoring.

HOUSEHOLD CONTROL DEVICES

The interfaces that allow a personal computer to help you out around the house are now commercially available from the firms listed below. For those with a hardware bent, schematics for a simple control latch system and A/D converter are included at the end of this chapter.

The firms have been divided into two groups, depending upon the type of product they offer: those listed under "Personal Computer Systems" offer products that are designed to work with one or more popular brands of personal computers; those listed under "Dedicated Systems" offer products that are made specifically for home control applications but can be interfaced to computers by electronic geniuses.

Personal Computer Systems

Circuit Science, 4 Townsend West, Nashua, NH 03063; (603) 880-4066. Circuit Science manufactures the CSI-1200, a controller interface that plugs into an RS-232 port. This system eliminates the BSR control box, but uses the BSR remote modules for each appliance controlled.

Compu-Home Systems, 3333 East Florida Ave., Denver, CO 80210; (303) 777-6600. This firm manufactures the Tomorrowhouse system, which controls lights, appliances, solar-heating systems, sprinklers, hot tubs, indoor heat, and air-conditioning. It guards against burglars and reminds you of appointments and important dates.

Cyberlynx Computer Products, 4828 Sterling Dr., Boulder, CO 80301 (303) 444-7733. Cyberlynx offers the Smarthome I system for connection to an RS-232 port. It can be attached to an infrared detector to sense heat or movement in a room and cause lights and appliances to turn on and off to scare off an intruder. The system is also configured to control appliances for convenience and energy saving.

HyperTek, P.O. Box 137, Route 22 East, Salem Industrial Park, Whitehouse, NJ 08888; (201) 874-4773. HyperTek manufactures the HomeBrain, a dedicated microprocessor for home control that uses sensor for heat, temperature, and motion. It uses Leviton wireless controllers and hardwired relays to integrate and schedule many home appliances. It can be connected with any personal computer via an RS-232 port.

Intelectron, 1275 A St., Hayward, CA 94543; (415) 581-4490. This firm offers The Control Center, a system operating on the same principle as the BSR system.

Infield Software, 2422 Alvin St., Suite 100, Mountain View, CA 94043. Infield sells the Home Controller, which incorporates the BSR home control unit to run appliances, lights, sprinklers, spa, and so on.

Dedicated Systems and Hardware

Anova Electronics, Three Waters Park Drive, San Mateo, CA 94403; (415) 572-9686. Anova sells three dedicated microprocessor-based systems for home control. These systems can be used for control via telephone; and offer timed or instant remote control of appliances, and protection against fire, burglary, and utility failure.

Audio Command Systems, 46 Merrick Road, Rockville Center, New York, NY 11570; (516) 766-2627. This firm offers remote control devices including low-voltage lighting-control systems, motorized drapery controllers, stereo components, and robots.

BSR, Route 303, Blauvelt, NY 10913; (914) 358-6060. This firm is the granddaddy of home control systems; their BSR System is used by a variety of other manufacturers as a component of their system. The BSR controller encodes a signal on the 60 Hz alternating current of the home electrical system, eliminating the need for special wiring throughout the house. Each controlled appliance is plugged into a remote unit that may be turned on and off the main control box of the BSR System.

Leviton, 59-25 Little Neck Parkway, Little Neck, NY; 11362 (212) 229-4040. Leviton manufactures electronic control devices that allow computer control of lighting and appliances.

Technicom International, 23 Old Kings Highway South, Darien, CT 06820; (202) 655-1299. This firm offers the Energy Control System (ECS), which can control up to eight devices in the home using BSR remote modules.

The Use of Home Control Systems

Users of these control systems report applications as diverse as energy conservation through keeping various rooms at desired temperatures for different times of day, sprinkling the lawn according to the amount of ground moisture, securing doors, signaling a baby's movements in a crib, making and logging phone calls, detecting the seepage of water into a basement, opening and shutting drapes and starting the roast by a phone call from the office.

The control system can be arranged in such a manner that one computer controls the entire house, or a network of computers (one in each area of the house) can be interconnected via RS-232 communications channels as shown in the diagram in Fig. 8-1.

MUSIC

A few music/voice synthesizers are now on the market as personal computer peripherals. Possible uses for these include the following:

- Use them with games for special sound effects.
- Use them with a music composing program to generate and play original music continuously.
- Use a music synthesizer as programmable drummer to accompany other instruments. Various drum sounds, speeds, and patterns including Latin, swing, jazz, waltz, and march, could be programmed. The metronome, cymbals, and other percussion devices could also be imitated.
- Use a voice synthesizer to "sing" the vocals of a music piece, producing a unique composition.

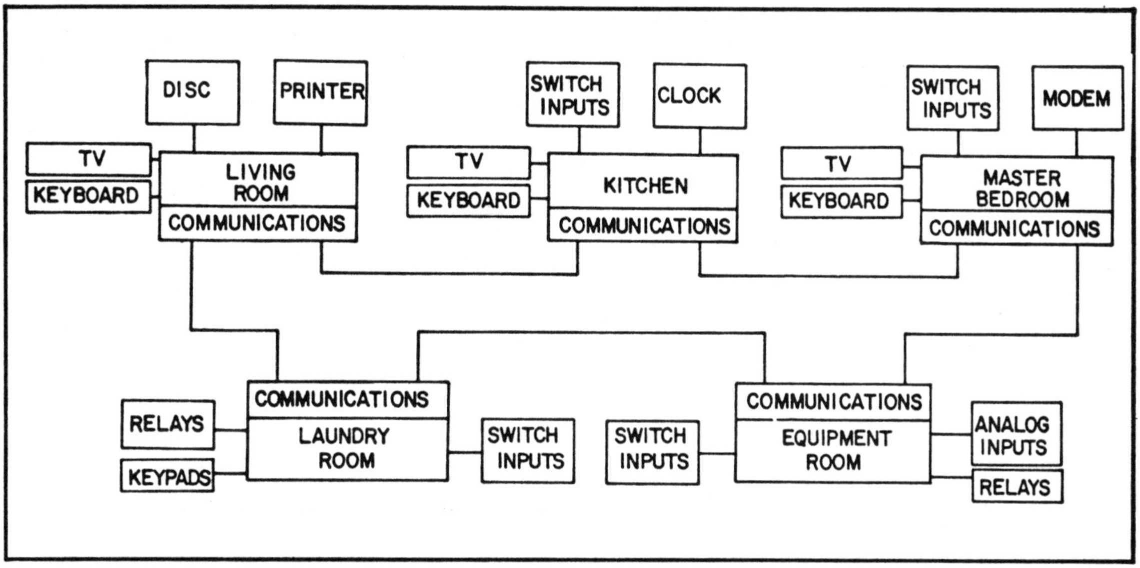

Fig. 8-1. Five areas of a computer-controlled house. Several microprocessor-based nodes communicate via an intelligent communications processor and an advanced data link controller.

- Use the standardized MIDI (Musical Instrument Digital Interface) to connect a home computer to one or more electronic musical synthesizers to play or digitally record your compositions on a standard electronic keyboard. Comprehensive information on MIDI is available from: MIDI Users Group, P.O. Box 593, Los Altos, CA 94022, phone (408) 253-4684.

Additional applications in the area of music include the following:

- If you have a plotter or a graphic printer or terminal, your musical compositions or those of the computer could be displayed in standard musical notation.
- Loops of the proper speed and duration will generate a specific audible frequency on an AM radio placed next to a CPU. A machine language or BASIC program to make use of this effect could produce sounds that resemble music.
- If music is digitized with the use of an A/D converter, it can be altered in various ways. Here are some examples:

  —Selected voices or instruments could be removed/added after an analysis of frequency content.

  —The music couldbe played at any selected rate without a change in pitch, or could be played backwards for special effect. You could transform a given composition into another style of your choice.
- Today's color organs, which produce a pulsating light in response to music, rely upon analog circuits and often do not produce good results. A dedicated microprocessor could be used to control the lights instead, resulting in a more favorable response.

AN EXTERNAL DEVICE CONTROLLER FOR YOUR COMPUTER

The project described below will allow the electronic enthusiast to economically interface his or her computer with external devices. For those not electronically inclined, controlling interface circuit boards are commercially available for under $200.

The controller described here will allow you to economically interface your computer with virtually any external electrical device; up to 16 devices (channels) can be controlled simultaneously.

This interface switches on and off a small amount of current to control relays that in turn can control larger electrical loads (see Fig. 8-2). Practically all 8-bit computers can drive the interface, and a 4-bit microprocessor could drive a modified interface for specialized control purposes.

The interface consists of three modules: a 16-channel demultiplexer, a 16-bit "memory," and 16 single transistor driver amplifiers (see Fig. 8-3); the construction cost should not exceed $30. The interface is designed to be connected directly with a parallel output port.

The four low-order bits of data coming from the parallel output port are inputted to the demultiplexer. The demultiplexer selects the appropriate output pin and pulls it low (for example, if the four bits are 0000, channel zero will be selected and pin one pulled low). Since only 16 individual signals are possible with four bits, 16 is the maximum number of channels that can be selected. Each output signal switches the state of one of the 16 flip-flop chips. Thus, the flip-flops act as a 16-bit memory to maintain the status of each channel continuously. Signals sent to one flip-flop will alternatively toggle the corresponding channel on and off. The fifth bit of the data byte is first buffered and then connected to the reset pin of each flip-flop. Thus, all channels may be reset (turned off) simultaneously through the use of the fifth bit.

The software must output the signal corresponding to the correct channel to control devices connected to the interface. However, channel can-

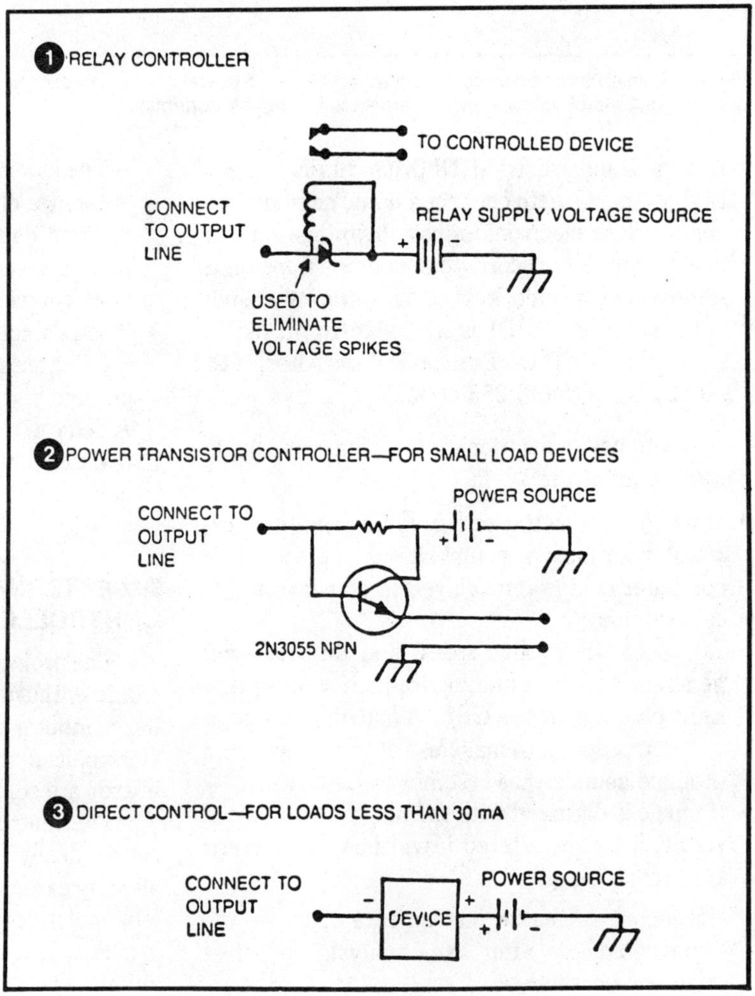

Fig. 8-2. Diagram of output devices that can be selected to match the controlled load.

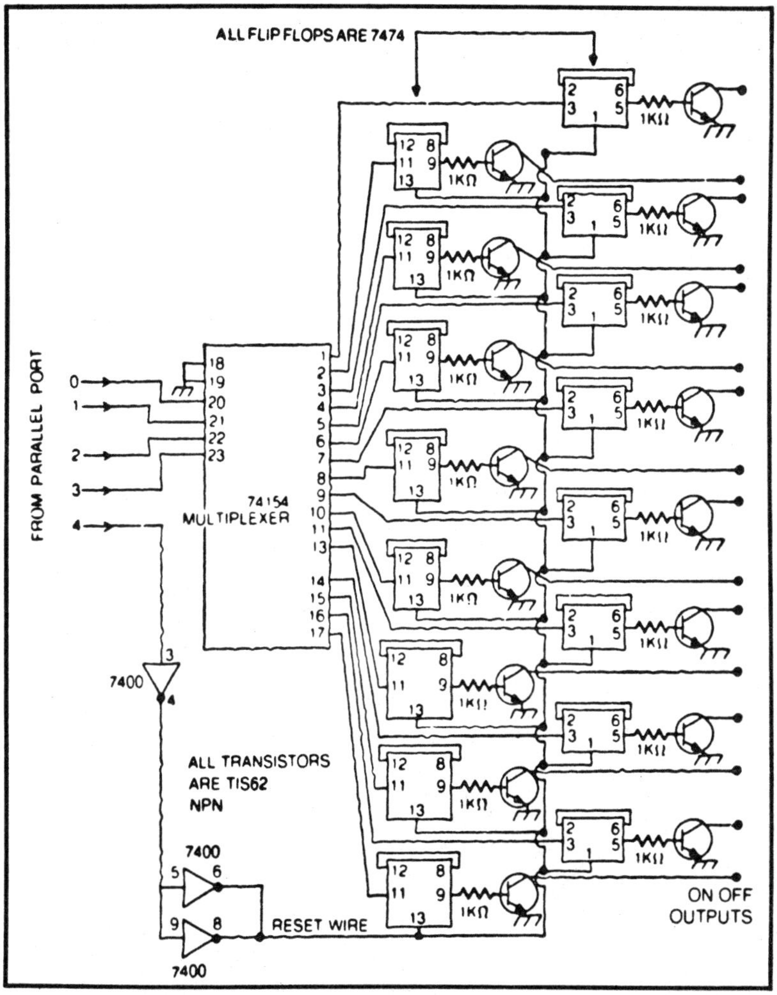

Fig. 8-3. A schematic diagram of the control latch system.

not be switched on and off continuously by selecting that channel over and over again. This restriction is due to the fact that the flip-flops only switch on rising edges from the demultiplexer, which occur only if the multiplexer has been changed to select a different channel. Therefore, to switch a given flip-flop on and then off, first select the channel with the proper data byte, then select any other channel (for example an unused channel), then wait for the first channel to toggle on, and finally reselect the first channel to turn it off.

AN A/D CONVERTER FOR YOUR COMPUTER

The A/D (analog to digital) converter has many applications for use with personal computers. It will allow you to interface joysticks or potentiometers with computers for use during editing, video drawing, or game playing. Automation of test equipment and control over robots or machines are among the many other possible applications.

The eight-channel interface described here is designed for use in converting signals in the range of about 0.1 Hz to 100 Hz, which is sufficient for the applications listed above (see Fig. 8-4). The "sample-and-hold" principle is used in the design to store an analog signal as a capacitor charge until it is processed. The two power supplies necessary should fall between 4.5 to 6.5 Vdc and 12 to 15, respectively.

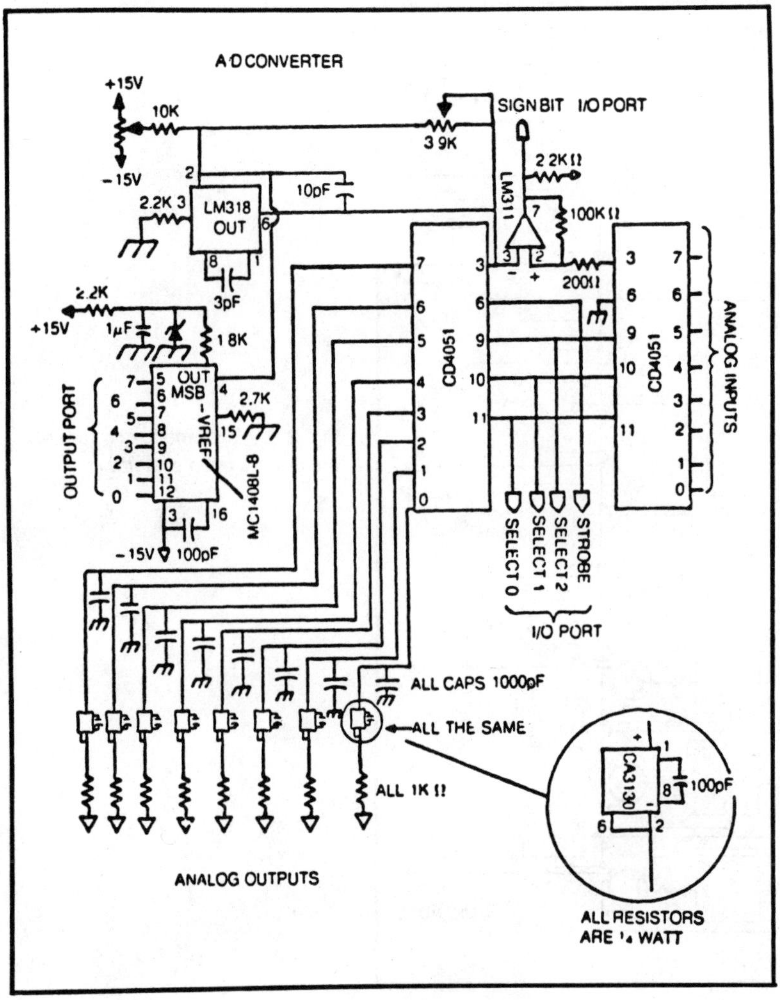

Fig. 8-4. A schematic diagram of the analog/digital converter.

An assembly language software description is provided below; you should supply the op codes for your microprocessor.

1. Initialize the pointer
2. Load the next byte for output
3. Output the byte
4. Set the accumulator equal to the pointer
5. Select the next channel and enable the sample and hold process
6. Turn off the sample and hold strobe
7. Turn off the selected sample and hold
8. Decrement the value of the pointer
9. If the pointer is greater then or equal to zero, loop back to step 2; otherwise return to the main program.

As you can see, the program sequentially addresses a channel, outputs the voltage that is to be held, disables that channel, repeats the process for the other channels, and then returns to the main program. You could arrange the program to act as an interrupt handler signaled by a clock strobe on an interrupt line.

A digital to analog (D/A) converter can also be built or purchased and used to produce speech, music, or sound effects or to control the speed of a motor, among many other applications.

PERSONAL ROBOTS

Today the development of personal robotics is at the stage personal computers development was in the early 1970s. It's a young field with great potential and much remaining to be explored. Personal robotics is discussed here as a control application for your personal computer, considering that many robots available on the market rely upon external microcomputers for partial or complete control over their actions.

The state of the art personal robot can locomote, talk, and perhaps perform crude manipulator functions or chores such as vacuuming the house or automatically finding the battery recharge unit when necessary. Capabilities such as setting the table like a maid, fetching a beer, or mowing the lawn like a loyal son are currently out of the question. As of this date, none of the available products even come close to replacing appliances or offspring. In fact, most of the robots for sale do not have functional arms, and few are self-contained; most communicate with their host computer by means of a cord or via radio transmissions. At present, personal robots serve little purpose other than entertainment and as an educational tool. However, advances are being made to allow more practical use of personal robots, and you could be part of that frontier!

Manufacturers of personal robots include:

Androbot, Inc.
101 E. Daggett Dr.
San Jose, CA 95134

Heath Co.
Benton Harbor, MI 49022

Microbot, Inc.
453-H Ravendale Dr.
Mountain View, CA 94043

RB Robot Corp.
14618 W. 6th Ave., Suite 201
Golden, CO 80401

Robotics International Corp.
2335 E. High
Jackson, MI 49203

Sandhu Machine Design, Inc.
308 S. State St.
Champaign, IL 61820

Technical Micro Systems, Inc.
366 Cloverdale
Box 7227
Ann Arbor, MI 48107

Terrapin, Inc.
380 Green St.
Cambridge, MA 02139

Chapter 9

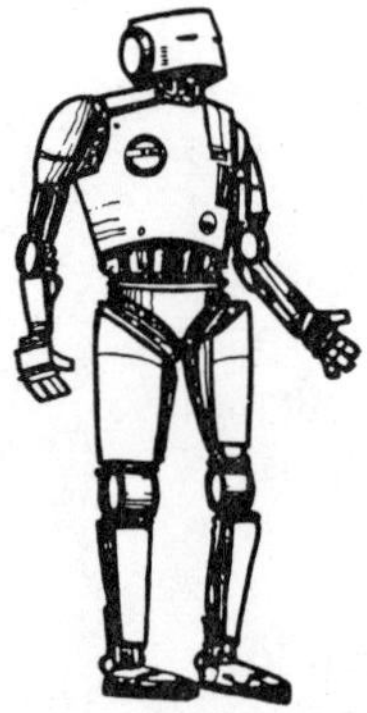

Artificial Intelligence, the Future Personal Computer, and Networking

In *Future Shock,* Alvin Toffler describes a future home computer system named OLIVER, the primary purpose of which is to help the owner deal with decision overload:

> In its simplest form, OLIVER would merely be a personal computer programmed to provide the individual with information and to make minor decisions for him. At this level, it could store information about his friends' preferences for Manhattans or martinis, and data about traffic routes, the weather, stock prices, and so on. The device could be set to remind him of his wife's birthday or to order flowers automatically. It could renew his magazine subscriptions, pay the rent on time, order razor blades and the like. As computerized information systems expand, they would tap into a worldwide pool of data stored in libraries, corporate files, hospitals, retail stores, banks, government agencies, and universities. OLIVER would thus become a kind of universal question answered for him. However, some computer scientists see much beyond this. It is theoretically possible to construct an OLIVER that would analyze the content of an owner's words, scrutinize his choices, deduce his value system, update its own program to reflect changes in his values, and ultimately handle larger and larger decisions for him.

FUTURISTIC APPLICATIONS THAT ARE FEASIBLE NOW

Although many of these applications will probably not be feasible within the coming decade, some ideas being put into practice include the following:

Medical Monitoring. A specially designed microcomputer could be programmed to make checks of your bodily functions. Information such as nutritional and caloric intake, pulse rate, blood pressure, and weight loss or gain could be entered into a program especially tailored for your metabolism. Specific conditions that warrant a visit to the doctor could be computed and outputted.

With a telephone modem, the computer could transmit such information to a larger data bank for processing. Additionally, answers to common medical questions could be provided by the data bank.

Information Research. The facilities to tap computerized information banks (for example, the information banks of the *New York Times* and the World Trade Center) are already available via telephone modems connected to such service companies as The Source[SM]. Such services are especially useful to businessmen, authors, and educators who need to locate specialized information. In addition, a home computer interfaced to a standard modem could tap the Library of Congress computerized card catalog as well as numerous other data banks.

Personalized News Service. A home computer on line with a news service could select news items by category and store them for review later by the home owner. The United Press International wire service provides all major national and world news; news items are coded by category, and thus, a computer on line could select items of interest.

Travel Information. A travel service data bank, filled with information regarding flights, schedules, prices, availability, reservations, and so on could supply all the information necessary for you to plan a vacation or an outing, via a telephone modem.

Stock Market Quotes. A continuous Dow Jones listing service could supply stock market quotes to the home computer via a telephone modem. Such a service would be a boon to those attempting stock market analyses with their computer.

Educational Programs. High-quality, comprehensive educational programs are being developed for the growing home computer/video tape player interface, which can be used in conjunction with the computer to provide television images that cannot be provided with conventional computer graphics. In addition, the computer can randomly access video images from a video disk to provide interactive education.

Business Extensions. Computer programmers, professional investors, and other professionals who do most of their work with a computer system are beginning to install home terminals; soon traveling to an office will be unnecessary.

Computer Networks. Numerous amateur and professional computer networks have been formed for the exchange of programs, ideas, tips, and other information. Commercially available "bulletin board" software allows anyone with a computer and auto-answer modem to form their own network. Consult Table 9-3 for a listing of computer bulletin board systems available in your area.

Intelligent Devices. A home computer interfaced with household devices could create a complete home management system. Climate control, solar energy system control, television set timing, cooking device control, and so on could all be done simultaneously by a properly equipped home computer. With falling costs for microcomputers, such control applications are becoming economical.

Other possibilities include a complete, computer-controlled diagnostic system for your automobile.

Artificial Intelligence? A popularly quoted assessment of computers and people goes like this: "Computers are fast, accurate, and stupid. People are slow, inaccurate, and brilliant. Together they can perform incredible feats beyond the imagination." With the advent of artificial intelligence, computers have begun to enter the "brilliant" category. So-called *expert systems* are capable of making informed decisions on the basis of hundreds of thousands of rules and relationships much as a human expert can. Although most artificial intelligence programs are intended for large computer systems, some of this technology will be available in the near future for the personal computer. Numerous applications in medicine, business, science, and education are foreseen. For further information and experimental programs for use on your personal computer, see *Artificial Intelligence,* by Neil Graham, TAB Books, Inc., Blue Ridge Summit, PA 17214.

NOT-YET-FEASIBLE FUTURISTIC APPLICATIONS

However, not all applications suggested by the media are practical, and in some cases may not be possible to accomplish with current technology.

The examples of impractical applications described below will serve to define the limits of personal computer control/peripheral applications.

Personal Security System. By determining heights, weights, and diameters of all who come to your doorstep, your computer will be able to recognize whether or not that person is an acquaintance (based on previously stored information).

The problems associated with this application are obvious; the equipment to determine heights and diameters of a person in motion would be difficult to interface with the computer, and no purpose is given for spending hundreds of dollars to accomplish such a feat.

Robot Maid. Some authors have claimed that domestic androids will be available within a few years to do such chores as vacuuming a home, walking the dog, washing dishes, preparing food, and so on and will have the capability of carrying on a natural conversation with the owner.

Although several robots are commercially available for home use, the application of these as useful household servants has not passed the point of tedious control of their every movement by humans. Some robots are available with sensors that enable them to avoid collisions with people and objects such as furniture. These robots can even vacuum a floor in a semirandom fashion, but further applications are limited by inadequate mechanics and the problem computers have in recognizing "universals."

Dennis Gabor described this problem in his book *Innovations.* "One can say that it is incomparably easier to design a computer for solving a wave equation beyond the reach of the best analyst than to design one that will pick up and empty ashtrays, because ashtrays come in so many shapes."

Presumably, the use of the television camera is the only way to give a robot "sight." Computer analysis of the thousands of individual pixels, or dots, in a television picture to determine what objects are in the picture is not yet practical for personal computers.

The problems of speech input are also numerous. A very large memory capacity and a high processing speed are necessary for "understanding" anything even approaching normal conversation.

However, hobbyists show considerable interest in robotics, and over the next few years they will produce increasingly sophisticated robots.

Controlling an Automobile. The problems associated with the computerized control (driving) of an automobile are much the same as those associated with the control of domestic androids.

NETWORKING

The world is your neighbor via your microcomputer. Within the past few years there has been a tremendous growth in *networking,* the connection of computers to other computers through the use of modems and phone lines. Many experts predict that networking will be one of the primary uses of personal computers in the future.

What services are available from networks, now and in the near future? One important application will be the creation of an electronic banking system. With this system, you will be able to make and receive payments via your home computer terminal, which would be the main computer system in your bank or supermarket. The so-called *cashless society* will become a reality.

Another important aspect of networking is that you will have access to vast amounts of information instantly—everything from stock market quotations to major newswires to journal and encyclopedia articles. You will also be able to exchange information, programs, and other forms of *electronic mail* with one or all of the thousands of users on a typical network. The applications of networking services for personal computer users is in its embryonic stage, and many new applications are forthcoming.

Modems

Modems are electronic devices that allow communication between your computer and another computer. They translate the electronic signals from a computer into audio tones that may be sent through an ordinary phone line and translate the incoming audio signals into digital signals. The cost for a modem ranges from $50 to over $600 depending upon its capabilities, but most personal computer users can find a modem to suit their needs for under $200.

A *direct-connect* modem patches into your phone line directly and is the simplest to use. An *acoustic-coupled* modem which cradles an ordinary telephone handset, is often less reliable, but it has the advantage of being usable at public phones. If you're willing to spend extra, a direct-connect modem can be equipped with a feature that will answer the telephone automatically and can dial numbers stored in the computer and then initiate data transmission; these features are called *auto-answer* and *auto-dial.*

The other consideration in buying a modem is the speed at which it can send and receive data. The normal telephone line is capable of sending 300 bits of information per second, or 300 *baud.* This rate is most commonly used by computer hobbyists, although higher speeds of data transmission can be had for a price.

Terminal Programs

As a final requirement, you must write or purchase software to communicate with the modem and the outside world; the required software is commonly called a *terminal* or *communications* program. Modems are often sold with these communication programs as a package designed for your brand of personal computer. This software will allow you to send messages or programs to the main network computer and display or store incoming data. Again, a wide price range exists, depending upon the capabilities you need; these factors should be reviewed with your salesman before purchase.

Available Networks

There are two principal networks of broad interest—CompuServe and The Source. Both of these services offer an extensive variety of information sources, which are outlined in Tables 9-1 and 9-2. Their addresses are:

CompuServe
5000 Arlington Centre Blvd.
P. O. Box 20212
Columbus, OH 43220

Source Telecomputing Corporation
The Reader's Digest Association, Inc.
1616 Anderson Road
McLean, VA 22102

Local Networks. A comprehensive listing of local networks or "bulletin board systems" (BBS), the computer era's answer to old-fashioned corkboards, for personal computerists is shown in Table 9-3. To post a notice, you dial the service and add your message to a list of notices that will appear on your screen. If any message interests you, you can reply—on your computer, of course. Usually, your only cost is the phone charges.

The codes printed next to each BBS phone number are explained here:

*24	denotes 24-hour operation
#1	denotes original system of that type
–rb	denotes call, let ring once and call back
–so	sexually oriented messages
–rl	religious orientation
!	new system or new number for existing system
1	Supports VADIC 1200 baud operation
&	Supports 212A 1200 baud operation

Start dialing and explore!

DATABASES

Would you like to know about the latest advances that doctors have made against arthritis? Or find out how long it takes to fly to Chicago? What about the addresses of all your competitors' offices in California? To get the answers to these and other obscure questions, it's not necessary to live or work near a large reference library.

All this information and more is available

Table 9-1. Partial List of CompuServe Services.

AAMSI Medical Forum
AID calculations
AMEX prices (MQUOTE)
ASCMD SIG
ASI Monitor
AVSIG.
Academic American Ency.
Access
Access phone numbers
Adult education
Adventure game
Advertisers, TODAY
Advertising:
For sale
Notices
TODAY Magazine
Want ads
Advertising, classified:
St. Louis Post-Dispatch
Advice:
Aunt Nettie
African weather
Agribusiness
Agricultural news
Air travel:
Firstworld Travel Club
Official Airline Guide
Pan Am
Travel Fax
Air travel delays
Aircraft
Airline guide
Airport delay guide
Amateur Radio
Analogies test
Annual reports
Apple, programs for
Apple User's Group
Appliances for sale
Archade (SIG)
Art Gallery
Articles, computer
Asian weather
Assoc. Press Access
Assoc. Viewdata Wire
Astrology Game
Astronautics
Atari Forum
Athletic equipment
Athletic's Outfitter
Atlas, shopping service
Attorneys
Author's (SIG)
Auto information:
Gov't publications
Investors Diversified
Popular Science
AutoNet
Autos, buying
AutoNet
St. Louis Post-Dispatch
Aviation:
ASI Monitor
EMI Flight Planning
NSW Aviation Weather
Official Airline Guide
Peak Delay Guide
Aviation Rules & Reg.
Aviation Safety Inst.
Aviation (SIG)
Aviation weather
Bacchua Data Services
Banking, electronic
Banks:
Central Trade Bank
First Tennessee Bank
Huntington National Bank
Shawmut Bank of Boston
Banshi game
Baseball (AP wire)
Basic CompuServe
Beef prices
Belmont Golf Association
Belmont's golf (SIG)
Billing, reviewing
Biorhythms
Blackjack game
Bliss language
Book, ordering:
Fifth Avenue Shopper
Howard Sams Books
Book, reviews:
AAMSI, medical journals
Rainbo's Reviews
Boston, Shawmut Bank
Bridge game
Brokerage
Budgeting, home:
CompuServe
Gov't publication
Bulletin Board
Business, farming
Business Information Wire
Business news:
AP Viewdata Wire
Business Wire
Canadian, U.S. Int'l
CompuServe
Middlesex Daily
St. Louis Post-Dispatch
Washington Post
CB Interest Group
CB Radio simulation:
Access to
Instructions
Introduction
CB Society
CEMSIG
CP/M user's group
Cameras for sale
Canadian:
Business news
Currency exchange
Stocks
Canning, home
Car care
Cars, comparison
Cattle prices
Central Trade Bank
Changing terminal type
Changing terminal type
Charges, monthly
Checking, banking
Child care
Children, education
Children's games
Cinema news
Clarke School for Deaf
Classified Ads:
St. Louis Post-Dispatch
Clothing, fashion
Clothing, sport
Cocoa news
Coffee news
College cost program
Color computer (SIG)
Color graphics
Columbus area
Banks
Chamber of Commerce
Education
SIG
Command level
Commentaries:
Investment
Video
Commodities calendar
Commodities future
Commodities glossary
Commodity News Service:
Agricultural news
Commodity prices
Economic news
Futures industry news
Futures market prices
General news
Metals news
Weather
Commodore newsletter
Commodore VIC (SIG)
Comm. Industry Forum
CompuServe command
Comp-U-Store
Computer, books
Computer club news:
Computers & Electronics
The Micro Advisor
Computer Magazine Index
Computers & Electronics
Concentration game
Consumer items for sale
Consumer news:
Software
Continuing education
Cooking (SIG)
Corporate news release
Copper futures prices
Copper news
Cotton futures prices
Cotton news
Court cases, aircraft
Cross Assemblers
Cruise line
Current rates
Database, how to use
Database searches
dataFamiliae
Decwars game
Decwars (SIG)
DEFALTS, setting
Department of State
Disk area
Document delivery
Document retrieval
Documentation ordering
Dress
Drugs
Drugs, medicine
EMI Flight Plans
Earnings forecasts
Economic news
Editorials:
Washington Post
Education:
Academic Encylcopedia
Clarke School for Deaf
The College Board
The Multiple Choice
Education, family
Educational games:
Super Brain Challenge
Witty Write-Ins
Educator's (SIG)
Electronic banking
Electronic Bounce Back.
Electronic Heath Catalog
Electronic mall
Electronic shopping
Eliza program
EMAIL
Emergencies, auto
Emergencies, health
Employee benefits
Encyclopedia
Energy conservation:
Gov't publication
Popular Science
Energy news
Entertainment:
AP Viewdata Wire
CompuServe
Hollywood Hotline
Environmental Forum
Equipment, mining
European weather
Executive, terminal
Expert, music
FAA reports
FAA rule changes
NOI Newsline
Facts, general
Family budget
Family life
Family Matters Forum
Fantasy game
Farming
Fashions
Federal gov't news:
Associated Press News
Washington Post
Federal publications
Fedwatch newsletter
Feedback, CompuServe
Fifth Avenue Shopper
FILGE Instructions
Finance
Financial advice
Financial aid, college
Financial forecasts
Financial information
Financial insurance
Financial news (AP)
Financial news, micros
Financial planning
Financial services
Fire Fighters' (SIG)
Fire prevention
Fireplaces, firewood
First Aid
First Tennessee Bank
Firstworld Travel Club
Fitness
Flight operations
Flight plans
Flowers, ordering
Focal
Food & Drug Admin
Food Buyline (SIG)
Food information:
FDA
Food storage
For fitness
Freezing
Menus
Football (AP wire)
Football game
For Sale:
Bulletin Board
Clothing, sport
Consumer goods
Fortran (XF4)
Funds Management
Fur Trader game
Futures industry news
Futures prices
Games, computer:
Adventure
Astrology
Backgammon
Banshi
Biorythms
Blackjack
Bridge
Chess
Civil War
Concentration
Decwars
Dice
Eliza
Fantasy
Fastermind
Football
Fur Trader
Golf
Gomoku
Hammurabi
Hangman
Kesmai
Lunar Lander
Magic Cube solution
Maze
Megawars
Mugwump
New Adventure
Othello
Real-Time Star Trek
Roulette
Scott Adams'
Scramble
Space War
Star Trek
Trivia test
Wumpus
Games (SIG)
Gandolf's Reports
Gardening
Gasoline, saving
General banking
Godiva chocolate
Gold:
Future prices
News
Golf, Belmont Golf Assn
Golf, Official PGA Tour:
Biographies
Players
Statistics
Golf (SIG)
Gomoku game
Good Earth (SIG)
Grain prices
Grains futures
Grolier's Encyclopedia
Ground water
Hammurabi game
HamNet (SIG)
Handelman's Athletic Sup
Handicapped, deaf
Hardware reviews
Health
Health and fitness
Health Care
Health Resources
Health-Tex
Heath User's Group
Heathkit Catalog
Heinold Commodities
Help
Help (documentation)
Hi-Tech Forum
Hockey (AP wire)
Hollywood Hotline
Home banking
Home finance
Home management
programs:
Amortize a loan
Calculate a raise
Checkbook balancer
Net worth
Home services
Horticulture
House plants
Howard Sams Books
Humor, satire
Huntington, bank
Husbandry
IBM-PC (SIG)
IDS
IRA
Immigration
Index:
AAMSI journals
CompuServe
Computer Periodical
Stock Market
Industries, farming
Information, music
Information on Demand
Information Retrieval Ser
Insurance:
Dental
Disability
Employee Benefits
Health
Life
Miscellaneous
Insurance, aircraft
Intelligence test
Interest rate
Investment news
Investment News & Views
Investments:
MicroQuote
Investors Diversified

Job. in the home
Jobs:
St. Louis Post-Dispatch
Jumbled words test
Kesmal
Kitbuilding
LDOS (SIG)
Languages on CompuServe:
Bliss
Focal
Fortran
Macro
Pascal
Snobol
Legal Forum
Legal issues
Library, electronic
Lineprinter art
Liquid Green
Literary (SIG)
Livestock futures
Livestock prices
Lobby Letters
MMS Financial Analysis
MNET-11 (SIG)
Macro
Magazine, advertisers
Magic Cube solution
Mainstreaming
Maintenance equip
Manuals, documentation
Manufacturer's newsletters:
Commodore
RCA
Tandy
Maps, road travel
Marine weather
Market prices
Market research
Massachusetts, banking
Medical:
AAMSI Forum
ASCMD Forum
FOI Newsline
Medical newsletter
Medical Records
Medicine consumer
Metals futures prices
Metals prices
Micro Advisor, The
Microcomputers:
Advice
Financial news
General
RCA
Tandy
What's new in
MicroQuote
Microsoft (SIG)
Middlesex Daily News
Mine-Equip
Money market
Money supply
Monthly charges
Mortgage budgeting
Movie reviews
CompuServe
Hollywood Hotline
Multiple Choice, the
Music
Music Forum
Music Information Service
Musus-Pascal (SIG)
Mutual Funds
NASA
NIPSIG
NOAA weather
NTSB cases (aviation)
NWS aviation (weather)
NYSE prices (MQUOTE)
Names of users
National Issues (SIG)
National Water Well Assn
National Weather Service
Netwitts
Netwits (SIG)
New product news:
Popular Science
The Micro Advisor
New services
News, CB
Newsletters:
AAMSI Communications
Commodore
RCA
Tandy
Newspapers
Node locations
North American weather
Norwegian Am. Cruises
Notices (Bullet)
Nutritional analysis
OK level
OTC drugs
OTC prices (MQUOTE)
Official Airline Guide
Ohio, banking
Ohio regional news
Ohio Scientific (SIG)
Options, stock
Orch-90 music (SIG)
PGA Official Tour Guide
PUG (Panasonic SIG)
Pan Am
Panasonic (SIG)
Parenting & Family Life
Pascal (SIG)
Password, changes
Peak Daisy Guide
Periodical Guide
Personal computing
Personal finance:
Gov't publications
Home Management
Investors Diversified
Personality profile
Pets
Pilot weather
Plants
Politics:
AP Viewdata Wire
Middlesex Daily
Washington Post
Popular Science
Magazine:
Automotive News
New Products
Science & Technology
Software reviews
Pork prices
Portfolio valuation
PowerSoft's XTRA-80
Precious metals
Precious metals news
Prescriptions
Prime Interest Rates
Primetime Radio Classics
Professional:
Agribusiness database
Eng Technical database
Environmental database
Programmer's SIG
Programming area
Programming languages
Programs for sale
Programs from users
Programs medical
Public access
Quick Quote
RCA Newsletter
RCA (SIG)
Radio:
Amateur
Old radio shows
Radio Shack computers
Rainbo's Reviews
Rates, CompuServe
Real estate, ads:
St. Louis Post-Dispatch
Recipes (SIG)
Recordkeeping, home
Reference guide
Referral Service, law
Regulatory Affairs Prof
Reservations, airline:
Firstworld Travel
Resource, water
Reviews, hardware
Reviews, movie
CompuServe
Reviews, software:
Popular Science
The Micro Advisor
SAT test information
SIGS:
AAMSI
ASCMD
AVSIG
Arcade
Atari
Author's
CBIG
CEMSIG
Commodore
Commodore Pet
Commodore 64
Commodore VIC 20
Communications
Cooks' Underground
CP/M Group
Decwars
Educators'
Environmental
Family Matters
FireNet
Food Buyline
Games
Golf
Good Earth
HamNet
Hi-Tech
HUG (Heath)
IBM-PC
LDOS TRS-80
Legal
Literary
MAUG (Apple)
Microsoft
MNET-11
MNET80 TRS-80
Music
Musus-Pascal
Netwits
NIPSIG
Orch-90
OSI
PowerSoft's XTRA-80
Programmer's
PUG (Panasonic)
RCA Group
Space
Sports
Telecomm
Travel
TRS-80 color
TRS-80 Model 100
Veternarians
Work-at-Home
St. Louis Post-Dispatch
Sams, Howard Books
Satire
Saving Accounts
Scott Adams' games
Scramble game
Securities:
Information
Self-employment
Services for the Deaf
Shawmut, bank
Shop-at-home
Shopping:
Cars
Musical
Radio Shows
Shuttle, space
Silly fill-ins
Silver-futures prices
Silver news
Ski conditions
Small business reports
Smoking and health
Snobol
SOFTEX
Software Authors' SIG
Software Exchange
Software revies:
Popular Science
The Micro Advisor
South America weather
Space (SIG)
Special interest Groups:
Access to
Commercial
Descriptions of
General
Hardware related
Instructions
Software/related
Sport, clothes
Sports news:
Golf
St. Louis Post-Dispatch
Scores (AP)
Sports quiz
Spotlight, CBers
Standard & Poors
Star Trek game
State capital games
Stereos for sale
Stevens Business Reports
Stocks, bonds:
MicroQuote
Quick Quote
Sugar futures prices
TMC for kids
TRS-80 color (SIG)
TRS-80 computers
TRS-80, MNET80 (SIG)
TRS-80 M odel 100 (SIG)
TRS-80, programs for
Tandy Corp. news
Technical books
Technical research
TeleComm (SIG)
Telephone access
Tennessee, banking
Terminal parameters
Terminal software
Terminal types
Tests, children
Tests, interactive
Tests, SAT
Text editors
The College Board:
Adult education
Choosing a college
Financial aid
Publications of
SAT test information
The National Satirist
Time used
Trading, commodities
Travel:
Department of State
Firstworld Travel Club
Norwegian A. Cruises
Pan Am
Travel Fax
TravelVision
Worldwide exchanges
Travel, abroad:
Department of State
Firstworld Travel Club
Norwegian Am. Cruises
Official Airline Guide
Pan Am
Travel Fax
Travel, advisories
Travel, airline guide
Travel Fax
Travel (SIG)
Traveler, airport guide
TravelVision
Treasury bills, yields
Trivia:
kids
Movie
Radio
Unlimited test
UCSD Pascal Group
USDA Grades
USDA standards:
Meat
Poultry
U.S. Department of State
U.S. News:
St. Louis Post-Dispatch
Washington Post
Used cars, buying
User directory
User directory
User information
User's programs
Vacationing
Value Line Database
Vegetables
Veterinarians Forum
Victory Garden
Video Information
Videotx, views on
VIDTEX executive
Viewpoint, CompuServe
Want ads (Bullet)
War games:
Decwars
Megawars
Space War
Washington, D.C. area
Middlesex Daily
St. Louis Post-Dispatch
Washington Post
Washington Post
Water, ground
WaterLine
Weather:
Weather:
AP Viewdata Wire
African weather
Asian weather
Aviation weather
Extended forecasts
N. American weather
S. American weather
State forecast
What's New
Wheat prices
Wine guide
Wire service news:
(see Associated Press Access)
Word processors
World news:
AP Viewdata Wire
Associated Press
Worldwide Exchanges
Yachts
Associated Press News Access
Financial wire:
Middlesex Daily News
St. Louis Post-Dispatch
Washington Post
Sports:
Middlesex Daily News
St. Louis Post-Dispatch
Washington Post
U.S. News:
Middlesex Daily News
St. Louis Post-Dispatch
Washington Post
Washington News:
Middlesex Daily News
St. Louis Post-Dispatch
Washington Post
World News:
Middlesex Daily News
St. Louis Post-Dispatch
Washington-Post

Table 9-2. Partial List of The Source Services.

- ADVANCED APPLICATIONS & PROGRAMS
- ADVICE COLUMN
- AIRSCHEDULES
  - Domestic
  - International
  - Inter-City
- ASTROLOGY LIBRARY
- AWARE FINANCIAL SERVICE GLOSSARY
- BARTER-TRADE NETWORK
- BUSINESS & FINANCE
    - Analysis Programming
    - Annuities Analysis
    - Aware Financial Service
    - Spreadsheet
  - PURCHASE VS. PRODUCTION COMPARISON
  - BUSINESS PROGRAMS
    - Complete Listing
    - Amortization of Loans
    - Amortization of Loan UNK Term
    - Annuity Debt Payment
    - Balancing Checkbook
    - Capital, Cost of Equity
    - Cashflow, Present Value
    - Commission, Sales Report
    - Depreciation Schedule
    - Equipment, Lease vs. Purchase
    - Equity Capital, Cost of
    - Inter-Industry Flow of Goods & Services
    - Interest, Bonds
    - Interest, Loans
    - Sales Commission Report
- CALCULATOR
- CAREER NETWORK
- CLASSIFIED ADS
- COMMODORE BUSINESS MACHINES
- COMMUNICATIONS
  - CHAT
    - Chat (live conversation with other subscribers)
  - TELECONFERENCING
  - SOURCEMAIL
    - To Check Mailbox
    - To Read Letters
    - To Scan Correspondence
    - To Send a Letter
    - General Information
    - Commands in Mail
    - Cross-Referenced Names
    - Operation of SourceMail
    - Timed-Mail Delivery
    - To Send a MAILGRAM
  - MISCELLANEOUS COMMUNICATION SERVICES
    - Contents of THE SOURCE
    - Personal Appointment Schedule
    - THE SOURCE Announcements
    - THE SOURCE Toll Charges
    - Suggestions for THE SOURCE
    - Subscribers Currently On-Line
    - TYMNET/TELENET Access Numbers
    - Subscriber Directory Services
    - The Common-Interest Directory
    - To Add Your Name and Number
- CONSUMER INFORMATION
- DINING OUT; WASHINGTON, D.C.
  - NEW YORK CITY
  - CONTINENTAL U.S. & CANADA
- DISCOUNT SHOPPING SERVICE (COMP-U-STORE)
  - Instructions
  - Overview
  - Bargains (the monthly listing)
  - Auction
  - Product and Manufacturer List
  - Begin Shopping

Covering the following product categories:

Appliances	Fine China	Sterling
Cameras	Furniture	Televisions
Cars	Pianos and Organs	Video Recorders
Crystal	Specialty Items	Watches
Figurines	Stereo & Audio	

- EDUCATION
- ENERGY SAVING NEWS & TIPS
- FINANCIAL MARKETS
  - UNISTOX REPORT INDEXES
    - Alphabetically
    - By Time
    - Dividends, Earnings
    - Earnings Reports
    - Exchange Rate
    - Federal Land Bank Bonds
    - Futures, Treasury Bills
    - Futures & Options
    - Glossary of Stock Investment Terms
    - Indexes, Stock Market Daily Avgs
    - Moody's Index
    - Standard & Poor's Index
  - AMERICAN STOCK EXCHANGE
    - Bonds
    - Closings (All Stock Exchanges)
    - Ten Most Active
    - Weekly Composite Prices
    - Weekend Bond Prices
  - BONDS
    - AMEX Daily Listing
    - Bond Yield Computations
    - Bond Price, Accrued Interest Computations
    - Federal Land Bank, Daily
    - NYSE Daily Listing
    - Treasury OTC, Daily
    - World Bank, OTC, Daily
    - Treasury OTC, Weekend
    - Weekend Listings
    - Commodities
  - METALS
    - Metals News
    - Gold News
    - Gold Spot Prices
    - NY/Chicago Mkt Prices
    - NY/London Mkt Prices
    - Platinum
    - Silver Coins
    - Silver Prices
    - Silver News
  - MONEY MARKET NEWS AND COMMENTS
    - Afternoon Lead
    - Futures
    - Markets at a Glance
    - Night Lead
    - Noon Lead
    - NYSE Trends
    - Opening Lead
    - Stock Pulse
    - What the Market Did
- FINANCIAL MODELING FOR BUSINESS PLANNING
- FINANCIAL NEWS
- GAMES
  - Adventure
  - Backgammon
  - Blackdragon
  - Cards
    - Blackjack
    - Super Blackjack
    - Bridge
    - Poker
    - Tricks
  - Checkers
  - Chess
  - Children's Programs
  - Civil War
  - Craps
  - Draw
  - Farmer
  - Fill in Letters
  - Football
  - Golf
  - Govern Sumeria
  - Guess Computer's Number
  - Hangman
  - Horse Race
  - I-Ching
  - IQ Test
  - Life
  - Lunar Landing
  - Market A Product
  - Mastermind
  - Maze Generation
  - Mind Reading
  - NIM
  - Patrol Streets (game)
  - Poster
  - Puzzles
  - Rule Sumeria
  - Score Four
  - Sinners
  - Slalom
  - Slot Machine
  - Sonnets
  - Statistics
  - Star-Trek
  - Super Adventure
  - Target Practice
  - Tic Tac Toe
  - Toro
  - Tricks
  - Vegas
  - Wumpus Hunt
- INFORMATION ON DEMAND
- INFORMATION ON UPDATES TO THE SOURCE
- MANAGEMENT CONTENTS
  - Overview
  - Instructions
  - The List of Journals

On the following Journals:

Across the Board	INC
Administrative Management	Institutional Investor
American Demographics	Journal of Retailing
The Banker	Medical Economics
Business and Society Review	Mergers & Acquisitions
Business Week	Monthly Labor Review
Cash Flow Magazine	Office, The
Dun's Review	Practical Accountant
Federal Reserve Bulletin	Sloan Management Review
Financial Executive	Taxes
Forbes	Venture
Fortune	Vital Speeches
Futurist	Wharton Magazine
Harvard Business Review	

- MEDIA GENERAL STOCK ANALYSES
  - Overview
  - Instructions
  - Categories of Stock Comparison
  - Definitions of Data Items
  - Industry Groups Numbers List
  - Creating Portfolio Files
  - **Stock Analysis and Tables**
- MEDICAL ADVICE
- MENU TO MANY DATA BASES ON THE SOURCE
- MOVIE REVIEWS BY JAY A. BROWN
- NEWS
- PERSONAL CALENDAR & NOTEBOOK
- PERSONAL FINANCE
- POLITICAL ACTION REPORT
- PORTFOLIO MANAGEMENT
- PROFESSIONAL BOOK CENTER
- PUBLISHERS WEEKLY BESTSELLERS LIST
- RADIO PROGRAMS TO ORDER
- RAYLUX FINANCIAL SERVICES
- SCIENCE & ENGINEERING
- SELF-PERCEPTION
- SMITHSONIAN EXHIBITS AND TOURING EXHIBITS
- SPECIAL APPLICATIONS
- STUDENT AID
- TAXES
  - Assets
  - Calculation of Income Statement
  - Computing Taxes
  - Contributions
  - Credits
  - Debts
  - Deductions
  - Dependents
  - Depreciation Schedule
  - Donations
  - Expenses
  - Income Statement, Pro Forms
  - Income Tax
  - Taxes
- TRAVEL CLUB
- UNISTOX
- UNITED PRESS INTERNATIONAL (UPI)
- USER PUBLISHING
- VOICEGRAM
- WEATHER
- WINE
- WISDOM OF THE AGES

Table 9-3. Some Computer Bulletin Board Services.

ABBS Apple-Mate, New York, NY	(201) 864-5345
ABBS CCNJ, Pompton Plains, NJ	(201) 835-7228
ABBS Livingston, NJ	(201) 994-9620*24
A-C-C-E-S-S Wyckoff, NJ	(201) 891-7441*24
Aphrodite-E	(201) 790-5910-so
CONFERENCE-TREE ?, Flagship, Denville, NJ	(201)627-5151*24
DIAL-YOUR-MATCH #14	(201) 272-3686-so
FORUM-80 Linden, NJ	(201) 486-2956*24
FORUM-80 Monmouth, Brielle, NJ	(201)528-6623*24
New Jersey TELECOM	#1(201)635-0705*24
PHOTO-80, Haledon, NJ	(201) 790-6795
PMS - Rutgers Univ. Microlab, Piscataway, NJ	(201)932-3887
PMS - Shrewsbury, NJ	(201) 747-6768
RATS ?, NJ #1	#1(201) 887-8874
RCP/M MCBBS Ken Stritzel, Flanders, NJ	(201) 584-9227*24
RCP/M RBBA Cranford, NJ	(201) 272-1874
RCP/M RBBA Ocean, NJ	&(201) 775-8705
RCP/M RBBS Paul Bogdanovich, NJ	(201) 747-7301
PCP/M RBBT New Brunswick, NJ	(201) 932-3879*24
ARMUDIC Washington, DC	#1(202) 276-8342
PSBBS Washington, DC	(202) 337-4694*24
BULLET-80 Danbury, CT	#1(203) 744-4644
BULLET-80 Seymour, CT	(203) 888-7952
Telcom 7 New Fairfield, CT	(203) 746-5763*24
FORUM-80 Montgomery, AL	(205) 272-5069
RCP/M RBBA Huntsville, AL	(205) 895-6749-rb
ABBS Apple Crate I, Seattle, WA	(206) 935-9119
A-C-C-E-S-S Olympia, WA	(206) 866-9043*24
Dial-Your-Match #16	(206) 256-6624-so
FORUM-80 Seattle, WA	(206) 723 3282
JCTS Redmond, WA	(206) 883-0403*24
MSG-80 Everett, WA	(206) 334-7394
Mail Board-82 Seattle, WA	(206) 527-0897*24
Mini-Bin Seattle, WA	(206) 762-5141*24
PMS - Software Unltd, Kenmore, WA	(206) 486-2368*24
RCP/M RBBS Yelm, WA	(206) 458-3086-rb
Seacomm-80 Seattle, WA	(206) 763-8879*24
DIAL-YOUR-MATCH #26, Clovis, CA	(209) 298-1328-so
ABBS (?) Queens, NY	(212) 896-0519
Bronx BBS, NY	(212) 933-9459
BULLET-80 New York, NY	(212) 740-5680*24
COMM-80 Queens, NY	(212) 897-3392*24
CONNECTION-80 Woodhaven, NY	(212) 441-3755*24
Leigh's Computer World, NY, NY (7PM)	!(212) 879-6257
NET-WORKS New York, NY	(212) 410-0949
Nybbles-80 NY	(212) 626-0375
Pat-100 System New York, NY	(212) 991-1664*24
PEOPLE-LINK	#1!(212) 877-7703*24
PMS - McGraw-Hill Books, New York, NY	(212) 997-2488
STUART-200 BBA Howard Beach, NY	(212) 835-5962*24
TCBBS AstroCom, New York, NY	#1!(212) 799-4649
TCBBS B.A.M.S. New York, NY	(212) 362-1040*24
TCBBS Leigh's Computer World, NY	(212) 897-7698
VTUGS NY, NY (VIC-20)	#1(212) 534-3149*24
All Night BBS	(213) 564-7636
ABBs Computer Conspiracy, Santa Monica, CA	(213) 829-1140
ABBS Pacific Palasades, Los Angeles, CA	(213) 459-6400
BBS B.R., Los Angeles, CA	(213)394-5950*24
Computer Connection	(213) 657-1799
CONFERENCE-TREE #4, Santa Monica, CA	(213) 394 1505
CONFERENCE-TREE Kelp Bed, Los Angeles, CA	(213) 372-4800
Datamate, Conoga Park, CA	#1(213) 998-7992-so
DIAL-YOUR-MATCH #1	(213) 842-3322-so
DIAL-YOUR-MATCH #11	(213) 242-1882-so
DIAL-YOUR-MATCH #22	(213) 990-6830-so
DIAL-YOUR-MATCH #4	(213) 783-2305-so
DIAL-YOUR-MATCH #9	(213) 345-1047-so
Dragons Game System (pass-DRAGON)	(213) 428-5206
Electric Line Connection, Sherman Oaks, CA	(213) 789-9512
Greene Machine Fricaseed Chicken, Arcadia, CA	(213) 445-3591*24
Greene Machine, Los Alamitos, CA	!(213) 431-1443
Greene Machine, Temple City, CA	!(213) 287-1363
Kluge Computer	$&(213) 947-8128*24
L.A. Interchange, Los Angeles, CA	(213) 631-3186*24
Long Beach Community Computer	(213) 591-7239*24
NET-WORKS Coin Games, Los Angeles, CA	(213) 336-5535
NET-WORKS Computer World, Los Angeles, CA	(213) 859-0894*24
NET-WORKS Softworx, West Los Angeles, CA	(213) 473-2754
Novation CO., Los Angeles, CA [pass-CAT]	(213) 881-6880
Oracle North Hollywood, CA	(213) 980-5643-so
PASBBS Torrance, CA	#1(213) 516 708
PMS - Los Angeles, CA	(213) 334-7614*24
PMS - O.A.C., Woodland Hills, CA	(213) 1849*24
RCP/M CBBS Pasadena, CA	(213) 799-1632*24
RCP/M RBBA BBA Valley	!(213) 360-5053
RCP/M RBBA GRRN Dta Exch. Palos Verdes, CA	$&(213) 541-2503*24
RCP/M RBBS Sofwaire Store, Los Angeles, CA	(213) 296-5927*24
ABBS Dallas Info Board	(214) 248-4539
ABBS Teledunjon II, Dallas, TX	(214) 530-0858
ABBS Teledunjon III, Dallas, TX	(214) 960-7654
ABBS The Moon, Dallas, TX	(214) 931-3437*24
BBS-80 DALTRUB, Dallas, TX	(214) 235-8784*24
BULLET-80 Hawkins, TX	(214) 769-3036
NET-WORKS Apple Grove, Dallas, TX	(214) 644 5197
NET-WORKS Apple Shack, Dallas, TX	(214) 644 4781*24
NET-WORKS Eclectic Computer, Dallas, TX	(214) 239 5842
NET-WORKS Hacker-net, Dallas, TX	(214) 824 7160
NET-WORKS Winesap, Dallas, TX	(214) 824 7455
RCP/M CBBS Dallas, TX	(214) 931-8274
BULLET-80 Langhorne, PA	(215) 364-2180
COMNET-80 North Wales, PA	(215) 855-3809
Hermes-80 Allentown, PA	(215) 434-3998
Lehigh Press BB, PA	#1(215) 435-3388
RCP/M RBBA Allentown, PA	(215) 398-3937*24
ABBS Akron Digital Group, Akron, OH	(216) 745-7855*24
BBS Computer Applications Co., Poland, OH	(216)757-3711
BULLET-80 Chesterland, OH	(216) 729-2769
COMNET-80 Akron, OH	&(216) 645-0827*24
FORUM-80 Cleveland, OH	&(216) 486-4176
INFOEX-80 Akron, OH	!(216) 724-2125*24
PMS - Massillon, OH	(216) 832-8392*24
PMS - RAUG, Akron, OH	(216) 867-7463*24
BULLET-80 Springfield, IL	(217) 529-1113
NET-WORKS C.A.M.S., Decatur, IL	(217) 429-5541
A-C-C-E-S-S Annapolis, MD	(301) 267-7666*24
ABBS Computer Crossroads, Columbia, MD	(301) 730-0922
ARMUDIC Computer Age, Baltimore, MD	(301) 587-2132
BBS IBM PC Beltsville, MD	!(301) 937-4339*24
BBS IBM PC Bethesda, MD	!(301) 460-0538*24
BBS IBM PC Gaithersburg, MD	!(301) 251-6293*24
BBS IBM PC Rockville, MD	!(301) 949-8848*24
CBBS CPEUG/ICST Gaithersburg, MD	(301) 948-5717
CONNECTION-80 Gaithersburg, MD	(301) 840-8588*24
HEX Silver Spring, MD	%(301) 593-7033*24
NET-WORKS COMM Center, Laurel, MD	(301) 953-3341
PMS - Baltimore, MD	(301) 764-1995*24
PMS - Ellicott City, MD	(301) 465-3176
PMS - Pikesville, MD	(301) 653-3413
PSBBS Baltimore, MD	(301) 994-0399*24
RCP/M RBBA Bethesda, MD	(301) 229-3196
RCP/M RBBA Laurel, MD	(301) 953-3753*24
Remote Northstar NASA, Greenbelt, MD	(301) 344-9156
ABBS Denver, CO	(303) 759-2625
BBA IBM PC Denver, CO	!(303) 773-2699*24
CONNECTION-80 Denver, CO	(303) 690-4566*24
FORUM-80 #2, Denver, CO	(303) 399-8858*24
HBBS Denver, CO	(303) 343-8401*24
RCP/M CUG-NOTE, Denver, CO	(303) 781-4937*24
RCP/M RBBS Arvada Elect., Colorado Springs, CO	(303) 634-1158*24
RCP/M RBBS Boulder, CO	(303) 499-9169
Remote Northstar Denver, CO	(303) 444-7231
NET-WORKS Charleston, WV	(304) 345-8280
ABBS Byte Shop, Ft. Lauderdale, FL	(305) 486-2983
ABBT Byte Shop, Miami, FL	(305) 261-3639
ABBS West Palm Beach, FL	(305) 848-3802
AMIS APOGEE Miami, FL	(305) 238-1231-rb
BBS Homestead, FL	(305) 246-1111
CONNECTION-80 Orlando FL	(305) 644-8327*24
CONNECTION-80 Winter Garden, FL	(305) 894-1886*24
FORUM-80 Ft. Lauderdale, FL	(305) 772-4444*24
Greene Machine Corsair, WPB, FL	!(305) 968-8653
Greene Machine, WPB, FL	(305) 965-4388-so
INFOEX-80 West Palm Beach, FL	(305) 683-6044*24
MOUSE-NET Orlando, FL	(305) 277-0473*24
Micro-80 West Palm Beach, FL	(305) 686-3695
NET-WORKS Big Apple, Miami, FL	(305) 948-8000
Personal Msg. System-80 Deerfield Bch, FL	&(305) 427-6300*24
TRADE-80 Ft. Lauderdale, FL	#1(305) 525-1192
PET BBS SE Wyoming PUG	(307) 637-6045*24
ABBS Peoria, IL	(309) 692-6502
NET-WORKS MAGIE, Galesburgh, IL	(309) 342-7178
RCP/M Geneseo, IL	(309) 944-5455
ABBS CODE, Glen Ellny IL	(312) 537-7063*24
ABBS Gamemaster, Chicago, IL	(312) 475-4884*24

ABBS Illini Microcomputer, Naperville, IL	(312) 420-7995
ABBS Rogers Park, Chicago, IL	(312) 973-2227
AMIS Chicago, IL	(312) 789-3610*24
ANESSY Chicago, IL	+1(312) 773-3308
BBS IBM PC Modem Chicago, IL	!(312) 259-8086*24
CBBS Chicago, IL	#1(312) 545-8086*24
MCMS C.A.M.S. Chicago, IL	#1&(312) 927-1020*24
MCMS L.A.M.S. Round Lake, IL	(312) 740-9128
MCMS Metro West Database, Chicago, IL	&(312) 260-0640*24
MCMS P.C.M.A. Wheaton, IL	!&(312) 462-7560*24
MCMS WACO Hot Line, Schaumburg, IL [pvt]	(312)4374*24
NET-WORKS Chipmunk, Hinsdale, IL	(312) 323-3741*24
NET-WORKS North Parks, Chicago, IL	(312) 745-0924
NET-WORKS Pirate's Ship, Chicago, IL	(312) 935-2933*24
PBBA Co-operative Comp Svc, Palatine, IL	(312) 359-9450*24
PET BBA Commodore, Chicago, IL	(312) 397-0871*24
PMS - Chicago, IL	(312) 373 8057*24
PMS - Downers Grove/SRT, Downers Grove, IL	(312) 964-6513
PMS - I.A.C., Lake Forest, IL	(312) 295-6926*24
RATS Homewood, IL	(312) 957-3924
RCP/M A.B. Dick Co., Niles, Il	&(312) 647-7636*24
RCP/M AIMS Hinsdale, IL	(312) 789-0499*24
RCP/M IBM PC, Niles, IL	(312) 259-8086
RCP/M Logan Square, Chicago, IL	(312) 252-2136
RCP/M NEI, Chicago, IL	(312)949-6189
RCP/M Palatine, IL	&(312) 359-8080*24
Scream Machine	(312) 680-9613-so
ABBS Detroit, MI	(313) 477-4471
ABBS Michigan Apple-Fone, Southfield, MI	(313) 357-1422
AMIS A.R.C.A.D.E. Sterling Heights, MI	(313) 978-8087*24
AMIS M.A.C.E. Detroit, MI	#1(313) 868-2064*24
Apple-Gram	)313) 295-0783*24
BBS Metro Detroit, MI	!(313) 455-4227-so
BULLET-80 Waterford, MI	(313) 683-5076*24
COMNET-80 Mt. Clemens, MI	&(313) 465-9531
Davy Jones Locket	(313) 764-1837
RCP/M Detroit, MI	(313) 584-1044-rb
RCP/M MCBBS Keith Petersen, Royal Oak, MI	(313) 759-6569-rb
RCP/M MCBBS TCBBS Dearborn, MI	(313) 846-6127*24
RCP/M RBBS Pontiac, MI	(313) 338-8575
RCP/M RBBS Southfield, MI	(313) 559-5326*24
RCP/M RBBS Westland, MI	(313) 729-1905-rb
Treasure Island	(313) 547-7903
Twilight Phone	(313)775-1649*24
Westside Download, Detroit, MI	(313) 533-0254
ABBS Century Next Computers, St. Louis, MO	(314) 442-6502
ABBS St. Louis, MO	(314) 838-7784*24
Midwest, St. Louis, MO	(314) 227-4312-so
NET-WORKS Computer Station, St. Louis, MO	(314) 432-7120
PET BBS Commodore Comm., Lake St. Louis, MO	(314) 625-4576*24
Greene Machine, Rome, NY	!(315) 337-7720
FORUM-80 Wichita, KA	&(316) 682-2113*24
NET-WORKS Greenfield, IN	(317) 326-3833*24
ONLINE Indianapolis, IN. [ID#-GUES, pswd-pass]	(317) 787-9881*24
PET BBA AVC Comline, Indianapolis, IN	(317) 255-5435*24
PMS - Indianapolis, IN	(317)787-5486*24
FORUM-80 Shreveport, LA	(318) 631-7107*24
ABBS Apple-Med, Iowa City, IA	(319) 353-6528
CBBS Cedar Rapids, IA	(319) 364-0811
NET-WORKS Computer City, Providence, RI	(401) 331-8450*24
ABBS Omaha, NE	(402) 339-7809
DIAL-YOUR-MATCH #23, Omaha, NE	(402) 571-8942-so
TRADE-80 Omaha, NE	(402) 292-6184
Lethbridge Gaming system, Lethbridge, Alta	(403) 320-6923
RCP/M RBBS Computron, Edmonton, Alta., Canada	(403) 482-6854*24
RCP/M RBBS Edmonton, Alberta, Canada	&(403) 454-6093*24
ABBS #X, Atlanta, GA	(404) 256-1549
ABBS AGS, Atlanta, GA	(404) 733-3461*24
ABBS Baileys Computer Store, Augusta, GA	(404) 790-8614
BBS IBM Hostcomm Atlanta, GA	!(404) 252-4146
BBS IBM PC Atlanta, GA	!(404) 252-9438*24
BBS IBM PC Atlanta, GA	!(404) 294-6879
BULLET-80 Fayetteville, GA	(404) 461-9686
CBBS Atlanta, GA	(404) 394-4220*24
Remote Northstar Atlanta, GA	#1(404) 926-4318*24
Telemassage-80, Altanta, GA	(404) 962-0616
HBBS Oklahoma City, OK	(405) 848-9329*24
BBS IBM PC Billing, MT	(406) 656-9624
AMIS GRAFEX Cupertino, CA	(408) 253-5216
AMIS IBBBS San Jose, CA	(408) 298-6930
AMIS T.A.B.B.S., Sunnyvale, CA	(408) 942-6975
BULLET-80 San Jose, CA	(408) 241-0769
NET-WORKS Computer Emprium, San Jose, CA	(408) 227-0227
PMS - Campbell, CA	(408) 370-0873*24
PMS - Santa Cruz, Aptos, CA	(408) 688-9629*24
RCP/M Collossal Oxgate, San Jose, CA	(408) 263-2588
RCP/M RBBS DataTech 004, Sunnyvale, CA	(408) 732-2433
RCP/M RBBS San Jose Exgate, San Jose, CA	(408) 287-5901*24
RCP/M Silicon Valley, CA	(408) 246-5014*24
? (Western Massachusetts)	(413) 637-3515
CBBS PACC, Pittsburgh, PA	(412) 822-7176*24
ABBS Colortron Computer, WI	(414) 637-9990*24
Big Top Games System, Milwaukee, WI	(414) 259-9475
CBBS MAUDE Milwaukee, WI	(414)241-8364*24
RCP/M RBBS Mike's, Milwaukee, WI	!(414) 647-0903
TBBS Canopus, Milwaukee, WI	!(414) 281-0545*24
Vanmil, Milwaukee, WI	!(414) 271-7580*24
ABBS Computerland, Fremont, CA	(415) 794-9314
ABBS Hayward, CA	(415) 881-5662
ABBS PCnet, San Francisco, CA	(415) 863-4703*24
ABBS South of Market, San Francisco, CA	(415) 469-8111-so
BBS Living Videotext, Menlo Park, CA	(415) 327-8876*24
Blue BOSS IBM PC, Berkeley, CA	(415) 845-9462*24
CBBS Lambda, Berkeley, CA	(415) 658-2919-so
CBBS Promima, Berkeley, CA	(415) 357-1130
CONFERENCE-TREE #3, Hayward, CA	(415) 538-3580
CONNECTION-80 Fremont, CA	(415) 651-4147*24
DIAL-YOUR-MATCH #17	(415) 991-4911
Drummer	(415) 552-7671-so
PMS - Pleasanton, CA	(415) 462-7419*24
PMS - Portola Valley, CA	(415) 851-3453*24
RCP/M RBBS DataTech 001, San Carlos, CA	#1$&(415) 595-0541*24
RCP/M RBBS DataTech 006, San Francisco, CA	(415) 563-4953
RCP/M RBBS Larkspur, CA	(415) 461-7726*24
RCP/M RBBS Marin County, CA	(415) 383-0473*24
RCP/M RBBS Piconet Oxgate, Mountain View, CA	(415) 965-4097*24
Sunrise System Oakland, CA	(415) 452-0350
System/80 San Leandro, CA	(415) 895-0699
BBS IBM Hostcomm Toronto, Ontario, CA	!(416) 499-7023*24
BBS NET Toronto, Ontario, CN	(416) 445-6696*24
KPri, Toronto, Ont., CN	#1(416) 624-5431*24
PET BBS TPUG, Toronto, Ontario, CN	(416) 223-2625*24
RPC/M HAPN Hamilton, Ontario, CN	(416) 335-6620*24
RCP/M Mississauga HUG, Toronto, Ont., CN	$&(416) 826-5394*24
ABBS ABACUS II, Toledo, OH	(419) 865-1594
ABBS Computer Store, Toledo, OH	(419) 531-3845
CONNECTION-80 Little Rock, AS	(501) 372-0576
PMS - Ft. Smith Comp. Club, Ft. Smith, AK	(501) 646-0197
CBBS NW, Portland, OR	(503) 646-5510*24
OARCS Portland, Oregon	(503) 641-2798
FORUM-80 Medford, OR	(503) 535 6883*24
PMS - Computer Solutions, Eugene, OR	(593) 689-2655*24
PMS - Portland, OR	!(503) 245-2536
ABBS Baton Rouge, LA	(504) 291-1360
CBBS Baton Rouge, LA	(504) 273-3116*24
NET-WORKS Crescent City, Baton Rouge, LA	(504) 454-6688
Baton Rouge Data System, Baton Rouge, LA	(504) 926-0181
ABBS Electro-Mart, Spokane, WA	(509) 534-2419*24
ABBS Rob Roy Computer, Yakima, WA	(509) 575-7704
CBBS Corpus Christi, TX	(512) 855-1512
CONFERENCE-TREE Victoria, TX	(512) 578-5833
FORUM-80 San Antonio, TX	!(512) 655-8143
NET-WORKS Sparklin' City, Corpus Christi, TX	(512) 882-6569
Bathroom Wall BBS, San Antonio, TX	(512) 655-8143
SATUG BBS, San Antonio, TX	(512) 494-0285
XBBS Hamilton, OH	(513) 863-7681*24
NET-WORKS Dayton, OH	(513) 223-3672
PMS - Cincinnati, OH	(513) 671-2753
CONNECTION-80 Laval BELE, Laval, Quebec, CN	(514) 622-1274*24
ONLINE Computerland, Montreal, Quebec, CN	(514) 931-0458*24
NET-WORKS Computer Emporium, Des Moines, IA	(515) 279-8863
ABBS Pirates Cove, Long Island, NY	(516) 698-4008
CBBS LICA LIMBS, Long Island, NY	(516) 561-6590*24
CBBS Long Island, NY	(516) 334-3134*24
CONNECTION-80 Centereach, NY	(516) 588-5836
CONNECTION-80 Great Neck, NY	(516) 8491*24
NET-WORKS Pirate's Trek	(516) 627-9048
Adventure BBS	(516) 621-9296
CONNECTION-80 Lansing, MI	(517) 339-3367
Capital City BBS, Albany, NY	(518) 346-3596*24
Remote Apple Jackson, MS	(601) 992-1918*24
A-C-C-E-S-S Phoenix, AZ	#1(602) 996-9709*24
A-C-C-E-S-S Phoenix, AZ	&(602) 957-4428*24
A-C-C-E-S-S Phoenix, AZ	(602) 274-5964
A-C-C-E-S-S Scotsdale,AZ	(602) 998-9411*24
ABBS Phoenix [AZ	(602) 898-0891
CBBS TSG, Tucson, AZ	(602) 746-3956*24
FORUM-80 Sierra Vista, AZ	(602) 458-3850*24
BBS Apollo, Phoenix, AS !	(602) 246-1432*24
CONNECTION-80 Peterborough, NH	(603) 924-7920
FORUM-80 Nashua, NH	(603) 882-5041
NET-WORKS Portsmouth, NH	(603) 436-3461
Software Referral Service	(603) 625-1919
ABBS Vancouver, B.C.	(604) 437-7001

CBBS Prince George, B.C., Canada	(604) 562-9515
RCP/M CBBS Frog Hollow, Vancouver, BC, CN	(604) 873-4007*24
RCP/M Terry O'Brien, Vancouver, BC, Canada	(604) 584-2543
RCP/M SJBBS Johnson City, NY	(607) 797-6416
AMIS Magic Lantern, Madison, WI	(608) 251-8538
BBS IBM PC Madison, WI	!(608) 262-4939*24
RATS Wenonah, NJ #2	(609) 468-3844
RATS Wenonah, NJ	(609) 468-5293
ABBS Calvary Mission Church, Mnpls, MN	(612) 471-0252-rl
CONFERENCE-TREE Minneapolis, MN	(612) 854-9691
MCMS NC Software, Minneapolis, MN	(612) 533-1957*24
PMS - Minneapolis, MN	(612) 929-6699*24
PMS - Twin Cities, Minneapolis, MN	!(612) 929-8966
ABBS Compumart, Ottawa, Ontario, Canada	(613) 725 2243
BULLET-80 Ironton, OH	(614) 532-6920
Applecrackers, Columbus, OH	(614) 475-9791*24
Ohio Valley BBS	(614) 423-4422
RCP/M CBBS Columbus, OH	(614) 272-2227*24
ABBS Computer Room, Kalamazoo, MI	(616) 382-0101
AMIS G.R.A.S.S. Grand Rapids, MI	(616) 241-1971*24
CONNECTIONS-80 W. Mich. Micro Group, MI	(616) 457-1840*24
AMIS Starbase 12 Philadelphia, PA	(617) 876-4885
BULLET-80 Boston, MA	&(617) 266-7789*24
CBBS Boston, MA	(617) 646-3610*24
CBBS Lawrence General Hospital, Boston, MA	(617) 683-2119
DIAL-YOUR-MATCH #18	(617) 334-6369-so
PMS - Apple Guild, Weymouth, MA	(617) 767-1303*24
Computer City, Danvers, MA	(617) 774-7516
New England COmp. Soc., Maynard, MA	(617) 897-0346
RCP/M MCBBS Superbrain, Lexington, MA	$&(617) 862-0781*24
Visiboard, Wellesley, MA	!(617) 235-5082
NET-WORKS Granite City, IL	(618) 877-2904
NET-WORKS Warlock's Castle St. Louis, MO	(618) 345-6638
CONNECTION-80 Escondido, CA	(619) 746-6265
ONLINE CDC, San Diego, CA	(619) 452-6011
ONLINE Saba, San Diego, CA	(619) 692-1961*24
ONLINE Santee, CA [ID#GUEST, pswd-PASS]	(619) 561-7271*24
PMS - Computer Merchant, San Diego, CA	(619) 582-9557
PMS - Datel Systems Inc., San Diego, CA	!(619) 271-8613*24
RCP/M RBBS San Diego, CA	$&(619) 273-4354*24
PMS - El Cajon, CA	(619) 579-0553
PMS - Lakeside, CA (type PMS to activate)	(619) 561-7271*24
PMS - Santee, CA	#1(619) 561-7277*24
NET-WORKS Armadillo, ND	(701) 746-4959
FORUM-80 Las Vegas, NV	(702) 362-3609*24
SIGNON Reno, NV [pswd-FREE]	(702) 826-7234
ABBS Software Sorcery, Herndon, VA	(703) 471-0610
BBS IBM Hostcomm Fairfax, VA	!(703) 425-9452*24
BBS IBM Hostcomm Fairfax, VA	!(703) 591-5120*24
BBS IBM Hostcomm Fairfax, VA	!(703) 978-0921*24
BBS IBM Hostcomm Fairfax, VA	!(703) 978-9592*24
BBS IBM Hostcomm Springfield, VA	!(703) 425-7229*24
C-HUG Bulletin Board, Fairfax, VA	(703) 360-3812*24
Carrier 2 Alexandria, VA	(703) 823-5210
Potomac Micro Magic Inc., Falls Church, VA	(703) 379-0303*24
RCP/M CBBS RLP, MacLean, VA	(703) 524-2549*24
Switchboard, Alexandria, VA	(703) 765-2161*24
TCUG BBS, Washington, DC	(703) 836-0384*24
RCP/M RBBS Napa Valley, CA	(707) 253-1523??
Armadillo Media Services, Houston, TX	(713) 444-7098
Compuque-80, Houston, TX	(713) 444-7041*24
PMBBS	(713) 441-4032
RCP/M RBBS Houston, TX	(713) 497-5433
Weekender, Houston, TX	(713) 492-8700
Zachary *Net, Houston, TX	(713) 933-7353*24
IDBN Info-Net, Costa Mesa, CA	(714) 545-7359
North Orange County Computer Club	(714) 633-5240
OCTUG Orange County, Garden Grove, CA	(714) 530-8226
Orange County Dta Exchange, Garden Grove, CA	(714) 537-7931
PIG-STY Costa Mesa, CA	(714) 545-4648
RACS V Fullerton, CA	(714) 524-1228
RCP/M RBBS ANAHUG, Anaheim, CA	(714) 774-7860*24
RCP/M RBBS GFRN Dta Exch. Garden Grove, CA	$&(714) 534-1547*24
RCP/M RBBS Rochester NY	(716) 223-1100*24
LITHO/NET	(800) 831-6964
ST80-CC Lance Micklus, Inc. Burlington, VT.#1	(802) 862-7023*24
Compusystems, Columbia, SC	(803) 771-0922
NBBS Norfolk, VA	(804) 444-3392
RCP/M RBBS Grafton, VA	(804) 898-7493
Remote Northstar Virginia Beach, VA	(804) 340-5246
Talk-80 ROBB, Portsmouth, VA	(804) 484-9636
RCP/M Net Simi Valley, CA	(805) 527-9321
Remote Northstar Santa Barbara, CA	(805) 682-7876
Remote Northstar Santa Barbara, CA	(805) 964-4115
Alpha, Tampa, FL [acct#-ABCD00, pwd-TRYIT]	(813) 251-4095*24
Apollo's Chariot, Apollo, FL	(813) 645-3669
BSBB Tampa, FL	(813) 885-6187
Bradley Computer BBS	(813) 734-7103
Micro Informer	(813) 884-1506
Remote Northstar Largo, FL	(813) 535-9341*24
TECOM-80 Tampa, FL	(813) 839-6746
RCP/M CUG-NODE, PA State College	(814) 238-4857*24
TRADE-80 Erie, PA	(814) 898-2952*24
PET BBS KCPUG, Kansas City, KS	(816) 356-2382*24
BBS Pensacola, FL	(904) 477-8783
PMS - Anchorage, AK	(907) 344-8558
DIAL-YOUR-MATCH #3	(912) 233-0863-so
PMS - Apple Bits, Kansas City, MO	!(913) 341-3502*24
PMS - Computer Connection Kansas City MO	!(913) 677-1299
Experimental-80 Kansas City, MO	(913) 676-3613
NET-WORKS ???	(914) 725-4060
NET-WORKS Pirate's Lodge	(914) 634-1268
Nybbles-80 Elmsford, NY	(914) 592-5385
OSUNA Scarsdale, NY	(914) 725-4060
RACS #3, Westchester, NY	(914) 942-2638
RCP/M RBBS Brewster, NY	(914) 279-5693
RCP/M RBBS Woodstock, NY	(914) 679-8734*24
RCP/M SJBBS Bearsville, NY	(914) 679-6559-rb
ST80-PBB Monroe Camera Shop, Monroe, NY	(914) 782-7605
RCP/M RBBS Comp. Tech. Assoc., El Paso, TX	(915) 533-2202*24
RCP/M RBBS El Paso, TX	(915) 598-1668
HBBS El Paso, TX	(915) 592-1910
Aviators Bulletin Board, Sacramento, CA	(916) 393-4459
RCP/M CBBS	(916) 483-8718*24
BULLET-80 Tulsa, OK	(918) 749-0059*24
CONNECTION-80 Tulsa, OK	(918) 747-1310*24
DIAL-YOUR-MATCH #20	(919) 362-0676-so
FORUM-80 Hull, England	(011) 44 482 059169
RCP/M RBBS Software Tools, Australia	(02) 997-1836
CBBS London, England (European standard)	(044) 1 399-2136

through computerized databases that are accessible through computers with modems, which allow communication across the country via phone lines. Indeed, just about everything that is available in print is also available on a database. There are now 1300 public databases, available to anyone willing to pay to use them, and at least 6000 private databases maintained by colleges, trade associations, and companies.

Most databases provide abstracts of materials that have already been published elsewhere, usually in a journal, magazine, newspaper, or conference proceeding. A few provide only citations, that is, the names of authors, the titles, and the publications in which the articles appeared. However, it has become increasingly popular for databases to contain the entire text of all articles.

The greatest advantage to the use of databases, aside from their ready availability, is their indexing and cross-referencing features. These features enable you to conduct a rapid search through thousands of periodicals and other information sources, spanning whatever years you specify, and give you the capability of finding an article based solely on the date of publication or the author's name. You can often search through "free text"—every word in an abstract or article—to determine whether or not they contain the words you specify. These features provide information-gathering capabilities transcending those possible or reasonable using a traditional approach.

One disadvantage of databases is a lack of common indexing terms (each system has its idiosyncrasies). Another disadvantage is that they may only be searched one at a time.

For a comprehensive review of over 1000 public database systems, consult the *OMNI Online Database Directory,* by Mike Edelhart and Owen Davies, MacMillan Publishing Co., 1983, and read the sampler of databases below.

A Sampler of Information Utilities.

BRS/After Dark
BRS, 1200 Rt. 7, Latham, NY 12110; (800) 833-4707. This service offers electronic mail, abstracts of books and magazine articles in science, finance, education, energy, and general reference. Hours: 6 P.M. to midnight Monday through Friday, and all day Saturday and Sunday. Rates: $6 to $15 per hour, plus $50 subscription fee.

CompuServe
CompuServe, Consumer Information Service, 5000 Arlington Center Blvd., P.O. Box 20212, Columbus, Ohio 43220; (800) 848-8199 or (614) 457-0802 in Ohio. This service offers hundreds of databases for both the consumer and business markets, including news, entertainment, electronic mail, programming languages, and user groups. Hours: 24 hours, 7 days. Rates $6 to $12.50 per hour, plus a subscription fee of $19.95 to $49.95, depending on where purchased.

Delphi
General Videotex Corp., 3 Blackstone St., Cambridge, MA 02139; (617) 491-3393. This consumer-oriented utility offers services and information similar to those offered by The Source and CompuServe. Hours: 24 hours, 7 days. Rates: $6 to $17 per hour, and a subscription fee of $49.95.

Dialog Information Retrieval Service
Dialog Information Services, Inc., 3460 Hillview Ave., Palo Alto, CA 94304; (800) 227-1927, or (800) 982-5838. This service offers a large collection of databases about business, government, current affairs, and the environment, among others. Hours: 22 hours, Monday through Saturday. Rates: $15 to $300 per hour, with no minimum.

Dow Jones News/Retrieval
Dow Jones and Company, P.O. Box 300, Princeton, NJ 08540; (800) 257-5114. This business-oriented service provides detailed financial information, including current and historical quotations from major stock exchanges, commodities prices, media general reports, and financial disclosure details on thousands of American corporations. Hours: 22 hours, 7 days. Rates: $6 to $72 per hour, plus subscription fees ranging from a one-time $50 to $50 per month.

ITT Dialcom
ITT Dialcom Inc., 1109 Spring St., Silver Spring, MD 20910; (301) 588-1572. This service offers a variety of databases with information about medicine, government, energy, and travel, as well as electronic mail. Hours: 24 hours, 7 days. Rates: $11 to $15 per hour, with a $100 per month minimum.

Knowledge Index
Dialog Information Services Inc., 3460 Hillview Ave., Palo Alto, CA 94304; (800) 528-6050, ext. 415 or (800) 227-1927. This service offers a subset of Dialog's more consumer-oriented databases, including business, engineering, psychology, magazines and computer information. Hours: 6 P.M. to 5 A.M. Monday through Thursday; 6 P.M. to midnight Friday; 8 A.M. to midnight Saturday; and 3 P.M. to midnight Sunday. Rates: $24 per hour, $35 subscription fee.

NewsNet
NewsNet, 945 Haverford Rd., Bryn Mawr, PA 19010; (800) 345-1301 or (215) 527-8030. This service offers the full text of over 100 newsletters on

a variety of subjects, plus electronic mail connections with the newsletter publishers. Hours: 24 hours, 7 days. Rates: $18 to $24 per hour, with a $15 per month minimum.

Nite-Line
National Computer Network, 1929 Harlem Ave., Chicago, IL 60635; (312) 622-6666. This service offers financial and business databases. Hours: 24 hours, 7 days a week. Rates: $9 to $20 per hour.

Orbit Information Retrieval System
SDC Information Services, 2500 Colorado Ave., Santa Monica, CA 90406; (800) 421-7229 or (800) 352-6689. This service offers reference databases covering business, chemistry, engineering, electronics, and other fields. Hours: 22 hours. Monday through Friday. Rates: $40 to $125 per hour, with a start-up fee of $125 to $400, depending on the training requested.

The Source
Source Telecomputing Corp., 1616 Anderson Road, McLean, VA 22102; (800) 336-3366. This service is a large general-interest utility offering consumer information, electronic mail and conferencing, programming languages, and other services. Hours: 22 hours, 7 days. Rates: $5.75 to $22.75 per hour, plus a $100 subscription fee and a $10 per month minimum.

Chapter 10

Askey Louis	**Freena Merla**
Auman Glen	**Gsel Tim**
Avey Mana	**Hamilton Angela**
Baer Egar	**Kerman Ed**
Bard Ellis	**Loche Ron**
Lundio P. Ron	
Barlup Helen	
Basorea Edwina	
Cosey Sid	
Covalt Mark	

Utility Programs

Although your computer system may not offer many of the useful features of larger systems, software can often be written to simulate many of these features. Such software is often referred to as *utility programs*. The category of *utility programs* also includes commonly used routines or subprograms that can be incorporated in a larger program. Through the use of utility programs, your personal computer can emulate its big brothers.

MULTIPURPOSE PROGRAMS

Although some computer systems provide the features found below, others don't. The person who develops programs to perform these and other utility functions will often have a readily salable product.

- Diagnostic programs: Programs that test all of the statements and commands found in given BASIC are useful in determining whether or not BASIC has loaded properly for execution. Programs to test memory by filling and reading all locations are also helpful.
- Memory-map programs: A machine-language program to output a memory map would be valuable.
- Menu selection programs: A machine-language routine to automatically find and execute any programs that are on line would make life easier for some operators.
- Routines for improved data file handling for floppy disks or cassettes are needed for some computers.
- Machine language programs that automatically convert one cassette/floppy disk standard to another are needed by a number of people.
- Variable list programs: A program to output the current value and location for all variables used in a program would be useful in large-program debugging.
- Renumber or resequence programs: A program to remember the statements in an assembly language program or BASIC program would be a convenient tool for programmers.

- Base conversion programs: This kind of program is useful in assembly language programming.
- BASIC patches that allow commands such as INKEY$ or GET, which permit program inputs without the pressing of the Enter or Return key and can limit the time allowed for a response.
- Vector graphic assembly language routines could be useful.
- Cross-assemblers or conversion programs between languages such as BASIC, Fortran, and APL would be a boon for programmers.
- Routines for handling fractions instead of decimals for greater precision in certain applications could be created.
- Specialized compilers for BASIC: although writing a complete BASIC compiler would be difficult, specialized compilers could be written to handle string, mathematical, or sorting functions. The advantage is the tenfold or more increase in execution speed.
- BASIC patches to provide increased debugging power could include error simulation routines to test a program (ERROR (code) and ON ERROR GOTO commands), TRACE commands to output a listing of each line number as it is executed, and powerful editing functions.
- Memory routines: Relocating memory loaders, which could be written in extended BASIC, could combine two programs, add machine language calls, and so on. A memory dump program could be provided to output programs in a variety of formats (decimal, hexadecimal, octal, and so on). A memory search program could be used to identify all occurrences of a specific byte value between any starting and ending addresses; such a program would be useful in disassembling and debugging.
- AUTO command: The AUTO command automatically provides line numbers when a program is being typed in.
- PLOT command: The PLOT command is useful in automatically displaying the values of a function or given set of data in graphical form.
- Multiple-precision routines: The scientific user of small computers (and some business users) needs multiple-precision capability.

In addition, a useful reference manual that included commonly used BASIC or assembly-language routines would simplify programming for the beginner.

UTILITY SUBROUTINES

Below are some practical routines that deal with matrices and string manipulation.

Matrix and String Utility Routines

Listing 10-1 is a simple string sort subroutine you can incorporate in your programs; Listing 10-2 is a program featuring subroutines that perform common matrix operations.

Sorting Routines

Among the different sorting routines listed here, the Quicksort (Listing 10-3) is the most efficient, although it requires more BASIC program lines than some of the other sorts require. Listing 10-4 shows the classic Shell-Metzner sort, and Listing 10-5 contains three additional sorting strategies. The bubble sort is the least efficient.

Listing 10-1. An INSTRING Subroutine.

```
1000  REM INSTRING SUBROUTINE
1010  FOR I=1 TO LEN(X$)-LEN(Y$)+1
1020  IF Y$=MID$(X$,I,LEN(Y$)) THEN RETURN
1030  NEXT I
1040  RETURN
```

Listing 10-2. Matrix Operations Program.

```
5      REM MATRIX FUNCTIONS
10     FULLW 2:CLEARW 2:GOTOXY 1,1
20     PRINT "This program consists of a series of utility subroutines
       useful"
25     PRINT "in working with matrix functions such as are used in mul
       tiple"
30     PRINT "element arrays."
40     PRINT "     to view these subroutines, list the program."
50     PRINT "You can stop the listing at any point by selecting STOP"

55     PRINT "from the menu.  These subroutines may be"
60     PRINT "used in programs you write for your own use."
70     STOP
100    REM Matrix Addition 3-D
110    FOR I=1 TO N1
120    FOR J=1 TO N2
130    FOR K=1 TO N3
140    C(K,J,I)=A(K,J,I)+B(K,J,I)
150    NEXT K
160    NEXT J
170    NEXT I
180    RETURN
190    REM ---------------------------------------------
200    REM MATRIX TRANSPOSITION 2-D
210    FOR I=1 TO N1
220    FOR J=1 TO N2
230    B(J,I)=A(I,J)
240    NEXT J
250    NEXT I
260    RETURN
270    REM
280    REM ------------------------------------------
290    REM
300    REM MATRIX MULTIPLICATION BY ONE VARIABLE 3-D
310    FOR I=1 TO N3
320    FOR J=1 TO N3
330    FOR K=1 TO N1
340    B(K,J,I)=A(K,J,I)*X
350    NEXT K
360    NEXT J
370    NEXT I
380    RETURN
390    REM --------------------------------------------
400    REM MATRIX INPUT ROUTINE 3-D
410    FOR I=1 TO N1
420    PRINT "PAGE ";I
430    FOR J=1 TO N2
440    PRINT "INPUT ROW ";J
450    FOR K=1 TO N3
460    INPUT X(J,K,I)
470    NEXT K,J:PRINT
480    NEXT I
490    RETURN
495    REM -----------------------------------------------
500    REM MATRIX INPUT SUBROUTINE (TWO DIMENSION)
```

```
510     FOR H=1 TO N
520     PRINT "ENTER ROW ";H
530     FOR I=1 TO N1
540     INPUT X(H,I)
550     NEXT I,H
560     RETURN
570     REM
580     REM -------------------------------------------------
590     REM
600     REM MATRIX PRINT SUBROUTINE 3-D
610     FOR I=1 TO N1
620     FOR J=1 TO N2
630     FOR K=1 TO N3
640     PRINT X(J,K,I),
650     NEXT K:PRINT
660     NEXT J:PRINT
670     NEXT I:PRINT
680     RETURN
690     REM -------------------------------------------------
700     REM MATRIX READ FROM DATA STATEMENT IN 3-D
710     FOR I=1 TO N1
720     FOR J=1 TO N2
730     FOR K=1 TO N2
740     READ X(J,K,I)
750     NEXT K,J,I
760     RETURN
770     REM DATA INSERTED HERE
780     REM
790     REM ----------------------------------------------
800     REM MAT=ZER MATRIX SET TO ZERO SUBROUTINE 3-D
810     FOR I=1 TO N1
820     FOR J=1 TO N2
830     FOR K=1 TO N3
840     X(K,J,I)=0
850     NEXT K,J,I
860     RETURN
870     REM
880     REM -------------------------------------------------
890     REM
```

Listing 10-3. A QuickSort Program.

```
5       REM QUICKSORT
6       REM N=NUMBER OF DATA ELEMENTS IN D( )
10      X=0:I=X+X:S(I+1)=1:S(I+2)=N:X=X+1
20      IF X=0 THEN RETURN
30      X=X-1:I=X+X:A=S(I+1):B=S(I+2)
40      Z=D(A):TP=A:BT=B+1
50      BT=BT-1
60      IF BT=TP THEN 110
70      IF Z<=D(BT) THEN 50 ELSE D(TP)=D(BT)
80      TP=TP+1
90      IF BT=TP THEN 110
100     IF Z>D(TP) THEN 80 ELSE D(BT)=D(TP):GOTO 50
110     D(TP)=Z
```

```
120   IF B-TP>=2 THEN I=X+X:S(I+1)=TP+1:X=X+1:S(I+2)=B
130   IF BT-A>=2 THEN I=X+X:S(I+1)=A:X=X+1:S(I+2)=BT-1
140   P=P+1:GOTO 20
1000  FOR X=1 TO 9:D(X)=X*-1:NEXT
1010  GOSUB 5
1020  FOR X=1 TO 9:PRINT D(X);:NEXT
```

Listing 10-4. The Shell-Metzner Sort.

```
5     REM SHELL-METZNER SORT
10    P=N:REM N=NUMBER OF DATA ELEMENTS IN D( )
20    P=INT(P/2)
30    IF P=0 THEN RETURN:REM ARRAY NOW SORTED; RETURN TO MAIN PROGRAM

40    K=N-P:J=1
50    I=J
60    L=I+P
70    IF D(I)<D(L) THEN 100
80    T=D(I):D(I)=D(L):D(L)=T:I=I-P
90    IF I>=1 THEN 60
100   J=J+1
110   IF J<=K THEN 50 ELSE 20
```

Listing 10-5. Three Sorting Subroutines.

```
5     REM THREE SORTING SUBROUTINES
10    FULLW 2:CLEARW 2:GOTOXY 1,1
20    PRINT "This program consists of three sorting subroutines you c
      an"
25    PRINT "use in your own programs.  Two of them, 'bubble sort' an
      d 'ripple sort'"
30    PRINT "can be viewed by listing the program.  The third, 'alpha
      betizer',"
40    PRINT "will automatically run when you press RETURN."
60    INPUT "Enter END at this point:",A$
70    IF A$="END" THEN END
100   REM IMPROVED RIPPLE SORT ROUTINE
110   C=0:N=N-1
120   IF N=0 THEN GOTO 200
130   FOR I=1 TO N
140   IF A(I)<=A(I+1) THEN 180
150   T=A(I)
160   A(I)=A(I+1)
170   A(I+1)=T
180   C=1
190   NEXT I
200   IF C=1 THEN 110
225   REM
250   REM -----------------------------------------------
275   REM
300   REM BUBBLE SORTING ROUTINE
```

```
310   FOR I=1 TO N-1
320   FOR J=I+1 TO N
330   IF A(I)<=A(J) THEN 370
340   T=A(I)
350   A(I)=A(J)
360   A(J)=T
370   NEXT J
380   NEXT I
390   REM ----------------------------------------------------
400   REM ALPHABETIZING PROGRAM
410   REM OUTPUTS LISTING ONLY (DOESN'T REARRANGE MEMORY)
430   DIM A$(100),N$(100)
440   PRINT "Enter STOP to end."
450   FOR N=1 TO 1000
460   INPUT "WORD ";N$(N)
470   IF N$(N)="STOP" THEN N=N-1:GOTO 490
480   NEXT N
490   REM
500   FOR I=1 TO N
510   A$(I)=N$(I)
520   NEXT I
530   K=0
540   I=1
550   FOR J=2 TO N
560   IF A$(I)<A$(J) THEN 570 ELSE I=J
570   NEXT J
600   K=K+1
610   IF K=N THEN 620 ELSE 540
620   PRINT:PRINT
630   END
```

Chapter 11

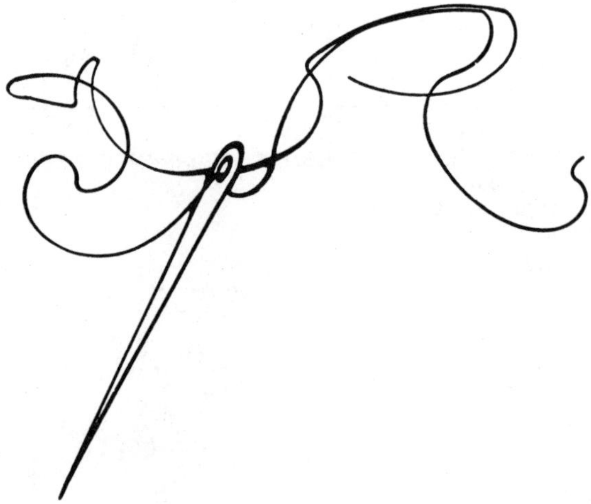

Miscellaneous Applications

There are a number of applications that don't fit easily in the categories already covered. These applications will be discussed in this final chapter.

COMPUTERS AND THE HUMANITIES

Amateur as well as professional scholars of history, language, literature, anthropology, archaeology, and other fields of the humanities may find personal computers useful in storing, organizing, analyzing, and indexing data.

History

The historian may wish to encode information of the following types for use with computers:

1. Census records.
2. Congressional voting records.
3. Election statistics.
4. Court records and decisions.
5. Ship sailing records—historical, geneological, and economic significance.
6. Diplomatic records.
7. Journalism statistics. A school of journalism has used a personal computer to record and plot the ratios of column inches devoted to various political parties or candidates in 15 major national newspapers, under the assumption that the amount of text space allotted to a candidate or party reflects the paper's views. You or your organization may wish to pursue similar lines of research.

Language

The microcomputer can be used to deal with languages in at least two ways.

Translations. It is possible to program a personal computer to act as a crude translating machine, capable of recognizing foreign vocabulary words and providing the English equivalent. Sentence structure and overall meaning are much more difficult to program, however, and are a current area of research in computer science. The pocket translating machines and spelling-checker programs available today may serve as models for such a program, which may provide an interpretable

English equivalent to a given foreign phrase. For example, if provided with the Spanish phrase, "Mucho gusto en conocerlo" (Pleased to meet you), the literal computer translation may read, "Very much in to meet you." A more sophisticated program could check for idiomatic expressions such as this and provide a better translation. A translating program may prove to be educational and useful to those with a minimum of familiarity with a language.

Compilation of Dictionaries. The dialects and languages of a speech community can be entered into a computer database for ease in compiling a dictionary.

Literature and Writing

There are a number of ways in which you can use your personal computer to help you in your writing and in analyzing literature.

Auto-Editor. A personal computer program capable of performing basic editing functions has been developed. The program balks at overly long sentences, or stilted, cumbersome expressions and suggests alternatives. For instance, it will suggest "absolutely" for "categorically," and "by" or "under" instead of "in accordance with." It proposes "now" instead of "at this point in time." It can detect spelling errors, improper punctuation, split infinitives, and other common grammatical errors.

Thesaurus. An on-line thesaurus can provide rapid, time-saving access to alternative word choices. This feature, in conjunction with a word processor, can serve as a powerful writing tool.

Automatic Table of Contents/Index Generation. In preparing a text on a word processor, the author need only flag with a special code the keywords to be indexed or the chapter headings for the table of contents. The computer will compile and organize these entries in desired form.

Writer's Outline Utility. A specialized word processor with database capabilities could assist the writer in preparing outlines.

Spelling Checker. Numerous spelling checker programs are available for personal computers. These are capable of checking documents for errors on the basis of 30,000-90,000 stored words. The user has the option of adding or deleting words, and special dictionaries are available (for example, medical terms).

Analysis of Literature. Computers can be used to prepare statistical analyses of literature that you have typed using your word processor. Such a program would calculate the number of lines, number of sentences, number of words, number of syllables, average word length, average sentence length, average sentence length, and the reading level based upon any of the standard formulas developed by Flesch, Fry, Raygor, Dale Chall, or Spache. For instance, the Fog index (FI) is given by

$$\text{FI} = \left(\frac{\begin{array}{c}\text{total no.}\\ \text{words}\end{array}}{\begin{array}{c}\text{sentences}\\ \text{total no.}\end{array}} + \frac{\begin{array}{c}\text{no. "hard"}\\ \text{words} \times 100\end{array}}{\begin{array}{c}\text{total no.}\\ \text{words}\end{array}} \right) \times 4$$

where "hard" words are considered to be those words with three or more syllables, except proper names, compounds of short words (for example, down-and-out), and words in which the third syllable ends in es or ed (for example, arrested). If the value of FI is 20 or more, you should consider the reading level advanced or difficult. To ensure that your message gets across to the masses, aim for a FI of around 10. A concordance table, listing all words used and their absolute or relative frequency of use can also be constructed; the list can be sorted alphabetically or by frequency. See *Microcomputing,* page 60, June 1981 for a sample BASIC program. Word-class distribution statistics, measures of redundancy of vocabulary (averages, medians, and so on), numbers of modifiers, adverb/verb and auxiliary verb/verb ratios, clause length statistics, distribution of clause types (simple, compound subject, and so on), distribution of sentence openers (prepositional phrase, subordinated clause, and so on), and style of sentence structure could also be analyzed by a more complex program.

Along similar lines, computers have been used to statistically determine whether works of indefinite authorship are typical of a given writer (for example works by Bacon and Shakespeare are compared), since the above statistical parameters tend to remain constant for one writer and may be compared with the figures for other writers.

Literature Database. A specialized database could store important manuscripts and be used to index, cross reference, and find given keywords or phrases quickly. QWIK-Indexes™ may also be generated.

AID TO THE HANDICAPPED

Use of microcomputers as aids to the handicapped is a very important and useful application; only the forefront has been explored, and the potential is tremendous. Examples of this application include the following:

The computer can act as a "robot" for the handicapped. One system was used by a paraplegic to communicate with others; the computer scanned the alphabet and once a particular letter was reached, the patient would make a certain movement to signal that that letter was to be typed out. In this manner, words and sentences were produced.

Voice synthesizers and decoders are especially helpful for those who cannot interact with a computer through a video terminal.

A computer with a printer (either dot matrix or daisy-wheel type) could be used to convert input text into braille. Each line of text would be reversed in computer memory and the braille equivalent (composed of periods or dots) printed in its mirror image. By turning over the output, the impressions left by the printer will form braille text.

The personal computer could be used to monitor people who are chronically ill, are predisposed to suffer heart attacks, or are in other life-threatening situations. Twice a day the patient would be required to input something into their computer; if they don't, medical personnel would be alerted by telephone dialing and vocal output peripherals.

Other areas in which the microcomputer can help the handicapped include the following:

- Sensory enhancement or translation: clarification of audio or visual information or translation of video information to and from audio information.
- Manipulator controls: powered prostheses or robots for individuals with severe motor impairment.
- Information amplification for the motion impaired: increase the amount of information that can be relayed with a given number of keystrokes, for example, a shorthand translater, as described in the first chapter.
- Recreation and development aids: games and educational programs allowing handicapped persons a reliable means to control, explore, and manipulate objects or learn about them.
- Communication aids: telephone dialers, computer-aided writing and filing systems, and phone communication through the use of speech synthesizers, for example.
- Security/monitoring systems: mechanisms for controlling locks and windows, emergency call systems, medication reminders, and monitoring systems that will periodically demand a response and signal if the individual fails to answer its queries.
- Information resource/management: Inability to quickly manipulate and scan materials may prevent the handicapped from making effective use of dictionaries, phone lists, calendars, filing systems, and books. These functions can be paralleled through the use of specifically designed microcomputer-based interfaces that work with residual physical and sensory capabilities.

TEST YOUR TYPING SPEED

Those learning to type will appreciate a measurement of their progress in speed. A program to test typing speed would have to be written in assembly language if your BASIC doesn't provide INKEY$, GET, ENTER (or RETURN) or WAIT-type commands.

MAINTENANCE OF ORGANIZATION RECORDS

Clubs and other organizations may find it worthwhile to purchase or use a member's small computer to ease paperwork. Anyone who develops software for this application may be able to sell it to local organizations or charge for computing services done on his own computer.

CO-OP SCHEDULING AND FINANCES

A computer analysis of costs and duties could help divide these responsibilities fairly between members of communal residence or cooperative organizations. A duty roster in calendar form as well as a financial summary of amounts owed could then be printed out.

TAILOR'S CALCULATIONS

Alterations to dress, suit, and other patterns for "tailor-made" clothing could be mathematically determined by your computer. If you have a printer with a line length large enough, the altered pattern could be printed in actual size.

PHONE CODE

A relatively simple program could be written to produce a listing of all the possible letter combinations on the phone dial for a given phone number. Businessmen may use this listing to find an appropriate, easy-to-remember word representing their phone number (for example, a computer store number was 266-7883 and COMPUTE was the corresponding telephone word). An interesting word may appear for you to use with your home phone.

BRAINSTORMER

A few years ago, a large sphere containing thousands of plastic squares with a different word printed on each was sold as a "brainstormer." The idea behind the device was to rotate the sphere, mix up the words, and then peek through a window at whatever words appeared. From this combination of adjectives and nouns, the user was to come up with a new invention or idea. The "brainstormer" could be useful in stimulating ideas; for instance, if the words *television* and *game* appeared, a properly prepared mind could have made the intuitive leap to invent video games. You could create your own computerized "brainstormer" by programming a large array of nouns and adjectives with a random number generator that calls them to the video screen 5-10 at a time.

A similar program could be called an "idea stimulator." Instead of miscellaneous words randomly appearing, a special set of adjectives or phrases describing possible improvements to an invention would appear individually and in random order on the screen. For instance, if you were trying to invent a new type of cooking pot and the word *slower* appeared, the brainstormed idea might be a slow crockpot cooker. The list of brainstorming questions below could be randomly arranged by your computer and individually called to the screen.

Brainstormer programs needn't be limited to products and inventions. Choreographer Merce Cunningham, Mozart, Oscar Wilde, and cartoonist Sergio Alverez, among others in the arts, have reported using similar random methods as an approach to artistic creation. One cartoonist reports use of a computer program to randomly mix cliches, locations, props, and various character types for possible cartoon ideas.

Brainstorm Chart for Products, Processes, or Services

In what other way can it be made more effective?
Is there a surer way to do it?
Is there a cleaner, neater way to do it?
Is there a more comfortable way to do it?
Is there a more healthful way to do it?
Is there a safer way to do it?
Is there a more durable form?
Is there a more pleasant way to do it?
Is there a quicker way to do it?
Is there an easier way to do it?
In what other way can it be improved?
Can the package be improved?
Can the distribution methods be improved?
Can it be made disposable or portable?
Can a combination with other devices be devised?
Can something be added to enhance its value?
Can it be adapted to some other use?
Is there a way to increase its usefulness; can

it become multipurposed?
Can it be made more attractive?
Is there a cheaper way to do it?
Can a similar result be obtained in any other way?

Inventor's Idea Stimulator

The program in Listing 11-1 can be very useful to those who have a creative and intuitive mind. A large list of "idea words" are shuffled and displayed three at one time. The object is to apply your thinking to these words in relation to another idea. For example, if you had to design a new product, such as a cigarette lighter, and the word *disposable* appeared, the idea of a disposable lighter would come to you.

Listing 11-1. The Inventor's Idea Stimulator.

```
10    REM LISTING11.01 - The Inventor's Idea Stimulator Program
15    FULLW 2:CLEARW 2:GOTOXY 1,1
20    PRINT "INVENTOR'S IDEA STIMULATOR"
30    DIM A$(98),M(98)
40    PRINT "The purpose of this program is to stimulate your creativ
      e"
50    PRINT "thinking when working on an invention or product.  A ser
      ies"
60    PRINT "of three words will be printed.  Think about each carefu
      lly"
70    PRINT "and try to apply them to your inventive process.  For ex
      ample"
80    PRINT "if you were trying to develop a product to improve offic
      e"
90    PRINT "communication and the word 'efficient' appeared, you mig
      ht"
100   PRINT "think of a dictating machine, etc."
110   INPUT "Press RETURN when ready ",A$
120   FOR X=1 TO 98:READ A$(X):NEXT X
130   N=98:FOR I=1 TO N
140   M(I)=I:NEXT I
150   FOR I=1 TO N-1
160   R=(N+1-I)*RND
170   R=INT(R)+I
180   T=M(R)
190   M(R)=M(I)
200   M(I)=T
210   NEXT I
220   PRINT "Press RETURN when finished with each word set."
230   FOR X=1 TO 33 STEP 3
240   PRINT A$(M(X))
250   PRINT A$(M(X+1))
260   PRINT A$(M(X+2))
270   INPUT B$
280   NEXT X
290   END
300   DATA LARGER,SMALLER,LONGER,SHORTER,THICKER,THINNER,DEEPER,SHALL
      OWER,STAND VERTICALLY/HORIZONTALLY,MAKE SLANTED OR PARALLEL
310   DATA STRATIFY,INVERT,CONVERGE,ENCIRCLE,INTERVENE,DELINEATE,BORD
      ER,MORE,LESS,CHANGE PROPORTIONS,FRACTIONATE,JOIN SOMETHING
320   DATA ADD SOMETHING,COMBINE,COMPLETE,CHANGE ARRANGEMENT,FASTER,S
      LOWER,LAST LONGER,CHRNOLOGIZE,MAKE PERPETUAL,SYNCHRONIZE
330   DATA RENEWABLE,ALTERNATING,STIMULATED,ENERGIZED,STRENGTHENED,LO
```

```
     UDER,LESS NOISE,COUNTERACTING,STRONGER,WEAKER,ALTERED
340  DATA CONVERTABLE,SUBSTITUTED,INTERCHANGED,STABILIZED,REVERSED,R
     ESILIENT,UNIFORM,CHEAPER,ADD/CHANGE COLOR,IRREGULAR DESIGN
350  DATA CURVED DESIGN,MODERN DESIGN,HARDER,SOFTER,SYMMETRICAL,NOTC
     HED,ROUGHER,SMOOTHER,DAMAGE AVOIDED,DELAYS AVOIDED
360  DATA THEFT AVOIDED,ACCIDENTS PREVENTED,CONFORMABILITY,ANIMATED,
     STILLED,DIRECTED MOTION,ATTRACTED/REPELLED MOTION,LOWERED
370  DATA BARRED,OSCILLATED,AGITATED,HOTTER,COLDER,OPENABLE,PREFORME
     D,DISPOSEABLE,INCORPORATED,SOLIDIFIED,LIQUEFIED,VAPORIZED
380  DATA PULVERIZED,ABRADED,LUBRICATED,WETTER,DRYER,INSULATED,EFFER
     VESCED,COAGULATED,ELASTICIZED,RESISTANT,LIGHTER,HEAVIER
390  DATA FOR MEN/WOMEN/CHILDREN,FOR ELDERLY/HANDICAPPED,FOREIGN MAR
     KETING
```

SOURCE INDEX

Addresses of manufacturers, institutions, organizations, and other sources of information or products can be stored in computer form and indexed for future reference. Any source of information or materials that you don't have use for at present, yet know you may need in the future, should be stored (for example, manufacturers and suppliers of peripherals for your system). These sources can be indexed under the material they can provide.

PEOPLE MATCHING

At a party or other social gathering it is often best to make arrangements so that those who are most similar will meet each other. Recently at a convention, a microcomputer was used to create special name cards for each guest. Everyone who attended had previously filled out a questionnaire indicating his or her occupation, hobbies, age, sex, likes and dislikes, and so on. This data was input to the computer, which subsequently produced a special name card with differently colored dots on it for each individual. Each color indicated a specific characteristic of that person, and thus, the guests could instantly find others who had the same color dots and thus the characteristics as themselves.

Computers have prepared seating charts for dinners, arranged blind dates, matched carpools, and paired athletes according to individual characteristics (partner or opponent matching). A bulletin board service for modem owners called Dial-Your-Match (213) 842-3322 allows computer dating for the would-be romantic.

An interesting people matching game would ask participants to rank their ideals. The list of common ideals below could be used for that purpose.

1. Active and satisfying life
2. Active and satisfying athletic life
3. Power over things (for example, automobiles, boats, and computers)
4. Socially significant activity
5. Good health
6. Opportunities for risk and adventure
7. Resilience (ability to "bounce-back")
8. Prestigious family life
9. Artistic ability
10. Ability to initiate and maintain friendships
11. Intellectual ability
12. Ability to draw love from others
13. Ability to influence others with your ideas
14. Ability to be a caring person
15. Ability to give love
16. Close and supportive relationships
17. Intellectual stimulation
18. Approval by opposite sex
19. Wealth
20. Ability to be self-sufficient
21. Physical attractiveness

Each particpant could rank each item in terms of its importance to him or her. Next, everyone would be allotted a certain number of tokens to use in bidding for the items of the most importance to themselves. Participants will realize what is of the most significance in their life and that of others.

Similarly two or more players could rank 1) what I think I am, 2) what the other player thinks I am, and 3) what the other player thinks I think I am (and 2 and 3 for the other player) for these characteristics: aggressive, dependent, enthusiastic, intelligent, honest, humorous, jealous, kind, rude, sensitive, sensual, and sociable. The personal computer would then compare and correlate responses in a useful, insightful way.

On a more personal basis, programs have been written to first determine the "personality" makeup of a couple and then suggest an appropriate "interlude." This is *not* a children's game and is an application to be used at your own risk.

Along similar lines, your local organization or business could use a computer car-pool matching program if there are many people involved.

GREETING CARD PRODUCER

Some clever hobbyists have written programs to produce assorted types of greeting cards, announcements, and invitations on their printers. One example is shown in Fig. 11-1. The cards can be personalized and can make use of computer art. One hobbyist uses his computer and printer to produce Christmas gift wrapping paper by printing designs of Christmas trees, snowflakes, and other patterns.

CONTESTS

For those who take sweepstakes seriously, a personal computer can be used to fill out multiple contest entry forms with name, address, and additional information required. One group of computerists entered a large national contest a few years ago, using a computer to print 10,000 entry forms; they won over 90 percent of the prizes. As a result, many contests now require hand-printed entry forms. However, peripherals are now available that can duplicate your handwriting or signature using a programmable "mechanical writing arm." Technology marches onward.

HANDWRITING ANALYSIS

Many major corporations are now using handwriting analysis as one instrument to evaluate prospective employees, although its usefulness remains controversial. The gaudy carnival "handwriting analysis computers" do little more than print

```
                    M
                  MERRY
                MERRYCHRI
              MERRYCHRISTMA
            MERRYCHRISTMASMER
          MERRYCHRISTMASMERRYCH
              MERRYCHRISTMA
            MERRYCHRISTMASMER
          MERRYCHRISTMASMERRYCH
        MERRYCHRISTMASMERRYCHRIST
      MERRYCHRISTMASMERRYCHRISTMASM
    MERRYCHRISTMASMERRYCHRISTMASMERRY
            MERRYCHRISTMASMER
          MERRYCHRISTMASMERRCH
        MERRYCHRISTMASMERRYCHRIST
      MERRYCHRSITMASMERRYCHRISTMASM
    MERRYCHRISTMASMERRYCHRISTMASMERRY
  MERRYCHRISTMASMERRYCHRISTMASMERRYCHRIS
 MERRYCHRISTMASMERRYCHRISTMASMERRYCHRISTMA
MERRYCHRISTMASMERRYCHRISTMASMERRYCHRISTMASMER
                  MERRY
                  MERRY
                  MERRY
                  MERRY
```

Fig. 11-1. A computer-generated greeting card.

out a random evaluation, as handwriting analysis is still on the cutting edge of computer science. However, a relatively simple program could print out the standard interpretations for handwriting characteristics after these have been encoded by an expert. Such a program could eliminate the drudgery of writing an explanation for each characteristic and could check for conflicting or concording results.

FIFTY MISCELLANEOUS APPLICATIONS

To further exemplify the scope of applications of personal computers in all walks of life, I have listed some of the more unusual uses readers have contributed:

- Design and animation of marching band patterns.
- Maintenance and inventory of equipment and instruments in small laboratories.
- Membership tracking for small organizations with the addition of dues accounting, questionnaire analysis, and mailing list capabilities.
- TV pattern generator for electronic technicians.
- Artistic pacifier for toddlers based on random graphical patterns, as a form of the stimulation necessary for the development of a normal IQ.
- Banner and sign generator to prominently display your message, created on ordinary lineprinters.
- Posters and calendars from lineprinter output.
- Translations of foreign words done by portable computers for travelers (or for educational purposes).
- Analysis of the cost-saving benefits of various solar collector designs.
- Calculation of home improvement costs by determining gallons of paint, rolls of wallpaper, or square yards of carpeting for a given job.
- Car maintenance reminder for routine tuneups and parts replacement according to miles driven.
- Car pool record keeping program which records car usage by driver, destination, and date with the ability to print schedules for each member.
- Bendo Kagawa, a Zen priest in Japan, uses his personal computer to help people meditate.
- Bob Waltz's personal computer at Smithers-Oasis can tell you all you ever wanted to know about geranium growing.
- Three Harvard professors writing a physiology text use their personal computers to exchange chapters by phone.
- Edward Adler arranged for his computer to rock his baby's cradle every time she cried.
- Architects can sketch new designs on personal computers that rival design systems formerly costing in the millions.
- For training purposes, companies are now using personal computers to instruct employees in everything from advanced optics to photocopier repair.
- A psychologist is using his computer to teach people self-relaxation techniques and self-hypnosis.
- Earth, Wind, and Fire use a computer to set off flash pots and explode small bombs on stage during their pyrotechnic rock performances.
- A German firm is using a personal computer to create new sweater patterns.
- Daryl Faud's personal computer sifts through hundreds of bacterial strains to assist in recombinant DNA experiments.
- Dr. Terry Pundiak uses a voice interface with his computer to give antismoking lectures.
- Experimental systems that are being developed to read ordinary text to the blind are based on personal computers.
- Boy Scouts across the nation are using personal computers for help in earning the Computer merit badge.
- Dr. Michael Lamb has adapted his personal computer for anesthesia monitoring during surgery.
- Colossal Pictures Corporation used a personal computer to create the title sequences for *The Black Stallion* and *One From The Heart.*
- Psychologist John McPhee developed a program to analyze Rorschach inkblot tests on his personal computer.
- The Sports Car Club of America, San Francisco office uses a personal computer to track race results instantly.
- David Curtis turned his personal computer into a lie-detector and analysis machine.
- One hobbyist creates personalized Christmas let-

ters by using a word processor, cutting the time required in half.

- A bar-code reader allows a hobbyist to rapidly input information concerning supermarket items purchased. A pantry inventory can easily be created.
- One thrifty personal computer owner devised a program to randomly match each person in his extended family for exchange of gifts.
- One family uses their system as a message board to store, word-process, and display messages to other family members.
- Traveling salesmen use their portable computers to maintain expense accounts.
- One hobbyist created a "drunkometer" program to evaluate residual cognitive function in those smashed by alcohol.
- A nighttime and vacation check-off program to remind the hobbyist that nights and vacations exist for a purpose and to ensure that all necessary duties have been taken care of could be a godsend to obsessive programmers.
- A citrus grower uses his personal computer to continuously monitor temperature and soil conditions to alert him of changes and automatically control heaters and sprinklers.
- An instrumentalist uses his personal computer to accompany him on the flute.
- A wrestling coach no longer tussles with the problem of pairing 500 boys by age and weight; he uses his personal computer.
- A personal computer owner about to marry created a database to map out chapel seating for 100 wedding guests and table arrangements for 220 lunch guests and to do tabulations on no-shows. He is also keeping a record of those who give gifts and what they send.
- A new minister was given information concerning the personal and familial problems of his flock stored in a database created by the retiring minister.
- Chicago Alderman Lawrence Bloom keeps a database of 6,000 voters on his computer. Precinct workers can make personalized calls and say "Alderman Bloom helped you get rid of that abandoned car. Now he needs your help."
- Carter Scholz used his personal computer to compute the lengths of a set of tuned wind chimes.
- The Osvoz family of New York, use their personal computer to maintain database of family medical information, including blood types, allergies, dates of checkups, poison antidotes, eyeglass prescriptions, insurance policies, check-up reminders, height, and weight.
- Professionally-prepared programs are available to plan a vacation trip for you, given the starting point and the destination; miles, costs, routes, and itinerary can be computed automatically.
- Dave Adams, a businessman, uses his personal computer with a modem to access on-line airline schedules and make reservations. The Source and CompuServe, among other networks, offer this service.
- Automotive expense records, including the following information, may be tracked using your personal computer: loan or lease payment records, accumulated gasoline costs, MPG average, maintenance and repair records, insurance records, depreciation, automotive tax deductibles, and accumulated cost per mile to operate.
- Bill Strozier uses his personal computer to operate a passive solar heating system in his home. The computer controls the opening and closing of movable partitions and shades and an air circulation system. Other personal computer owners have controlled active solar heating collectors, directed air or liquid to areas where it was needed, and analyzed the performance of the system.
- One hobbyist uses a program to organize his elaborate home workshop; he maintains a tool and equipment inventory and lists of parts and supplies, projects completed, and future projects (with tentative starting dates).
- Bird watcher Edward Mair uses a personal computer to store his lifetime, year, state, property, and feeder lists and for exchanging information with other birdwatchers across the nation via a network.
- Several executives, computer programmers, and writers can now do their work at home, rather than traveling to the office, thanks to personal computers linked with their company's computer via modems.

Index

Edited by Stephen Moore

1001 Things to Do with Your ATARI® ST™

If you are intrigued with the possibilities of the programs included in *1001 Things to Do with Your ATARI® ST™* (TAB Book No. 2776), you should definitely consider having the ready-to-run disk containing the software applications. This software is guaranteed free of manufacturer's defects. (If you have any problems, return the disk within 30 days, and we'll send you a new one.) Not only will you save the time and effort of typing the programs, the disk eliminates the possibility of errors that can prevent the programs from functioning. Interested?

Available on disk for ATARI 520 ST and 1040 ST with one 3 1/2″ diskette drive and TOS operating system at $24.95 for each disk plus $1.00 shipping and handling.

I'm interested. Send me:

__________disk for ATARI 520/1040 ST with 3 1/2″ diskette drive and TOS (6325S)

__________TAB BOOKS catalog

Check/Money Order enclosed for $__________ ($24.95 plus $1.00 shipping and handling for each disk ordered.)

__________ VISA __________ MasterCard

Account No. ____________________ Expires ____________________

Name ____

Address ____

City ____________________ State _______________ Zip __________

Signature ____

Mail To: **TAB BOOKS Inc.**
P.O. Box 40
Blue Ridge Summit, PA 17214

(Pa. add 6% sales tax. Orders outside U.S. must be prepaid with international money orders in U.S. dollars.)

TAB 2776